The European Union:
How does it work?

FOURTH EDITION

Daniel Kenealy, John Peterson, and Richard Corbett

OXFORD
UNIVERSITY PRESS

OXFORD

UNIVERSITY PRESS

Great Clarendon Street, Oxford, OX2 6DP,
United Kingdom

Oxford University Press is a department of the University of Oxford.
It furthers the University's objective of excellence in research, scholarship,
and education by publishing worldwide. Oxford is a registered trade mark of
Oxford University Press in the UK and in certain other countries

© Oxford University Press 2015

The moral rights of the authors have been asserted

First Edition 2003
Second Edition 2008
Third Edition 2012

Impression: 2

Published in the United States of America by Oxford University Press
198 Madison Avenue, New York, NY 10016, United States of America

British Library Cataloguing in Publication Data
Data available

Library of Congress Control Number: 2014960113

ISBN 978–0–19–968537–0

Printed in Great Britain by
Ashford Colour Press Ltd, Gosport, Hampshire

▮ OUTLINE CONTENTS

PART I   Background

PART II   Major Actors

PART III   Policies and Policy-Making

▌ DETAILED CONTENTS

PART I   Background

PART II   Major Actors

PART III   Policies and Policy-Making

PART IV   **The EU and the Wider World**

■ PREFACE AND ACKNOWLEDGEMENTS

Change is a constant. That has always been one of the themes of this book and it certainly applies to the European Union since the third edition was published in 2012. At that time, we were still coming to grips with the new 'EU-27' (now 28). The Union was in the first few years of operating under a new (Lisbon) Treaty, which created a permanent European Council President as well as something like an EU Minister of Foreign Affairs, while extending majority voting to a significantly larger number of policies. Since the *first* edition of this book was published, the Union has twice overhauled its founding Treaties (once successfully), and expanded to a population of over 507 million. It has increased its land mass by around 30 per cent, while nearly doubling its membership.

Today, our task is arguably even more daunting. The EU's size is not the only thing to have expanded. The Union is now involved in far greater array of policy areas, or involved more intensely in existing ones. It has suffered the body blow of the post-2008 global economic crisis, which itself contributed to an existential economic crisis in the Eurozone after 2010. One consequence has been dramatic steps to create a vast emergency assistance fund to help rescue states in severe economic difficulty and even a European banking union.

But another upshot has been rising Euroscepticism across the European continent, with anti-EU parties making significant gains in the 2014 European Parliament election. For the first time, the prospect of an existing member state—the United Kingdom (UK)—voting to leave the Union has become a real one. Meanwhile, Europe's recovery from more than five years of economic woe has stalled, with even its powerhouse economy, Germany, subject to gloomy growth forecasts.

We, and our authors, can offer little more than educated guesses about what the effects of these institutional, political, and economic changes will be. But the status quo looked very fragile as we went to press, suggesting that more changes were likely to be in the offing. We (or most of us) are, by now, battle-hardened as to how much and fast the ground can shift in European integration. What the Union does, how it does it, and with what consequences, have all altered or intensified in some (usually significant) way since the last edition of each edition of this volume was published.

We have tried to reflect the most important of these changes in this new edition. Each individual chapter has been significantly updated (three years is a long time in EU affairs), especially to take account of the EU's responses to the Eurozone crisis and the UK's debate about its European future. We've added several new authors to be sure that, even as we offer a basic introduction to the Union, our book reflects findings from the very latest and most perceptive research on European integration. We've also taken on a new co-editor, Daniel Kenealy, while retaining Richard

Corbett, fresh from a five-year stint in the *cabinet* of the European Council's first permanent President, Herman Von Rompuy, and just recently elected as a Member of the European Parliament. Richard gives us that insider's eagle eye that Alexander Stubb, Prime Minister of Finland as we went to press, contributed to earlier editions. It is tempting to conclude that there's no limit to how far one can go after contributing to this volume!

Even more important is what we have *not* changed. Our core mission remains the same: to produce a clear, concise, truly introductory text for students and the curious general reader. No experience required. We know the EU is important; we demonstrate why and how. We also know that it can be made both comprehensible and interesting; our aim is to show how. If we succeed, it is in great part due to our team of star contributors, support and publishing staff.

First, the contributors. One of the book's most distinctive and strong qualities is its blend of academics and practitioners. All chapters were either co-authored or reviewed by both an academic and practitioner. We thank our team of authors for working to make this blend workable and even enjoyable. Special thanks are owed to the authors or co-authors who contributed to the *first* three editions: Prime Minister Alex, Laura Cram, Lynn Dobson, Lykke Friis, David Martin, John D. Occhipinti, Michael E. Smith, Michael Shackleton, Rory Watson, Albert Weale, and the late, great Sir Neil MacCormick. Above all, the lead editor of all three previous editions, Elizabeth Bomberg, has done more than anyone to establish this book's credentials as the first one to assign to inquiring minds trying to make sense of this strange and often baffling political beast.

A second batch of thanks goes to the editorial and production team. Marlene Gottwald deserves our thanks in advance for editing the Online Resource Centre page that accompanies this volume. As always, we are in debt to series editor Helen Wallace, who has offered not only excellent substantive guidance but also unflagging and essential encouragement in the production of this and past volumes. Thanks also to the production team at OUP, especially Martha Bailes and Sarah Iles, both of whom demonstrated patience and skill in seeing the project through.

Thirdly, our readers. The advantage of doing multiple editions is that we are able to benefit from the feedback from the last one as we plough ahead with the next. We've profited enormously from comments offered by reviewers of the first two editions, by practitioners in Brussels, and by the many EU studies colleagues who have used this book in their teaching. An extremely useful range of comments, criticisms, and suggestions came directly from end users themselves—including students using the earlier editions in their courses at the University of Edinburgh and College of Europe.

Finally, amidst all the tumultuous change, there is always one constant: the support offered by our partners and families, and presumably those of our authors. Like last time, only more so: we could not have done it without you.

Daniel Kenealy, John Peterson, and Richard Corbett
Edinburgh and Leeds

▮ LIST OF FIGURES

∎ LIST OF BOXES

LIST OF TABLES

▮ ABBREVIATIONS AND ACRONYMS

ACP	African, Caribbean, and Pacific
APEC	Asia Pacific Economic Cooperation
ASEAN	Association of South-east Asian Nations
BEUC	Bureau Européen des Union de Consommateurs (European Consumers Organization)
CAP	common agricultural policy
CEPOL	European Police College
CFSP	Common Foreign and Security Policy
CIA	Central Intelligence Agency (US)
COPA	Committee of Professional Agriculture Organizations
CoR	Committee of the Regions and Local Authorities
COREPER	Committee of Permanent Representatives
DG	Directorate-General (European Commission)
EAW	European Arrest Warrant
EC	European Community
ECAS	European Citizen Action Service
ECB	European Central Bank
ECHO	European Community Humanitarian Office
ECHR	European Convention on Human Rights
ECJ	European Court of Justice
ECOFIN	(Council of) Economic and Finance Ministers
ECSC	European Coal and Steel Community
EDC	European Defence Community
EDF	European Development Fund
EEA	European Economic Area
EEC	European Economic Community
EEW	European Evidence Warrant
EFTA	European Free Trade Association
EMU	Economic and Monetary Union
EMS	European Monetary System
ENP	European Neighbourhood Policy
EP	European Parliament
EPACA	European Public Affairs Consultancies Association

EPC	European Political Cooperation
ERF	European Refugee Fund
ERM	Exchange Rate Mechanism
ESC	Economic and Social Committee
ESDP	European Security and Defence Policy
ESS	European Security Strategy
ETUC	European Trades Union Confederation
EU	European Union
EURATOM	European Atomic Energy Community
FBI	Federal Bureau of Investigation (US)
FD	Framework Decision
FRG	Federal Republic of Germany
FTA	Free Trade Area
FYROM	Former Yugoslav Republic of Macedonia
GAERC	General Affairs and External Relations Council
GATT	General Agreement on Tariffs and Trade
GDP	Gross Domestic Product
GMOs	Genetically Modified Organisms
GNP	Gross National Product
IGC	Intergovernmental Conference
IO	International Organization
IR	International Relations
JHA	Justice and Home Affairs
MEP	Member of the European Parliament
MEPP	Middle East Peace Process
MFA	Minister for Foreign Affairs
NAFTA	North American Free Trade Agreement
NATO	North Atlantic Treaty Organization
NGO	Non-governmental Organization
NSS	National Security Strategy
OEEC	Organization for European Economic Cooperation
OMC	Open Method of Coordination
OSCE	Organization for Security and Cooperation in Europe (formerly CSCE)
PCTF	Police Chiefs Task Force
PNR	Passenger Name Record
QMV	Qualified Majority Voting
REACH	Registration, Evaluation, Authorization, and Restriction of Chemicals

SAP	Stability and Association Process
SCIFA	Strategic Committee on Immigration, Frontiers, and Asylum
SEA	Single European Act
SGP	Stability and Growth Pact
SIS	Schengen Information System
SME	Small and Medium-sized Enterprise
TEC	Treaty establishing the European Community
TEU	Treaty on European Union
UK	United Kingdom
UN	United Nations
UNICE	Union of Industrial and Employers' Confederations of Europe
US	United States
VIS	Visa Information System
VWP	Visa Waiver Program (US)
WEU	Western European Union
WTO	World Trade Organization
WWF	World Wide Fund for Nature

▌ LIST OF CONTRIBUTORS

GRAHAM AVERY	St Antony's College, Oxford
RICHARD CORBETT	Member, European Parliament
DESMOND DINAN	George Mason University
ANDREW GEDDES	University of Sheffield
MARLENE GOTTWALD	Steinbeis Foundation, Stuttgart
FIONA HAYES-RENSHAW	College of Europe, Bruges
DANIEL KENEALY	University of Edinburgh
BRIGID LAFFAN	European University Institute
JOHN PETERSON	University of Edinburgh
ALBERTA SBRAGIA	University of Pittsburgh
FRANCESCO STOLFI	University of Nottingham Malaysia Campus

New to this Edition

- Richard Corbett, former member of the European Council President's *Cabinet*, and now Member of the European Parliament for Yorkshire and Humber (UK), returns to the editorial team to ensure that it continues to offer a practitioner's perspective.

- Several new authors have been added to the line-up of contributors to ensure that the book—albeit a basic introduction to the European Union—continues to reflect findings from the most recent and perceptive research on the EU.

- All chapters have been revised and updated in light of the post-2009 Eurozone crisis.

- The book includes extensive coverage of the UK's debate about its future membership of the EU, and the historically unprecedented possibility that an existing member state of the EU might choose to exit from it.

FIGURE 0.1 Map: The European Union's member states

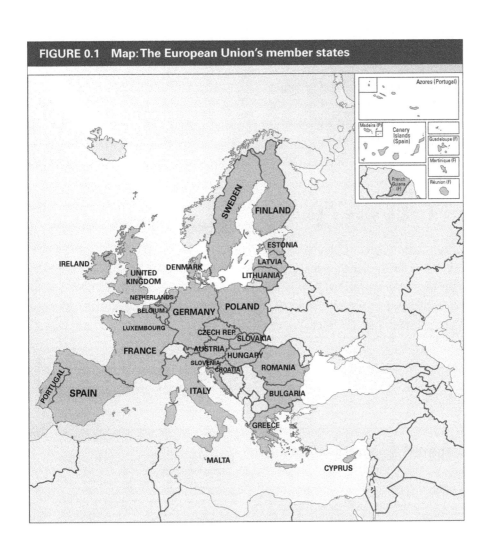

This book is enriched with a number of learning tools to help you reinforce your knowledge and further your understanding of European Union politics.

Chapter summaries

Each chapter opens with a brief summary which sets the scene for the themes and issues to be discussed, and indicates the scope of the chapter's coverage.

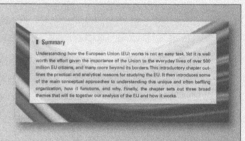

▌ Summary

Understanding how the European Union (EU) works is not an easy task. Yet it is well worth the effort given the importance of the Union to the everyday lives of over 500 million EU citizens, and many more beyond its borders. This introductory chapter outlines the practical and analytical reasons for studying the EU. It then introduces some of the main conceptual approaches to understanding this unique and often baffling organization, how it functions, and why. Finally, the chapter sets out three broad themes that will tie together our analysis of the EU and how it works.

'How it really works' boxes

'How it really works' boxes connect theory with reality, clearly explaining how the EU works in practice. Additional boxes and tables provide you with extra information to help reinforce your understanding of the main text and key terms.

BOX 10.3   How it really works

The EU and the Libyan crisis

The Union's response to the 2011 Libyan crisis was widely criticized for being slow, incoherent and ineffective. Constituting the first major foreign policy crisis since the entry into force of the Lisbon Treaty, expectations that the EU could deliver a decisive response were high. However, the crisis revealed yet another gap between the Union's rhetoric and action, and showcased how 'uncommon' its foreign, security and defence policies continued to be.

The EU's response to a potential humanitarian disaster on its Mediterranean doorstep revealed an imbalance between its military and civilian crisis management capacities and a lack of any integrated civilian-military capacity. The Union was at least partially successful in civilian crisis management by implementing 'soft' security actions, such as civil protection and humanitarian assistance. European heads of state and government also agreed to impose sanctions authorized by the United Nations Security Council on the Gaddafi regime and went even beyond them with tougher measures. However, while member states eventually agreed on the need for Gaddafi to cede power, they remained at odds on the use of military force. Germany refused to support a UN Security Council Resolution (1973) authorizing (amongst other measures) the implementation of a no-fly zone over Libya, abstaining on the vote and withdrawing its military assets from the Mediterranean once a NATO military action began. After an extraordinary European Council failed to endorse the no-fly zone, the UK Prime Minister, David Cameron, told the press ('Of course the EU is not a military alliance and I don't want it to be a military alliance. Our Alliance is NATO' (Nicholas and Traynor 2011). An attempt to set up a CSDP military mission, EUFOR Libya, to support the UN in the delivery of humanitarian aid

'Compared to what?' boxes

Throughout the text, 'Compared to what?' features broaden your understanding of the subject by comparing the EU with other political systems.

BOX 10.5   Compared to what?

The EU and Russia

The EU's relationship with Russia is a classic glass half-empty or half-full story. A pessimist would note the EU's dependence on Russia for energy, particularly since price disputes between Moscow and former Soviet republics or client-states led to repeated interruptions (or threats of them) in flows of Russian natural gas in the 2000s. The EU's concern for its energy security is often viewed as making it the weaker partner in its relationship with Moscow. One upshot, according to this view, is that the Union is reluctant to speak truth to power about the erosion of Russian democracy, the 2007 cyber-war waged (apparently) by Russia on Estonia (an EU member state), and Russia's 2014 annexation of the Crimean region of Ukraine.

In practice, the EU and Russia are mutually and heavily interdependent. The EU relies on Russia to supply more than a quarter of both its oil and natural gas. Russia equally relies on its sales of raw materials to the EU for most of its hard currency earnings, which fund nearly 40 per cent of Russia's federal budget. Around 60 per cent of Russia's export earnings come from sales of energy, most of it to the EU.

The EU needs to co-exist with Russia but it is difficult to imagine that the two could ever be 'partners'. Russia's intervention in Ukraine in 2014 followed the overthrow of a pro-Russian Ukrainian government by citizens motivated in large part by the rejection of an agreed EU-Ukraine trade deal by President Viktor Yanukovych. The contempt of the Russian President, Vladimir Putin, for the EU was reflected in his courtship of far right,

Discussion questions

Carefully devised discussion questions at the end of each chapter are designed to help you assess your understanding of core themes, and may also be used as the basis of seminar discussion or coursework.

? DISCUSSION QUESTIONS

1. What are the most important features determining an EU member state's attitudes towards integration?
2. Which is more powerful: the impact of the EU on its member states, or the impact of the member states on the EU?
3. How useful is theory in explaining the role of the member states in the EU?
4. How different are EU member states from 'ordinary' nation-states?

Further reading

Take your learning further with the authors' recommended further reading lists at the end of each chapter, which help you to identify the key literature in the field.

→ FURTHER READING

Some of the key themes introduced in this chapter are inspired by leading, general studies of the EU including Scharpf (1999), Weiler (1999), Hooghe and Marks (2001), Jørgensen et al. (2006), and Wallace et al. (2015). Wiener and Diez (2009) feature a collection of works on European integration theory and practice. Good overviews of integration theory include Rosamond (2000, 2013), Ekstrup-Sangiovanni (2006), Pollack (2010), and the relevant chapters of Jones et al. (2012). An excellent recent addition to the literature, written by the speechwriter to a former European Council President, is Van Middelaar (2013).

Web links

To help you with further research, annotated summaries of useful web links are provided at the end of each chapter.

⊕ WEB LINKS

- The EU's official website 'The European Union online' (http://europa.eu/) is a valuable starting point. It provides further links to a wide variety of official sites on EU policies, institutions, legislation, Treaties, and current debates.
- Precisely because the EU's website is so large, the Europa Information Services website provides a nice index of where to find answers on the Europa website (http://europa.eu/geninfo/info/guide/index_en.htm).
- You can also use the web to access the *Official Journal* (OJ) which is updated daily in several languages. The OJ is the authoritative and formal source for information on EU legislation, case law, parliamentary questions, and documents of public interest (http://eur-lex.europa.eu/).
- For pithier reporting, the *Economist* (www.economist.com) provides useful general articles, while *European Voice* (www.european-voice.com) offers insider coverage of EU policies and news.

Chronology

A useful chronology of key dates in the history of European integration is provided in an appendix for easy reference.

▌ APPENDIX: Chronology of European Integration*

1945 May	End of World War II in Europe
1946 Sept.	Winston Churchill's 'United States of Europe' speech
1947 June	Marshall Plan announced
	Organization for European Economic Cooperation established
1949 Apr.	North Atlantic Treaty signed in Washington
1950 May	Schuman Declaration

Glossary terms

Key terms appear in colour in the text and are defined in the glossary at the end of book to aid your exam revision.

Absorption capacity (see Box 8.1) Refers to the EU's ability to integrate new members into its system.

Accession (see Box 8.1) The process whereby a country joins the EU and becomes a member state.

Acquis communautaire (see Box 4.1) Denotes the rights and obligations derived from the EU treaties, laws, and Court rulings. In principle, new member states joining the EU must accept the entire *acquis*.

Candidate countries (see Box 8.1) Refers to a country whose application is confirmed by the EU but is not yet a member.

Charter of Fundamental Rights Adopted at the Nice Summit in 2000 but not legally binding, the Charter was made binding on the EU's institutions and law by the Lisbon Treaty. It seeks to strengthen and promote the fundamental human rights of EU citizens.

Civil society (see Box 6.1) The collection of groups and associations (such as private

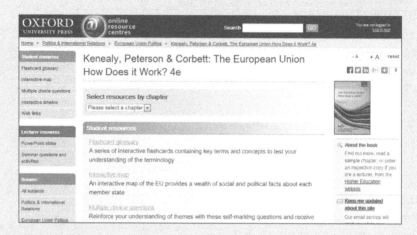

www.oxfordtextbooks.co.uk/orc/kenealy4e/

The Online Resource Centre that accompanies this textbook provides students and lecturers with ready-to-use teaching and learning materials. These resources are free of charge and designed to maximize the learning experience.

For students

Flashcard glossary

Interactive flashcards containing key terms from the text allow you to test your knowledge of the terminology of EU politics, and provide a useful revision tool.

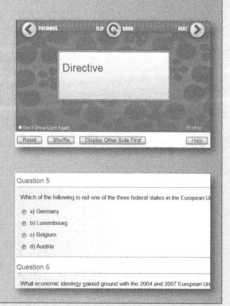

Multiple-choice questions

Each chapter is accompanied by a bank of self-marking multiple-choice questions, which provide instant feedback on your answers to aid your learning and revision.

Interactive map

An interactive map of the EU provides a wealth of social and political facts about each member state.

Interactive timeline

An interactive timeline is provided to help reinforce your knowledge of the history of European integration. Simply click on each date for a summary of key events.

1945-1949	1950-1954	1955-1959	1960-1964	1965-1969	1970-1974

2000 **2001**

February An Intergovernmental Conference (IGC) is launched to discuss reforms left uncompleted after the Treaty of Amsterdam. These include the size and composition of the Commission, the weighting of votes in the Council of Ministers and Qualified Majority Voting.

March The institutions of European Security and Defence Policy (ESDP) begin provisional operation. The same month, a special European Council held in Lisbon agrees to a new EU strategy on employment, economic reform, and social cohesion, and makes a commitment to turn the EU into 'the most competitive knowledge-based economy in the world' 2010. This becomes known as the 'Lisbon Agenda'.

Web links

To help you further your research, annotated web links direct you towards important treaties, working papers, articles, and other relevant sources of information on EU politics.

The Europa website provides a historical overview of the p
http://europa.eu/abc/history/1945-1959/index_en.htm

The European Navigator website offers excellent coverage history. Use the link 'history' for summaries of the historical documents and multimedia clips.
www.ena.lu

The website of the Jean Monnet Foundation contains excer memoirs describing the construction of Europe and include 1950-1952 period:

For further online resources about EU politics also visit our European Union Politics resource centre at **www.oxfordtextbooks.co.uk/orc/eupolitics/**

For registered adopters of the textbook

Chapter 3: The EU's Institutions

Institutions in treaty and practice

Power Point® slides

Each chapter of the book is accompanied by customizable PowerPoint® slides to assist with preparing lectures and handouts.

Chapter 6

1. Why is the European Union's budget so small?
2. Can the European Union have an effect beyond the scope of its treaty competencies?
3. What are the most important types of policies in the European Union?
4. How do policies evolve to address current problems facing the Europe
5. On which types of policy should the European Union concentrate? W

Seminar questions

A set of carefully devised seminar questions is provided for use in assessment or to stimulate class debate.

PART I

Background

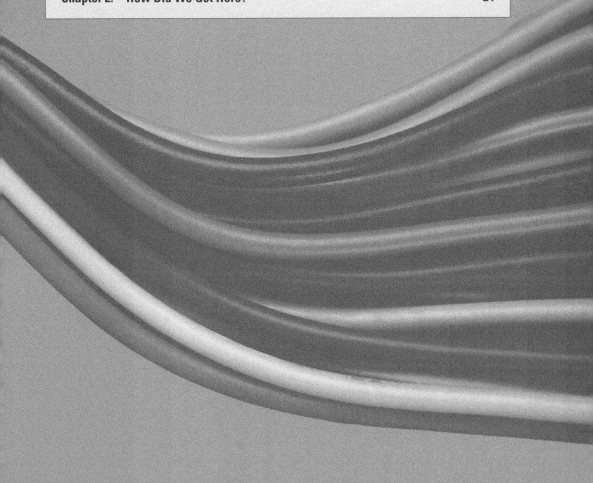

CHAPTER 1

Introduction

Daniel Kenealy, John Peterson, and Richard Corbett

▌ Summary

Understanding how the European Union (EU) works is not an easy task. Yet it is well worth the effort given the importance of the Union to the everyday lives of over 500 million EU citizens, and many more beyond its borders. This introductory chapter outlines the practical and analytical reasons for studying the EU. It then introduces some of the main conceptual approaches to understanding this unique and often baffling organization, how it functions, and why. Finally, the chapter sets out three broad themes that will tie together our analysis of the EU and how it works.

Studying the EU

The years 2009–15 have been particularly turbulent ones for the EU. It has struggled to deal with the fallout of a global financial crisis that crystallized towards the end of 2008. From 2010–12, there was almost daily turmoil in the Eurozone, comprising the (now 19 of 28) EU member states that share the single currency: the euro. The governments of Greece, Ireland, and Portugal successively required emergency loans from their partners to cover their financing needs. Spain and Italy teetered, for many months, on the brink of requiring similar treatment. In Athens, Lisbon, Rome, and Madrid, street protests in response to stagnating economies, high unemployment, and austerity policies brought to the fore significant issues of legitimacy. Anti-EU parties made unprecedented gains in the 2014 European Parliament election, topping the polls in France, the United Kingdom, and Denmark and achieving historically high votes elsewhere. Put simply, the second decade of the twenty-first century already appears to qualify as the most challenging time in the history of European integration. Yet, the EU's defenders can plausibly argue that European integration has been the most successful experiment in international cooperation in human history. In the midst of some of its most difficult days ever, the Union was awarded the Nobel Peace Prize in 2012.

The EU is not easy to grasp. To the uninitiated its institutions seem remote, its remit unclear, and its policies perplexing. Such bewilderment is unsurprising as, on a fundamental level, the EU defies simple categorization. It is less than a federal state, but clearly more than a standard international organization. Yet, it shares certain characteristics with both. The EU's development is shaped by an increasing number of players: 28 member states, seven EU institutions including a Central Bank, two consultative bodies with legal status, an External Action Service, and an Investment Bank. A clutch of agencies, and countless private interests, experts, foreign actors and citizen groups try to influence what the EU does (or does not do). 'What the EU does'

BOX 1.1   What's in a name?

Even the question of what to call the EU can cause confusion. What became the European Union was originally established as the European Coal and Steel Community in 1951, followed by the main **European Economic Community** (EEC, colloquially known as the Common Market) by the 1957 Treaty of Rome. Its remit was widened and its name shortened to **European Community** (EC) in 1992. That year's Maastricht Treaty created a **European Union**, consisting of the EC as well as two other 'pillars' of cooperation in the areas of common and foreign policy and justice and home affairs. The Lisbon Treaty formally merged all three pillars into a single legal entity, called the European Union, in December 2009. We use the label European Community (or EC) to refer to the organization in the pre-Maastricht period (see especially Chapter 2), but 'European Union' to refer to all periods—and the activities of all pillars—thereafter. As we will see, vocabulary in the EU can be a sensitive matter (see Box 11.1).

has expanded enormously since its origins. Originally concerned principally with establishing a common market, at first just for coal and steel, its policy remit has expanded to cover agricultural, monetary, regional, environmental, social, immigration, foreign and security policy, and the list does not stop there (see Box 1.2).

BOX 1.2   The three pillars of the European Union

The 1992 Maastricht Treaty organized the activities of the EU into three areas, or 'pillars'. When the Lisbon Treaty came into force in 2009 the pillars were collapsed into one common institutional structure and the EU as a whole was given a single legal personality. However, important differences between the 'non-existent' pillars persisted, especially for pillar 2. It remains the case that the EU cannot be fully understood without understanding the previous pillar system.

FIGURE 1.1.   The (pre-Lisbon Treaty) 'pillar structure' of the European Union

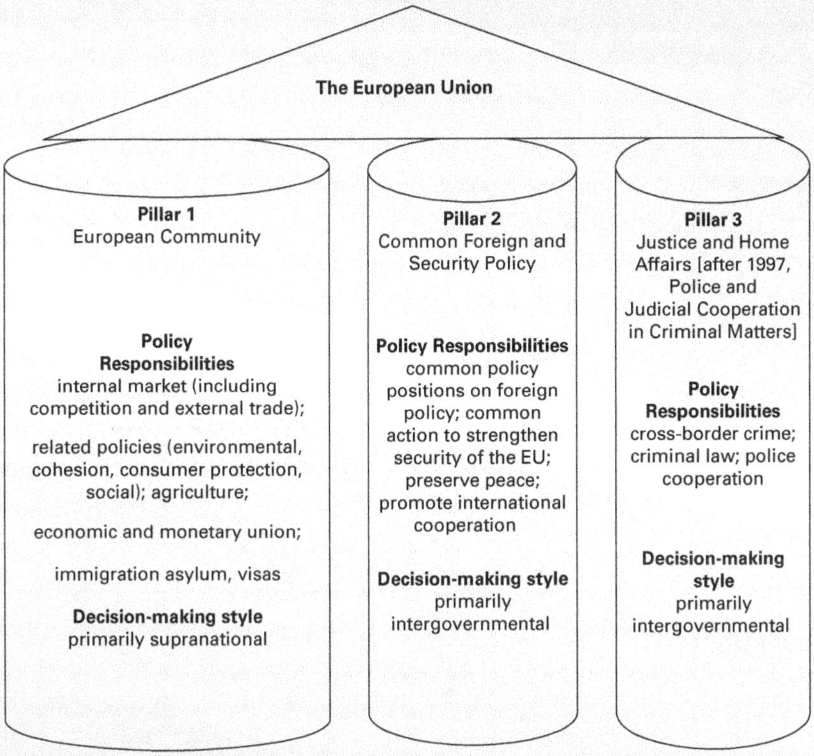

The European Union

Pillar 1 European Community	Pillar 2 Common Foreign and Security Policy	Pillar 3 Justice and Home Affairs [after 1997, Police and Judicial Cooperation in Criminal Matters]
Policy Responsibilities internal market (including competition and external trade); related policies (environmental, cohesion, consumer protection, social); agriculture; economic and monetary union; immigration asylum, visas **Decision-making style** primarily supranational	**Policy Responsibilities** common policy positions on foreign policy; common action to strengthen security of the EU; preserve peace; promote international cooperation **Decision-making style** primarily intergovernmental	**Policy Responsibilities** cross-border crime; criminal law; police cooperation **Decision-making style** primarily intergovernmental

PILLAR 1: EUROPEAN COMMUNITIES—

The first pillar was the biggest, incorporating the vast majority of EU responsibilities. It covered internal market policies as well as trade, agricultural, and competition policy

Cont. ➤

Cont.

amongst others. Eventually, it was extended to cover some immigration and asylum policy, and economic and monetary union. In this pillar the EU's common institutions (Commission, Council, Court, and Parliament) could act with a significant degree of autonomy from national governments.

PILLAR 2: COMMON FOREIGN AND SECURITY POLICY—

In the second pillar, member states attempted to forge common positions and take joint action in areas of foreign and security policy. Decision-making was primarily intergovernmental (that is, between governments), by unanimity, and without a separate legal framework. Neither the Commission nor the Parliament had much direct influence.

PILLAR 3: JUSTICE AND HOME AFFAIRS (FROM 1997, POLICE AND JUDICIAL COOPERATION IN CRIMINAL MATTERS)—

The objective of the third pillar was to increase cooperation in the area of internal security, including the fight against international crime and the drugs trade. As in pillar 2, decision-making was essentially intergovernmental. Unanimity of member governments was required for virtually all important decisions.

Sometimes Treaty reforms or specific decisions could shift policy responsibility from one pillar to another, changing the nature of decision-making. For instance, the 1997 Treaty of Amsterdam moved policy on visas, immigration, and asylum from the third to the first pillar, signalling a shift towards more supranational decisions in this area. A decade later the Lisbon Treaty (signed in 2007) abolished the separate pillars entirely, while keeping some of their special features.

The dramatic expansion of EU competences over time—especially into areas traditionally seen as the responsibility of elected national governments—has meant that debates about European integration have become wrapped up in larger debates about sovereignty, democracy, and the future of the nation state. To study the EU is thus to study a lot more than its institutions and their operations. Studying integration means posing questions about legitimacy, democracy, law, state-society relations, international politics, bureaucracies, and much more. And the EU never stands still for long, making it a dynamic topic of study.

Why bother?

Although understanding the EU is a daunting intellectual challenge, there are three reasons why it has major pay-offs. First, on a practical level, no student of politics can make sense of European politics without understanding an organization that has daily and powerful effects on European (and non-European) governments, markets, and citizens (Box 1.3). The way it works often lacks political drama: yet the EU is responsible for practical, everyday things that make a tangible difference to European citizens such as a cap on mobile roaming charges and a right to compensation

BOX 1.3	The practical significance of the EU

The EU's practical impact is felt in a wide range of areas including:

- **Market:** The EU now regulates the world's largest market, including over 500 million consumers, around 60 per cent more than the United States.

- **Legislation:** it is not easy to measure and estimates vary, but in most years something between 6 and 35 per cent of the domestic legislation enacted by the Union's member states originates from EU legislation.

- **Currency:** In 2002, 12 national currencies—some dating back 600 years—ceased to be legal tender and were replaced by the euro. By 2015, 19 countries and 335 million consumers used this single currency.

- **Wealth:** The EU's collective wealth (Gross National Income) accounts for about 30 per cent of the world's total.

- **Trade:** Not counting intra-EU trade, the EU's share of world trade (imports and exports) exceeds that of the United States, accounting for almost 20 per cent of all global trade.

- **Aid:** The EU and its member states are the world's largest donors of development aid, accounting for over 55 per cent. They are also the world's largest importer of goods from less developed countries (see Chapter 10)

While the wisdom or desirability of EU policies and actions are hotly contested, few would deny their practical importance.

Sources: figures available from the websites of the European Commission:

- http://ec.europa.eu/economy_finance/euro/index_en.htm
- http://ec.europa.eu/economy_finance/index_en.htm
- http://trade.ec.europa.eu/doclib/docs/2006/september/tradoc_122531.pdf

Eurostat:

- http://epp.eurostat.ec.europa.eu/portal/page/portal/eurostat/home/

and from the World Trade Organization:

- http://stat.wto.org/CountryProfile/WSDBCountryPFView.aspx?Language=E&Country=E27

when airline flights are delayed or cancelled. For students reading this book that are studying within the EU, but in a state other than that of which they are a national, the Union has been instrumental in establishing and securing that right.

In 2009–14, members of the European Parliament (MEPs) voted, amongst other things, to:

- reject the Anti-Counterfeiting Trade Agreement, which sought to curb piracy on the internet but that many activists claimed lacked safeguards to protect freedom of expression;

- to cap bankers' bonuses and introduce new, more stringent financial services regulations;
- to mandate that more information was provided for consumers on food products; and
- to support an EU tax on financial transactions, often called a 'Robin Hood' tax because it would take from the rich—such as banks—and potentially generate billions to tackle poverty.

At the more dramatic end, the EU has played a leading role over recent years in international action on climate change, fighting piracy off the Horn of Africa, and in negotiations over Iran's nuclear programme.

Second, as the most advanced experiment ever in multilateral cooperation (see Box 1.4), the EU is important analytically. Understanding the EU helps us frame questions about the future of the nation-state, the prospects for international cooperation, the effects of globalization (see Box 1.5), and the proper role of governments in advanced industrial societies. Put another way, what makes the EU challenging to study—its dynamic character, complexity, and expanding activities—also makes it fascinating.

BOX 1.4	Constitutional reform or Lisbon Treaty?

The Constitutional Treaty, the result of a special Convention on the Future of Europe (see Chapter 8), was unanimously endorsed and signed by EU government leaders in 2004. It was eventually abandoned... or was it? Debates persist even about the answer to this most basic of questions.

The Constitutional Treaty comprised three basic elements: institutional reform, a Charter of Fundamental Rights and the consolidation of existing Treaties. The primary **institutional measures** included:

- increased majority voting on the Council of Ministers (where each member state is represented), simplified to represent a double majority based on states and population;
- more legislative powers for the Parliament;
- a full-time president of the European Council (where heads of state and government are represented). This post replaced the previous six-month rotation between Presidents or Prime Ministers of member states;
- a smaller European Commission; and
- a new EU minister of foreign affairs

The second section of the Treaty codified a **Charter of Fundamental Rights** (a wide-ranging statement of 'rights, freedoms, and principles' including the right to life, free expression and the right to strike, binding on the Union's institutions and in the field of EU law; see Chapter 7).

Cont. ➤

Cont.

The third part (by far the longest) consisted of a consolidated and amended version of all previous Treaties. It formally designated the Treaty as a constitution for the first time and gave the Union a single 'legal personality'. However, the term 'Constitutional Treaty' was a typical Eurofudge: yes, it had been prepared by a 'Convention' but it was finally agreed between member states as any Treaty would be. Designed to streamline and bring the EU closer to its citizens, the Treaty ended up stretching to 300 pages of text, not all of them comprehensible. Thus the French government's decision to post copies of the entire text to all voters in advance of France's referendum was not a successful 'vote yes' strategy.

Treaty change requires ratification by all member states. By mid-2007 18 of the 27 had ratified the Treaty. But voters in two founding member states—France and the Netherlands—had rejected the Treaty in referenda held in 2005. An alternative solution had to be found.

In 2007, European leaders finally agreed to abandon the idea of a 'constitution' and instead amended the pre-existing Treaties. They avoided all references to constitutional symbols such as a European flag or anthem, and dropped the idea of giving the title (EU) 'Minister of Foreign Affairs' to a more powerful foreign policy chief. But the new Treaty maintained the bulk of the institutional reforms that were contained in the Constitutional Treaty. The Treaty was initially referred to as the 'Reform Treaty'—after all, everyone is in favour of reform—but the designation was dropped when, like most Treaties, it took on the name of the city where it was signed in late 2007: Lisbon. Eventually ratified by all member states by the end of 2009, Lisbon actually leaves the Union with two main Treaties. The first is called Treaty on European Union (TEU) and contains the basic aims, principles, and instruments of the EU, as well as its provisions on foreign and security policy. The second is called Treaty on the Functioning of the EU, which contains detailed policy provisions and procedures. However, the two are often referred to in the singular as the Lisbon Treaty. Its close substantive resemblance to the Constitutional Treaty prompted debates about whether the original was a 'constitution' in anything but name and whether Lisbon was more than an ordinary 'Treaty'.

Third, the EU is a political puzzle. On the one hand, EU governments and institutions have transformed it from a common market of six countries into a peaceful, integrated Union of 28 states. The EU's economy is considerably bigger than that of the United States. EU trade with the rest of the world accounts for around 20 per cent of global exports and imports. It has its own currency and a fledgling foreign policy. A queue of applicant states waits at its borders.

Yet a growing number of citizens appear disillusioned with the EU, and not just in the traditionally more 'Eurosceptic' states such as the United Kingdom (UK). In 2005 citizens in two founding member states—France and the Netherlands—rejected a Constitutional Treaty designed to make the EU more efficient and bring it closer to its citizens. Eurobarometer public opinion surveys conducted since the

---

BOX 1.5   **Key concepts and terms (listed alphabetically)**

globalization is the idea that the world is becoming increasingly interconnected and interdependent because of increasing flows of trade, technology, ideas, people, and capital. Globalization is usually presented as reducing the autonomy of individual states, although whether its impact is essentially positive or negative, inevitable or controllable, are hotly debated questions (see Wolf 2004; Rodrik 2011).

governance means 'established patterns of rule without an overall ruler'. Even though there is no government, the EU undertakes the sort of activities that have traditionally been the responsibility of governments. The EU is thus said to be a system of governance without a government (or an opposition).

integration is the process whereby sovereign states partially relinquish, or pool, national sovereignty to maximize their collective power and interests.

intergovernmentalism is a process or condition whereby decisions are reached by specifically defined cooperation between or among governments. Formally, at least, sovereignty is not relinquished. The term intergovernmentalism is usually contrasted with supranationalism.

multilevel governance is often used to describe the EU. It means a system in which power is shared between the supranational, national, and subnational levels. The term also suggests there is significant interaction and coordination of political actors across those levels. How they interact and with what effect helps determine the shape of European integration (see Hooghe and Marks 2001).

sovereignty refers to the ultimate authority over people and territory. It is sometimes broken down into internal (law-making authority within a territory) and external (international recognition) sovereignty (see Krasner 1999). Opinions vary on whether state sovereignty is 'surrendered' to, or merely 'shared' or 'pooled' in the EU.

supranationalism means above states or nations. Processes or institutions that are largely (but never entirely) independent of national governments make key decisions. The subject governments (in the case of the EU, the member state governments) are then obliged to accept these decisions. The Court of Justice of the European Union (Chapter 3) is a supranational institution. The term supranationalism is usually contrasted with intergovernmentalism.

---

onset of the Eurozone crisis have shown a marked fall in levels of trust in EU institutions (although trust in national institutions has also fallen) and a greater tendency to identify as a 'national' of a specific country than as 'European'.

Meanwhile, Brussels bureaucrats make easy targets for almost every ill. Populist political parties often gain electoral success through EU-bashing. In fact, the mobilization of their supporters may help explain why 2014 marked the first time ever that voter turnout in a European Parliament election did not fall from the level seen at the previous election. The EU's institutions—the European Commission, the European Council (representing national governments), and even the directly elected European Parliament—are viewed as remote and complex, or just not worth bothering about. The EU certainly is not a well-understood body, and it is difficult even for diligent students to see just how (or if) it works.

This book addresses a central question: 'how does it work?' But the question has two separate meanings and constitutes what is known (in French) as a *double entendre*. One meaning is how it does what it does: who are the main actors, and what are the main processes, dynamics and explanations for what the EU does? But we also want to address the more rhetorical question: 'how (in the world) does it work?!' How can such a massive, complex, unwieldy amalgam of states, institutions, lobbyists, languages, traditions, legal codes, and so on, possibly do much of the governing of Europe, let alone do so both efficiently and legitimately? Why have sovereign states agreed to relinquish part of their sovereignty (see Box 1.5)? Why do European policies emerge looking as they do? Why does the EU elicit such strong demonstrations both of support and antipathy? The primary purpose of this book is to address these questions in a lively and comprehensible way.

Each of our contributors is an expert with research, teaching or policy-making experience (some with all three). Students need to understand both the formal rules of EU practice (what the Treaties say, what EU legislation stipulates, and so on), but also how it really works (how are the Treaties interpreted, what informal rules guide action, and other such unofficial 'rules of the game'). A series of boxes entitled 'How it Really Works' appear throughout the book and are designed to capture this dual dynamic. They illustrate how a particular actor, policy or process actually works, regardless of the formal rules.

Most chapters also include a 'Compared to What?' box. Its purpose is to place the institutions, structures and policies of the EU in a comparative perspective, and help readers better understand the EU by underlining how it is like, or unlike, other systems of governance (Box 1.5). Finally each chapter offers 'Key Concepts' boxes that define important terms, and also provides guides to further reading and useful Internet sites. All of these features are designed to bring the EU to life for our readers.

Understanding the EU: Theory and Conceptual Tools

There is, and can be, no single theory of the EU. Some years ago one of us (Peterson 2001) argued that EU theorists faced 'a choice'. That is, anyone seeking to theorize about European integration had to choose at which level to engage with the EU. For example, at one level the EU remains a system of international relations in which states bargain, cooperate, and compete to achieve their national interests. At another level, the EU is a political system that can usefully be studied using concepts and approaches from comparative politics and public policy. There is also an ever-expanding literature that adopts a constructivist approach, and focuses on how the rules of the game—formal or informal—are 'constructed' as different kinds of EU actor interact with one another at all levels of analysis.

When studying anything as complex as the EU, we need conceptual tools to guide us. Theories simplify reality and allow us to see relationships among the things we observe. When utilizing theories, it is important to specify what about the EU we are seeking to explain before choosing a theory that seems appropriate to the task.

Sketched in the section that follows are some leading theoretical frameworks and approaches, including their key assumptions and insights. The chapters that follow use these insights to elaborate and explain how the EU works. Many of these theories have been developed and refined over many years and readers are encouraged to explore them further through the suggested readings at the end of the chapter.

International Relations (IR) approaches

Several classic theories of European integration draw from IR theory. The basic unit of analysis for most (not all) IR theories is the state. When applied to the EU, they are primarily concerned with explaining how and why states choose to form European institutions, and who or what determines the shape and speed of the integration process.

In 1958, coinciding with the establishment of the EEC, Ernst Haas published *The Uniting of Europe*, a classic work of neofunctionalist theory. Haas and other neofunctionalist scholars sought to explain how a merger of economic activity in specific economic sectors (starting with coal and steel) across borders could 'spill over' and provoke wider integration in related areas (Haas 1961, 1964; Lindberg and Scheingold 1970). One form of spill over was functional: for instance, a single EU market wasn't truly possible without a single EU environmental policy. Moreover, neofunctionalists posited that political spill over would supplement functional spill over. Political spill over referred to the possibilities created by new institutions at the European level. Actors at the national level (such as interest groups) could align their interests across borders and interact directly with EU institutions (say, the European Commission) and press for further integration. Through this process, a new field of political action—in addition to already existing national fields—would be created. Over time, and incrementally, interests and loyalties would gradually shift from the national to the supranational (Box 1.5) level.

Neofunctionalism appeared well suited to explaining the successful early years of integration. However, by 1965 the French President Charles de Gaulle had appeared on the scene. De Gaulle was symbolic of the ongoing importance, to many, of state sovereignty and national interests. The mid-1960s were characterized by the so-called Empty Chair Crisis in which De Gaulle withdrew French participation from meetings of the Council of Ministers (hence the empty chair). Supranational institutions were weakened during this period. The nation state had seemingly reasserted itself. Neofunctionalist theory possessed a unidirectional logic (suggesting that integration could only go forward), which damaged its credibility as events of the 1960s and 1970s unfolded.

Dissatisfaction with neofunctionalism in the 1960s was reflected in Hoffmann's (1966) assertion that the nation state was 'obstinate, not obsolete', in Europe as well as globally. The phrase captured the notion that a logic of diversity amongst national interests might just as easily impede the development of European integration as it might further it. Interestingly, Hoffmann (1995: 1–6) identified himself as a realist.

Realism, a prominent theory within IR, has had surprisingly little to say about European integration. Realism's emphasis on the importance of the structure of the international system, on states as unitary and rational actors possessing fixed and often conflictual goals, and its pessimism about the positive impact of international institutions, jars with the complexity of the EU and its densely institutionalized mechanisms of interstate cooperation. Recently, Rosato (2011, 2012) has offered a realist account of European integration that identifies the Cold War threat posed by the Soviet Union as the key factor determining decisions by the original 6 member states (and then more member states later) to press ahead with integration. Rosato's highly provocative account has been criticized on both historical and methodological grounds (Moravcsik 2013).

A more credible account is offered by Moravcsik's (1993, 1998) liberal intergovernmentalism. It contends that it is the preferences and power of EU member states that drive forward the integration process. The approach is 'liberal' because it assumes that economic interests, and not just security interests (as realists sometimes argue), motivate and drive European states. Liberal intergovernmentalism disaggregates the state and considers how national governments bargain with various domestic interest groups (especially economic ones) to produce a coalition of support broad enough to support its agenda. It is an 'intergovernmental' theory because, at the EU level, Moravcsik conceptualizes national governments as bringing their preferences to a bargaining table with the outcome being a reflection of the relative power of each member state. Moravcsik emphasizes national power, package deals, and the ability to make side-payments to reluctant partners. EU institutions and transnational alliances of interest groups are afforded little role, marking a key distinction between his approach and neofunctionalism.

Moravcsik's (1998) historically impressive work, *The Choice for Europe*, confines itself to major choices in the history of the EU—what Peterson (1995) calls 'history making decisions'. It does not account for much of what might be called the day-to-day activities of the Union. Along with other IR theories, it approaches the Union as a sub-system of international relations and one that is overwhelmingly dominated by states.

A comparative politics approach

Works drawing on comparative politics approaches have challenged the primacy of the state in shaping European integration. Foremost amongst them is the so-called new institutionalism (Hall and Taylor 1996; Pollack 2004), which emerged as part of a broader move in political science in the late 1980s and 1990s. What was new about institutionalism was that it brought 'back in' to the study of politics how institutions matter in determining outcomes, after a long period when they were neglected. It has been applied fruitfully to the study of the EU to the point where, arguably, institutionalism has become *the* leading theory of EU politics and policymaking (see Cowles and Curtis 2004).

Institutionalism insists that the EU's institutions are more than impartial arbiters in the policymaking process; they are key players with their own agendas and priorities (Armstrong and Bulmer 1998; Pollack 2009). Institutionalists contend that the Union's policies are not simply the results of bargaining between governments. Its institutions are unusually powerful compared to those of other international organizations. They thus play a key role in the formulation and adoption of EU policy. To illustrate, almost nothing can become EU legislation unless the Commission tables a proposal. The European Court of Justice has been able to shape EU integration even, at times, against the wishes of member states. The Parliament can kill off proposals that are supported by the governments of member states.

Many institutionalists focus on the impact of institutions over time and specifically how institutions, once established, can shape and even constrain the behaviour of the actors who established them (Pierson 1996, 2000). Political institutions and even policies, once established, can become subject to path dependency. Political actors often naturally stick with established institutions and policies as they increasingly learn how to operate with, and within, them. Institutions, and policies, are thus said to be 'sticky'; that is, once established, they tend not to change. Consider the EU's common agricultural policy (CAP), which has survived—with incremental adaptations—for many years despite intense criticism. The idea of starting again on a long, time-consuming and expensive process of renegotiating the CAP has been resisted.

Obviously, institutions matter far more for institutionalists than they do for liberal intergovernmentalists. Inevitably, perhaps, institutionalism is better at explaining developments after the fact than it is at offering predictive hypotheses. Still, its advocates are on strong ground in insisting that institutions can alter the incentives that actors face when making decisions about how best to pursue their preferences, and must be taken into account.

A sociological/cultural approach

One theoretical approach to the EU claims to be able to generate equally plausible explanations at all levels of analysis. Constructivism is strikingly diverse but at its core is an attempt to focus on the 'social construction' of the collective rules and norms that guide political behaviour (Eilstrup-Sangiovanni 2006: 393). At its most radical, a constructivist approach argues that reality does not exist outside of human interpretation and language. In the study of the EU, however, a less radical or abstract form of constructivism is prevalent (see Risse 2009). Constructivism shares neofunctionalism's concern with new arenas for socialization, transfers of loyalty, and processes in which actors redefine their interests as a result of interacting with the EU and its institutions (Haas 2006). Along with institutionalists, social constructivists suggest that informal rules and norms (such as reciprocity or good will) can shape or even determine the behaviour of political actors (Checkel 2006).

Of course, it is extremely difficult to show that abstract ideas or norms actually cause a change in behaviour, as many constructivists argue. Consider this: during 2013–14 the idea emerged that the individual appointed as President of the European Commission should be the 'lead candidate' of the political party that won the most seats in the 2014 European Parliament elections. The national interests of at least some member states stood contrary to that idea. And yet, ultimately, the idea prevailed and the lead candidate of the centre-right European People's Party—Jean Claude Juncker—was appointed President. A more cynical perspective might argue that those promoting the idea (such as the political party groups, leading members of the European Parliament) were simply seeking to advance their own interests and using the power of an idea, in this case the idea of a more democratic process of appointment, to attain their desired outcome.

Constructivists can, therefore, often correlate ideas with behaviour but they have trouble proving that ideas matter more than interests (Aspinwall and Schneider 2000; Checkel 2004). Nevertheless, sociological/constructivist approaches to the EU offer insight into, for example, the extent to which EU Commission officials are socialized in a supranational way (Hooghe 2005; Kassim et al. 2014), or the extent to which actors can learn from prior interactions and alter their preferences accordingly (Checkel 2001). In recent years, sociological approaches to the EU have proliferated and offered new insights into the nature of political protests across the EU as well as which citizens are most likely to identify as 'European' (see Merand and Saurugger 2010; Roche 2010; Risse 2010).

A public policy approach

A fourth theoretical approach useful to those studying the EU is the policy network framework (Jordan and Schout 2006; Peterson 2009). Unlike neofunctionalism and liberal intergovernmentalism, this approach does not tell us much about the grand bargains struck between national governments, nor the history-making decisions, such as Treaty reform, that set the broad direction of European integration. But policy network analysis helps guide exploration of the behind-the-scenes negotiation and exchange that shapes EU policy day-to-day. A policy network is a 'cluster of actors, each of which has an interest or stake in a given EU policy sector and the capacity to help determine policy success or failure' (Peterson and Bomberg 1999: 8).

Policy networks at the EU level bring together institutional actors (from the Commission, Council, Parliament) and other stakeholders such as representatives of private firms, public interest groups, technical or scientific experts, political campaigners and national officials. Networks lack hierarchy. There is no one actor in charge. They rely instead on resource exchange. As a result, participants need to bring to Brussels (or Strasbourg) some valued resource with which to bargain. That resource could be information, ideas, money, constitutional-legal power, or political legitimacy. According to network analysts, bargaining and resource exchange among these actors, rather than strictly intergovernmental bargaining, determine the shape of actual EU policies.

Different theories, different insights

Each of these theoretical approaches has a set of assumptions, strengths and weaknesses (Table 1.1). No one theory can explain everything treated in this book. But each offers different insights about different key features of the EU: how integration evolves; the way policies are made; the role of different actors in the process; and so on. Readers need not master all these theories to use this book. Rather, these theoretical insights—and their application in subsequent chapters—are meant to

TABLE 1.1   Theories of European integration and the EU

Theory/approach	Proponents/ major works	Assumptions	Shortcomings
Neofunctionalism	Haas (1958)	Supranational institutions crucial; spill over drives integration	Cannot explain stagnation
Liberal intergovernmentalism	Moravcsik (1998)	Member states control integration	Too state-centric, neglects day-to-day policymaking
New Institutionalism	Pollack (2009)	Institutions matter, path dependencies and sunk costs make institutions and policies 'sticky'	Over-emphasizes the power of the EU's institutions
Social Constructivism	Checkel (2004)	Ideas matter, interests are constructed and not pre-determined	Methodological weaknesses
Policy Networks	Peterson (2009)	Resource exchange within networks shapes policy	Cannot explain big decisions

encourage thinking about theory and its role in helping us understand and evaluate European integration and EU politics.

Themes

To help the reader make sense of the EU, this text is held together by three common themes. Each highlights a key, distinctive feature of the EU as:

1. An 'experiment in motion', an ongoing process without a clear end-state;
2. A system of shared power characterized by growing complexity and an increasing number of players;
3. An organization with an expanding scope, but limited capacity.

We will now introduce each of these themes.

Experimentation and change

Since its conception in the early 1950s, European integration has been an ongoing process without a clear end-state (see van Middelaar 2013). In one sense its development has been a functional step-by-step process: integration in one area has led to pressures to integrate in others. As neofunctionalists would point out, the EU has developed from a free trade area to a customs union, from a customs union to a single market, and from a single market to an economic and monetary union. These developments, however, have not been smooth or automatic. Rather, the EU's development has progressed in fits and starts, the result of constant experimentation, problem-solving, and trial and error. European foreign policy—from the failed attempts of the 1950s (see Chapter 2), to the creation of a Common Foreign and Security Policy (CFSP) in the early 1990s and a Common Security and Defence Policy (CSDP) in the late 1990s—is a good example of this evolution. With no agreed end goal (such as a 'United States of Europe'), the EU's actors have reacted to immediate problems, but they have done so neither coherently nor always predictably.

The nature and intensity of change are also varied. Constitutional change takes place through Intergovernmental Conferences (IGCs)—special negotiations in which government representatives come together to hammer out agreements to adapt or alter the EU's founding Treaties. The first (resulting in the 1951 Treaty of Paris) created the ECSC with six members. Most recently, the Lisbon Treaty (ratified in 2009) was designed to consolidate and streamline a Union of (then) 27 members, with the possibility of it growing still further to 30 or more (see Box 1.6). Less spectacularly, legislative change has taken place through thousands of EU directives and regulations. Finally, the EU's institutions, especially the European Commission and Court of Justice, and the member states have themselves acted as instigators of change,

> **BOX 1.6** **The Treaties**
>
> When practitioners and academics use the term 'the Treaties', they are referring to the collection of founding treaties and their subsequent revisions. The founding treaties include the Treaty of Paris (signed in 1951, establishing the European Coal and Steel Community) and two Treaties of Rome signed in 1957, one establishing the European Economic Community and the other the European Atomic Energy Community (Euratom). The Treaty of Paris became void in July 2002. The Euratom Treaty never amounted to much. But the **Treaty of Rome** that established the EEC became absolutely central. It has been substantially revised, notably in the:
>
> - **Single European Act** (signed 1986)
> - Treaty on European Union, more commonly termed the **Maastricht Treaty** (signed 1992)
> - **Treaty of Amsterdam** (signed 1997)
> - **Treaty of Nice** (signed 2001)
> - **Treaty of Lisbon** (signed 2007)
>
> As Box 1.1 explained, the intergovernmental conference leading up to the Maastricht Treaty not only revised the Treaty of Rome (which it re-named the Treaty establishing the European Community), it also agreed the broader Treaty on European Union (TEU, or Maastricht Treaty), which included two new pillars covering foreign policy and justice and home affairs (see Box 1.2). The Amsterdam and Lisbon Treaties subsequently collapsed the pillars into a single framework.
>
> The EU's Treaties are the basic toolkit of ministers, European Commissioners, parliamentarians, and civil servants dealing with EU matters. Each piece of legislation is based on one of these Treaty articles (of which there are more than 400). The Treaties have grown increasingly long and complex. To improve the presentation, and facilitate the reading of the Treaties, the articles were renumbered in the Amsterdam IGC of 1997. But the Treaties are hardly an easy read. Even many legal scholars would agree that some of their language borders on the incomprehensible. The failed Constitutional Treaty of 2004 was intended to simplify the existing texts and make them more readable. The Lisbon Treaty made a more modest attempt at simplification, although the term 'constitution' was dropped.

through their interpretations of the Treaties and of legislation as well as through informal agreements and practices supplementing them. The point is that change is a constant in the EU. This book will explore its main sources and implications.

Power sharing and consensus

Our second theme concerns power and how it is shared between different actors and across layers of government. The EU policy-making system lacks a clear nexus of power: there is no 'EU government', nor is there any 'opposition'. Instead, power is dispersed across a range of actors and levels of governance (regional, national and supranational). Deciding which actors should do what, and at what level of governance, is a matter of on-going debate within the EU. But, whenever possible, the Union seeks to act on the basis of broad consensus.

The three most important sets of actors are the member states, the EU institutions, and organized interests. Certainly, much about the evolution of the EU has been determined by the member states themselves, and in particular their different approaches to integration. Some member states want deeper integration, others do not, and this division continues to shape the speed and form of the integration process. Meanwhile, EU institutions have shaped its development as they vie for power with the member states, as well as among themselves. Finally organized interests—including representatives of sub-national levels of governance, private interests, and citizens groups—now play an increasing role.

Part of what makes the EU unique—and certainly different from its member states—is that these actors exist in a complex web where there are established patterns of interaction but no overall 'ruler', government, or even dominant actor. Instead, actors must bargain and share power in an effort to reach an agreement acceptable to all, or at least most. This dynamic has been captured in the term multi-level governance (see Box 1.5), which suggests a system of overlapping and shared powers between actors on the regional, national and supranational level (Hooghe and Marks 2001). EU governance is thus an exercise in sharing power between states and institutions and seeking consensus across different levels of governance. Coming to grips with this unique and changing distribution of power is a key task of this book.

Scope and capacity

Our final theme concerns the expanding remit of the EU and its ability to cope with it. The EU has undergone continuous (in a phrase used by insiders) 'widening and deepening'. The widening of its membership has been astonishing. It has grown from a club of six member states (West Germany, France, Italy, the Netherlands, Belgium and Luxembourg) to nine (UK, Denmark and Ireland joined in 1973), to 12 (Greece in 1981; Portugal and Spain in 1986), to 15 (Austria, Finland and Sweden joined in 1995). Then in 2004 the EU jumped to 25 following the accession of ten mainly central and eastern European states. The accession of Bulgaria and Romania in 2007 took the EU to 27, with Croatia becoming the 28th in 2013. Additional countries—the Former Yugoslav Republic of Macedonia, Montenegro, and Serbia plus Albania, Iceland and Turkey—are candidate states. The institutional, political, economic, and even linguistic challenges that enlargement poses are immense (Box 1.7).

The EU has also 'deepened' in the sense that the member states have decided to pool sovereignty in an increasing number of policy areas, including, most dramatically, in sensitive policy areas associated with the Area of Freedom, Justice

> ### BOX 1.7   Lost in interpretation?
>
> Following the accession of Croatia in 2013, the EU boasted 24 official languages: Bulgarian, Croatian, Czech, Danish, Dutch, English, Estonian, Finnish, French, German, Greek, Irish, Hungarian, Italian, Latvian, Lithuanian, Maltese, Polish, Portuguese, Romanian, Slovak, Slovene, Spanish, and Swedish.
>
> The EU's translation service is the largest in the world by far (over twice the size of the UN's) and the cost of translation and interpretation is over €850m a year, or around €1.70 for every person in the EU. In Parliament alone, where interpreters in soundproof boxes attempt to translate words such as gobbledygook (the word doesn't exist in Polish), and avoid confusing frozen semen with frost-bitten seamen (as occurred in one parliamentary debate), the cost and potential confusion is immense. But being able to communicate with your electors and fellow representatives in your own language is also seen as a fundamental right. After all, it is difficult for EU citizens to feel close to an institution that does not operate—at least officially—in their own language. In practice, most of the work of the EU is carried out in just three languages, English, French and German. Meanwhile, the rising cost of translation has had one positive effect—it has forced practitioners to limit official texts to fewer than 15 pages.
>
> *Sources:* Commission 2007b, 2007c; query to Commission DG Translation.

and Security (see Chapter 7). The sovereign debt crisis led the EU to become more actively involved in the sensitive area of national budgets. Such developments mean that the EU is managing tasks that have traditionally been the exclusive preserve of the nation state.

At the same time, the EU continues to try to dispose of its image as 'economic giant, a political dwarf, and a military worm', a depiction attributed to the Belgian Foreign Minister, Mark Eyskens. The EU is trying to stamp its authority on the international scene through its leadership on issues such as climate change and the Iranian nuclear programme. A CFSP has been developed that, according to the Treaties, 'might lead to a common defence' (Article 24 TEU). These developments have challenged the EU's capacity—its practical and political ability to realize its ambitions. While the EU has taken on more members and more tasks, its institutional and political development has not kept pace. This mismatch—between the EU's ambitions on the one hand and its institutional and political capacity on the other (see Hill 1993)—raises questions about the EU's future and ability to adapt. It also represents the third theme of the volume.

Taken together these three themes address:

- How the EU has developed and why (experimentation and change);
- Who the main players are and how they interact (power sharing and consensus);
- What the EU does, and how it does it (scope and capabilities).

These three themes provide the glue necessary to hold together our investigation of the EU and how it works.

Chapter Layout

Any book on European integration that aims to be at all comprehensive is bound to cover a lot of ground, both theoretical and practical. In explaining how the EU works, it is necessary to look at the historical background of European integration, the major actors involved, the key policies and their impact, and the EU's global presence. The book's layout reflects this logic. Chapter 2 tells us 'how we got here' by providing a concise historical overview of the EU's development. The next section (Chapters 3–4), focuses on the major actors: the EU's institutions and member states. Section III focuses on policy and process. It provides an overview of key economic and related policies (Chapter 5), how policies are made (Chapter 6), and the wider constitutional issues arising from these policy processes (Chapter 7). Chapters in the last section examine the EU's relations with the wider world. Chapter 8 covers EU enlargement and its policy towards states in its geographical neighbourhood. Chapter 9 focuses on the EU's foray into the sensitive area of security policy. Chapter 10 explores the EU's growing role as a global actor. A conclusion draws together the main themes of the volume and ponders how the EU might work in the future.

DISCUSSION QUESTIONS

1. The EU can be seen as one of the most successful modern experiments in international cooperation, yet it is increasingly unpopular amongst its citizens. Why?

2. Which theory appears to offer the most compelling account of recent developments in European integration?

FURTHER READING

Some of the key themes introduced in this chapter are inspired by leading, general studies of the EU including Scharpf (1999), Weiler (1999), Hooghe and Marks (2001), Jørgensen et al. (2006), and Wallace et al. (2015). Wiener and Diez (2009) feature a collection of works on European integration theory and practice. Good overviews of integration theory include Rosamond (2000, 2013), Eilstrup-Sangiovanni (2006), Pollack (2010), and the relevant chapters of Jones et al. (2012). An excellent recent addition to the literature, written by the speechwriter to a former European Council President, is Van Middelaar (2013).

Eilstrup—Sangiovanni, M. (ed.) (2006), *Debates on European Integration: A Reader* (London: Palgrave).

Hooghe, L. and Marks, G. (2001), *Multi-Level Governance and European Integration* (Lanham and Oxford: Rowman and Littlefield Publishers, Inc).

Jones, E., Menon, A., and Weatherill, S. (eds) (2012), *The Oxford Handbook of the European Union* (New York and Oxford: Oxford University Press).

Jørgensen, K. E., Pollack, M., and Rosamond, B. (eds) (2006), *Handbook of European Union Politics* (London: Sage)

Pollack, M. (2010), Theorizing EU Policy-Making in Wallace, H., Pollack, M., and Young, A. (eds), *Policy-Making in the European Union*, 7th edn. (Oxford and New York: Oxford University Press): 15–44.

Rosamond, B. (2000), *Theories of European Integration* (Basingstoke and New York: Palgrave Macmillan).

Rosamond, B. (2013), 'Theorizing the EU After Integration Theory', in M. Cini and N. Pérez-Solórzano Borragán (eds), *European Union Politics*, 4th edn. (Oxford and New York: Oxford University Press).

Scharpf, F. W. (1999), *Governing in Europe: Effective and Democratic?* (Oxford and New York: Oxford University Press).

Van Middelaar, L. (2013), *The Passage to Europe: How a Continent Became a Union* (New Haven CT and London: Yale University Press).

Wallace, H., Pollack, M., and Young, A. (eds) (2015), *Policy-Making in the European Union*, 7th edn. (Oxford and New York: Oxford University Press).

Weiler, J. H. H. (1999), *The Constitution of Europe* (Cambridge and New York: Cambridge University Press).

Wiener, A. and Diez, T. (eds) (2009), *European Integration Theory*, 2nd edn. (Oxford and New York: Oxford University Press).

WEB LINKS

- The EU's official website 'The European Union online' (**http://europa.eu/**) is a valuable starting point. It provides further links to a wide variety of official sites on EU policies, institutions, legislation, Treaties, and current debates.
- Precisely because the EU's website is so large, the Europa Information Services website provides a nice index of where to find answers on the Europa website (**http://europa.eu/geninfo/info/guide/index_en.htm**).
- You can also use the web to access the *Official Journal* (OJ) which is updated daily in several languages. The OJ is the authoritative and formal source for information on EU legislation, case law, parliamentary questions, and documents of public interest (**http://eur-lex.europa.eu/**).
- For pithier reporting, the *Economist* (**www.economist.com**) provides useful general articles, while *European Voice* (**www.european-voice.com**) offers insider coverage of EU policies and news.

- To follow current events and developments within the EU, the following sites are useful:

  - EurActiv reports EU current affairs with analysis, and has an easy to navigate system of 'dossiers' which provide an overview of different policy areas (**http://www.euractiv.com**).

  - EUobserver offers coverage of EU current affairs with a very useful email bulletin service (**http://euobserver.com/**).

  - Current debates and topics are also addressed in series of think-tank websites. Some of the better known include the Centre for European Policy Studies (**http://www.ceps.be**); the European Policy Centre (**http://www.epc.eu**); the Centre for European Reform (**www.cer.org.uk**); and the Trans European Policy Studies Association (**www.tepsa.be**).

  - The Institute for European Politics (Berlin) website offers an overview of current thinking on EU policies and issues in all the member states (**http://www.iep-berlin.de/index.php?id=publikationen&L=1**).

 Visit the Online Resource Centre that accompanies this book for additional material: **www.oxfordtextbooks.co.uk/orc/kenealy4e/**

CHAPTER 2

How Did We Get Here?

Desmond Dinan

▌ Summary

European governments responded to a series of domestic, regional, and global challenges after the Second World War by establishing new transnational institutions in order to accelerate political and economic integration. These challenges ranged from post-war reconstruction, to the Cold War, and then to globalization. Driven largely by mutually compatible national interests, Franco-German bargains, and American influence, politicians responded by establishing the European communities in the 1950s and the European Union in the 1990s. Yet the increasing political salience of European integration generated seemingly insurmountable challenges for the EU, touching on identity, sovereignty, and legitimacy. At the same time, successive rounds of enlargement, which saw the Union grow in size from its original six member states, generated institutional and policy challenges that have shaped the contours of European integration.

Introduction

Continuity or change? Individual initiative or unstoppable momentum? Ideology or self-interest? Questions such as these help frame the debate about the origins and evolution of the European Union (EU). Specifically, to what extent do the vicissitudes of institutionalized economic and political integration in the post-World War II period represent a decisive break from previous patterns of international relations? Has the EU been shaped more by human agency than by profound, impersonal forces? How important are ideational as opposed to material motives?

Historians have grappled with these and other questions, large and small, since the emergence of EU history as a sub-field of modern European history (see Box 2.1). Consensus remains elusive, although differences among mainstream historians are mostly of degree rather than of dogma. Antecedents of **European integration** existed well before the end of World War II. Economic, political, and strategic challenges in the post-war period facilitated the rise of European integration, which committed and influential politicians helped to bring about. Often strongly sympathetic to European federalism, however vaguely understood, these individuals mostly operated within the framework of nation states. Without a realistic sense of what constituted the national interest, proponents of European integration would not have seen their ideas come to fruition.

BOX 2.1	Interpreting European integration

Historians have offered different interpretations of how European integration has developed and why. Alan Milward (1984, 2000) was the foremost historian of European integration. He argued that economic interests impelled Western European countries to integrate, but that national governments shared sovereignty only to the extent necessary to resolve problems that would otherwise have undermined their effectiveness, legitimacy and credibility. Paradoxically, European states rescued themselves through limited **supranationalism**. Andrew Moravcsik (1998) has complemented Milward's thesis by claiming that national governments, not supranational institutions, controlled the pace and scope of integration. Moravcsik uses historical insights from a series of case studies from the 1950s to the 1990s to develop **liberal intergovernmentalism** as a theory of European integration. Intergovernmentalism generally is in the ascendant in the historiography of European integration, in contrast to the early years of the EC when the arguments of neofunctionalist scholars such as Ernst Haas (1958) and Leon Lindberg (1963) dominated academic discourse on the EC (see Chapter 1).

Post-War Problems and Solutions

One of the most pressing problems at the end of the Second World War was what to do about Germany. The question became acute with the onset of the Cold War. As the Soviet Union consolidated its control over the eastern part of the country, the Western Powers—the United Kingdom (UK), France, and the United States (US)—facilitated the establishment of democratic and free market institutions in what became the Federal Republic of Germany (FRG, or West Germany). The German question then became how to maximize the economic and military potential of West Germany for the benefit of the West while allaying the understandable concerns of Germany's neighbours, especially France.

The US championed integration as a means of reconciling old enemies, promoting prosperity, and strengthening Western Europe's resistance to communism. The Marshall Plan (see Box 2.2) was the main instrument of American policy. European governments wanted American dollars for post-war reconstruction, but without strings attached. For their part, the Americans insisted that European recipients coordinate their plans for using the aid. That was the extent of European integration in the late 1940s. The UK had no interest in sharing sovereignty. France wanted to keep the old enemy down and prevent (West) Germany's coal-rich Ruhr region from becoming a springboard to remilitarization. Few countries were willing to liberalize trade. Winston Churchill's famous call in 1946 for a United States of Europe belied the reality of politicians' unwillingness to change the status quo.

It was West Germany's rapid economic recovery, thanks in part to the Marshall Plan, which made the status quo untenable. The US wanted to accelerate German recovery in order to reduce occupation costs and promote recovery throughout Europe. A weak West Germany, the Americans argued, meant a weak Western Europe. France agreed, but urged caution. France wanted to modernize its own economy before allowing West Germany's economy to rebound. Indeed, France agreed to the establishment of West Germany only on condition that its coal production (a key material for war-making) remained under international control.

German resentment of French policy resonated in Washington. As the Cold War deepened, the US intensified pressure on France to relax its policy so that West German economic potential could be put at the disposal of the West. Yet the US was not insensitive to French economic and security interests. Instead of imposing a solution, Washington pressed Paris to devise a policy that would allay French concerns about the Ruhr region, without endangering West Germany's full recovery. Given its preference for European integration, the US hoped that France would take a supranational tack.

BOX 2.2	Key concepts and terms

The **Empty Chair Crisis** was prompted by French President Charles de Gaulle's decision to pull France out of all Council meetings in 1965, thereby leaving one chair empty. De Gaulle staunchly opposed the Commission's plans to extend the EC's powers generally and the application of the Treaty provisions on the extension of **qualified majority voting (QMV)**.

The **Luxembourg Compromise** resolved the empty chair crisis. Reached during a foreign ministers' meeting in 1966, the Compromise was an informal agreement (issued only in the form of a press release) stating that when a decision was subject to QMV, the Council would postpone a decision if any member states felt 'very important interests' were under threat, and would 'endeavour, within a reasonable time' to find a solution acceptable to all. Although France and the Five disagreed on what would happen if no such solutions were found within a reasonable time (continue discussions or proceed to a vote), in practice the compromise meant that QMV was used far less often, and unanimity became the norm.

The **Marshall Plan** (1947) was an aid package from the US of $13 billion (equivalent to five per cent of US GNP at that time) to help rebuild West European economies after the war. The aid was given on the condition that European states cooperate and jointly administer these funds.

Qualified Majority Voting (QMV) is the voting system most commonly used in the Council. Decisions require a high level of support but do not need unanimity. The formula, revised by the Lisbon Treaty, can be found in Table 3.2.

The **Schengen Agreement** was signed by five member states in 1985 (Belgium, France, Germany, Luxembourg, and the Netherlands) and came into effect ten years later. It removed all border controls among its signatories, and now includes most member states as well as Iceland, Liechtenstein, Norway, and Switzerland. Ireland and the UK are not in the Schengen area.

Subsidiarity is the idea that action should be taken at the level of government that is best able to achieve policy goals, as close to the citizens as possible. According to its logic, local councils (of towns and cities) should handle rubbish removal, while the EU as a whole should make trade policy (see Chapter 10).

Originally, the US wanted the UK to lead on 'the German question'. The UK had already taken the initiative on military security in Europe, having pressed the US to negotiate the Washington Treaty (which founded NATO, the North Atlantic Treaty Organization). Yet the UK was reluctant for reasons of history, national sovereignty, and economic policy to go beyond anything but intergovernmental cooperation. Absent British leadership and under mounting American pressure, France came up with a novel idea to reconcile Franco-German interests by pooling coal and steel resources under a supranational High Authority.

The Schuman Plan

This idea became the Schuman Plan, drafted by Jean Monnet, a senior French civil servant with extensive international experience. Monnet faced intense American pressure to devise a new policy towards West Germany but also believed in European unity and saw the Schuman Plan as a first step in that direction. More immediately, it would protect French interests by ensuring continued access to German resources, although on the basis of cooperation rather than coercion. The new plan bore the name of the French Foreign Minister, Robert Schuman, who risked his political life promoting it at a time when most French people deeply distrusted Germany.

The West German Chancellor, Konrad Adenauer, endorsed the plan, which provided a means of resolving the Ruhr problem and rehabilitating West Germany internationally. Schuman and Adenauer trusted each other. They were both Christian Democrats, came from the Franco-German borderlands, and spoke German together. Aware of the UK's attitude towards integration, Schuman did not bother to inform London of the plan. By contrast, the Americans were in on it from the beginning.

The Schuman Plan was a major reversal of French foreign policy. Having tried to keep Germany down since the war, France now sought to turn the inevitability of West Germany's economic recovery to its own advantage through the establishment of a common market in coal and steel. The Schuman Declaration of 9 May 1950, announcing the plan, was couched in the language of reconciliation rather than *realpolitik*. In fact the initiative cleverly combined national and European interests. It represented a dramatic new departure in European as well as in French and German affairs (see Box 2.3).

Participation in the plan was supposedly open to all the countries of Europe. In fact, the list of likely partners was far shorter. The Cold War excluded Central and Eastern Europe from the plan. In Western Europe, the UK and the Scandinavian countries had already rejected supranationalism. Ireland was isolationist; Spain and Portugal, under dictatorial regimes, were international outcasts; and Switzerland was resolutely neutral. That left the Benelux countries (Belgium, the Netherlands, and Luxembourg)—which were economically tied to France and West Germany— and Italy, which saw integration primarily as a means of combating domestic communism and restoring international legitimacy. Consequently the European Coal and Steel Community (ECSC), launched in 1952, included only six countries. The ECSC soon established a common market in coal and steel products, with generous provisions for workers' rights.

The European Defence Community

The same six countries ('the Six') signed a Treaty to establish a defence community in 1952. The rationale for both communities was the same: supranational institutions provided the best means of managing West German recovery. In this case, the

BOX 2.3	How it really works

Rhetoric versus reality in the Schuman Plan

Jean Monnet's drafting of the Schuman Plan in 1950 marked a diplomatic breakthrough on the contentious German question. More generally, the plan's proposal for a coal and steel community also advanced the goal of European unity. When outlining the proposal in the Schuman Declaration—a highly publicized initiative—Monnet emphasized the European and idealistic dimension of the proposal. Issued on 9 May, the Schuman Declaration proclaimed that:

World peace can only be safeguarded if constructive efforts are made proportionate to the dangers that threaten it ... France, by advocating for more than twenty years the idea of a united Europe, has always regarded it as an essential objective to serve the purpose of peace ... With this aim in view, the French government proposes to take immediate action on one limited but decisive point. The French government proposes that Franco-German production of coal and steel be placed under a common 'high authority' within an organization open to the participation of the other European nations ... [This step] will lay the first concrete foundation for a European federation, which is so indispensable for the preservation of peace.

But Monnet was also concerned to defend French national interests. He wanted to ensure French access to German raw materials and European markets in view of West Germany's economic resurgence. In a private note to Schuman some days before the Declaration's release, Monnet explained that France had little choice but to safeguard its interests by taking a new approach. On 1 May, Monnet informed Schuman that:

Germany has already asked to be allowed to increase its output [of steel] from 10 to 14 million tons [French output was 9 million tons at the time]. We will refuse but the Americans will insist. Finally, we will make reservations and give way ... There is no need to describe the consequences [of not giving way] in any detail.

(quoted in Duchêne 1994: 198)

Instead of trying to block West Germany's advance, Monnet advocated a European initiative—the Schuman Plan—that also catered for French interests.

outbreak of the Korean War in June 1950, perceived as a possible precursor to a Soviet attack on Western Europe, made West German remilitarization imperative. France at first resisted, and then acquiesced on condition that German military units were subsumed into the proposed European Defence Community (EDC). Like the Schuman Plan, the plan for the EDC sought to make a virtue (European integration) out of necessity (German remilitarization). Although the EDC was a French initiative, most French people fiercely opposed German remilitarization. The EDC became the most divisive issue in the country. In view of the Treaty's unpopularity, the government delayed ratification for two years, and the French parliament rejected the Treaty in 1954.

Ironically, West Germany formed an army anyway, under the auspices of the Western European Union (WEU), an intergovernmental organization established by the UK and the Six established in 1954. West Germany joined NATO via the WEU in May 1955 and effectively regained full sovereignty. Whereas the intergovernmental WEU endured (until it was folded into the EU, beginning in 2000), the EDC was a bridge too far for European integration. At a time when the Six were setting up the ECSC, the launch of a similar initiative in the much more sensitive defence sector was too ambitious. Even if it had come into existence, in all likelihood the EDC would have been unworkable. Resistance to its implementation, especially from the far left and far right, would have been intense. Although ratified by the others, the EDC brought the idea of supranationalism into disrepute in France. The end of the affair allowed supporters of supranationalism to jettison the baggage of West German remilitarization and concentrate on first principles: economic integration.

It is remarkable how quickly the idea of European integration bounced back to life. The ECSC was operating fully, but its political and economic impact was slight. Despite what some observers (and neofunctionalist theorists) predicted, there was little 'spill over' from supranational cooperation in coal and steel to other sectors. Monnet, who became President of the High Authority, was bored in Luxembourg, the ECSC's capital. He left office and returned to Paris in 1955, where he set up a transnational organization, the Action Committee for the United States of Europe, to advocate further integration. His pet scheme was an Atomic Energy Community (Euratom), created along the same lines as the ECSC. The French government was interested, but not for the same reasons as Monnet. Whereas Monnet saw Euratom as a further step towards European unity, the government saw it as a means of bolstering France's nuclear programme for civil and military purposes. Not surprisingly, this idea held little appeal for France's partners.

The European Community

The relaunch of European integration after the EDC's collapse was due largely to changes in international trade relations in the mid-1950s. Thanks to liberalization measures in the Organization for European Economic Cooperation (OEEC) and the General Agreement on Tariffs and Trade (GATT), intra-European trade was on the rise. With it, prosperity increased. European governments wanted more trade, but disagreed on the rate and range of liberalization. The British favoured further liberalization through the OEEC and the GATT, as did influential elements in the West German government (notably Ludwig Erhard, the economics minister). The French were instinctively protectionist, although some prominent politicians advocated openness. The Dutch, with a small and open economy, wanted full liberalization and were impatient with progress in the OEEC and the GATT, where each member's veto power constrained decision-making.

The Dutch had proposed a common market for all industrial sectors in the early 1950s. The idea was to combine a customs union (the phased abolition of tariffs—taxes on imports—among member states and erection of a common external tariff, see Box 2.4) with the free movement of goods, people, services, and capital, as well as supranational decision-making in areas such as competition policy. The Netherlands revived the proposal in 1955, arguing that the international economic climate was more propitious than ever for the launch of a common market.

Successful negotiations to establish the European Economic Community (EEC or EC) in 1956, so soon after the collapse of the EDC, owed much to the leadership of politicians such as Paul-Henri Spaak in Belgium, Guy Mollet and Christian Pineau in France, and Konrad Adenauer in West Germany. Because of France's political weight in Europe and traditional protectionism, Mollet and Pineau played crucial roles. But their advocacy of the EC came with a price for the other prospective member states. In order to win domestic support they insisted on a special regime for agriculture in the common market, assistance for French overseas territories (France was then in the painful process of decolonization), and the establishment of Euratom.

The negotiations that resulted in the two Rome Treaties, one for the EC and the other for Euratom, were arduous. The UK opposed supranationalism generally and the proposed agricultural regime in particular, so chose not to participate. West Germany succeeded in emasculating Euratom and grudgingly accepted the EC's overseas territories provisions. In the meantime, Adenauer resisted Erhard's efforts to jettison the common market in favour of looser free trade arrangements, arguing that the EC was necessary for geopolitical as well as economic reasons. French negotiators fought what they called the 'Battle of Paris', trying to assuage domestic criticism of the proposed common market while simultaneously driving a hard bargain in the negotiations in Brussels.

The ensuing Treaty of Rome establishing the EC was a typical political compromise. Its provisions ranged from the general to the specific, from the mundane to the arcane. Those on the customs union, calling for the phased abolition of tariffs between member states and erection of a common external tariff, were the most concrete. The Treaty did not outline an agricultural policy, but contained a commitment to negotiate one in the near future. Institutionally, the Treaty established a potentially powerful Commission, a parliamentary Assembly (of appointed, not elected, members) with limited powers, a Council to represent national interests directly in the decision-making process, and a Court of Justice (see Chapter 3).

The Rome Treaties were signed on 25 March 1957, and the EC came into being on 1 January 1958. Most Europeans were unaware of either event. Apart from the EDC, European integration had not elicited much of a reaction in terms of public opinion. Yet the ECSC and EC were highly significant developments. The Coal and Steel Community represented a revolution in Franco-German relations and international organization more generally, while the even more consequential EC had the potential to reorder economic and political relations among its member states.

BOX 2.4   Compared to what?

Regional and economic integration

Economic integration in Europe has proceeded in a number of steps or stages. A similar trajectory has occurred in other regions of the world, although nowhere else has the level of economic cooperation matched that found in the EU.

In a **free trade area** (FTA) goods travel freely among member states, but these states retain the authority to establish their own external trade policy (tariffs, quotas, and non-tariff barriers) towards third countries. By allowing free access to each other's markets and discriminating favourably towards them, a free trade area stimulates internal trade and can lower consumer costs. But the lack of a common external tariff means complicated rules of origin are required to regulate the import of goods. One example of an FTA outside the EU is the European Free Trade Association (EFTA), which was established under British leadership in 1960 to promote expansion of free trade in non-EC western European countries. The UK left EFTA to join the EC in 1973, but Iceland, Liechtenstein, Norway, and Switzerland are still members. Canada, Mexico, and the US signed the North American Free Trade Agreement (NAFTA) in 1992.

Regional organizations elsewhere have created closer economic ties, which may develop into FTAs. For instance the Association of South-east Asian Nations (ASEAN) was established in 1967 to provide economic as well as social cooperation among non-communist countries in the area. A wider forum for regional economic cooperation is found among Pacific Rim countries within APEC (Asia Pacific Economic Cooperation), which includes Australia, China, Indonesia, Japan, Mexico, the Philippines, and the US.

A **customs union** requires more economic and political cooperation than an FTA. In addition to ensuring free trade among its members, a customs union has a common external tariff and quota system, and a common commercial policy. No member of a customs union may have a separate preferential trading relationship with a third country or group of third countries. A supranational institutional framework is required to ensure that it functions. Customs unions generally create more internal trade and divert more external trade than do free trade areas. The six founding members of the EC agreed to form a customs union, which came into being in 1968, two years ahead of schedule. A customs union also exists in South America. Mercosur (the Southern Cone Common Market) was established in 1991 by Argentina, Brazil, Paraguay, and Uruguay.

A **common market** represents a further step in economic integration by providing for the free movement of services, capital, and labour in addition to the free movement of goods. For various economic and political reasons, the EC Six decided to go beyond a common market by establishing additionally a common competition policy; monetary and fiscal policy coordination; a common agricultural policy (CAP); a common transport policy; and a preferential trade and aid agreement with member states' ex-colonies. Not all of these elements were fully implemented. By the 1980s it was clear that the movement of labour and capital was not entirely free, and a host of non-tariff barriers still stymied intra-Community trade in goods and services. The '1992 project' or single market programme was designed to achieve a true internal market in goods, services, labour, and capital.

Cont. ➤

Cont.

An **economic and monetary union (EMU)** is far more ambitious. It includes a single currency, a single monetary policy, and close coordination (if not unification) of fiscal policy. In the EU, plans to introduce EMU, outlined in the Maastricht Treaty, were successfully implemented in January 1999, with euro notes and coins circulating by January 2002. No other region in modern times has come close to this level of economic cooperation.

Consolidating the European Community

The big news in Europe in 1958 was not the launch of the EC but the collapse of the French Fourth Republic and the return to power of General Charles de Gaulle. Events in France had a direct bearing on the EC. De Gaulle helped consolidate the new Community by stabilizing France politically (through the construction of the Fifth Republic) and financially (by devaluing the franc). On the basis of renewed domestic confidence, France participated fully in the phased introduction of the customs union, the cornerstone of the common market, so much so that it came into existence in 1968, 18 months ahead of schedule.

De Gaulle also pushed for completion of the common agricultural policy (CAP). With a larger farming sector than any other member, France had most to gain from establishing a single agricultural market, based on guaranteed prices and export subsidies funded by the Community. France pressed for a generous CAP and had the political weight to prevail. Nevertheless the construction of the CAP, in a series of legendary negotiations in the early 1960s, proved onerous. What emerged was a complicated policy based on protectionist principles, in contrast to the liberalizing ethos of Community policies in most other sectors (see Chapter 6). The contrast represented the competing visions of the EC held by its members, potential members, and the wider international community (see Box 2.5).

Implementation of the customs union and construction of the CAP signalled the Community's initial success, obscuring setbacks in other areas such as the failure to implement a common transport policy. The customs union and the CAP had a major international impact. For instance, as part of its emerging customs union the EC developed a common commercial policy, which authorized the Commission to represent the Community in international trade talks, notably the GATT. The CAP tended to distort international trade and irritate the EC's partners. It is no coincidence that the first transatlantic trade dispute was over the CAP, the so-called 'Chicken War' of 1962–3, sparked by higher tariffs on US chicken imports.

The EC's fledgling institutions also began to consolidate during this period. The Commission organized itself in Brussels under the presidency of Walter Hallstein, a former top official in the German foreign ministry and a close colleague of

BOX 2.5	How it really works

British accession and competing visions of Europe

The integration of Europe is sometimes portrayed (not least in the popular press) as an inexorable process following some overarching, agreed plan. But in practice integration has proceeded in fits and starts, the result of domestic and international pressures and competing visions of what the EU is or should be. The debates surrounding the UK's first application to join the EC illustrate very different visions of Europe competing for dominance during the Community's early years.

In a remarkable reversal of policy, the UK applied to join the EC in 1961. The UK wanted unfettered access to EC industrial markets, but also wanted to protect trade preferences for Commonwealth countries (former British colonies) and turn the emerging CAP in a more liberal direction. De Gaulle was unsympathetic to the UK's application. Economically, he wanted a protectionist CAP. Politically, he espoused a 'European Europe', allied to the United States but independent of it. By contrast, the UK acquiesced in America's so-called Grand Design—espoused by the Kennedy administration in the early 1960s—for a more equitable transatlantic relationship built on the twin pillars of the US and a united Europe centred on the EC. Arguably, the Grand Design (at least in French eyes) disguised America's quest for continued hegemony in NATO. The US supported British membership in the EC as part of its Grand Design. By vetoing the UK's application in January 1963, de Gaulle defended the CAP and thwarted American ambitions in Europe. The episode suggests how international pressure, domestic politics, and competing visions of Europe have shaped the evolution of European integration.

Adenauer's. There were nine Commissioners, two each from the large member states and one each from the small member states (this formula would remain unchanged for nearly 50 years). The Commission's staff came initially from national civil services and from the ECSC's High Authority, which continued to exist until it merged into the Commission in 1967. In the Council of Ministers, foreign ministers met most often, indicating the EC's predominantly political nature. The Council formed a permanent secretariat in Brussels to assist its work. Member states also established permanent representations of national civil servants in Brussels, whose heads formed the Committee of Permanent Representatives (Coreper), which soon became one of the Community's most powerful bodies. The Assembly, later known as the European Parliament (EP), tried to assert itself from the beginning, demanding for instance that its members be directly elected rather than appointed from national parliaments. But the EP lacked political support from powerful member states. Working quietly in Luxembourg, the Court of Justice began in the 1960s to generate an impressive corpus of case law. In several landmark decisions, the Court developed the essential rules on which the EC legal order rests, including the supremacy of Community law (see Chapter 3).

Crisis and compromise

De Gaulle's arrival had a negative as well as a positive effect on the fledgling EC. De Gaulle openly opposed supranationalism. He and his supporters (Gaullists) had resisted the ECSC and the EDC. They tolerated the EC, but primarily because of its economic potential for France. In de Gaulle's view, states could and should form alliances and collaborate closely, but only on the basis of intergovernmentalism, not shared sovereignty. De Gaulle thought that the Community could be useful politically as the basis of an association of European states.

A clash over supranationalism was likely to arise in 1965 as, under the terms of the Rome Treaty, a number of decisions in key policy areas, including agriculture, were due to become subject to qualified majority voting. QMV (as it became known) is a key instrument of supranationalism because member states on the losing side agree to abide by the majority's decision. De Gaulle rejected this idea in principle, seeing QMV as an unacceptable abrogation of national sovereignty. The looming confrontation erupted in June 1965, when de Gaulle triggered the Empty Chair Crisis (see Box 2.2) by withdrawing French representation in the Council ostensibly in protest against Commission proposals to strengthen the EC's budgetary powers, but really in an effort to force other member states to agree not to extend the use of QMV. De Gaulle had a compelling practical reason to resist QMV: he wanted to protect the CAP against a voting coalition of liberal member states.

The crisis ended in January 1966 with the Luxembourg Compromise (see Box 2.2). The Treaty's provisions on QMV would stand, but the Council would not take a vote if a member state insisted that its very important interests were at stake. The Luxembourg Compromise tipped the balance toward intergovernmentalism in the Community's decision-making process, with unanimity becoming the norm. This development had a detrimental effect on decision-making until the Single European Act took effect in 1987.

The EC after De Gaulle

By 1969, when de Gaulle resigned, the EC was economically strong but politically weak. The Commission and Parliament were relatively powerless, and unanimity hobbled effective decision-making in the Council. De Gaulle had twice rebuffed the UK's application for EC membership, in 1963 and in 1967, after London decided by the early 1960s that, for economic reasons, it was better off inside the common market. Following de Gaulle's departure, British membership became inevitable, although **accession** negotiations were nonetheless difficult. Ireland, Denmark, and Norway negotiated alongside the UK, but a majority of Norwegian voters rejected membership in a referendum in 1972. The UK, Ireland, and Denmark joined the following year.

The EC's first enlargement was a milestone in the organization's history. Unfortunately it coincided with international financial turmoil and a severe economic downturn that slowed momentum for further integration. Moreover, the UK's early membership was troublesome. A new Labour government insisted on renegotiating the country's accession terms, much to the annoyance of France and West Germany. Based on the outcome of the renegotiation, a majority voted in favour of continued EC membership in the UK's first nation-wide referendum, in 1975. At the end of the decade a new Conservative government, under Margaret Thatcher, demanded a huge budget rebate. The UK had a point, but Thatcher's strident manner when pushing her case incensed other member states. The British budgetary question dragged on until 1984, overshadowing a turnaround in the Community's fortunes after a decade of poor economic performance.

A difficult decade

Because of the UK's early difficulties in the EC and prevailing stagflation in Europe (weak economic growth combined with high inflation and unemployment), the 1970s is generally seen as a dismal decade in the history of integration. Yet a number of important institutional and policy developments occurred at that time. On the policy side, the 1979 launch of the European Monetary System (EMS), the precursor to the single currency, was especially significant. Concerned about America's seeming abdication of international financial leadership, and eager to curb inflation and exchange rate fluctuations in the EC, Commission President Roy Jenkins and the French and German leaders devised the EMS, with the Exchange Rate Mechanism (ERM) designed at its core to regulate currency fluctuations. The sovereignty-conscious UK declined to participate. By the mid-1980s, the inflation and exchange rates of ERM members began to converge, thus helping to keep their economies stable and Thatcher decided to join it in 1989. The Lomé agreement of 1975, providing preferential trade and development assistance to scores of African, Caribbean, and Pacific countries, was another important achievement for the beleaguered Community, as was the launch of European Political Cooperation (EPC), a mechanism to coordinate member states' foreign policies (see Chapter 10). In terms of closer European integration, the expansion of EC environmental policy in the 1970s was even more important.

Institutionally, the 1970s saw a gradual improvement in the Commission's fortunes, especially later in the decade under the presidency of Roy Jenkins. The first direct elections to the EP took place in 1979, raising the institution's profile and enhancing the EC's formal legitimacy. The inauguration of the European Council (regular meetings of the heads of state and government) in 1975 strengthened intergovernmental cooperation. The European Council soon became the EC's most important agenda-setting body (see Chapter 3), while direct elections laid the basis for the EP's institutional ascension in the 1980s and 1990s. The Court of Justice continued in the 1970s to build an impressive body of case law that maintained the momentum for deeper integration.

By the early 1980s, the EC had weathered the storm of recession and the challenge of British accession. The end of dictatorial regimes in Greece, Portugal, and Spain in the mid-1970s presaged the EC's Mediterranean enlargement (Greece joined in 1981, Portugal and Spain in 1986). By that time the EC was more than a customs union but still less than a full-fledged common market. A plethora of non-tariff barriers (such as divergent technical standards) hobbled intra-Community trade in goods and services, and the movement of people and capital was far from free. Intensive foreign competition, especially from the US and Japan, began to focus the attention of political and business leaders on the EC's ability to boost member states' economic growth and international competitiveness. This focus became the genesis of the single market programme, which spearheaded the EC's response to globalization and ushered in the EU.

The Emerging European Union

The single market programme for the free movement of goods, services, capital, and people emerged as a result of collaboration between big business, the Commission, the Parliament and national leaders in the early 1980s. Several European Councils endorsed the idea. But the initiative only took off when the Commission, under the new presidency of Jacques Delors, unveiled a legislative roadmap (a White Paper on the 'completion' of the internal market) in 1985. To ensure the programme's success, the European Council decided to convene an Intergovernmental Conference (IGC) to make the necessary Treaty changes. Chief among them was a commitment to use QMV for most of the White Paper's proposals, thereby ending the legislative gridlock that had hamstrung earlier efforts for full market liberalization.

As well as covering the single market programme, the Single European Act (SEA) of 1986 brought environmental policy into the Treaty, strengthened Community policy in research and technological development, and included a section on foreign policy cooperation. It also committed the EC to higher expenditure on regional development (cohesion policy), partly as a side payment to the poorer member states, including new entrants Portugal, Spain, and Greece, which were unlikely to benefit as much from market integration as were their richer counterparts. Institutionally, the SEA's most important provisions enhanced the EP's legislative role as a means of improving the EC's democratic accountability.

The single market programme, with a target date of 1992, was a success. Business responded enthusiastically to the prospect of a fully integrated European marketplace. '1992' unleashed a wave of europhoria. The EC was more popular than at any time before or since. Eager to remove barriers to the free movement of people even before implementation of the single market programme, France and West Germany agreed in 1984 to press ahead with the abolition of border checks. This pledge led to the Schengen Agreement (see Box 2.2) for the free movement of people, which gradually added other member states and formally became part of the EU under the terms of the 1997 Amsterdam Treaty.

Economic and Monetary Union

The popularity of the single market programme emboldened Delors to advocate Economic and Monetary Union (EMU) and a single European currency arguing, as did many businesses, that a single market would work better with a single currency. He had the strong support of German Chancellor Helmut Kohl, an avowed 'euro-federalist'. The Commission publicly justified EMU on economic grounds, but Delors and Kohl saw it primarily as a political undertaking. French President François Mitterrand also supported EMU, for both political and economic reasons. Thatcher opposed EMU vehemently, seeing it as economically unnecessary and politically unwise. Far from turning the tide against EMU, Thatcher's obstructionism in Brussels contributed to her political downfall at home.

The European Council authorized Delors to set up a committee, composed mostly of Central Bank Governors, to explore the road to EMU. The Delors Report of 1989 proposed a three-stage programme, including strict convergence criteria for potential participants and the establishment of a European Central Bank with responsibility primarily for price stability. The report largely reflected German preferences for EMU. That was understandable, given West Germany's economic weight and obsession with inflation. Even so, opinion in Germany remained sceptical about EMU, with the politically influential West German central bank (Bundesbank) opposed to it.

Planning for EMU was well on track by the time the Berlin Wall came down in November 1989. By raising again the spectre of the German question, the end of the Cold War increased the momentum for EMU. Fearful of the prospect, however remote, of a rootless and reunified Germany in the post-Cold War world, other leaders were determined to bind Germany fully into the new Europe, largely through EMU. Kohl was more than happy to oblige and cleverly exploited the concerns of Germany's neighbours to overcome domestic misgivings about EMU.

Maastricht and beyond

EC leaders convened two Intergovernmental Conferences in 1990, one on EMU and the other on political union, meaning institutional and non-EMU policy reforms. Both conferences converged in the Maastricht Treaty of 1992, which established the European Union with its three-pillar structure (see Box 1.2). The first pillar comprised the EC, including EMU; the second comprised the Common Foreign and Security Policy (CFSP), a direct response to the external challenges of the post-Cold War period; the third covered cooperation on justice and home affairs, notably immigration, asylum, and criminal matters. This awkward structure reflected several members' unwillingness to subject internal security and foreign policy to supranational decision-making. Thus the Commission and the EP were merely associated with Pillar 2 and 3 activities. Within Pillar 1, by contrast, the Maastricht Treaty extended the EP's legislative power by introducing the far-reaching co-decision procedure, which made the Parliament a legally and politically equal co-legislator with the Council of Ministers (see Chapter 3).

The further extension of the EP's legislative authority, and the introduction of the principle of subsidiarity (see Box 2.2), demonstrated EU leaders' concerns about the organization's legitimacy. Those concerns were fully vindicated in tough ratification battles in several countries, including the UK, France, and Germany, but especially in Denmark, where a narrow majority rejected the Treaty in a referendum in June 1992. Voters approved the Treaty, with special concessions for Denmark, in a second referendum, in May 1993, allowing the EU to come into being six months later.

At issue in Denmark and elsewhere was the so-called democratic deficit: the EU's perceived remoteness and lack of accountability (see Chapter 7). This issue remained a major challenge for the EU into the twenty-first century. The resignation of the Commission under the Presidency of Jacques Santer in March 1999, amid allegations of fraud and mismanagement, increased popular scepticism, although it also demonstrated the Commission's accountability to the EP (the Commission resigned before being sacked by the Parliament). Yet many Europeans saw the EP as part of the problem: few understood exactly its role, and the turnout in EP elections declined yet again in 1999, 2004, 2009, and 2014. For its part, the Commission launched successive rounds of reform, while EU leaders attempted to improve policy-making and delivery. Nevertheless, as illustrated by the negative results of five EU-related referenda since the Maastricht Treaty, and the strong support for anti-EU parties in the 2014 EP election, public opinion grew increasingly sceptical of the EU.

Hand-in-hand with public unease, the post-Maastricht period saw substantial EU policy development. The launch of the final stage of EMU in January 1999, in keeping with the Maastricht timetable, was one of the EU's most striking achievements. Euro notes and coins came into circulation in January 2002. The strengthening of the CFSP and the initiation of a European Security and Defence Policy, largely in response to the Balkan wars of the 1990s and uncertainty about US involvement in future European conflicts, was another important EU policy development. Reform of CFSP was an outcome of the 1997 Amsterdam Treaty, which nevertheless ducked increasingly pressing questions of institutional reform necessitated by impending enlargement.

Enlargement, constitution building, and the Eurozone crisis

Enlargement was a major challenge for the new EU. Following the end of the Cold War, three militarily neutral European states (Austria, Finland, and Sweden) joined in 1995. Norway, a non-neutral, again chose not to join in a referendum held in 1994. The newly independent states of Central and Eastern Europe soon applied for EU membership, as did Cyprus and Malta. For the Central and Eastern European states the road to membership would be long and difficult, involving major political, economic, and administrative reforms. The slow pace of enlargement disappointed the applicant countries and their supporters in the US, who criticized the EU for being too cautious. The Union countered that enlargement, an inherently complicated process, was even more complex than (say) the enlargement of NATO in view of the applicants' history, political culture, and low level of economic development. The EU's approach reflected a widespread lack of enthusiasm for enlargement among politicians and the public in existing member states. Even so, negotiations with the Central and Eastern European applicants eventually began in 1998, with the five front-runners and in 2000, with the five others. Cyprus also began accession negotiations in 1998 and Malta in 2000.

Eight of the Central and Eastern European countries joined in 2004, together with Cyprus and Malta; the other two, Bulgaria and Romania, joined in 2007. The EU reluctantly acknowledged Turkey as a candidate in December 1999 and, no less reluctantly, opened formal accession negotiations with it in October 2005. However, Turkey's unpopularity throughout the EU, as well as specific issues such as the unresolved Cypriot question, bedevilled the country's membership prospects. Meanwhile, the EU acknowledged the 'European perspective' of the Western Balkans, suggesting that every country in the region stood a reasonable chance of eventually becoming a member. Croatia was first to join, in 2013.

As Chapter 8 explains, enlargement greatly altered the EU. The accession of so many relatively poor countries, with comparatively large agricultural sectors, was bound to have a major effect on the CAP and cohesion policy. The Union reformed both policies as part of its Agenda 2000 initiative, in anticipation of enlargement, but the results were patently inadequate. Further reform inevitably fuelled bitter budgetary disputes, such as the one preceding implementation of the 2014–20 financial framework.

The EU's institutions also required reform because of enlargement. Member states avoided the contentious question of institutional reform in the Amsterdam Treaty, agreeing instead to undertake an institutional overhaul in another IGC in 2000. That conference resulted in the Nice Treaty of 2001, which changed the modalities of QMV in anticipation of enlargement, but in a way that complicated rather than clarified legislative decision-making. In other institutional areas the outcomes of the 2000 IGC were equally disappointing. The messy compromises that were struck illustrated the growing difficulty of reaching agreement among member states on institutional issues, especially those that tended to drive a wedge between France and Germany, or between the small and large member states.

Appreciating the inadequacies of the Nice Treaty, the European Council decided in December 2001 to hold a convention of national and EU-level politicians to draft a new Treaty that would supersede and supposedly simplify the existing Treaties. That was the genesis of the Convention on the Future of Europe of 2002–3 and ensuing IGC, which resulted in the Constitutional Treaty of June 2004. Amongst other things, the Constitutional Treaty altered the system of QMV, giving more power to the big member states; incorporated the previously negotiated Charter of Fundamental Rights into the EU's legal system; called for a standing president of the European Council; and provided for an EU foreign minister. Although it was ratified by most member states, voters in referenda held in the Netherlands and France, two of the EU's founding member states, rejected the Constitutional Treaty in spring 2005, for a variety of reasons mostly unrelated to the Treaty itself, ranging from domestic political considerations to concerns about the consequences of globalization and fear of further enlargement. The results of the Dutch and French referenda were a severe blow to the image and prestige of the EU. But they did not derail the process of European integration, to which most European politicians, if not all their publics, remained committed, as was revealed in December 2007 when EU leaders signed the Lisbon Treaty, which incorporated most of the changes in the unratified Constitutional Treaty. While apparently less far-reaching than the Constitutional Treaty, in fact the Lisbon Treaty, which came into effect in 2009, marked another historically significant step towards 'ever closer union'.

Implementation of the Lisbon Treaty coincided with the onset of the economic crisis, which had a devastating impact on the EU's credibility, on relations among member states, and on the euro. The weakness of EMU's fiscal foundations became abundantly clear as banking and/or sovereign debt crises engulfed the weaker Eurozone members. Germany, at the centre, enjoyed a boom in exports to the increasingly less competitive peripheral countries. As the banking and debt crises threatened the survival of the euro and exacerbated the economic recession, Germany's insistence on EU-wide deficit reduction alienated political and public opinion in the worst affected countries. Fissures in the EU widened between Germany and the rest; between the stronger and weaker Eurozone members; and between Eurozone and non-Eurozone countries. The fallout from the chronic crisis fuelled pervasive Euroscepticism, and boosted support for extremist parties in the 2014 EP election.

The economic crisis exacerbated another festering problem: the UK's relationship with the EU. Driven by concerns about immigration and the economy, a virulent strain of Euroscepticism propelled the United Kingdom Independence Party (UKIP) to prominence and pushed the Conservative Party farther to the right. Responding to these pressures, Prime Minister David Cameron, the Conservative leader, called for wide ranging EU reform as a prelude to another referendum, more than 40 years after the 1975 referendum, on whether the UK should remain a member state of the EU. Other EU leaders agreed on the importance of reform but doubted that the British could be conciliated. Though business elites in the UK generally advocated keeping the country in the Union, anti-EU opinion seemed to be in the ascendant. For the first time in EU history, there was a real possibility that a member state might leave.

Conclusion

The history of the EU presents a fascinating puzzle: why did national governments, traditionally jealous of their independence, agree to pool sovereignty in an international organization that increasingly acquired federal attributes? The answer may be as simple as it is paradoxical: because it was in their national interests to do so. Political parties and interest groups did not always agree on what constituted the national

interest, and governments themselves were sometimes divided. But at critical junc-
tures in the post-war period, for various strategic and/or economic reasons, national
leaders opted for closer integration.

This chapter has approached the history of European integration by focusing on
national responses to major domestic and international challenges since the end of
the Second World War, responses that gave rise to the European Communities and
later the EU. France and Germany played key roles. The EC was a bargain struck
primarily between them for mutual economic gain. In strengthening post-war
Franco-German ties, the EC also had an important political dimension. Indeed,
West Germany conceded much to France in the negotiations that led to the EC in
order to deepen Franco-German solidarity, a key step towards binding West Germany
to the West. Franco-German bargaining was also crucial at subsequent milestones in
the history of European integration, such as EMU.

Yet the dynamics of Franco-German relations and leadership in the EU have changed,
not least because of enlargement in 2004 and 2007, which shifted the geopolitical balance of the EU eastward, in favour of Germany. As various rounds of post-Maastricht
Treaty negotiations have shown, France and Germany are often far apart on institutional issues, and increasingly differ on a range of core policy issues as well. Whereas
united Germany is more assertive in the EU, France seems unsure of its place in world.
Far from joining France and Germany in a tripartite leadership structure, or replacing
France as Germany's favoured interlocutor in EU affairs, the UK never wholeheartedly
embraced European integration and became decidedly semi-detached.

Ideology—the quest for a united Europe—has not been a major motive for
European integration. The Preamble of the Rome Treaty, the EC's charter, called for
'ever closer union', a vague aspiration for European unity that hardly constituted a
guiding principle. Some national and supranational leaders were (and remain)
strongly committed to a federal EU, but managed to move Europe in that direction
only when ideological ambition coincided with national political and economic
preferences. The language of European integration, redolent of peace and reconciliation,
provided convenient camouflage for the pursuit of national interests based on rational
calculations of costs and benefits. Apart from spectacular episodes such as the Empty
Chair Crisis, however, member states' perceptions of their national interests and of a
common European interest generally converged. In the post-Maastricht period, by
contrast, these perceptions have increasingly diverged, to the detriment of today's EU.

Nevertheless the history of European integration shows that countries can overcome institutional and policy differences for the sake of common economic and political interests. Over time, the context of European integration has greatly changed, but
not necessarily its substance. With global challenges more pressing than ever before,
arguably it is in the interest of all member states—including the UK—to manage the
single market, make a success of monetary union, and increase the EU's effectiveness as
an international actor. Member states may have little choice but to perpetuate European
integration, while striving to improve the EU's operation and output. Regardless of
whether the UK stays or leaves, the EU is likely to survive, perhaps even thrive.

DISCUSSION QUESTIONS

1. Are France and Germany bound to lead in Europe?

2. Why is the UK an outlier?

3. How significant have federalist aspirations been in the history of European integration?

4. Is the United States a 'federator' of Europe?

5. What economic factors impelled European integration during various stages of its history?

FURTHER READING

Dinan (2014a) provides a thorough history of the EU, while Dinan (2014b) examines key developments in EU history and includes a chapter on the historiography of European integration. For a neofunctionalist analysis of the EC's development, see Haas (1958) and Lindberg (1963). Milward (1984, 2000) is the most influential historian of European integration. Moravcsik (1998) blends political science and historical analysis to produce liberal intergovernmentalism and explain major developments in the history of the EU. Duchêne (1994) is excellent on Jean Monnet, and Gillingham (1991) provides an authoritative account of the origins of the ECSC. Gillingham (2003) describes the history of European integration as a struggle between economic liberalism and centralization, personified in the 1980s by Delors and Thatcher. Vanke (2010) provides an excellent counterpoint to Milward and Moravcsik by emphasizing the importance of ideas and emotions—'Europeanism'—and not just economic interests in the history of European integration.

Dinan, D. (2014a), *Europe Recast: A History of European Union* (Basingstoke: Palgrave).

Dinan, D. (ed.) (2014b), *Origins and Evolution of the European Union*, 2nd ed. (Oxford and New York: Oxford University Press).

Duchêne, F. (1994), *Jean Monnet: The First Statesman of Interdependence* (New York: Norton).

Gillingham, J. (1991), *Coal, Steel and the Rebirth of Europe, 1945–1955* (Cambridge and New York: Cambridge University Press).

Gillingham, J. (2003), *European Integration, 1950–2003* (Cambridge and New York: Cambridge University Press).

Haas, E. (1958), *The Uniting of Europe: Political, Social and Economic Forces* (Stanford, CA: Stanford University Press).

Lindberg, L. (1963), *The Political Dynamics of European Economic Integration* (Stanford, CA: Stanford University Press).

Milward, A. (1984), *The Reconstruction of Western Europe, 1945–51* (Berkeley: University of California Press).

Milward, A. (2000), *The European Rescue of the Nation-State*, 2nd ed. (London: Routledge).

Moravcsik, A. (1998), *The Choice for Europe: Social Purpose and State Power from Messina to Maastricht* (Ithaca, NY, and London: Cornell University Press and UCL Press).

Vanke, J. (2010), *Europeanism and European Union: Interests, Emotions, and Systemic Integration in the Early European Economic Community* (Palo Alto, CA: Academica Press).

WEB LINKS

- The EU's official portal site has its own useful history page: **http://europa.eu/abc/history/index_en.htm**
- The Florence-based European University Institute (EUI)'s European Integration History Index provides internet resources (in all languages) on post-war European history, with a particular emphasis on the EU: **http://vlib.iue.it/hist-eur-integration/Index.html**

Visit the Online Resource Centre that accompanies this book for additional material: **www.oxfordtextbooks.co.uk/orc/kenealy4e/**

PART II

Major Actors

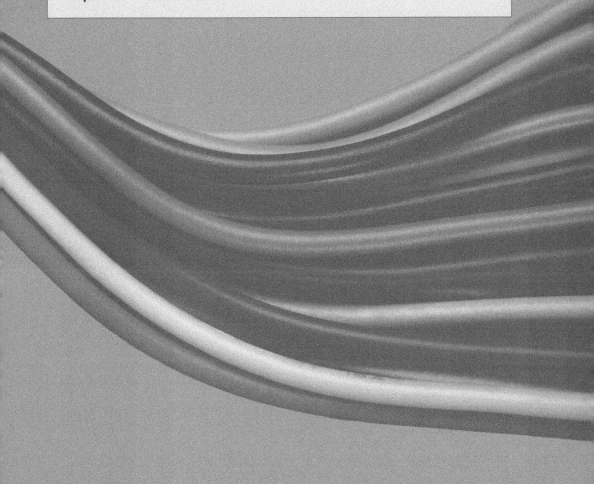

CHAPTER 3

The EU's Institutions

Richard Corbett, John Peterson, and Daniel Kenealy

■ Summary

No student of the EU can understand their subject without careful study of its key institutions and how they work. EU institutions are not just dry (and complex) organizations; they are dynamic organisms exercising a unique mix of legislative, executive, and judicial power. We begin by introducing the EU's five most important institutions. We outline their structures and formal powers—that is, what the Treaties say they can do—but we also focus on how they 'squeeze' influence out of their limited Treaty prerogatives. We then explore why these institutions matter in determining EU politics and policy more generally.

Institutions in Treaties and in Practice

What makes the EU unique, perhaps above all, is its institutions. This chapter explores the five that exercise the most power and influence: the European Commission, the Council (of Ministers), the European Council, the European Parliament, and the European Court of Justice. We draw analogies to their counterparts at the national level, but also show how they are distinct and unique. It is important to understand not just the formal powers conferred on the EU's institutions, but also how informal powers have accrued to them over time, and how incremental power shifts occur between rounds of Treaty reform. The informal institutional politics of European integration are lively and important (see Chapter 6).

The European Commission

One of the EU's most powerful and controversial institutions is the European Commission. The EU's founders were faced with a challenge. If the member states wanted to pursue common policies in certain fields, should they hand over responsibilities to a common institution, and leave it to get on with it, which would pose major questions of democratic accountability? Or should policies be settled by agreement between national governments, thus risking endless intergovernmental negotiations and lowest common denominator agreements?

In the end they opted for a compromise: a common institution—the European Commission—was charged with drafting policy proposals (and implementing policies once agreed). But a separate institution—the Council—consisting of ministers representing national governments, would take (most) decisions on the basis of those proposals. This interplay of an institution charged with representing the common interest and those composed of representatives of national governments (Council) or citizens (Parliament) is the essence of what became known as the 'Community method' (see Chapter 4).

Tasks and powers

The Treaties allocated to the Commission other important tasks besides the right to propose policies. The Commission is charged with representing the general interest of the Union, and in this capacity, does a variety of jobs:

- It acts as guardian of the Treaties (to defend both their letter and spirit) verifying the correct application of EU legislation;
- It can be given powers to implement EU legislation and manage its programmes

- It is the competition authority for the single market, with powers to vet and veto mergers, even of companies located outside the EU
- It manages and negotiates international trade and cooperation agreements.

Above all, nothing (or very little) can become EU legislation unless the Commission proposes it. All of this makes the Commission perhaps the most powerful international administration in existence (see Kassim et al. 2013), and many of its decisions are contentious. Perhaps controversy is unavoidable for an institution that is designed to act independently of the EU's member states and in the general, supranational interest of the Union as a whole.

The Commission's powers are not far short of those enjoyed, in the economic field, by national governments. But its capacity to act autonomously is more limited than that of a government in a national context. And it does not have the powers that national governments have over armed forces, police, and the nomination of judges or foreign policy. The Treaties limit the Commission's powers and autonomy.

How the Commission is organized

'The Commission' rather confusingly refers to two arms of the same body: the College of Commissioners (or executive Commission) and the administrative Commission (its permanent 'services'). The College is the powerhouse of the Commission. Each of the 28 Commissioners—one from each member state—is, like a minister in a national government, nominated by the prime minister or president of their country. Commissioners are not directly elected, but they are more like politicians than civil servants (most have held high office in national politics before becoming Commissioners) and hold office only with the approval of the European Parliament (EP). The permanent civil servants (in French, the *fonctionaires*), who are recruited normally through competitive examination, work under the College's authority. Here we find a unique feature of the EU: its institutions recruit their own civil servants and do not rely (much) on national appointees.

The Commission President is elected by the EP on a proposal of the European Council, which itself is obliged to take account of EP election results in making that nomination (Corbett 2014). In other words, heads of government have to choose a candidate capable of commanding a parliamentary majority much in the same way that a head of state in a national context has to when nominating a prime minister. This was interpreted by several European political parties to mean that the European Council should first send for the nominee of the EP party with the most seats, and they proceeded each to propose their own candidate ahead of the 2014 European elections. After the elections, the European Council indeed nominated the candidate of the "winning" party (the centre-right European People's Party), the former Luxembourg Prime Minister, Jean-Claude Juncker, though not without controversy as the UK Prime Minister strongly opposed this interpretation of the Treaty provisions.

Once elected by the EP, the President must then agree with each head of government on the nominee from each country for the remaining members of the Commission. It is then up to the President to distribute policy responsibilities—known as 'portfolios'—to individual Commissioners (for Transport, Agriculture, and so on). The one exception is the EU High Representative for Foreign Affairs and Security Policy, who is also a Vice President of the Commission (see later).

The prospective Commission must then present itself to the Parliament for a vote of confidence. This vote is on the Commission as a whole—again, much in the same way as a vote of confidence in a government in a national context. However, prior to this vote, the EP holds public hearings for each Commissioner before the parliamentary committee corresponding to their portfolio (which does not happen to ministers in most European countries). The Commission's fixed, five-year term is linked to that of the European Parliament, which is elected every five years. The Parliament—and only the Parliament—can dismiss the Commission earlier in a vote of no confidence.

The distribution of portfolios can be controversial. Portfolios dealing with international trade, the internal market, competition policy, agriculture, regional development funds and, in recent times, environment and energy are particularly sought after. The 2009 appointment of the Frenchman, Michel Barnier, as Internal Market Commissioner (including financial regulation) was seen by some as a move by France to gain regulatory powers over the City of London. In reality, how much an individual Commissioner can shape policy is limited by the principle of collegiality: the entire College agrees all policy proposals. Once it takes a decision, if necessary by majority vote (but nearly always by consensus), it becomes the policy of all of the Commission. Each Commissioner must support it or (in principle) resign. Moreover, key legislative and policy decisions have to be approved by other EU institutions. The Commission illustrates one of the ironies of the EU: its institutions are more powerful than they are autonomous.

The growing size of the Commission with successive enlargements has risked turning it from a compact executive into a miniature assembly. The 2009 Lisbon Treaty had provisions for a smaller Commission but also allowed member states to vary its size, leading to a decision to stick with one Commissioner per country. The move shows that there remains more concern for the Commission's legitimacy—with, for instance, one member of the College who speaks each country's language and can appear in the national media—than with its efficiency.

Commissioners each have their own private office—or (in French) *cabinet*—of around seven personal advisers. These officials are chosen by the Commissioner and may be drawn from inside or outside the Commission. They perform a very demanding and important role, keeping the Commissioner informed about their own policy area(s) as well as wider developments in the Commission and Europe more generally. Most cabinets are composed largely of members of staff of the same nationality as the Commissioner, but the Head or Deputy Head of each must hail from a member state different from that of the Commissioner. Member states are often accused of seeking to appoint their own national officials to Commission cabinets to ensure that their interests are not overlooked. However, after new rules were imposed by President Romano Prodi (1999–2004), cabinets became more 'European'—with nearly all having at least three nationalities—and less male-dominated, with around 40 per cent of appointees being women (see Peterson 2012a).

Controversy surrounding portfolio assignments and cabinet appointments shows that the defence of national interests in the Commission can never be entirely removed. Commissioners take an oath of independence when they are appointed, but never abandon their national identities. Indeed, many consider it to be an advantage that they bring knowledge of their respective countries to the Commission, even if they are not there to represent them—that job belongs to ministers in the Council.

The independence of Commissioners can sometimes be a matter of contention. A Commissioner who simply parrots the position of her national government would soon lose credibility within the Commission. However, one that too obviously ignores major national interests may be liable for criticism at home. Famously, the UK Prime Minister, Margaret Thatcher, despaired at the alleged failure of 'her' Commissioner—Lord Cockfield—to defend the interests of the Thatcher government. Thus Commissioners face a tough balancing act: they must be sensitive to the interests of the member state that (in Brussels speak) 'they know best', but must not undermine the independence of the Commission.

Each Commissioner is responsible for one or more Directorate General (DGs)—or services—which relate to their portfolio. These DGs, the equivalent of national ministries, cover the EU's main policy areas such as competition, the environment, or agriculture. A Director General, who reports directly to the relevant Commissioner, heads each. There are about 30 or so services that together make up the administration of the Commission.

The Commission is far smaller than is often portrayed in the popular press, where it is frequently characterized as an enormous body intent on taking over Europe. In fact, it has roughly as many officials (in policy-making posts) as work for a medium-sized national government department, such as the French Ministry of Culture, or for a medium-sized city council. Of the Commission's approximately 33,000 officials, only about one-fifth are in policy-making posts, with a huge proportion involved in translating or interpreting into the 24 official languages of the EU.

In day-to-day work, the dividing line between administrative civil servants and Commissioners is not always self-evident. While the College is ultimately responsible for any decisions that emanate from the institution, in practice many matters are handled much further down in the administration. Furthermore, the Commission's agenda is to a large extent set for it by the EU's Treaties or other commitments (see Box 3.1). In turn, some Commissioners are more interventionist than others in seeking to influence the day to day functioning of 'their' Directorate General, in much the same way as occurs in relations between ministers and civil servants in a national context.

The major challenge for the Commission is stretching its limited resources to cover the wide range of tasks that member states have conferred upon it. At times,

---

BOX 3.1 **How it really works**

Who initiates policy?

The formal right to initiate policies is one of the Commission's most precious and funda-mental powers. But the origins of its initiatives are diverse. In practice, most initiatives emanating from the Commission are a response to ideas, suggestions, or pressures from other sources. While figures vary from year to year, the Commission has estimated that only about one-fifth of its proposals are entirely of its own initiative. Of course, it decides the shape and form of all of its proposals. However, an even greater proportion amend existing EU law, rather than legislating in new fields. For example, of all (416) Commission proposals in the year 2008:

- 52 per cent were to amend, replace, codify, or recast existing EU laws;
- 8 per cent were further measures arising from existing law;
- 21 per cent arose from the EU's international obligations;
- 10 per cent were proposals for trade defence measures (such as anti-dumping duties); and
- the remainder (9 per cent) technically were original Commission proposals, but over half came from the (European) Council or the Parliament.

The Lisbon Treaty added a new, direct source of proposals: one million EU citizens can invite the Commission to submit a proposal. The Commission is not legally obliged to act on the initiative, but it would most certainly have to take it into account.

(Figures derived from Answer to Parliamentary Question E3775/2010)

---

the Commission can be adept at making the most of the powers given to it. For example, the Commission was among the first institutions to conduct detailed research on climate change, which highlighted the necessity of new initiatives such as an emissions trading scheme and a stronger role for the EU. Thus, the Commission is not simply the servant of the member states but can sometimes 'squeeze' more prerogatives despite its limited competence.

The Council (of Ministers)

The Council of Ministers was created as the EU's primary decision-making body. The Treaties state that the Council shall consist of 'a representative of each member state at ministerial level, who may commit the government of the member state in question and cast its vote' and that it 'shall, jointly with the European Parliament, exercise legislative and budgetary functions' and 'carry out policy making and co-ordinating functions'.

It is thus both a legislative chamber of states (as half of the Union's bicameral legislative authority, together with the EP) and at the same time the body in which the governments of the member states come together to meet, resolve issues of Union or foreign policy and coordinate policies, such as macroeconomic, that are primarily a national responsibility. It is in the Council that national interests, as seen by the government of the day in each member state, are represented and articulated.

The Council is a complex system. The Treaties speak of only one Council, but it meets in different configurations depending on what policy area is being discussed. For example, when agriculture is discussed, agriculture ministers meet; when the subject is the environment, it is environment ministers, and so on. There are altogether ten different configurations of the Council, with the General Affairs Council (now largely Europe Ministers to relieve the burden on Foreign Ministers, so the latter can concentrate on foreign policy) holding a coordinating brief. The General Affairs Council is responsible for the dossiers that affect more than one of the Union's policies, such as enlargement or the EU's budget and for preparing meetings of the European Council.

The Council is aided by a Secretariat of around 2,800 officials. It plays an important role in brokering deals and crafting compromises between member states. Even with the help of the Secretariat, the burden on EU Ministers has increased enormously. The agricultural, foreign, and economic ministers meet at least once a month, others from one to six times a year.

Given their core function—representing member states—it is easy to conclude that the Council and its preparatory bodies are purely intergovernmental. But, as constructivists would note (see Lewis 2003), regular ministerial meetings, informal contacts, and routine bargaining have provided the grounds for continual and close cooperation between executives from different member states. As a result, the Council has constructed a sort of collective identity that is more than an amalgamation of national views. That identity has helped push the Union forward.

Majority voting can be used in the Council in most areas of EU business. In fact, votes rarely take place (see Box 3.2), although more often now than before the 2004–7 enlargements. Council deliberations on legislation now take place in public: they are web-streamed or televised (there is no physical public gallery). Previous to the Lisbon Treaty, the Council legislated behind closed doors, which made negotiations easier but left the Council vulnerable to the charge that it was the only legislative body in the democratic world that enacted legislation without the public being able to see how members voted. The Council still meets behind closed doors on some non-legislative matters such as foreign policy and security discussions.

Vice President of the Commission/High Representative for Foreign & Security Policy

In 2010, a major innovation was the merging of two previously separate posts: the Commissioner for External Relations and the Council's High Representative for (the Common) Foreign and Security Policy (CFSP). The creation of the latter post in the late 1990s reflected the reluctance of member states to extend the Commission's role in external representation. France and the UK in particular were averse to the idea of the Commission representing the Union beyond its existing remit in trade, development, and humanitarian aid. Thus, the top civil servant of the Council, its Secretary General, was designated High Representative for the CFSP. This division of labour, however, proved problematic and confusing. Non-EU countries were not always sure of whom to turn to in the first instance. In many situations, the Union had to be represented by both the High Representative and the External Relations Commissioner.

For these reasons, the Lisbon Treaty merged the two posts. Still called the High Representative—although now also a Vice President of the Commission—the European Council chooses the appointee, with the agreement of the Commission President. The High Representative is charged with chairing meetings of the Council of Foreign Affairs Ministers. She (and to date it has always been a 'she') also has assumed authority for a new European External Action Service (EEAS), intended as something like a EU 'foreign ministry' (see Chapter 10).

Is the High Representative a Council cuckoo in the Commission nest or a Commission cuckoo in the Council nest? Some see it as a logical step towards bringing the tasks of the former Council High Representative fully into the Commission, ending the anomaly of foreign policy being different from other external policy sectors. Others see it as a smash and grab raid by the Council on the Commission's external representation role. The reality is an uneasy compromise, although one that potentially enables the Union's external relations to draw on both its traditional methods in a more unified way. The appointment of a sitting Commissioner, Catherine Ashton, as the first incumbent was not without significance. Interestingly, the post—in identical guise—was labelled the EU 'Minister of Foreign Affairs' in the Constitutional Treaty before that label was abandoned. Recycling the more anodyne title 'High Representative' for the post did not necessarily affect the likelihood of its holder becoming a high profile figure representing the EU to the world. In any case, the High Representative is the most explicit case of seeking to combine the supranational and intergovernmental in one institutional post.

The Council presidency

Except for meetings of Foreign Affairs Ministers, a minister from the member state holding the rotating 'Presidency of the Council' chairs the Council. Member states take it in turns to chair Council meetings for six months each. Although often referred to in the media as the 'EU Presidency', Presidencies are, in fact, simply the chair of just one of the Union's institutions. Assuming the Presidency does not confer any additional powers on the holder. Rather, the Presidency's job is to build consensus and move decision-making forward.

Holding the Presidency places the country concerned in the media spotlight and can give it added influence. For instance, the Presidency arranges meetings and can set the Council's agenda, determining which issues will be given priority.

But holding the Presidency also has disadvantages. The time required of national officials is daunting, especially for smaller states. Much can go wrong in six months, whether or not the country holding the Presidency is responsible. Despite the media hype, the Presidency's scope for action is limited and its agenda is largely inherited, or dictated by events.

Voting in the Council

The Treaties provide, in most policy areas, that a qualified majority (see Boxes 3.2 and 3.3) can approve a Commission proposal, whereas unanimity is required to amend it—a crucial feature of the 'Community method' (see Chapter 4). Some policy areas, however, require unanimity to approve any measure. Unanimity applies to sensitive matters such as tax harmonization, anti-discrimination legislation and non-legislative decisions on foreign and security policy and constitutional questions such as the accession of new member states (see Chapter 8). A simple majority, with one vote per member state, is used rarely, primarily for procedural questions.

The chair of the Council decides whether and when to call for a vote, whatever decision rule applies (see Box 3.2). Even though consensus is always sought, and usually achieved, formal votes are sometimes needed. Successive enlargements of the EU, adding mostly smaller or medium-sized member states, had led to a situation where—in theory—a qualified majority could be obtained by the representatives of a minority (or a small majority) of the EU's population. Larger member states felt they were becoming under-represented in the system, which eventually led to its reform (see Box 3.3).

Under the pre-2014 rules, a 'triple majority' was required: not just the requisite number of weighted votes, but also positive votes from a majority of member states that represented at least 62 per cent of the Union's population. The Lisbon Treaty ushered in a simpler system, applying as of 1 November 2014, which works on the basis of a 'double majority': 55 per cent of member states are required representing 65 per cent of the EU's population (see Box 3.3).

Coreper

Council decisions are preceded by extensive negotiation. Each EU member state has its own Permanent Representation ('Perm Rep') in Brussels, headed by a Permanent Representative who has ambassadorial status. The national civil servants who staff the Perm Reps sit on all manner of preparatory working groups within the Council system. Much policy substance is thrashed out at these levels, particularly by the Committee of Permanent Representatives, known by its French acronym Coreper. Composed of national Ambassadors to the EU and their staffs, Coreper's job is to prepare the work of the Council and try to reach consensus or suitable majorities ahead of Council meetings. Items on which agreement is reached at Coreper are placed on the Council's agenda as so-called 'A points' for formal approval: if no minister objects they are nodded through. Coreper is split (confusingly) into Coreper II,

BOX 3.2   How it really works

Reaching decisions in the Council

Qualified majority voting (QMV) now applies to most areas of Council decision-making, and any national representative on the Council can call for a vote on any measure to which it applies. In practice, only a small number of decisions subject to QMV are actually agreed that way. Pushing for a formal vote too early or often creates resentment that disrupts the mood and effectiveness of the Council. Thus, whatever the formal rules say, decision-making in the Council—even one accommodating 28 states—usually proceeds on the understanding that consensus will be sought, but equally that obstructionism or unreasonable opposition could be countered by a vote.

How is consensus achieved between 28 (now very disparate) states? Imagine a contentious item on the Council's agenda (say, dealing with work and safety regulations). Perhaps a majority of states support the initiative but some are opposed or ambivalent. Before proceeding to a vote, several attempts will be made to achieve some sort of consensus. Bargaining is most intense at the level of Coreper (the committee in which member state ambassadors to the EU meet). Phone calls or informal chats between national representatives prepare the ground for subsequent meetings where agreements can be struck. Informal agreements might also be reached at the meals that are very much a part of both Coreper and Council meetings. Ostensibly a time for break and refreshment, these lunches provide opportunities for a delicate probing of national positions. Similarly, a good Chair can make use of scheduled or requested breaks in the proceedings to explore possibilities for a settlement. These breaks may feature off-the-record discussions or 'confessionals' between the Chair and national representatives or amongst representatives themselves. Lubricating these discussions is the familiarity and personal relationships national representatives have built up over time. In the end, the objections of opposing states might be assuaged by a redrafting of certain clauses, a promise of later support for a favoured initiative, or the possibility of a derogation (or postponement) of a policy's implementation for one or more reluctant states. The point is that day-to-day practice in Coreper and the Council is characterized far more by the search for a consensus than by any straightforward mechanism of strategic voting.

made up of the permanent Ambassadors, who deal primarily with the big political, institutional, and budgetary issues, and Coreper I led by Deputy Ambassadors who deal with most other issues. Some sensitive or especially busy policy areas—such as security, economic and financial affairs, and agriculture—have their own special preparatory committees, composed of senior officials from the member states.

To the uninitiated (and many of the initiated), Coreper and its various working parties are shadowy and complex. National ambassadors and senior civil servants preparing Council meetings are assisted by numerous (around 140) working groups and committees of national delegates who scrutinize Commission proposals, put forward amendments and hammer out deals in the run up to the Council meetings. The vast majority of Council decisions (around 70 per cent) are settled here, before ministers become directly involved (Hayes-Renshaw and Wallace 2006: 14). Some see

---

BOX 3.3	**Voting in the Council of Ministers**

In 2014 a system known as 'double majority voting' was introduced. For a proposal to go through, it requires the support of two types of majority: at least 55 per cent of the member states of the Council (at least 15 out of 28) that must represent, collectively, at least 65 per cent of the EU's population. A blocking minority must include at least four Council members. Article 238 of the Treaty on the Functioning of European Union sets out a few exceptions to this general voting rule.

However, until 31 March 2017, a member state can request that the previous QMV rules are used for any individual vote. The previous system gave each member state a certain number of 'weighted' votes. The weighting of votes is set out in the Treaties and roughly reflects the population of member states—the bigger a country's population, the more votes it has, although the numbers are weighted in favour of the less populous countries as follows:

- France, Germany, Italy, United Kingdom: 29 votes each
- Spain, Poland: 27 votes each
- Romania: 14 votes
- Netherlands: 13 votes
- Belgium, Czech Republic, Greece, Hungary, Portugal: 12 votes each
- Austria, Bulgaria, Sweden: 10 votes each
- Croatia, Denmark, Ireland, Lithuania, Slovakia, Finland: 7 votes each
- Cyprus, Estonia, Latvia, Luxembourg, Slovenia: 4 votes each
- Malta: 3 votes

There are, in total, 352 votes. A qualified majority is reached if a majority of member states (15 of 28) vote in favour, and a minimum of 260 votes out of the total 352 votes are cast in favour. A member state can also request confirmation that the votes cast in favour represent at least 62 per cent of the total EU population and, if that threshold is not reached, the decision is not adopted.

Coreper as a real powerhouse: 'the men and women who run Europe'. For others, including Coreper's civil servants themselves, their role is merely that of helping ministers. A civil servant's quote from some years ago remains apt: 'If ministers want to let Coreper decide, that is a ministerial decision' (*Economist*, 6 August 1998).

European Council (of Heads of State or Government)

The European Council began in the 1970s as occasional informal fireside chats among Heads of Government (or, in the case of member states with executive Presidents, such as France, Heads of State). It became a regular get together, and known as the European Council, in the mid-1970s (although the term 'summit' is still frequently heard). For a long time, the European Council was seen simply as the pinnacle of the Council system, comprising Prime Ministers rather than sectoral ministers. However, its composition is formally different—the President of the Commission is a member of the European Council alongside the Heads of State or Government—and the very nature and dynamics of its meetings give it an unmistakably distinct character. The Lisbon Treaty formally made it a separate institution.

The European Council must meet at least four times a year, although six has been the norm in recent years. The Treaties state that the European Council 'shall provide the Union with the necessary impetus for its development and shall define [its] general political directions and priorities'. Even prior to recognition of its role in the Treaties, it became the major agenda setter of the Union. Initiatives such as direct elections to the European Parliament, monetary union, successive enlargements, strategy on climate change, and major Treaty reforms have all been agreed or endorsed at European Council level. Meeting at 'the summit' of each member state's hierarchy guarantees that its conclusions, even when not legally binding, are acted upon by the Council, the member states and, in practice, the European Commission.

In the words of its own President, 'the European Council works by keeping out of day-to-day business which the other institutions do much better' (in the well-tested framework of the '**Community Method**'), 'yet springing into action to deal with the special cases—changing the Treaty, letting new members in the club, dealing with a crisis. In all these cases it draws upon the collective legitimacy of its members' (Van Rompuy 2012).

The European Council's other broad function is more mundane problem-solving. Issues that cannot be resolved within Coreper or the Council are often settled at this elevated political level, at times through informal persuasion. At other times, European leaders strike package deals that trade off agreement on one issue (say regional spending) in exchange for concessions on another (say agricultural reform), deals that sectoral ministers cannot easily make. Serious deadlocks on the finances of the Union have often been resolved only through such deals in late night sittings. The Lisbon Treaty also recognizes what has become, over time, an important role of the European Council: to nominate the President of the Commission, the Governor and Board members of the European Central Bank, and so on.

The Presidency of the European Council once rotated in tandem with that of the Council. With the Lisbon Treaty, it was agreed that Heads of State or Government would choose their own chairman for a two-and-a-half year (once renewable) period. The first such President, Belgium Prime Minister, Herman Van Rompuy, took office on 1 January 2010 (see Barber 2010). Donald Tusk was announced as Van Rompuy's successor on 30 August 2014. Tusk left the post of Prime Minister of Poland to serve as President and his term of office commenced on 1 December 2014.

A number of factors led to the creation of a 'permanent' and full-time President. Previously, the six-month term of office meant a new President every second or third meeting: a recipe for discontinuity and inconsistency. The preparation of European Council meetings, involving consultation of all Heads of Government, was, especially with successive enlargements, becoming increasingly onerous for any President or Prime Minister with their own national government to run. Also, the task of representing the EU externally at summit meetings on foreign policy issues, whilst at the same time representing their own country, was felt to be inappropriate.

Member states with an intergovernmentalist view of the EU saw the European Council President as a useful counterweight to the President of the Commission. Many French observers, given their domestic institutional system, see the President of the European Council as a sort of *Président* of Europe, with the Commission President demoted to the status of a French Prime Minister, devoted largely to internal affairs and even then deferring on major decisions to the President. That view is not shared by all. The first European Council President, Van Rompuy, described himself as being less than a *Président* but more than a chairman: a facilitator, not a dictator.

The European Parliament

The EU is unique among international organizations in having a parliament: the European Parliament (EP) is the only directly elected multinational parliament with significant powers in the world. The reasons for its unique status are twofold. Some saw the creation of a directly elected parliament as a means towards a more 'federal' system in which the Union would derive legitimacy directly from citizens instead of exclusively via national governments. Others simply saw the need to compensate the loss of national level parliamentary power, which is inherent in pooling competences at European level.

To its admirers, the Parliament is the voice of the people in European decision-making. To its critics, it is an expensive talking shop. Both of these portraits carry elements of truth. In contrast with most national parliaments, the EP cannot directly initiate legislation and its budgetary powers cover only spending, not taxation. The EP is dogged by image problems. Its housekeeping arrangements are clumsy and expensive: it is obliged by the member states to divide its activities between Brussels (three weeks out of four) and Strasbourg (for four days a month). The multiplicity of languages means that its debates lack the cut and thrust found in many national parliaments. Until 2014 there was no visible link between the outcome of the parliamentary elections and the composition of the executive, which is what voters are used to at the national level (see earlier for discussion of the appointment of Juncker to the post of Commission President in 2014). Turnout in EP elections is lower than in most national elections in Europe (although about the same as for mid-term, that is non-Presidential, elections in the US).

But the EP exercises its legislative powers forcefully compared to national parliaments, which rarely amend or reject government proposals. Because the EP is not controlled by the executive or any governing majority, it can use its independence to considerable effect. Each successive Treaty change has strengthened the role of the Parliament. The Parliament is a legal and political equal to the Council in deciding almost all legislation as well as the budget and ratification of international Treaties. It elects the President of the Commission and confirms (and can dismiss) the Commission as a whole. Its members are able to network across the institutions and with national governments, interest groups and NGOs.

The Lisbon Treaty caps the EP at 751 members with a minimum of six and a maximum of 96 seats per member state, degressively proportional to population. The members of the parliament (MEPs) sit in political groups, not in national blocs. Although there are over 150 national parties, they coalesce into seven groups, most of which correspond to familiar European political families: Liberals, Socialists, Christian Democrats, Greens and so on. Of course, national allegiances do not disappear. Nonetheless, EP political groups have become more cohesive over time (Hix, Noury and Roland 2009). The EP lacks the strict whipping system found in national parliaments, but positions taken by the groups—and the negotiations between them—are what count in determining majorities. And choices at stake when dealing with legislation are indeed typical political choices: higher environmental standards at greater cost to those regulated, or not? Higher standards of consumer protection, or leave it to the market? On these subjects, there are nearly always different views within each member state, irrespective of the position taken by their ministers in the Council. These various views are represented in the Parliament, which contains members from opposition parties as well as governing parties in every member state. There is a considerably higher degree of pluralism in the Parliament than in the Council.

The leaders of each political group, along with the Parliament's President, constitute the Conference of Presidents, which sets the EP's agenda. But, like the US Congress, the detailed and most important work of the Parliament is carried out in some 20 standing committees, mostly organized by policy area (such as transport, agriculture, or the environment) and some cross-cutting (such as budgets or women's rights). The committee system allows detailed scrutiny of proposals by members who are, or become, specialists.

The powers of the EP

The Parliament's powers fall under four main headings: legislative, budgetary, scrutiny, and appointments. The Parliament's legislative powers were originally very weak, having only the right to give an opinion on proposed legislation (see Box 3.4). After successive Treaty changes the EP now co-decides nearly all EU legislation in what amounts to a bicameral legislature consisting of the Council and the Parliament. What is now, revealingly, called the Ordinary Legislative Procedure requires

BOX 3.4	How the European Parliament 'squeezes' power

The EU's Parliament has tended to make the most of whatever powers it has had at any given moment. Even when it was merely consulted on legislation it developed techniques, such as the threat of delay, to make its influence felt. In budget negotiations the EP uses its power to sign off—or not—on the annual budget selectively but effectively.

Similarly, the EP has stretched its powers to oversee the Commission. Formally, the Parliament has only a collective vote of confidence in the Commission before it takes office. The EP has no right to hire or fire individual Commissioners. Yet, for example, in the parliamentary confirmation hearings of 2004 the EP objected to Italian Commissioner-designate Rocco Buttiglione's statements that homosexuality was 'a sin' and that women 'belonged in the home' (Peterson 2012a: 108). These comments caused widespread consternation, especially as his portfolio was to include civil liberties. As it became clear that Parliament might vote to reject the entire Commission, President-elect Barroso formally withdrew the team on the eve of the vote and came back a few weeks later with a new College from which Buttiglione had been dropped. Note that the Parliament did not have *de jure* power to sack Buttiglione, but de facto, it did just that. It did the same in 2009 and 2014.

Of course the EP's threats must seem real, and for that to happen it must stay united. Such unity is not easy to come by in such a large and diverse institution with 751 members from a vast array of parties and backgrounds. Thus, despite its ability to 'squeeze' power, the Parliament does not always get its way.

that both agree a text in identical terms before it can be passed into law. Similarly, international Treaties or agreements are subject to the consent procedure: the Parliament has the right—in a yes or no vote—to approve or reject the agreement. When it comes to budgetary matters, the Lisbon Treaty provides also for a sort of co-decision.

The Parliament also exercises scrutiny of the Commission (and to a degree other institutions). Its oversight is exercised via its right to question (through written questions or orally at question time), to examine and debate statements or reports, and to hear and cross-examine Commissioners, ministers, and civil servants in its committees. The Parliament also approves the appointment of the Commission and, more spectacularly, can dismiss it (as a whole) through a vote of no confidence. The latter is considered to be a 'nuclear' option—a strategic, reserve power that requires an absolute majority of all MEPs and a two-thirds majority of all votes cast. As in most national parliaments, which do not make daily use of their right to dismiss the government, its very existence is sufficient to show that the Commission must take due account of Parliament.

This power effectively was exercised only once, when it resulted in the fall of the Commission under the Presidency of Jacques Santer in 1999. Even then, the Commission resigned prior to the actual vote, once it was clear that the necessary majority would be obtained. One upshot of this episode was a Treaty change to allow the President of the Commission to dismiss individual members of the Commission (which the EP cannot do). Thus, if the behaviour of a particular Commissioner gives rise to serious parliamentary misgivings (as Edith Cresson's did in the Santer Commission; see Peterson 2012a), the President of the Commission can take action before events move to the stage where the Parliament might dismiss the Commission as a whole. Besides the Commission, the Parliament also elects the European Ombudsman and is consulted on appointments to other EU posts (see Box 3.8).

In short, the European Parliament's powers have grown significantly since direct elections were first held in 1979 (Hix and Høyland 2013). However, some still question its ability to bring legitimacy to EU decision-making. Its claim to represent the peoples of Europe is undermined by low turnouts for its elections (around 43 per cent in recent EP elections). In the 2014 election, voters elected an unprecedentedly high number of Eurosceptic MEPs, who question the very existence of the EU, with such parties topping the poll in some member states (including France and the UK). The relative lack of citizen engagement, combined with the Parliament's image (accurate or not) as a 'gravy train' does not help. Ultimately, the Parliament's future role is tied up with larger questions of democracy and power in the EU (see Chapter 7).

European Court of Justice

At first glance, the European Court of Justice (ECJ) seems neither a particularly powerful nor controversial institution. It is located in sleepy Luxembourg and comprised of 28 judges (one from each member state) plus nine Advocates-General who draft Opinions for the judges. It is supported by the General Court (previously known as the Court of First Instance), a lower tribunal created in 1989 to ease a growing workload (it had dealt with nearly 17,000 cases by 2010). The ECJ, the General Court, and the specialist Civil Service Tribunal (created in 2004) are collectively referred to as the Court of Justice of the European Union (CJEU). The ECJ's profile is generally low, apart from within European legal circles.

Simply put, the role of the ECJ is to ensure that, in the interpretation and application of the Treaties, the law is observed. The Court is thus powerful: it is the final arbiter in legal disputes between EU institutions or between EU institutions and member states or between citizens and EU institutions. The Court ensures that the EU institutions do not go beyond the powers given to them. Conversely, it also ensures national compliance with the Treaties and to legislation that flows from them. The ECJ even has the right to fine member states that breach EU law.

The Court is sometimes accused of having a pro-integration agenda, a reputation that derives mainly from its landmark decisions in the 1960s. In practice, the Court has to interpret the texts as they have been adopted. Significantly, its members are not appointed by EU institutions, but by member states. The ECJ therefore differs from the US Supreme Court, whose members are appointed by American federal institutions (see Box 3.5).

EU law is qualitatively different from international law in that individuals can seek remedy for breaches of the former through their domestic courts, which refer points of European law to the EU Court. The process allows national courts to ask the ECJ for a ruling on the European facet of a case before them. The national courts, in judging cases, use such preliminary rulings. This method has shaped national policies as diverse as the right to advertise abortion services across borders, roaming charges for mobile phones, and equal pay for equal work. If the Court has a pro-integration agenda, it is primarily to integrate national courts into a cooperative system for applying EU law. Otherwise, what would be the point of EU law?

Its critics sometimes claim that the Court has, in effect, become a policy-making body (see Weiler 1999: 217). Its defenders point out that it can only rule on matters referred to it, and then only apply texts adopted by legislators. Certainly, the Court's role in the 1960s was crucial in giving real substance to the EU legal system. Two landmark decisions stand out. In the 1963 *Van Gend en Loos* case, the Court established 'direct effect': the doctrine that EU citizens had a legal right to expect their governments to adhere to their European obligations. In 1964 (*Costa v ENEL*), the Court established the 'supremacy' of EU law: if a domestic law contradicts a EU obligation, European law prevails.

Later, in the 1979 *Cassis de Dijon* case, the Court established the principle of 'mutual recognition': a product made or sold legally in one member state—in this case a French blackcurrant liqueur—cannot be barred in another member state if there is no threat to public health, public policy, or public safety. This principle proved fundamental to the single market because it established that national variations in standards could exist as long as trade was not unduly impeded.

These judgments took place in a period normally characterized as one of stagnation and 'Eurosclerosis', when political integration seemed paralysed. Scholars who take inspiration from neofunctionalist thinking often cite evidence from this period to undermine the intergovernmentalist claim that national governments alone dominate the rhythm of integration. But the Court's power is limited: it must rely on member states to carry out its rulings. The powers of the Court—and how they should be wielded—remain contested in EU politics.

What is also contested is the relationship between the main institutional players—Commission, Parliament, Council, European Council and Court—which is constantly changing. Power shifts across and between institutions not only as a result of formal Treaty changes, but also due to changes in practice, the assertiveness of the various actors, agreements between EU institutions, and Court judgments. For instance, the ability of the Council to impose its view has declined as the bargaining power of Parliament has increased. The European Council's growing power to set the EU agenda has usurped the Commission's traditional and legal right of initiative.

BOX 3.5	Compared to what?

The ECJ and the US Supreme Court

The European Court of Justice—like the EU more generally—is in many ways *sui generis*: an international body with no precise counterpart anywhere in Europe or beyond. But interesting parallels, as well as contrasts, can be drawn between the ECJ and the US Supreme Court.

The US Supreme Court exists to uphold the US Constitution, whereas the EU has no such constitution. Yet even here the difference may not be as stark as it appears. The ECJ must uphold the EU's Treaties. For some legal scholars, the cumulative impact of Court decisions that have interpreted the Treaties amount to a 'quiet revolution' that effectively transformed the Treaties into a constitution insofar as they constitute the basic rule book of the EU (see Weiler 1999).

One difference is jurisdiction, or the power to hear and decide cases. The jurisdiction of the US Supreme Court is vast. It can hear all cases involving legal disputes between the US states. Even more important is its power to hear cases raising constitutional disputes invoked by any national treaty, federal law, state law or act. The ECJ's jurisdiction is far more confined. Its rulings on trade have had a fundamental impact on the single market and the EU more generally. But many matters of national law and most non-trade disputes between states fall outside its remit. Moreover, the ECJ cannot 'cherry pick' the cases it wants to hear, as the US court can. Finally, recruitment, appointment, and tenure differ. Following nomination by the President and confirmation by the Senate, US Supreme Court justices are appointed for life. Their appointments are highly politicized. In contrast, the member state governments appoint judges to the ECJ, with little publicity. They remain relatively unknown for their six-year renewable term.

Still, we find parallels between the two. The rulings of both the ECJ and Supreme Court take precedence over those of lower or national courts. Lower courts must enforce these rulings. Like the US Supreme Court in its early decades, the ECJ's early decisions helped consolidate the authority of the Union's central institutions. But perhaps the most interesting similarities involve debates surrounding these courts' powers and political role. In the case of the US Supreme Court, concerns about its politicization and activism are well known, especially in its rulings on abortion, racial equality, and campaign spending (see Martin 2010). In the EU too, concerns about the Court's procedure, its ability to push forward or limit integration, and the expansion of its authority have propelled the Court into the heart of political debates about the future of the Europe. Thus, whatever their differences, both courts raise fundamental questions about the proper limits of judicial activism and the role of courts in democratic societies more generally.

The establishment of a full time President of the European *Council* challenges the primacy of the President of the *Commission*.

Both formal and informal institutional change has contributed to a blurring of powers among core institutions. This blurring does not mean that the formal rules do not matter. Rules and Treaty provisions serve as the basis of authority from which the institutions can and do act. But formal powers are starting points only: knowing how the institutions exploit, compete for, and ultimately share power is also crucial for grasping how the EU works (see Box 3.6).

Why Institutions Matter

Examining its institutions and how they work is essential to understanding the EU. First, it gives us a starting point from which to examine the EU's policy process. Second, it helps us to identify the diversity of actors involved and to understand how together they determine the shape and speed of integration. Finally, it reminds us that there are many interesting questions still to be answered about European integration. Is it heading towards a European federal state? Or a looser, more intergovernmental body? Or a multi-tiered system? How democratic or efficient will it be? Who or what will determine the pace and shape of integration?

More particularly, the EU's institutions help illustrate the three central themes of this book: (1) the extent to which the EU is an experiment in motion; (2) the importance of power sharing and consensus; and (3) the capacity of the EU structures to cope with the Union's expanding size and scope.

BOX 3.6   **How it really works**

Turf wars!

Relations between EU institutions are both consensual and conflictual. Cooperation is unceasing because of the shared recognition that all institutions must compromise and work together to get a policy through or decision agreed. Even those final decisions that rest with one institution usually involve proposals from or consultation with another.

Yet inter-institutional rivalry is also fierce. Each institution usually guards its prerogatives (to initiate policy or control budgets) jealously. New institutionalist scholars such as Armstrong and Bulmer (1998) and Pollack (2009) have underlined the importance of this dynamic. Perceived attempts by one institution to encroach on another's 'turf' often elicit heated responses or fierce demonstrations of institutional loyalty. For example, in 2010, the Commission disliked the fact that the European Council had set up a Task Force, chaired by the European Council's President, to make proposals on the reform of economic governance procedures—something the Commission felt should be its job. Although represented on the Task Force, and broadly in agreement with its emerging recommendations, the Commission insisted on tabling them as its own legislative proposals to Parliament and Council only one week before their final approval by the Task Force.

Experimentation and change

The EU's institutional system has evolved considerably since the establishment of the European Coal and Steel Community in 1951. As we have seen, the institutions have adapted over time. The founding Treaties, and subsequent changes to them, formally mandate some of their tasks. Others have emerged as more informal experiments in cooperation. A variety of pressures have combined to encourage a sort of task expansion and the reinvention of institutions over time. In particular, gaps in the capacity of the EU to respond to events and crises have resulted in an ad hoc expansion of the informal powers of the institutions. For example, the need for common action on the environment meant that informal environmental agreements predated formal advances introduced by the Treaties. Sometimes member states agreed on the need to establish informal cooperation in new areas, but were not initially ready to be legally bound by the Treaties, as in the gradual expansion of the powers of the EU institutions in the area of justice and home affairs (see Chapter 9). Studying the institutional dynamics of the EU allows us not only to understand the extent to which the EU is subject to experimentation and change, but also to pose questions about where this process might be headed.

Power sharing and consensus

Scholars of European integration have long and fiercely debated where power lies in the EU. Do the EU's institutions drive the integration process forward? Or do national governments remain in control? Neofunctionalists and intergovernmentalists have taken up the two sides of this debate respectively. Both sides can cite changes in formal EU rules to buttress their case.

For example, as the Parliament has gained powers and member states have accepted more proposals on the basis of QMV, it could be claimed that supranationalism is on the rise. Equally, as the European Council has come to dominate high-level agenda setting, and some EU states have opted out of certain policies (such as monetary union), it could be said that intergovernmentalism is holding strong. But depicting integration as a pitched battle between EU institutions and the member states misses the point. Dividing lines are often within each of the above. And competition is fierce, but so, too, is the search for consensus. Enormous efforts go into forging agreements acceptable to all.

The overall trajectory of integration is thus a result of to-ing and fro-ing between a rich variety of actors and external pressures. This image is quite neatly captured in Wallace's (2000) description of EU governance as a pendulum, swinging sometimes towards intergovernmental solutions and other times towards supranationalism, but not always in equal measure. In this system, power is often a product of how well any institution engages with other actors—lobbyists, experts, governments, and other international organizations—at different levels of governance. Focusing on the institutions and how they cooperate or compete with each other and other actors helps us to begin to make sense of the EU as a complex policy-making process.

Scope and capacity

The step-by-step extension of the scope of the EU's activities is one thing. Its capacity to deal with those subjects that fall within its remit and to cope with successive enlargements is another. Have the institutional structures, originally conceived for a Community of six member states, been sufficiently adapted to deal with the demands of an EU of 28 or more (see Box 3.7)? In most policy fields, the EU has managed to avoid decision-making gridlock following each successive enlargement, though arguments continue as to whether enlargement has been at the cost of

---

BOX 3.7   Enlargement's institutional impact

Enlargement has brought both opportunities and headaches to the EU's institutions. The impact has varied across institutions, with some adapting more smoothly than others. The European Parliament, despite real linguistic challenges (see Box 1.7), seems to have had the least difficulty absorbing new members (see Donnelly and Bigatto 2008). Decisions are based on majority votes and the EP has shown that it is still able to deal with difficult legislation even with more than 700 MEPs. Moreover, the quality of MEPs from new (that is, post-2004) states generally has been high, with many having held important positions (including Presidents and Prime Ministers).

In the Commission, new and generally younger officials from states that recently joined the EU hold out the prospect of revitalizing and renewing the institution with fresh ideas and reform-minded Europeans (see Kassim et al. 2013: 245–72). However, a college of 28 Commissioners has resulted in a less cosy and, arguably, more **intergovernmental** and less collegial body (see Peterson 2008). With one per member state, its membership is now like that of the Council. Finding a sufficient number of responsible and interesting portfolios of relatively equal importance has proved difficult.

The Council and European Council have felt the effects of enlargement most keenly, especially where unanimity is required or desired. Since 2004, the Council has found it increasingly difficult to push through important decisions in areas such as foreign policy and police cooperation. National vetoes are not necessarily more common in an enlarged EU (see House of Lords 2006; Hagemann and De Clerck-Sachsse 2007). But Council meetings are more time-consuming and not always as productive. On important questions, all or most member states still want to present their positions and may insist on lengthy interventions. The result is less time for real discussion and compromise-seeking, which is the essence of what makes the Council and European Council function.

The impact of enlargement on the institutions reflects its wider impact on the EU. It has brought a mix of logistical headaches, challenges, doubts, and crises. But it also promises fresh impulse, drive, and energy for a Union otherwise threatened by stagnation and inertia.

having to settle for lowest common denominator solutions. Certainly in areas that require unanimity within the Council, the EU now is vulnerable to slow, cumbersome decision-making and even total blockage at the instigation of one or another member state.

Strengthening European cooperation may appear to equate to empowering its institutions. Yet, policy cooperation has been extended in a variety of different ways that have expanded the scope of the EU without necessarily expanding the powers of institutions. The careful exclusion of the ECJ, and the weaker role of the Commission and the EP, in most aspects of foreign and security policy are examples. So is the gradual bonding together of European leaders outside the formal confines of the European Council but also not, strictly and exclusively speaking, as representatives of purely national interests, (see Van Middelaar 2013). Finally, if there is one lesson to be learned from the study of EU institutions, it is their remarkable ability to adapt as new requirements are placed upon them. This chapter has tried to show that while the capacity of EU institutions may be limited, their ability to adapt often seems limitless.

Conclusion

The EU's institutional system is complex. But so, too, is the diverse polity it helps govern. We have attempted to cut through this complexity by focusing on the powers of the institutions, and what they do with them. We have stressed the importance of both cooperation and rivalry between the institutions. Each institution may have its own agenda, but nearly all of the important decisions require some (and usually, quite a large) measure of consensus spanning the EU's institutions (see Peterson and Shackleton 2012). The institutions are as interdependent as the member states that make up the EU.

Moreover, EU institutions do not operate alone. Today they must deal with an ever-broader range of actors, including an increasing number of member states (see Chapters 4 and 8), but also increasingly active groups of organized interests. Above all, understanding institutions helps us to explore broader questions of how and why the EU works the way it does.

As the EU takes on new tasks, the burden on its institutions will increase. The EU's growing role in areas such as migration, foreign and defence policy, food safety, and climate change means that other agencies and bodies (including international ones that transcend Europe itself) will join the institutional mix that helps govern EU politics (see Box 3.8). Further institutional reform may prove both necessary and inevitable to cope with the increasing size and policy scope of the EU. But given the challenge of obtaining unanimous support for institutional change, institutional reform—like so much else in the EU—is likely to be incremental and pragmatic rather than spectacular or far-sighted.

BOX 3.8	Other institutions and bodies

Several smaller institutions and bodies carry out a variety of representative, oversight, or managerial functions in the EU. By far the most significant of these specialized institutions is the **European Central Bank (ECB)**. Based in Frankfurt and modelled on the fiercely independent German Bundesbank, the ECB is charged with a fundamental task: formulating the EU's monetary policy, including ensuring monetary stability, setting interest rates, and issuing and managing the euro (see Chapter 5). The ECB is steered by a governing council (made up primarily of national central bank governors) and headed by a President and executive board chosen by member states although they cannot formally be removed by member states. The Bank's independence and power undoubtedly help ensure monetary stability but also have raised concerns about transparency and accountability. It must report to the EP several times a year. But its deliberations were until recently not made public and it enjoys considerable independence from other institutions or member states. While still a young institution, the Bank is certain to become a more important, but also controversial player in EU politics (see Hodson 2010). Its remit was expanded in 2014 to include supervision of banks.

The **Court of Auditors**, with 28 members, is charged with scrutinizing the EU's budget and financial accounts. Acting as the 'financial conscience' of the EU, the Court has increased its visibility in recent years as public concern over mismanagement, and occasionally fraud, has mounted. Its annual and specialized reports consist mainly of dry financial management assessment. But it has also uncovered more spectacular and serious financial misconduct (see Karakatsanis and Laffan 2012).

Several smaller bodies not classified as institutions (therefore having fewer rights at the Court) carry out a primarily representative function (see Jeffrey and Rowe 2012). For instance the **European Economic and Social Committee (EESC)** represents employers, trades unions, and other social or public interests (such as farmers or consumers) in EU policy-making. Chosen by the national governments, these representatives serve in a part-time function advising the Commission and other institutions on relevant proposals. Their opinions can be well researched but are not usually influential. The **Committee of the Regions and Local Authorities** suffers from a similar lack of influence. Created by the Maastricht Treaty, the Committee must be consulted on proposals affecting regional interests (cohesion funding, urban planning) and can issue its own opinions and reports. However, its membership is debilitatingly diverse (powerful regional ministers from Germany and Belgium sit alongside representatives from English town parishes). It has yet to exert the influence its proponents originally envisioned. But perhaps its real role is as a channel of communication across several layers of governance.

The EU **Ombudsman** is empowered to receive complaints from any EU citizen or any natural or legal person residing in the member states concerning instances of maladministration in the activities of the Union institutions or bodies (other than the Court in its judicial capacity). The EP chooses the Ombudsman after each parliamentary election for the duration of its term of office.

The **European Investment Bank (EIB)** is the world's biggest, public, long-term lending institution. It supports the development of infrastucture and economic development projects. The EIB's shareholders are the member states. It borrows on capital markets to finance capital projects. In 2013 it lent over €70bn.

DISCUSSION QUESTIONS

1. Which EU institution is most 'powerful' in your view and why?

2. Why has the balance of powers between the EU's institutions shifted over time?

3. In what ways has enlargement affected the EU's main institutions?

4. Is the relationship between the EU's institutions characterized more by cooperation or conflict?

FURTHER READING

For comprehensive analysis of all of the EU's institutions, see Peterson and Shackleton (2012a). Helpful examinations of individual institutions include Kassim et al.'s (2013) analysis of the Commission; Hayes-Renshaw and Wallace's (2006) classic study of the Council of Ministers (which also includes analysis of the European Council); Corbett et al.'s (2011) account of the workings of the Parliament; and Weiler's (1999) provocative and thoughtful essays on the Court and EU's legal identity. Van Middelaar (2013) offers a perceptive treatment of how the EU's institutional system has developed over time.

Corbett, R., Jacobs, F., and Shackleton, M. (2011), *The European Parliament*, 8th ed. (London: John Harper).

Hayes-Renshaw, F. and Wallace, H. (2006), *The Council of Ministers*, 2nd ed. (Basingstoke and New York: Palgrave).

Kassim, H., Peterson, J., Bauer, M., Connolly, S., Dehousse, R., Hooghe, L., and Thompson, A. (2013), *The European Commission of the Twenty-First Century* (Oxford and New York: Oxford University Press).

Peterson, J. and Shackleton, M. (eds) (2012a), *The Institutions and Policies of the European Union*, 3rd ed. (Oxford and New York: Oxford University Press).

Van Middelaar, L. (2013), *The Passage to Europe: How a Continent Became a Union* (New Haven: Yale University Press).

Weiler, J.H.H. (1999), *The Constitution of Europe* (Cambridge and New York: Cambridge University Press).

WEB LINKS

Most of the EU's institutions have their own website which can be accessed through the EU's official portal site, 'The European Union online' (**http://www.europa.eu/**). Here are the specific official websites of some of the institutions introduced in this chapter:

- European Commission: **http://ec.europa.eu/**
- Council of Ministers: **http://www.consilium.europa.eu/**
- European Parliament: **http://www.europarl.europa.eu/**
- European Council: **http://www.european-council.europa.eu/**
- European Court of Justice: **http://curia.europa.eu/**
- Court of Auditors: **http://www.eca.europa.eu/**

- Economic and Social Committee: **http://eesc.europa.eu/**
- Committee of the Regions: **http://www.cor.europa.eu/**
- European Central Bank: **http://www.ecb.int/**

Anyone brave enough to consider working as an intern or *stagiaire* in one of the EU's institutions can find out more at: **http://ec.europa.eu/stages/** For recent updates on institutional developments, especially in relation to Treaty reform, see: **http://www. euractiv.com/** The London-based University Association for Contemporary European Studies (UACES) (**http://www.uaces.org/**) announces regular workshops and lectures on the EU institutions held in the UK and (occasionally) on the European continent. For information on conferences and lectures held in the US, see the website of the US European Union Studies Association (EUSA) which can be found at: **http://www.eustudies.org**

 Visit the Online Resource Centre that accompanies this book for additional material: **www.oxfordtextbooks.co.uk/orc/kenealy4e/**

CHAPTER 4

Member States

Brigid Laffan

▌ Summary

This chapter focuses on the European Union's (EU's) most essential component: its member states. It examines six factors that determine how a state engages with the EU: date of entry, size, wealth, state structure, economic ideology, and integration preference. We then explore how member states behave in the Union's institutions and seek to influence the outcome of negotiations in Brussels. We focus throughout on the informal as well as formal activities of the member states. The final section explores the insights offered by theory in analysing the relationship between the EU and its member states.

Introduction

States are the essential building blocks of the EU. Without states there is no European Union. All EU Treaties are negotiated and ratified by the 'high contracting parties': that is, the governments of the member states. By joining the EU, the traditional nation-state is transformed into a member state. This transformation involves an enduring commitment to participate in political and legal processes that are beyond the state but embrace the state. Membership of the Union has significant effects on national systems of policy-making, national institutions, and national identity, **sovereignty**, and democracy. Put simply, once a state joins the Union, politics may begin at home but they no longer end there. National politics, polities, and policies become 'Europeanized' (see Box 4.1).

Member states shape the EU as much as the EU shapes its member states. The decision to join the Union is a decision to become locked into an additional layer of **governance** and a distinctive form of 'Euro-politics', which is neither wholly domestic nor international but shares attributes of both. This chapter explores this interactive dynamic. We tackle questions such as: what is the role of member states in the EU system? What is it about the EU that has led the member states to invest so much in the collective project? How do member states engage with the EU? What factors determine how any member state behaves as a EU member?

BOX 4.1   **Key concepts and terms**

Acquis communautaire is a French phrase that denotes the sum total of the rights and obligations derived from the EU Treaties, laws, and Court rulings. In principle, new member states joining the EU must accept the entire *acquis*.

Demandeur is the French term often used to refer to those demanding something (say regional or agricultural funds) from the EU.

Europeanization is the process whereby national systems (institutions, policies, governments, and even the polity itself) adapt to EU policies and integration more generally, while also themselves shaping the European Union.

Flexible integration (also called 'reinforced' or 'enhanced cooperation') denotes the possibility for some member states to pursue deeper integration without the participation of others. Examples include EMU and the **Schengen Agreement** in which some member states have decided not to participate fully. The Amsterdam and Nice Treaties institutionalized the concept of **flexible integration** through their clauses on enhanced cooperation.

Tours de table allow each national delegation in a Council of Ministers meeting to make an intervention on a given subject. In a EU of 28 member states *tours de table* have become less common. If every minister or national official intervened for even five minutes on each subject, it would take nearly two and half-hours.

Six Determining Features

The 28 (as of 2015) member states bring to the Union their distinctive national histories, state traditions, constitutions, legal principles, political systems, and economic capacity. A variety of languages (there are 24 official working languages in the EU) and an extraordinary diversity of national and sub-national tastes and cultures accentuate the mosaic-like character of Europe. The enlargement of the Union (13 new states since 2004) has deepened its pre-existing diversity. Managing difference is thus a key challenge for the Union. To understand how the EU really works, we must seek to understand the multinational and multicultural character of the European Union and its institutions.

Classifying the member states—including how and why they joined and how they operate within the EU—is a good first step towards understanding their relationship with the EU. Six factors are extremely important. No one factor determines the relationship between the Union and a member state, but together they provide a guide to understanding the engagement of member states with the EU.

Entry date

It is useful to deploy the metaphor of an onion to characterize the expansion of the Union from its original six states to nine, ten, 12, 15, and finally to 28 or more states in the years ahead (see Figure 4.1). France, Germany, and the four other founding members form the core of the onion. What is now the EU was originally the creation of six states that were occupied or defeated in the Second World War. It is the creation especially of France, a country that needed to achieve a settlement with its neighbour and historical enemy, Germany. From the outset the key relationship in the EU was between France and West Germany. As explained in Chapter 2, the Franco-German alliance and the Paris–Bonn axis—now Paris–Berlin—has left enduring traces on the fabric of integration. The **Elysée Treaty** (1963) institutionalized very strong bilateral ties between these two countries. The intensity of interaction should not be taken as evidence of continuous agreement between France and Germany on major European issues. Rather, much of the interaction has worked to iron out conflicts between them.

Close personal relationships between West German Chancellor Helmut Schmidt and French President Valery Giscard d'Estaing in the 1970s and Chancellor Helmut Kohl and President François Mitterrand in the 1980s and early 1990s were key to the most ambitious steps forward in **European integration**, including the creation of the European Monetary System (a precursor to EMU), the **single market** programme, and the euro. The Franco-German relationship was challenged by geopolitical change in Europe following the collapse of communism. German unification and the opening up of the eastern half of the continent altered the bilateral balance of power, with Germany no longer a junior

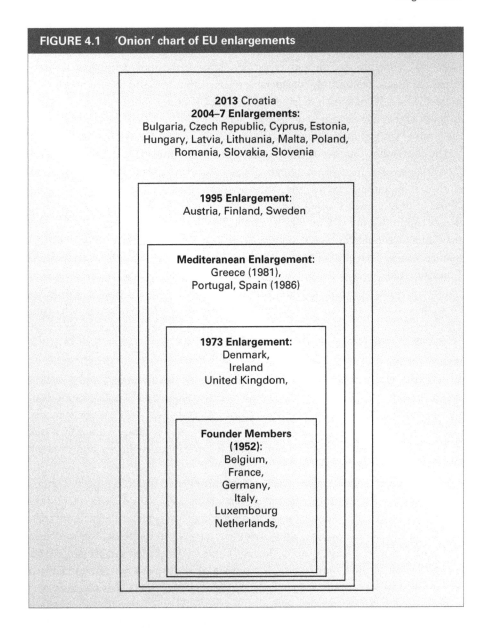

FIGURE 4.1   'Onion' chart of EU enlargements

2013 Croatia
2004–7 Enlargements:
Bulgaria, Czech Republic, Cyprus, Estonia,
Hungary, Latvia, Lithuania, Malta, Poland,
Romania, Slovakia, Slovenia

1995 Enlargement:
Austria, Finland, Sweden

Mediteranean Enlargement:
Greece (1981),
Portugal, Spain (1986)

1973 Enlargement:
Denmark,
Ireland
United Kingdom,

**Founder Members
(1952):**
Belgium,
France,
Germany,
Italy,
Luxembourg
Netherlands,

political partner to France. The change was symbolically captured by the reloca-
tion of the German capital to Berlin.

It is premature to talk of the demise of the Franco-German relationship; it remains
important. But changing geopolitics, enlargement to the east, and Germany's strong
economic performance have profoundly altered the context within which it is played
out. To illustrate, France and the UK—not Germany—have been in the forefront of EU
defence cooperation. Germany, the UK, and many of the new member states have

driven market liberalization against a more protectionist France. The most important shift however is the relative economic performance of the two countries since 2009. During the acute phase of the euro crisis, Germany was the dominant state in devising policy responses. Significantly considerable uncertainty attaches to the future of the UK in the EU. In a major speech in January 2013, the UK Prime Minister, David Cameron announced that if re-elected in the 2015 general election, he would seek to renegotiate the terms of UK membership and put the results to an 'in' or 'out' referendum.

The four other founder member states—Italy, Belgium, Luxembourg, and the Netherlands—see themselves as part of the hard core of the Union. The Benelux countries (Belgium, Luxembourg, and the Netherlands) were traditionally at the centre of developments, often ready to push for deeper integration. They were all deeply committed to the '**Community method**' of law-making (institution-led rather than intergovernmental) and supportive of a strong, supranational Union. This dynamic, however, has changed in recent times. Since 2005 and Dutch rejection of the Constitutional Treaty, Benelux cooperation has been at best lukewarm, at worst non-existent. For example, the 2007 EU summit that agreed the text of what would become the Lisbon Treaty featured a blazing row between the Belgian and Dutch Prime Ministers, with one attendee commenting: 'we thought they might come to blows' (*Financial Times*, 25 June 2007) over the issue of scrutiny rights for national parliaments (see Chapter 7).

Italy has oscillated between active involvement in EU diplomacy and a passive presence in the system. It has traditionally been enthusiastic about European institution-building, but not consistently so (see Bindi and Cisci 2005). More generally, Italy's relationship with the EU and other member states is hampered not by a lack of enthusiasm but by endemic instability in its governing coalitions and its weak capacity for internal reform.

All states joining the EU after its initial formative period had to accept the Union's existing laws and obligations (or *acquis communautaire*; see Box 4.1), its institutional system, and way of doing business, all of which had been formed without their input. Thus for all latecomers, adjustment and adaptation to the EU was a process that began before their date of **accession** and continued well after membership. With the expansion of the Union's tasks, the burden of adjustment has grown for each successive wave of accession. As Chapter 5 demonstrates, the EU has taken on new policy areas over the years ranging from environmental policy to police cooperation (the *acquis communautaire* has grown to cover over 80,000 pages of legislation). This expansion has made it even more difficult for outsiders to catch up and adapt to membership (see Chapter 8).

Size

As in all political systems, size matters in the EU. The distinction between large and small states is often evoked in political and media discussions about representation in the EU. At the cumbersome negotiations on the Treaty of Nice, which focused on

TABLE 4.1 Clusters of member states by size

Current member states

(figure in brackets = approximate population in millions in 2012)

Large	Medium	Small	Very Small
Germany (81.8)	Romania (21.3)	Sweden (9.5)	Cyprus (0.8)
France (65.3)	Netherlands (16.7)	Austria (8.4)	Luxembourg (0.5)
UK (63.0)	Greece (11.3)	Bulgaria (7.3)	Malta (0.4)
Italy (60.8)	Belgium (11.1)	Denmark (5.6)	
Spain (46.2)	Portugal (10.5)	Finland (5.4)	
Poland (38.5)	Czech Rep (10.5)	Slovakia (5.4)	
	Hungary (10.0)	Ireland (4.6)	
		Croatia (4.4)	
		Lithuania (3.0)	
		Latvia (2.0)	
		Slovenia (2.0)	
		Estonia (1.3)	

Eurostat 2012. **http://epp.eurostat.ec.europa.eu/portal/page/portal/population/documents/Tab/ESSQR_Mar2013_demogr_suppl_final.pdf**

the re-weighting of votes in the Council and the number of Commissioners each state could appoint, tensions between large and small states escalated. Nice settled little, and battles between large and small states marked negotiations surrounding the 2004 Constitutional Treaty and its eventual replacement (the Lisbon Treaty).

In any event, a more nuanced approach to understanding the impact of size is warranted. The EU really consists of four clusters of states—large, medium, small, and very small (see Table 4.1). The first cluster contains six large states: Germany, the UK, France, Italy, Spain, and Poland. Together they make up about 70 per cent of the population of EU-28 (although even here we find dissent: Germany, France, and the UK are certainly seen as the 'big three', with Italy seen as less powerful, and some would dispute Spain's and Poland's categorization as large states). The next cluster consists of medium-sized states: Romania, the Netherlands, Greece, Belgium, Portugal, the Czech Republic, and Hungary, whose populations range from 10 to 22 million. The third cluster is one of small states: Sweden, Austria, Bulgaria, Croatia, Denmark, Finland, Slovakia, Ireland, Lithuania, Latvia, Slovenia, and Estonia, which all have populations of between one and nine million. The fourth category, very small states, consists of Cyprus, Luxembourg, and Malta. Recent enlargements have brought mainly an increase of medium, small, and very small states (Poland being the exception). Indeed, one of the reasons Turkish membership of the EU is so contested is that its large population—larger than any EU state besides Germany and growing fast—would have a profound impact on the size balances within the Union (see Chapter 8).

Size has implications for power and presence in the Union's political and economic system. The power of large states is not just expressed in voting power in the Council. It manifests itself in political, economic, and diplomatic influence (see Wallace 2005: 38ff). Large states can call on far more extensive and specialized administrative and technical resources in the policy process than small states, and their diplomatic presence is far stronger throughout the world. The German Chancellor, regardless of who holds the post, is usually the most powerful politician at European Council meetings. Small states, however, enjoy important advantages in EU negotiations. They tend to have fewer vital interests than larger states, their interests can be aggregated with much greater ease, and the potential for conflict and competing claims among different social groups is reduced. Luxembourg, for example, can concentrate all of its diplomatic energy on protecting its traditional industries, its liberal banking laws, and its presence in EU institutions.

Although size matters, it has little bearing on national approaches to substantive issues of EU policy that are formed by economic considerations, domestic interests, and the proposed nature of the change. Thus, small states are unlikely to band together against the large states in substantive policy discussions. Their interests, just like those of the larger states, diverge. Coalition patterns in the Council have always consisted of a mix of large and small states in any particular policy domain.

Small states do, however, have a common interest in maintaining the EU's institutional balance and they can deploy a variety of strategies to cope with the structural disadvantage they face (Panke 2010). For instance small EU states can band together to oppose proposals that privilege a small group of larger states. They are keen supporters of procedural 'rules of the game' which protect their level of representation in the system. The key point here is that the multilateral, institutionalized, and legal processes of the Union have created a relatively benign environment for small states.

In the past, the EU successfully managed to expand its membership to include both large and small states without undermining the balance between them or causing undue tension. This balance began to shift in the 1990s. The 1995 enlargement and the prospect of further enlargement to the east and south heightened the salience of the small-state/large-state divide in the Union. The struggle for power—as reflected in number of Commissioners, votes in the Council, or seats in the European Parliament each member state receives—figured on the EU agenda for over a decade, from 1995 to 2009. Negotiating the relative power of member states has not been easy. Many would argue that the institutional debate has been the poisoned chalice of the EU over the past few years.

Wealth

The original European Economic Community had only one serious regional poverty problem: the Italian Mezzogiorno (Italy's southern regions). As such, 'cohesion' (or regional development) was not an important concern. The first enlargement in 1973 to include the UK, Denmark, and Ireland increased the salience of regional disparities in the politics of the Union. The UK had significant regional problems, with declining industrial areas and low levels of economic development in areas such as Northern England, Scotland, Wales, and Northern Ireland. The Republic of Ireland had per capita incomes that were about 62 per cent of the EU average at the time. The Mediterranean enlargements in the 1980s to include Greece, Spain, and Portugal (all relatively poor states) accentuated the problem of economic divergence.

By the 1980s, the Union as an economic space consisted of a 'golden triangle', which ran from southern England, through France and Germany to northern Italy and southern, western, and northern peripheries. Although committed to harmonious economic development from the outset, the Union did not have to expand its budgetary commitment to poorer Europe until the single market programme in the mid-1980s. At that point, Europe's poorer states successfully linked the economic liberalization of the 1992 programme with an enhanced commitment to greater cohesion in the Union. This commitment manifested itself in a doubling of the financial resources devoted to less prosperous regions, especially those with a per capita income less than 75 per cent of the EU average (see Table 4.2). In addition, four member states whose overall gross domestic product (GDP) was low—Spain, Portugal, Greece, and Ireland—were granted extra aid (in the form of a Cohesion Fund) as a prize for agreeing to monetary union. Of the four states, Ireland was the first to lose its cohesion status.

With eastern enlargement in 2004 and 2007, and the accession of Croatia in 2013, the poverty gap between the member states grew considerably wider. Today GDP per capita in all new member states and **candidate countries** remains under the EU-28 average (see Table 4.2). Cyprus and Slovenia rank as the richest of the new members, while Romania and Bulgaria—the 2007 entrants—are the poorest. Most candidate countries are even poorer (see Chapter 8).

The promotion of economic and social cohesion will continue to resonate in the politics of integration well into the future. During the 2007–13 financial framework period, **cohesion policy** accounted for around 35 per cent of the total EU budget (see Chapter 5). After eastern enlargement, many of the former recipients of cohesion funds (including Spain and Ireland) were no longer eligible for many EU funds, which were now funnelled towards the newer and poorer member states.

Economic divergence has a significant impact on how the EU works. First, it influences the pecking order in the Union. The poor countries are perceived as *demandeurs* in the Union, dependent on EU subsidies. Secondly, attitudes towards the size and distribution of the EU budget are influenced by contrasting views between net beneficiaries and net contributors. With the growth of the EU budget, a distinct 'net contributors club' has emerged in the Union, which is led by Germany but joined also by the UK, the Netherlands, Austria, Sweden, Finland, and Denmark. These

TABLE 4.2 Member states' gross domestic product in 2013			
GDP Per Capita in Purchasing Power Standards (PPS)			
European Union average	100		
Luxembourg	264	Malta	87
Austria	129	Slovenia	83
Ireland	126		
Netherlands	127	Czech Republic	80
Sweden	127	Portugal	75
Denmark	125	Slovakia	76
Germany	124	Greece	75
Belgium	119	Lithuania	74
Finland	112		
France	108		
UK	106		
Italy	98	Estonia	72
Cyprus	86	Hungary	67
Spain	95	Poland	68
		Latvia	67
		Croatia	61
		Romania	54
		Bulgaria	47

Eurostat 2013: Volume Indices of GDP per capita: http://epp.eurostat.ec.europa.eu/tgm/table.do?tab=table&init=1&plugin=1&language=en&pcode=tec00114

states are committed to controlling increases in the EU budget and limiting the budgetary costs of cohesion. As more states become 'net contributors', this club is set to grow. The poor countries as beneficiaries of financial transfers tend to argue for larger budgetary resources and additional instruments.

Thirdly, relative wealth influences attitudes towards EU regulation, notably in relation to environmental and social policy. The richer states have more stringent, developed systems of regulation that impose extra costs on their productive industries. They thus favour the spread of higher standards of regulation to peripheral Europe. By contrast, the poorer states, in their search for economic development, often want to avoid imposing the costs of high standards regulation on their industries. Overall, environmental and social standards have risen in Europe, particularly in peripheral Europe, but not to the extent desired by the wealthier states.

State structure

The internal constitutional structure of a member state has an impact on how it operates in the EU and not just in terms of whether it has a Presidential or parliamentary led system. The Union of 28 has three federal states—Germany, Austria, and Belgium. Others are unitary states or quasi-unitary, although the line is not always easy to draw. Unitary states can have subnational governments, self-governing regions, and autonomous communities. For example, Spain and the UK are in some ways de facto federations. The subnational units in all three federal states have played a significant role in the constitutional development of the Union. The German Länder, in particular, insisted in the 1990s that they be given an enhanced say in German European policy. They have been advocates of **subsidiarity** (see Box 2.2) and the creation of the Committee of the Regions. In the 1992 Maastricht Treaty, they won the right to send Länder ministers and officials to represent Germany in the Council of Ministers when matters within their competence are discussed. Representatives of the German and Austrian Länder, representatives of the Belgian regions and cultural communities, as well as ministers of the Scottish government now sit at the Council table and can commit their national governments.

In addition to direct representation, there has been an explosion of regional and local offices in Brussels from the mid-1980s onwards (Tatham and Thau 2014). Increasingly, state and regional governments, local authorities, and cities feel the need for direct representation in Brussels. Their offices act as a conduit of information from the EU to the subnational level within the member states. They engage in tracking EU legislation, **lobbying** for grants, and seeking partners for European projects. Not unexpectedly, there can be tension between national governments and the offices that engage in para-diplomacy in the Brussels arena (see Chapter 6).

Economic ideology

Much of what the EU does is designed to create the conditions of enhanced economic integration through market-building. The manner in which this economic liberalization has developed has been greatly influenced by the dominant economic and social paradigms of the member states. Different visions of the proper balance between public and private power, or between the state and market have left their traces on how the EU works.

Although all six founding member states might be regarded as adhering to a continental or Christian democratic model of capitalism, there are important differences amongst them. For instance, France traditionally has supported far more interventionist public policies than the German economic model would tolerate. But differences between France and Germany fade in comparison to differences between continental capitalism and the Anglo-Saxon tradition. The accession of the UK in 1973 and the radical deregulatory policies of successive Conservative governments brought the so-called Anglo-Saxon economic paradigm into the

Union. The UK has been a supporter of deregulation and economic liberalization in the Union but not always of re-regulation at Union level, particularly in the social and environmental fields. The Anglo-Saxon tradition, however, has been somewhat balanced by the accession of the Nordic states with a social democratic tradition of economic governance and social provision, combined with a strong belief in market liberalization. The Anglo-Saxon economic model gained further ground with the 2004 and 2007 enlargements. The new Eastern states generally favour a more liberal economic agenda. They were instrumental in pushing for a more liberal services **directive** in 2006. However, as Goetz (2005) argues, the new member states brought a diverse set of interests to EU policy-making and intraregional cooperation between them is weak, making any notion of an 'eastern bloc' more myth than reality.

A battle of ideas continues in the Union, based on competing views about the right balance between state and market, the role of the EU in regulation, and questions of economic governance more generally. These differences were sharply exposed during the 2010 financial crisis when it became apparent that the public finances of a number of member states, notably Greece, Spain, Portugal, Cyprus, Italy, and Ireland were on an unsustainable trajectory, in some cases because of problems in their banking systems. Following considerable disagreement, the (then) 16 euro member states (with Germany as primary paymaster) agreed to €500 billion of loan guarantees and emergency funding to address the Greek crisis. Following the intervention in Greece, three further member states were rescued: Ireland, Portugal and Cyprus. Spain received assistance for its banking system and Italy came under very strong market pressure. One important result was unprecedented involvement by the President of the European Central Bank (ECB), Mario Draghi, who pledged in June 2012 to do whatever it took to support the euro. His intervention appeared to calm the financial markets and ended the acute phase of the euro crisis.

Integration preference

The terms pro- and anti-European, or 'good' European and awkward partner, are frequently bandied about to describe national attitudes towards the EU. The UK, Denmark, Poland, and the Czech Republic are usually portrayed as reluctant Europeans (see Table 4.3). Whilst not entirely false, such categorizations disguise several facts. First, attitudes towards European integration are moulded not just by nationality but also (and often more powerfully) by factors such as socio-economic class, age, or educational attainment. Secondly, in all states we find a significant split between the attitudes of those who might be called 'the top decision-makers' and the mass public. A very high proportion of elites accept that their state has benefited from EU membership, and that membership is in their state's national interest. The wider public, in many states, does not share these sentiments. For instance, the comparative Table 4.3 illustrates the particular impact of the economic crisis.

TABLE 4.3 Support for EU membership

| Member state | Per cent responding that EU membership is a 'good thing'* | |
	2007	2011
Netherlands	77	68 (-9)
Ireland	76	63 (-13)
Luxembourg	74	72 (-2)
Spain	73	55 (-18)
Belgium	70	65 (-5)
Poland	67	53 (-14)
Romania	67	57 (-10)
Denmark	66	55 (-11)
Estonia	66	49 (-17)
Germany	65	54 (-11)
Slovakia	64	52 (-12)
EU AVERAGE	57	47 (-10)
Slovenia	58	39 (-19)
Greece	55	38 (-17)
Portugal	55	39 (-16)
Bulgaria	55	48 (-7)
France	52	46 (-6)
Italy	51	41 (-10)
Malta	51	42 (-9)
Sweden	50	56 (+6)
Czech Republic	46	31 (-15)
Cyprus	44	37 (-7)
Finland	42	47 (+5)
UK	39	26 (-13)
Hungary	37	32 (-5)
Latvia	37	25 (-12)
Austria	36	37 (+1)

*Question: 'Generally speaking, do you think that (YOUR COUNTRY)'s membership of the European Union is a good thing, a bad thing, or good and bad?' Note that this question has not been asked since Eurobarometer 75 in August 2011.

NB: In the figure for Cyprus, only the interviews conducted in the part of the country controlled by the government of the Republic of Cyprus are recorded.

Eurobarometer Report 67: Public Opinion in the European Union (Nov. 2007) **http://ec.europa.eu/public_opinion/archives/eb/eb67/eb67_en.pdf**

Eurobarometer Report 75: Public Opinion in the European Union (Aug. 2011) **http://ec.europa.eu/public_opinion/archives/eb/eb75/eb75_publ_fr.pdf**

Public opinion in most member states has shown a significant decline in those saying that membership of the EU has been good for their states. The decline is particularly sharp in those states—Ireland, Spain, Greece and Italy—that have confronted a public finance crisis as well as in Germany, the member state that will be (most) asked to come to the aid of those states. Most of the new member states are also characterised by a sharp decline. Attitudes towards the EU in the UK have been of particular interest over 2013 and 2014 as senior UK politicians have talked openly about the prospect of the UK's exit from the EU. Polling in the UK in late 2014 suggested that more UK voters were in favour of remaining in the EU than leaving. Furthermore, when asked how they would vote if the prime minister were able to secure membership of the EU on renegotiated terms, a majority of poll respondents said that they would vote for the UK to remain as a member.

Of course, governments must take public opinion into account. When coherent, public opinion sets the broad parameters of what is acceptable policy. But public opinion toward the EU—however reluctant—is only one of several factors shaping a government's position.

Some states certainly are more enthusiastic about certain developments (say, enlargement or greater **transparency**) than are others. But there is often an important difference between rhetoric and reality in EU negotiations. Some member states, including France and Germany, tend to use grandiose language in calling for deeper integration. However, around the negotiating table they are often the ones blocking an increase in **qualified majority voting (QMV)** on issues such as trade or justice and home affairs. The opposite can be true for states such as the UK. British ministers and officials are inclined to language that makes them seem reluctant about European integration. Yet, in negotiations on, for example, trade liberalization, they are often in the forefront of more or closer cooperation. In short, member states' attitudes towards integration are far more nuanced than is implied by the labels 'pro' or 'anti' Europe.

Different national preferences and attitudes are expressed most vividly during the Intergovernmental Conferences (IGCs) leading to Treaty reform. These events traditionally have been managed by the states holding the Council presidency and finalized—amidst much media fanfare—at a meeting of the European Council by the heads of state and government. In each IGC, member states need to decide what is negotiable and what is non-negotiable, or what they could trade in one area in return for concessions in another. The outcome has inevitably been a series of complex package deals (see Box 4.2).

An important feature of EU Treaty change since the early 1990s has been the greater frequency with which states have been allowed to 'opt-out' of certain policy developments. For example, Denmark has opted out of the euro, parts of the **Schengen agreement** on the free movement of people, and defence aspects of the Common Foreign and Security Policy. Similarly, the UK is not part of the euro, and neither it nor Ireland is a full participant in Schengen. Of the new member states, only Slovenia, Slovakia, Malta, Lithuania, Cyprus, Estonia, and Latvia are so far part of the

BOX 4.2   How it really works

Intergovernmental Conferences

The EU's Treaties state that the government of any member state, the European Parliament or the Commission may submit proposals for the amendment of the Treaties. If the European Council, after consulting the EP and the Commission, decides (by a simple majority) that such a proposal has legs, it then must convene 'a Convention composed of representatives of national parliaments, the Heads of State or Government of the member states, of the European Parliament and of the Commission' (unless the European Parliament decides that such a Convention is unnecessary because the extent of proposed changes are limited).

In any case, any proposed changes must be submitted to a 'conference of representatives of the governments', or what in EU-speak is called an **Intergovernmental Conference (IGC)**. An IGC is the means by which the EU changes its Treaties or enlarges.

IGCs are often long and tedious. In most cases, after months of discussions and seemingly endless *tours de table* (which allow the delegations to state and restate their national positions, see Box 4.1), the Council's General Secretariat and Presidency draft a proposed set of Treaty amendments. Member states then suggest changes to the draft. Finally, a compromise is hammered out. Ministers can solve some issues. The most difficult questions are left to be resolved at the infamous all-night sessions of the European Council.

An IGC usually affects many different policy areas and has an impact on the entire administrations of member governments. A sound relationship between administrations in national capitals and their Permanent Representation in Brussels is crucial. In many instances, the actual IGC negotiators have positions that are closer to each other's than those between ministries at home. During negotiations it is usually not difficult to detect when a negotiator has been unable to get agreement for a proposal from their home administration. The code phrase is often: 'we are still studying the question back home'.

An IGC may be avoided for minor Treaty changes that do not increase the competences of the EU. In such cases, the Lisbon Treaty's 'Simplified Revision Procedure' may be used. The European Council may adopt, unanimously, minor amendments, although they still require ratification by national parliaments.

After some 8 years of negotiations and ratifications in the run-up to the entry into force of the Lisbon Treaty in 2009, it was widely assumed that there was no appetite to change the Treaties again for a long time. However, two revisions took place after the Lisbon Treaty came into effect. A short IGC was held (without a Convention) in 2010 adjusting the number of MEPs per member state. The European Council also used the Simplified Revision Procedure in 2011 to amend the Treaty to permit the establishment of the permanent European Stability Mechanism to give loans to member states of the Eurozone with debt repayment difficulties.

Eurozone. Membership and non-membership of the Eurozone has become more significant as the euro states have had to engage in deeper policy integration to combat the euro crisis (see Box 4.3).

When member states hold referendums on European Treaties (of which there have been over 30), there is often a blurring of the boundaries between domestic

---

Box 4.3   Rescuing the euro

The 2008 global financial crisis morphed into a Eurozone crisis in autumn 2009 when it became apparent that Greece had a serious public finance crisis. Between December 2009 and May 2010, the euro states, particularly Germany, struggled politically to come to terms with the consequences of the crisis and the need to bailout Greece. By May 2010, the situation within the Eurozone had become sufficiently serious that Greece was rescued on May 2nd. Full programmes for Ireland, Portugal, and Cyprus followed. Spain avoided a full bailout but received support for its banks. The Eurozone crisis underlined the deep interdependence among member states in the single currency.

The crisis was the most serious ever experienced in the EU. The Union's laws, institutions and policy capacity were stretched to the limit. During the crisis, Germany emerged as the dominant state as its support was necessary for every rescue. German Chancellor Angela Merkel became the leading politician in the EU. Policy developed along two tracks. First, there were bailouts for the most troubled countries. They became programme countries subject to very strict conditionality from the so-called Troika—the Commission, ECB and International Monetary Fund (IMF). Second, the Eurozone developed a range of new policy instruments to prevent the crisis re-occurring and agreed very stringent new laws to govern member state public finances. These laws were known as the 'Six Pack', 'Two Pack', and Fiscal Compact. Taken together, these laws amounted to much stronger surveillance by the Commission and other member states of the public finances and macro-economic management of each member state. In addition, the Eurozone states agreed to establish a Banking Union bringing financial supervision under the control of the ECB. The severity of the crisis pitted the creditor states in the North against the debtor states in the South (Ireland became an honorary member of Club Med). The latter—Greece, Portugal, Spain, Italy, and Ireland—bore the brunt of the austerity policies that were imposed. The crisis also created tension between the members of the euro and those outside.

---

politics and the future of the EU. The Constitutional Treaty was the subject of four referendums in 2005 and was defeated in two of those, held in France and the Netherlands. This round was followed by the defeat of the first referendum on the Lisbon Treaty in 2008 in Ireland. Three dramatic referendum defeats in as many years meant that the stakes in the second Irish referendum held in October 2009 were very high.

Taken together, the six factors introduced in this section tell us a great deal about how the EU works. Styles of economic governance and levels of wealth have a major influence on national approaches to European regulation, and on just how much regulation each state favours at EU level. A hostile or favourable public opinion will help to determine the integration preferences of particular states. How states represent themselves in EU business is partially determined by their state structure and domestic institutions. The point is that EU member states vary across several cross-cutting dimensions, there are different cleavages on different issues and this mix is part of what makes the EU unique.

Member States in Action

Member states are not the only players in town (see Chapters 3 and 6), but national governments retain a privileged position in the EU. What emerge, as national interests from domestic systems of preference formation, remain central to how the EU works. But member states are not unitary actors. Rather, each consists of a myriad players who project their own preferences in the Brussels arena. National administrations, the wider public service, key interests (notably, business, trades unions, farming organizations, and other societal interests) all seek voice and representation in EU politics. A striking feature of European integration is the extent to which national actors have been drawn out of the domestic arena into the Brussels system of policy-making.

As Chapter 3 highlighted, the national and the European meet in a formal sense in the Council, the EU institution designed to give voice and representation to national preferences. On a midweek day, there are usually around 20 official meeting rooms in use in the Council building (named after the sixteenth-century Belgian philosopher, Justus Lipsius), apart from the month of August when the Brussels system goes on holiday. Formal meetings are supplemented by bilateral meetings on the margins of Council meetings, informal chats over espressos, and by media briefings. Thus considerable backroom dealing, arbitrage, and informal politics augment the formal system of policy-making. In the evenings, national officials (from some member states more than others) frequent the many bars near the Rond Point Schuman, the junction in Brussels where several EU institutions are housed. The evening buses to Zaventem (the Brussels airport) are often full of national officials making their way back to their capitals after a long day in Council working groups. Those within earshot can pick up good anecdotal evidence of how the EU actually works when member state officials pick over the details of EU proposals.

All member states have built up a cadre of EU specialists in their diplomatic services and domestic administrations who are the 'boundary managers' between the national and the European. Most are at home in the complex institutional and legal processes of the Union, have well-used copies of the EU Treaties, may read *Agence Europe* (a daily bulletin on European affairs) every morning, and know their field and the preferences of their negotiating partners. The EU is a system that privileges those with an intimate knowledge of how the Union's policy process works and how business is conducted in the Council, the EP, and the Commission.

National representatives in Brussels seek to exploit their political, academic, sectoral, and personal networks to the full. With more member states, a widening agenda, and advanced communications technology, there has been a discernible increase in horizontal interaction between the member states at all levels—prime-ministerial, ministerial, senior official, and desk officer. Specialists forge and maintain links with their counterparts in other member states on a continuous basis. Deliberations are no longer left primarily to meetings at working-group level in Brussels. Sophisticated networking is part and parcel of the Brussels game. Officials who have long experience of it build up extensive personal contacts and friendships in the system.

In addition to a cadre of Brussels insiders, many government officials in national capitals find that their work also has a European dimension. For most national officials, however, interaction with the EU is sporadic and driven by developments within a particular sector. A company law specialist may have intense interaction with the EU while a new directive is being negotiated, but may then have little involvement until the same directive is up for renegotiation.

The nature of EU membership demands that all member states must commit resources and personnel to the Union's policy process. Servicing Brussels—by committing time and resources to EU negotiations—has become more onerous with new areas of policy being added, such as justice and home affairs or defence. Once a policy field becomes institutionalized in the EU system, the member states have no choice but to service the relevant committees and Councils. An empty seat at the table undermines the credibility of the state and its commitment to the collective endeavour. Besides, the weakest negotiator is always the one who is absent from the negotiations.

Managing EU Business

All member states engage in internal negotiations and coordination, above all between different national ministries and ministers, in determining what their national position will be in any EU negotiation. The coordination system in most member states is organized hierarchically. National ministers and/or the head of government will usually act as the arbiter of last resort.

In addition, all member states have either a Minister or a State Secretary of European Affairs. The Ministry of Foreign Affairs plays an important role in all member states, and most central EU coordination takes place here. However, there are a number of member states, such as Finland, where the Prime Minister's Office takes the leading role. With the increasing prominence of EU policy in national administrations, more EU business is generally shifting to the offices of heads of government.

As discussed in Chapter 3, each member state also has a Permanent Representation in Brussels, a kind of embassy to the EU. In most cases it is the most important and biggest foreign representation the country maintains anywhere in the world. It is, for example, usually much bigger than an embassy in Washington DC or Moscow or a representation to the United Nations. Although the official role of the Permanent Representation of each member state varies, they all participate actively in several stages of the policy-making process. In certain member states they are the key player in the whole process.

Explaining Member States' Engagement

We have looked at the factors that determine the engagement of different states in the EU, and at the member states in action. What additional purchase do we get from theory in analysing member states in the Union? The relationship between the EU and its member states has been one of the most enduring puzzles in the literature on European integration. From the outset, the impact of EU membership on statehood and on individual states has been hotly contested. At issue is whether the EU strengthens, transcends, or transforms its member states. Is the Union simply a creature of its member states? Are they still the masters of the Treaties? Or has the EU irrevocably transformed European nation-states? The relationship between the EU and its member states is a live political issue and not simply a point of contention amongst scholars. The theories and approaches introduced in Chapter 1 provide different lenses with which to analyse the member states in the Union.

Liberal intergovernmentalism provides a theoretical framework that enables us to trace the formation of domestic preferences in the member states and then to see how they are bargained in Brussels. It identifies the domestic sources of the underlying preferences and the subsequent process of interstate bargaining. The approach rightly concludes that the EU is an 'institution so firmly grounded in the core interests of national governments that it occupies a permanent position at the heart of the European political landscape' (Moravcsik 1998: 501). This approach is less helpful in tracing the impact of the EU on national preference formation or the cumulative impact of EU membership on its member states. Its focus on one-off bargains provides a snapshot of the Union at any one time rather than a film or 'moving picture' of how membership may generate deep processes of change (see Pierson 1996).

Contemporary theorists who view the EU through the lenses of **multilevel** (Hooghe and Marks 2003) or **supranational governance** (Sandholtz and Stone Sweet 1998) emphasize how the national and the European levels of governance have become fundamentally intertwined. Similarly, Bartolini (2005) links the dynamics of European integration to state formation, concluding that the EU represents the latest stage in the emergence and adaption of the European nation state and state system. These approaches point to the influence of the supranational institutions—notably the Commission, Court, and Parliament—on the EU and its member states. The EU may be grounded in the core interests of the national governments, but the definition of core interest is influenced by membership of the EU and its continuous effects at the national level. Put another way, the EU has evolved into a political system in its own right that is more than the sum of its member states.

The **new institutionalism** offers at least two crucial insights concerning member states in the EU political system. First, its emphasis on gradual change captures the give-and-take nature of EU negotiations and the manner in which norms and procedures are built up over time. Secondly, its concern with **path dependency** highlights the substantial resources that member states have invested in the Union (Meunier and McNamara 2007). The costs of exit are very high, so high that no state (perhaps, besides the UK) would seriously contemplate it. At best, member states have the choice of opting out of various policy regimes. Even then there are costs associated with having no seat at the table.

A **policy network** approach captures the fragmented and sectorized nature of the EU. It highlights that the degree and nature of national adaptation differs from one policy area to another, and according to the different mix of players involved. Some policy fields, and the networks that preside over them, have been intensely Europeanized (agriculture) while others have not (transport). This approach helps us to gauge such variation and the varying involvement of different layers of government and public and private actors in different EU policy fields.

Finally, social **constructivism** helps us to analyse how national participants are socialized into the 'rules of the game' that characterize intergovernmental bargaining (Bulmer and Lequesne 2005a: 15). For constructivists, national interests are not predetermined but are shaped (or 'constructed') by interaction with EU actors and institutions (see Checkel 1999). In fact, the very identities of individual players in EU negotiations are viewed largely as being constructed within those negotiations, and not fixed, leading constructivists to question whether national identities and interests are gradually being replaced by European ones.

Conclusion

It is impossible to understand how the EU works without understanding the member states and their central role in the establishment and operation of the Union. In turn, the EU has altered the political, constitutional, economic, and policy framework within which the member state governments govern. Each enlargement is different and each has changed the dynamics of the EU. Many were afraid that the Union's decision-making would grind to a halt with the latest enlargement. Generally, it seems that these fears were unfounded. As a matter of fact the pace of EU decision-making was not noticeably slower than before, despite (or perhaps because of?) its expansion to 28 member states (see Box 4.4), although it was widely agreed that it needed new rules to streamline decision-making to avoid paralysis in the longer term.

BOX 4.4	How it really works

Decision gridlock?

Taking decisions in a big group is never easy. When the EU almost doubled its membership from 2004–7, many feared that it would face permanent gridlock. How did things actually turn out? Studies show that from 2004–6, the amount of legislation decreased compared to the rate prior to the 'big bang' enlargement (Hagemann and DeClerck-Sachsse 2007; Heisenberg 2007). Yet at the same time the EU was able to hammer out compromises at approximately the same pace as before. The average time from a Commission initiative to an approved legal act remained approximately the same for an EU of 28 as it was for an EU of 15 (Settembri 2007).

Enlargement has, however, changed the political dynamic of the EU institutions and the role of member states within them. All of the main institutions—the Commission, the European Council, the European Parliament, and the Council of Ministers—are less cosy than before. There are simply more players around the table. The dynamic of working groups, committees, and the actual Council meetings has also changed. In Council meetings member states no longer have the ability to express their view on all issues all the time. It would simply take too long. Member states raise issues when they have a serious problem.

Every enlargement is preceded by a debate about the EU's capacity to integrate or 'absorb' new member states. The debate is focused on whether the EU's institutions, budget, and policies can accommodate a larger membership. Those who want to slow down enlargement often argue that the EU is not ready to take on board new member states before it has revised its own institutions and working methods. Previous enlargements, however, seem to indicate that while the EU is never fully prepared to enlarge, it manages just the same.

All EU member states, along with some states that aspire to join the EU, are part of a transnational political process that binds them together in a collective endeavour. Their individual engagement with the Union varies enormously depending on their history, location, size, relative wealth, domestic political system, and attitudes towards the future of the Union. Yet, all member states are actively engaged on a day-to-day basis in Brussels. National ministers, civil servants, and interest groups participate in the Commission's advisory groups, Council working groups, and meetings of the European Council. All member states engage in bilateral relations with each of their partners, the Commission's services, and the Council presidency in their efforts to influence EU policy-making. In national capitals, officials and ministers must do their homework in preparation for the continuous cycle of EU meetings. National political parties interact with their MEPs. Brussels is thus part and parcel of contemporary governance in Europe. The member states are essential to how the EU works. Being a member of the Union, in turn, makes a state something rather different from an 'ordinary' nation-state.

DISCUSSION QUESTIONS

1. What are the most important features determining an EU member state's attitudes towards integration?

2. Which is more powerful: the impact of the EU on its member states, or the impact of the member states on the EU?

3. How useful is theory in explaining the role of the member states in the EU?

4. How different are EU member states from 'ordinary' nation-states?

 FURTHER READING

The literature on the member states of the Union is very diffuse. There are a large number of country studies (see, for example, Closa and Heywood 2004, and Papadimitriou and Phinnemore 2007, Laffan and O'Mahony 2008), a more limited number of comparative works (including Wessels et al. 2003, Bulmer and Lequesne 2005b, and Henderson 2007), and a very extensive body of policy-related work that throws some light on the EU and its member states (see, for example, Falkner 2000 and Baun et al. 2006). For discussions of the relationship between statehood and integration, see Hoffmann (1966), Milward (1992), Moravcsik (1998) and Bartolini (2005). On national management of EU business and the impact of the Union on national institutions, see Rometsch and Wessels (1996) and Kassim et al. (2001).

Bartolini S. (2005), *Restructuring Europe: Centre Formation, System Building and Political Restructuring between the Nation State and the European Union* (Oxford and New York: Oxford University Press).

Baun, M., Dürr, J., Marek, D., and Šaradín, P. (2006), 'The Europeanization of Czech Politics', *Journal of Common Market Studies*, 44/2: 249–80.

Bulmer, S., and Lequesne, C. (2005b), *The Member States of the European Union*. 2nd edn. (Oxford and New York: Oxford University Press).

Closa, C., and Heywood, P. S. (2004), *Spain and the European Union* (Basingstoke and New York: Palgrave).

Falkner, G. (2000), 'How Pervasive are Euro-Politics? Effects of EU Membership on a New Member State', *Journal of Common Market Studies,* 38/2: 223–50.

Henderson, K. (2007), *The European Union's New Democracies* (London and New York: Routledge).

Hoffmann, S. (1966), 'Obstinate or Obsolete: The Fate of the Nation-state and the Case of Western Europe', *Daedalus, 95/3:* 862–915 (reprinted in S. Hoffmann (1995), *The European Sisyphus: Essays on Europe 1964–1994* (Boulder, CO, and Oxford: Westview Press)).

Kassim, H., Peters, B. G., and Wright, V. (eds) (2001), *The National Co-ordination of EU Policy: The European Level* (Oxford and New York: Oxford University Press).

Laffan, B. and O'Mahony, J. (2008), *Ireland in the European Union* (Palgrave: London).

Milward, A. (1992), *The European Rescue of the Nation-state* (London and Berkeley: Routledge and University of California Press).

Moravcsik, A. (1998), *The Choice for Europe: Social Purpose and State Power from Messina to Maastricht* (Ithaca, NY, and London: Cornell University Press and UCL Press).

Papadimitriou, D., and Phinnemore, D. (2007), *Romania and the European Union* (London and New York: Routledge).

Rometsch, D., and Wessels, W. (1996), *The European Union and Member States: Towards Institutional Fusion?* (Manchester: Manchester University Press).

Wessels, W., Maurer, A., and Mittag, J. (eds) (2003), *Fifteen Into One? The European Union and its Member States* (Manchester and New York: Manchester University Press).

WEB LINKS

The Institute for European Politics' (Berlin) website features an enormously useful 'EU 28 watch' which offers a round-up of current thinking on EU policies and issues in all the member states: **http://www.eu-28watch.org/** The best place to search for websites of the member and candidate states' national administrations is: **http://www.europa.eu/abc/european_countries/index_en.htm**
Other useful links can also be found on the homepage of the European Commission: **http://ec.europa.eu/index_en.htm**

Visit the Online Resource Centre that accompanies this book for additional material: **www.oxfordtextbooks.co.uk/orc/kenealy4e/**

PART III

Policies and Policy-Making

CHAPTER 5

Key Policies

Alberta Sbragia and Francesco Stolfi

■ Summary

European Union policies affect the lives of millions of people in Europe and beyond. Because of the variety of actors involved, the wide range of policy capacities in different policy areas, and its constant evolution, policy-making in the EU is a challenging but fascinating area of study. This chapter describes some of the most important areas of policy-making in the European Union. We begin by explaining how EU policy-making differs from national policy-making, and then describe the most important policies aimed at building the **internal market** and limiting its potentially negative impact on individuals, society, and the environment. We show how these policies are made and also why and how they matter.

Introduction: Policies in the EU

The EU sets policies in so many areas that it is difficult to think about national policy-making in Europe in isolation from Brussels. While the euro—the common currency used by 19 of the EU's 28 member states (as of 2015)—is perhaps the most visible manifestation of European integration, a diverse set of public policies affecting the everyday lives of Europeans are shaped by the decisions taken at the EU level. Agriculture, environmental standards, consumer protection and other social regulations, international trade, and the movement of goods, services, labour, and capital across borders are all affected by the decisions taken in Brussels.

Yet the role of the EU should not be overestimated; it is not a 'superstate' exercising control over all areas of policy. It should be thought of as a selective policy-maker whose power varies significantly across policy areas. Most of the policies for which it is responsible are related to **markets** (see Box 5.1): some build markets, some protect producers from market forces, some try to cushion the impact of market forces.

The differentiated role of the EU across policy areas is not unusual if we compare it to **federal** systems where power is shared between the national and subnational level (see Box 5.1). In such systems the national level may not be allowed to legislate in certain areas, leaving policy discretion to the constituent units. Canadians, Australians and Americans, for example, take for granted that many decisions affecting their lives will be taken at the state or provincial level rather than at the national level. In the EU, citizens are becoming accustomed to such a system of differentiated policy responsibilities. Just as Washington lets each state decide whether to allow the death penalty within its borders, the EU does not legislate on Ireland's abortion policy, Sweden's alcohol control policy or Spain's policy on bullfighting. Citizens of a federal polity accept that at least some unequal treatment comes with living in a federation. In a similar vein, it matters a great deal—and will continue to matter— where one lives within the EU.

However, the impact of the EU is such that its member states are, in many ways, much more alike now than they were 60 years ago. In certain policy areas, especially those related to economic activity, member state governments as well as private firms either have had to engage in new activities (such as environmental protection) or alternatively change their traditional practices. And of course the introduction of the euro in 19 member states has not only changed the landscape of monetary affairs but also made EU citizens constantly aware of that changed landscape in their everyday life.

The world of money and business has been changed by EU policies in very fundamental ways, but so have many related areas. Environmental protection, gender equality in the workplace, and occupational health and safety have all moved the EU toward a system in which many of the negative consequences of market activity are addressed in Brussels rather than in national capitals. This expansion in the EU's remit is the result not of some well-orchestrated plan but rather the product of constant problem solving, bargaining and experimentation that marks the EU as a

---

BOX 5.1	Key concepts and terms

Benchmarking is the use of comparisons with other states or organizations (for instance on issues such as pension reform and employment practices) with the aim of improving performance by learning from the experience of others.

A **directive** is the most common form of EU legislation. It stipulates the ends to be achieved (say, limiting the emissions of a harmful pollutant) but allows each member state to choose the form and method for achieving that end. It can be contrasted with a regulation, which is directly binding on all citizens.

The **Eurozone** refers to the countries that are part of the Economic and Monetary Union (EMU). EMU was launched in 1999 (with notes and coins entering into circulation in 2002) and included 19 member states by 2015. All remaining new EU member states are expected to join once their economies are ready. The UK, Sweden, and Denmark have thus far chosen not to join.

Federalism is a constitutional arrangement in which the power to make decisions and execute policy is divided between national and subnational levels of government. In a federal system, both national and subnational units wield a measure of final authority in their own spheres and neither level can alter or abolish the other.

A **market** is a system of exchange bringing together buyers and sellers of goods and services. In most markets, money is used as means of exchange. Markets are regulated by price fluctuations that reflect the balance of supply and demand. To function properly, markets require the existence of law, regulation, and property rights. Virtually all markets are subject to some sort of regulation.

Non-tariff barriers refer to regulations, such as national standards or requirements (for instance health requirements) that increase the cost of imports and thus have the equivalent effect of tariffs. Often these regulations do not only serve bona fide social purposes (such as the protection of the environment or of consumer health), but also protect national producers from foreign competition.

Public policy is a course of action (decisions, actions, rules, laws, and so on) or inaction taken by government in regard to some public problem or issue.

---

unique policy-making system (see Chapter 1). The crisis that engulfed the euro in the early 2010s and fiscal governance in the EU is yet another case where decisions made by the Union's institutions and member states under the pressure of events developing by the hour will probably have lasting consequences on the shape and nature of European integration.

This chapter introduces some of the EU's key policies. Since economic integration is at the core of what the Union does, we focus on economic and related policies. The inclusiveness of these policies—how open they are to a large set of actors—varies. But a constant across policies is the preference for consensus building rather than conflict. Furthermore, we show how the remit of the EU has dramatically increased over time, but also how in many policy areas its capacity has remained limited when compared to that of a 'traditional' nation-state.

Key Features of EU Policies

Differences between national and EU policies

Policies in the EU differ in some important ways from policies decided at the national level by member state governments. At their most basic level, policies are different because the EU and its member states are structured and financed very differently. These varying financial structures lead to three wider differences between national and EU policies:

- with a few exceptions, EU policies typically involve the spending of very little money, whereas national policy typically involves spending a good deal of it;
- the distance between those who formulate policy and those who actually execute it in practice is far greater in the EU than it is in most of the national systems which make up the Union;
- the EU is active in a narrower range of policies than are national governments.

Thus, knowing about national policies is not a particularly good template for understanding EU policies. Let us examine each of these differences in more detail.

Money

One way to understand the EU's relative poverty in the area of public finance is to compare its budget with the budgets of central governments in its member states. As Table 5.1 illustrates, even though the central governments of France, Germany, and the United Kingdom are each responsible for only a fraction of the EU's total population, each of those central governments spends a great deal more than does Brussels. Another useful comparison is with the federal government's budget in the United States. The EU has a larger population than does the United States, but the budget of the US federal government is roughly 30 times as large as the EU's budget.

The Union therefore relies on the power of law (as embodied in legislation and court decisions) rather than money to carry out most of its policies. The lack of

TABLE 5.1	Compared to what? EU and national budgets compared			
EU Budget (2013)	**Germany Federal Budget (2011)**	**France Central Budget (2011)**	**UK Central Budget (2011)**	**US Federal Budget (2011)**
€ 152 billion	€ 1,060 billion*	€ 928 billion*	€ 787 billion*	€ 4,526 billion*

*US dollars converted to Euros at average exchange rate for 2011 (**http://www.ecb.europa.eu/stats/exchange/eurofxref/html/eurofxref-graph-usd.en.html**).
For the EU, Commission 2013a. For the national budgets, OECD 2013.

money shapes what the content of policies can be. The Union can have only a small number of policy areas that cost a great deal, whereas national systems typically have a large number of expensive policy areas, including those that fall under the rubric of the welfare state. The Union, given its current fiscal structure, could not, for example, finance health care for EU citizens or provide old age pensions or finance systems of public education. Overwhelmingly, the EU regulates economic activity; that is, it subjects it to rules and standards. However, and in spite of the relatively small size of the EU budget, the approval of the revenues and expenditures of the European Union can become contentious (Neheider and Santos 2011; see Box 5.2).

Legislation vs. execution

In most national systems, the national government makes policy decisions and then has numerous ways of ensuring that those policies are actually executed 'on the ground'. Although that link is far from perfect in actual practice, it is much tighter in

---

BOX 5.2   How it really works

Budget bargaining

Unlike national governments, the EU cannot run a deficit; its revenues limit the amounts it can spend. Various economic formulae are used to help determine the EU's overall budget revenue (derived primarily from custom duties, value added tax, and national contributions) and budget allocation (who gets what?). As in the past, Germany remains the 'paymaster of Europe,' being by far the largest net contributor to the European coffers, followed by France and Italy. On the expenditure side, two documents are important: the Financial Framework, decided by unanimity in the Council and with Parliament's consent, which sets the overall expenditure level and how it is to be divided between the various policy areas; and the annual budget, co-decided by majorities in Parliament and Council, which determines the detailed amounts spent on every item each year within the ceilings.

Formulae aside, the EU's budget is a result of politics as much as mathematics. Reaching a decision over the financial framework can be a highly contentious and a decidedly intergovernmental affair. Although the absolute amounts involved are not large—the overall EU budget equals only around 1 per cent of the member states' GDP—no government wants to appear weak in the eyes of its voters during the negotiations with other member states. Moreover, and especially in the case of the CAP, the amounts involved can mean a great deal to strong domestic constituencies.

The negotiations for the 2014–20 framework were especially acrimonious, pitting the UK, in favour of substantial cuts, against France, which supported spending increases to counter the effects of recession in many member states. Only at the second meeting of heads of state, in February 2013, was an agreement finally reached. For the first time ever, the new long-term budget of the EU was reduced—by 3 percent compared to the previous seven-year budget. Besides irritating the French government, with French President François Hollande anxious to claim that France had shifted less than the UK, the agreement was harshly condemned by the President of the European Parliament (Schultz 2013).

most national systems than it is when EU policy is involved. Policy decided in Brussels faces several unique hurdles before it can be successfully executed on the ground.

The first step is known as 'transposition'. That is, laws (known as directives, see Box 5.1) adopted by the Council of Ministers, and (usually) the EP, need to be 'transposed' into national legal codes before they can be executed by the member states' public administration or formally shape the behavior of private actors in significant ways. The Commission monitors that transposition is timely and correctly implements the European legislation. Member states that fail on these accounts can be taken before the European Court of Justice. Although transposition has become increasingly timely, differences still exist among the member states. Interestingly, at least in this area the division between older and newer member states does not seem to apply: based on the latest available data (for 2012, Commission 2013b), the four best and the four worst performers include both new and old member states (the Netherlands, Sweden, Ireland and Slovakia being the best, and Poland, Belgium, United Kingdom and Cyprus the worst).

In sum, Union policies do not become 'policy' at the national level uniformly across the member states. For example, a directive transposed in Finland shortly after its adoption in Brussels may not be transposed in France or Greece until several years after the Finnish action. These differences suggest that while Brussels formulates and adopts policy, its actual impact will be shaped by national systems of **governance**. National governments play a central role in the EU's policy process because they hold a monopoly of power in the actual execution of most policies adopted in Brussels. The EU has no administrative presence within the member states. While the Commission has its 'delegations' in all national capitals, and even sub-national ones like Edinburgh, they are not tasked with monitoring the execution of EU law. It must instead rely on complaints from citizens, firms, and non-governmental organizations. Even then, it first tries to persuade errant governments, taking them to Court only as a last resort.

The difficulties surrounding execution and monitoring mean that policies that affect a dispersed set of actors are less likely to be executed uniformly than are those policies that affect a few. For example, environmental policy, which attempts to shape the behaviour of huge numbers of both public and private actors, is executed with a tremendous degree of variability within the Union. By contrast, the Commission's decisions about mergers and acquisitions are implemented uniformly. The number of firms affected by any single Commission decision is very small and a non-complying firm would be very visible.

Jurisdiction

A third difference between EU and national policies concerns policy competencies (see Box 5.3). While certainly broader than other international organizations, the EU's policy remit is narrower than that of national governments. Health care, urban regeneration, family assistance, old age pensions, public health, industrial relations, child care, poverty alleviation, abortion, prison administration and education, for example, are not subject to EU legislation because the Union has not been given competence in those areas by the member states. Other areas remain under national control because of the decision-making rules that apply to that area. In the area of taxation, for example, the decision-making rule is one of unanimity (although pressures for a common EU energy policy are increasingly powerful). Since the member states have been unable to agree on any single policy, those policy areas effectively remain under national control.

Recently, various 'soft' measures such as benchmarking (see Box 5.1) or the 'open method of coordination' (OMC) of national policies have been used to encourage national governments to address issues such as their pension burden. Generally, however, the welfare state and the direct provision of social services are primarily under national control.

Policies that have a moral or cultural dimension also remain under national control. The Irish do not permit abortion except in cases where a mother's life is at risk, for example, and the EU does not have the power to tell the Irish either to change their abortion law or to keep it. The Swedish and Finnish alcohol control system has been under strain due to the ability of individual revelers to bring liquor in from other EU countries. But alcohol control policy in both Sweden and Finland is under national control.

> **BOX 5.3**   **The policy competences of the EU**
>
> Policy competence refers to the primary legal authority to act in particular policy areas. After the Lisbon Treaty, policy areas are divided into three categories depending on the degree of EU competence: (1) exclusive competence; (2) shared competence between the EU and the member states; (3) competence to support, coordinate and supplement the actions of the member states.
>
> 1. The EU has exclusive competence in few, but important, policy areas: external trade in goods and services, monetary policy (for the Eurozone), customs, and conservation of marine resources.
>
> 2. Shared competences include, for example, agriculture and fisheries, justice, environmental policy, consumer protection, mergers and acquisitions, research, development aid, transport policy, energy, visas, asylum, and immigration.
>
> 3. Finally, there are policy areas where the member states are the main players, even if the EU is involved in some general coordination or is engaged in a few specific projects. Education, culture, sport, employment, public health, and research policies fall into this domain.
>
> In some policy areas it is difficult to place policies in one of these categories because the line between shared competencies and member state competencies is blurred. In foreign and security policies, for instance, it is often unclear how much weight the EU has because the member states in the final analysis must allocate the resources necessary to execute the EU's foreign and security policy.

However, and in spite of the circumscribed jurisdiction of the Union, it is important to note that the EU can and often does have important indirect effects beyond the immediate scope of its competencies. For instance, key aspects of energy policy are still under national control. However, the energy market is being liberalized, as the EU requires national governments to allow consumers more choice of electricity suppliers. Similarly the commitment of the EU to meet the Kyoto Protocol requirements to combat global climate change stimulated the creation of a European market where industrial producers can trade carbon emissions permits, with the purpose of limiting overall emissions. To take another example, education at both pre-university and university level are under national control, but the EU has been a prime mover in encouraging university students to study in another EU member state. These Commission programmes on student mobility within the Union have led to major changes in the administrative structures of universities and have encouraged universities to work towards much greater cross-national standardization in degree programmes (such as the length of time required to receive a first degree). The lack of formal competence at the EU level does not mean that Brussels lacks influence in shaping the terms of debate within a policy area. The programmes that Brussels adopts, while not legally binding in the way that legislation is, are very important in providing incentives to national and subnational governments to carry out certain activities.

The Primacy of Economic Integration

The EU's unique history and development has privileged some areas as important for the Union while leaving others aside. As Chapter 2 explained, in the 1950s European states chose to defend each other within a transatlantic rather than a European organization (NATO includes Canada and the US). Policy areas concerning defense as well as foreign policy and security, therefore, were not central to the integration process and have become salient only recently (see Chapter 9).

By contrast, economic cooperation was viewed as a politically acceptable way of increasing integration while laying the groundwork for political cooperation at a future date. Consequently, policy areas related to economics have been privileged from the very beginning. The 1957 Treaty of Rome, by calling for a customs union and a common market (now referred to as a single or internal market), steered the process of European integration toward the liberalization of cross-border trade, a unitary trade policy vis-à-vis non-members, and the free movement of capital, goods, services, and labour. The centrality of that effort to European integration symbolizes the importance that economic integration has within the EU.

'Market-building' Policies

The focus on liberalization and creation of a single market highlights the EU's concern with 'market building' and what is sometimes termed 'negative integration'. Building markets involves both *removing* barriers to trade and carrying out regulatory reform. So negative integration includes eliminating various tariff and non-tariff barriers (see Box 5.1) to trade, regulatory reform in the area of economic regulation, and ensuring that competition among firms is encouraged. The goal is to facilitate cross-border economic transactions with the expectation that the resulting greater efficiency will lead to higher levels of prosperity for the citizens of Europe. This same aim is pursued globally within the World Trade Organization (WTO).

The political economy of the member states has been profoundly affected by the privileging of economic policies at the EU level (Sbragia 2001). In this arena, policies adopted in Brussels usually 'pre-empt' national policies and the EU is said to have 'exclusive competence'. Monetary policy falls under this category, although it only applies to the members of the Eurozone (see Box 5.1).

In general, the kind of negative integration which characterizes the EU is far more penetrating than that found at the global (WTO) level or in other regional arrangements such as the North American Free Trade Agreement (NAFTA) (Söderbaum and Sbragia 2010). The EU's ambitions in 'market building' are very serious and their scope very wide. The very foundation of the single market involves the 'four freedoms'—freedom in the movement of capital, goods, services, and labour. However, a single market such as that envisaged by the founders of the Community does not occur simply by removing obstacles to trade. A whole host of interventions must be put into place to ensure that the hoped-for market will operate smoothly and efficiently. The construction of the European market has led to such widespread regulation from Brussels that Majone (1999) has termed the EU a 'regulatory state'. Whereas a welfare state engages in redistribution and spends a great deal of money in providing social welfare (such as social security), a regulatory state exercises its influence primarily by passing legislation that regulates the behavior of actors in the economy.

The development of a far-reaching regulatory regime in Brussels also has led to frequent complaints from those affected by such regulation, negatively affecting the legitimacy of the EU among European voters (Schmidt 2013). Firms often complain that the EU over-regulates, fails to legislate fast enough to keep up with rapid technological change, or that a truly internal market simply does not exist. To illustrate, more than 80 per cent of the chairpersons of top (FTSE 100) British companies surveyed in 2014 backed the Conservative Party's determination to renegotiate the terms of the UK's EU membership, with most citing a desire for economic policy reforms (*Financial Times*, 28 July 2014).

Competition policy

One of the most important market-building powers given to the EU—the Commission specifically—is that of competition policy. The Commission operates as an independent institution in this area, and the Council of Ministers is not usually involved in these policy decisions. In essence, competition policy—known as anti-trust policy in the United States—is about encouraging competition among firms and battling monopolistic or oligopolistic practices or those which privilege national producers over those in other EU member states. The requirements can be tough for any member state, but competition policy poses particular challenges for the new member states from Central and Eastern Europe. Moving from economies which were largely under public control to ones in which the market is dominant has been difficult, and the rigor of the EU's competition policy has made that transition in some respects even more onerous.

The Commission has the authority to rule on many mergers and acquisitions, fight cartels, and rule on the appropriateness of many forms of state aid given by national or regional authorities to firms. In this policy area, the Commission is an international actor as well as an EU actor, and its Directorate-General (DG) for Competition has become one of the most powerful, and controversial, competition authorities in the world (Aydin and Thomas 2012). The Commission has the power to sanction the strategies of American firms with extensive operations in Europe even if American anti-trust authorities have approved them. Just to mention a few high-profile cases, the Commission vetoed the proposed merger between General Electric and Honeywell, fined Microsoft for abuse of dominant position a total of €780 million and Intel a staggering €1.06 billion. In 2014 it issued a decision mandating that Google modify how it displays its search results, with the ancillary consequence that searches done in Europe will produce different results than searches done elsewhere in the world.

Trade associations and firms as well as member state authorities and ministers (and at times prime ministers and presidents) lobby, especially informally, before decisions on specific competition cases. However, the Commission needs to engage in far less negotiation than is required in other policy domains and has turned a deaf ear to lobbying by very important national politicians. In this area, DG Competition and the Commissioner for Competition are the central actors.

Commercial policy (trade policy)

The key goal of the Treaty of Rome was to create a common market across national borders. The objective required liberalizing many national markets (that is, allowing imports to compete with domestically-produced goods), which had been heavily protected for many decades. Over time, the national economies of the member states have become far more interdependent. In 2010 trade within the EU accounted for 64 percent of the overall trade of the member states (Eurostat 2012). However, trade with countries outside the Union is still very important for many EU member states.

The application of a single external tariff to non-EU producers in the late 1960s led to the decision that the European Economic Community (as the EU was then known) would need to speak 'with one voice' in negotiations involving international trade policy. The Treaty of Rome gave the EEC competence in international trade negotiations involving trade in goods. The Commission was granted the power to act as sole negotiator for the Community in, for example, world trade talks and that power was strengthened in the Treaty of Nice, which gave the Commission the right to negotiate (with certain exceptions) trade in services. However, the competence to decide the EU's position in international trade negotiations was given to the Council of the European Union, not to the Commission acting on its own. Therefore, although the Commission is the negotiator, it is the Council, and thus ultimately the member states, which defines the Commission's negotiating mandate. In practice, the relationship between the member states (or at least selected ones) and the Commission is sometimes conflictual, especially when powerful national constituencies see their interests threatened by trade liberalization. Moreover, the Commission itself may be internally divided, with DG Agriculture, for instance, being more protectionist than DG Trade (Conceição-Heldt 2011).

Economic and Monetary Union (EMU)

At Maastricht, EU member states decided to create an Economic and Monetary Union, with a common currency and centralized responsibility for monetary policy. For the first time since the Roman Empire, Western Europe was to have a common currency. It was thought that a common currency would help keep a unified Germany tied to the project of European integration, help increase economic efficiency in the EU and thereby raise the standard of living, and develop a sense of 'European' identity. A common currency requires a single central bank in charge of monetary policy, and the European Central Bank was created to run monetary policy with the goal of price stability (anti-inflation) as its top priority.

Part of the bargain that underpinned the decision to move to a single currency by 1999 was an agreement that states wishing to adopt the euro had to meet certain requirements (informally known as the Maastricht criteria) on the level of inflation and of interest rates, and the size of the government deficit and debt. The heads of state and government took the decision, but finance ministers and a relatively small group of national civil servants and central bank staff undertook the preparation that underpinned the decision. Private businesses such as banks were not intimately involved, and the policy process was relatively closed.

The decision to move towards a single currency had profound implications for the member states, as the budget deficit requirements forced the restructuring of public finances in several states adopting the euro (the so-called Eurozone countries). In the Italian case, the restructuring was so profound that the country's ministerial organization and budgetary process were radically transformed in part to meet the requirements of participation in the euro project (Stolfi 2008). In some cases, the desire to join the EMU was so strong that countries—Greece for instance—resorted to questionable budgetary tricks in order to qualify. The original members of the EMU were Germany, France, Luxembourg, Belgium, the Netherlands, Spain, Portugal, Austria, Italy, Finland, and Ireland. Greece joined in 2001, while the UK, Sweden, and Denmark have chosen to remain outside the EMU for the time being. All new member states of the EU are expected eventually to join the

EMU (only Denmark and the UK possess a formal 'opt-out' from the euro). However, so far only a minority has done so: Slovenia (2007), Cyprus (2008), Malta (2008), Slovakia (2009), Estonia (2011) and Latvia (2014). Lithuania applied to join in 2006, but its application initially was rejected by the ECB before it was cleared to become the 19th member of the Eurozone in 2015.

Membership of the euro means these countries no longer have an independent monetary policy. The European Central Bank (ECB), headquartered in Frankfurt, makes decisions about monetary policy that apply to all member states using the euro. National governments therefore can no longer control the level of interest rates, a control that previously gave national governments (or national central banks) some leverage over the direction of their economy. The ECB is mandated to privilege price stability and thereby avoid inflation. But some actors—particularly those who would prefer it to adopt lower interest rates so as to stimulate the Eurozone economy and hopefully create more employment (e.g. the French government)—are critical of the bank. The ECB, however, has argued that job creation requires the adoption of a more flexible labor market and more liberalization of markets in general. It has not tailored its interest rate policy to the wishes of the member states, nor to societal actors. The ECB has become an important, and very independent, actor in the field of economic policy-making.

Even after the creation of the EMU, the stringent fiscal requirements remained, as EMU members committed to respect a Stability and Growth Pact (SGP), which includes financial penalties for the countries that violate it. Following the adoption of the euro in 1999 (notes and coins became available on 1 January 2002), several member states found their macro-economic policies under scrutiny as they struggled to meet the budget deficit requirements of EMU membership. By 2003, four countries, including the three largest economies of the Eurozone (Germany, France, and Italy), were in breach of the fiscal requirements set by the SGP. In the case of Germany, the breach was attributed to ongoing problems of German unification, and in any case Germany's finances were in a good shape. However, France seemed to show a willful disregard of the SGP, as if to signify that respecting the SGP rules was beneath its status (Ludlow 2010). When the Commission recommended to the ECOFIN the application of the penalties mandated by the SGP, the member states demurred.

In 2005 the SGP was modified to make it more flexible, in particular to allow more fiscal leeway to countries in better financial shape. The reform, however, did not make the SGP any more able to impart discipline on the member states. The main problems were that the European statistical agency (Eurostat) was prevented from scrutinizing fiscal data provided by the governments of the member states, thus opening the door to fraudulent accounts as in the case of Greece, and the imposition of fines proved politically difficult, so that the deterrent power of the SGP was low. The financial, fiscal and economic crisis that began in 2010 when Greece revealed that its deficit was much higher than previously reported is far from over. However, the ECB under its current President, Mario Draghi, has adopted a very pro-active approach to the crisis. It has been extremely helpful in calming the markets and giving troubled European economies room to address the crisis (Stolfi 2013). This has included the adoption by Treaty (known as the Fiscal Compact) of a more stringent set of rules with greater automaticity in imposing fines (the Commission recommendation is deemed to have been approved by Council unless rejected by a qualified majority).

'Market-correcting' and 'Cushioning' Policies

Although policies related to building markets have been a central feature of the Union's policy activity, the EU has also been very active in policy areas where the central goals might be viewed as 'market correcting' and 'market cushioning'. Market correcting policies, such as the common agricultural policy (CAP) and **cohesion policy**, attempt to compensate for the cost to particular groups imposed by the building of a single market and to limit inequality. Market cushioning policies, such as environmental and social regulation, attempt to limit the potentially harmful effects of the market on human beings and the environment.

Common agricultural policy

Perhaps the best-known policy designed to offset market forces is the CAP—for which the EU has almost exclusive competence. The CAP, with its system of agricultural support and subsidies, has, since its inception, been 'an integral part of the west European welfare state' (Rieger 2005: 182). However, reforms in the past ten years have attenuated criticism of the CAP and introduced new goals that go beyond supporting the livelihoods of European farmers (Roederer-Rynning 2010).

The CAP is unique in the amount of money it receives from the EU budget (see Figure 5.1; the CAP forms the bulk of EU expenditure under the heading 'Sustainable growth: natural resources'), the degree of power the Union exercises, and the amount of contestation it causes. Although the CAP created a market for agricultural goods within the EU, its market correcting properties have been the most controversial outside the EU because third parties have found their agricultural goods subject to high tariffs when exported to the EU. Unsurprisingly, many countries find the EU's attitude, praising free markets and providing development aid, hypocritical when the EU does not open its own markets to the agricultural products coming from developing countries (Elgström 2007).

The CAP stirs up plenty of internal debate as well. The benefits of the CAP are distributed very unequally across member states. Although new member states depend much more on agriculture than do older members, the largest recipients are still all older member states (see Table 5.2). However, some redistribution of agricultural funds from the older to the new member states has already occurred: from 2007 the funds for farmers in the old member states began to decline in order to make room for greater allocations for the farmers in the new member states.

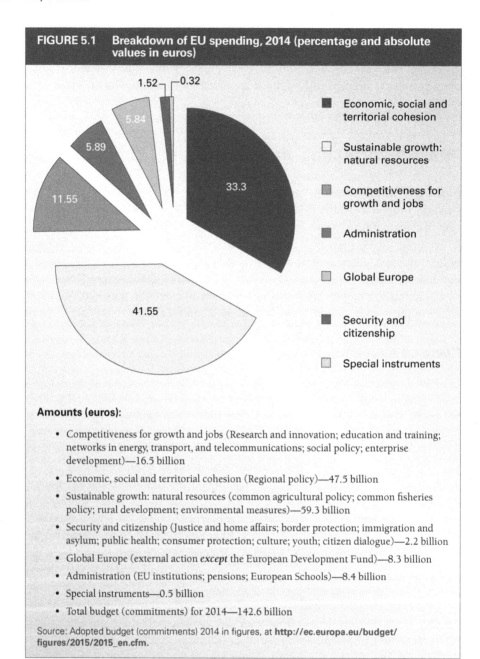

FIGURE 5.1   Breakdown of EU spending, 2014 (percentage and absolute values in euros)

1.52 ⌐ 0.32

5.84

5.89

11.55

33.3

41.55

- ■ Economic, social and territorial cohesion
- ☐ Sustainable growth: natural resources
- ■ Competitiveness for growth and jobs
- ■ Administration
- ▨ Global Europe
- ■ Security and citizenship
- ☐ Special instruments

Amounts (euros):

- Competitiveness for growth and jobs (Research and innovation; education and training; networks in energy, transport, and telecommunications; social policy; enterprise development)—16.5 billion
- Economic, social and territorial cohesion (Regional policy)—47.5 billion
- Sustainable growth: natural resources (common agricultural policy; common fisheries policy; rural development; environmental measures)—59.3 billion
- Security and citizenship (Justice and home affairs; border protection; immigration and asylum; public health; consumer protection; culture; youth; citizen dialogue)—2.2 billion
- Global Europe (external action *except* the European Development Fund)—8.3 billion
- Administration (EU institutions; pensions; European Schools)—8.4 billion
- Special instruments—0.5 billion
- Total budget (commitments) for 2014—142.6 billion

Source: Adopted budget (commitments) 2014 in figures, at **http://ec.europa.eu/budget/figures/2015/2015_en.cfm.**

More generally, pressure from enlargement has spurred some CAP reform including a shift from supporting production, which in the past had often led to overproduction and waste, to supporting rural development and rural environment (Grant 2010). The Council, Commission, and EP reached a political agreement in 2013 on the latest round of CAP reforms, whose goals include eliminating the

TABLE 5.2   CAP spending breakdown: top recipients

This table shows France is still the big winner from CAP spending, even increasing its share from the recent past. More generally, highly industrialized Member States have also increased their share of CAP spending. The largest of the new Member States, Poland, has seen its share decline.

Member State	Percentage of CAP expenditure (2009)	Percentage of CAP expenditure (2012)	Member State	Percentage of CAP expenditure (2009)	Percentage of CAP expenditure (2012)
France	13.3	15.8	Poland	9.0	8.3
Germany	11.3	11.5	United Kingdom	6.1	7.1
Spain	11.4	11.4	Greece	5.3	4.8
Italy	9.1	10.3	Romania	2.1	3.6

Source: Commission 2013 and 2010.

current reliance on historical reference levels to determine the direct payments to farmers, a policy that has over time created large differences across member states in per capita support to farmers (European Commission - MEMO/13/937). However the CAP remains a politically fraught policy area, where the interests of member states, European institutions, farmers and other stakeholders continually collide (Daugbjerg 2013).

Cohesion policy

Cohesion policy was introduced to reduce inequality among regions and compensate governments of poor countries for the costs of economic integration. Cohesion policy, introduced after the first enlargement (UK, Denmark, and Ireland), has increased in importance over time. It now represents one of the most important areas for public expenditure (see Figure 5.1).

The budget for cohesion policy represents approximately 36 per cent of the EU's budget (the CAP, including funding for rural development and natural resources, accounts for roughly 40 per cent). However, every member state receives some cohesion funding; regions with specific problems (such as a declining industrial base) also receive funding even if they are part of a wealthy member state, which makes this policy politically acceptable to all. However, most of the funding is spent in the regions with the highest need, where per capita GDP is below 75 per cent of the EU average, even though the distribution of funds is also influenced by the domestic politics of the member states (Chalmers 2013).

The distribution of structural funding across many member states has rendered it one of the most visible of the EU's policies, with road signs often advertising that a road or other public work is being financed with EU funds. It also features actors across levels of governance: regional, national and EU policymakers are all centrally involved in decisions surrounding the allocation of regional funds and their implementation. The interaction of actors from several levels of governance, and the sharing of power between them gives rise to the notion of the EU as a system of **multilevel governance** (Bache 2008) (see Chapter 1). Because regions in all member states have benefited from some form of regional spending, cohesion policy has escaped some of the intense controversy surrounding CAP.

However, enlargement has made cohesion policy more controversial, pitting net contributors against new recipients, or 'old' versus 'new' member states. Because the new member states are significantly poorer than the old ones, the poorest regions of Europe are now all concentrated in the new member states, with clear implications for the distribution of European funds. For instance, Poland is now by far the largest recipient of cohesion funds (Commission 2013).

Environmental and social regulation

Although the CAP and cohesion policy are probably the best known of the EU's policy areas outside of the single market, other policies have been initiated as relatively marginal and become far more important over time. Such policy areas are grouped under the rubric of 'social regulation': that is, they are designed to 'cushion' the impact of the market on society. Occupational health and safety legislation is one such area where the EU acted rather early.

As for environmental policy the EU became active (especially in the area of pollution control) after a customs union had been created, but before many of its member states had become environmentally conscious. Environmental policy was initially put on the agenda both because of international salience and because it would affect trade in goods such as motor vehicles. Over time, the focus was enlarged into areas that are not market-related, such as the protection of environmentally sensitive habitats.

EU regulation has significantly improved environmental standards in Europe (Holzinger and Sommerer 2011). Moreover, in many areas of environmental policy (primarily those outside of pollution control), national governments are free to supplement EU legislation. Some do. In general, the Scandinavian member states, Austria, the Netherlands, and Germany are the most active in supplementing EU legislation with their own. But most member states choose not to act unilaterally, thereby leaving the EU as the de facto primary actor in this area. In the face of persistently slow economic growth, the EU's 7th Environmental Programme sees environmental policy also as an instrument for economic growth and job creation (Decision No 1386/2013/EU).

Consumer protection is another area in which the EU is very active. For instance, a series of food scares and concern over genetically modified organisms (GMOs) has propelled this issue up the EU's agenda and resulted in the establishment of a Food Safety Agency. It has also caused conflict with the United States, which is the largest producer of GMOs, and which accuses the EU of using unscientific concerns as a way to shield European agriculture from foreign competition. Social regulatory policies that are related directly to the single market (such as regulations on product safety) pre-empt national policies, whereas in other areas (such as hygiene standards) the EU stipulates minimum standards that national governments can exceed if they so wish.

The EU has also been active in the area of gender equality. National pension systems have had to be restructured to treat men and women equally. More generally, the EU has been a significant actor in the move toward equal pay (both in terms of income and benefits) in the workplace (Caporaso 2001). Most recently, the EU passed laws against sexual harassment. While some member states already had tough laws, Spain, Portugal, Greece and Italy had no laws that held employers responsible for harassment within the workplace, and Germany defined sexual harassment more narrowly than did the EU legislation. Member states can adopt stricter definitions of harassment, but now European legislation provides a 'floor' for any national legislative activity in that area.

Comparing Policy Types in the EU

How can we make sense of all these policies? To start, note each category of policy has certain characteristics that distinguish it from others. While the categories are clearly not watertight in the real world, they do differ in significant ways along a number of dimensions highlighted in Table 5.3. First, those policies that fall under 'market-building' stimulate market forces and encourage regulatory reform. Because of their emphasis on competition, such policies tend in practice to favour (although not require) privatization and the withdrawal of the state from those areas in which it has protected national producers. Many of the policies in this category are regulatory. In general, they also tend to be made by the Community method in which the EU's supranational institutions are normally most active, the Union's competence tends to be most comprehensive, and national policy activity is largely pre-empted.

A variety of political dynamics, and a range of political actors, also mark the creation of markets. The different theoretical approaches introduced in Chapter 1 shed light on these different dynamics. A few policy areas, such as energy and pharmaceuticals, feature what Peterson and Bomberg (1999: 81) conclude is 'a relatively stable and cohesive policy network'. That is, policies are shaped by a tight and insular group of actors. Similarly, the area of monetary policy is quite insulated from actors

TABLE 5.3	Policy types in the EU			
Type	**Level of EU competence**	**Key features**	**Primary actors**	**Examples**
Market-building	Nearly exclusive; covering an extensive range of economic policies	Emphasis on liberalization and increasing economic efficiency; strong role for supranational institutions	Business actors; EU institutions; national finance officials; central bankers	Internal market policies (such as telecommunications or air transport); EMU
Market-correcting	Often exclusive but only in limited areas	Controversial; has redistributive implications; EP mostly excluded	Farm lobbies, national officials; Commission	CAP; cohesion policy; fisheries
Market-cushioning	Shared with member states	Significant implementation problems	Supranational institutions; sectoral ministers; public interest groups	Environmental protection; occupational health and safety; gender equality in the workplace

outside the central banking community. But most other areas related to trade do not exhibit such single-mindedness among the key actors who interact in what are often fragmented and internally divided networks.

Market correcting policies differ from market building policies in that they tend to protect producers from market forces. Most are redistributive: from consumers to farmers, and from rich to poor regions. Because they are so overtly redistributive rather than regulatory, they tend to be very difficult to change as the impact of any change is quite transparent. For this reason, market-correcting policies tend to be dominated by intergovernmental bargaining rather than by the EU's institutions. Liberal intergovernmentalists show how major decisions in these areas are dominated by national governments, responding to strong societal actors (say, agricultural lobbies), but national ministers ultimately decide when other considerations will trump the demands of those lobbies.

Market cushioning policies try to minimize the harm economic activities impose on nature and humans. These policies tend to be regulatory in nature, impose demands on private actors, and fall under the 'shared competence' of the EU because both Brussels and national capitals typically co-govern in these areas. The role of institutions in propelling these areas forward, often with strong support from a variety of representatives of **civil society**, provides fertile ground for the new institutionalists' claim that 'institutions matter'.

Conclusion

If institutions and member states are the skeleton of the EU, policies are its flesh. It is through its policies that the EU affects people's lives, within and beyond its own borders. The Italian retailer who can sell non-durum wheat pasta against the opposition of the Italian authorities or the British holidaymaker who may pay less for his mobile phone calls when holidaying in Spain both feel the influence of the EU in their daily lives. So does the American shareholder who sees the price of her Microsoft stocks affected by the competition policy decisions of the European Commission or the Indian farmer adversely affected by the high tariffs the EU imposes on agricultural products.

What makes studying EU policies enormously challenging, as well as fascinating, is that each policy has its own features and trajectory, as this chapter has illustrated. But amidst all that variation, common themes also emerge. In particular, policies and policy-making in the EU reflect the three major themes of this volume: experimentation as a driving force of European integration; the astonishing array of actors and power sharing and consensus-building amongst them; and the contrast between the scope and the capacity of the EU.

Thus, for instance, the creation of the EMU was in part the result of dramatic experimentation. One of the main reasons for moving to a common currency was that the old status quo, with exchange rate agreements that had proved prone to collapse, was no longer tenable. Yet monetary union as the way forward was an untested course. As the former chief economist of the ECB has argued, European governments met the challenge by consciously choosing to take a risk and take 'the big leap into monetary union' (*Financial Times*, 27 October 2006).

Different policy areas also show different levels of inclusiveness and power sharing. In some, such as competition policy and monetary policy, power is concentrated in a limited set of actors. In many others, however, a larger set of actors is involved. Both environmental and cohesion policy involve a large number of actors at different levels of governance—including EU institutions, national governments and private stakeholders—and exhibit a preference for consensus-building. But consensus building at Brussels comes at a price: decisions made by the EU, no matter how well thought-out, to many Europeans seem to be made too far away from their control. That citizen control is still largely exercised through the democratic process in each member state rather than through citizen participation in European decision-making. Although the Lisbon Treaty has tried to address this concern, many Europeans still feel disconnected from the way decisions are made in the EU.

Finally, the policy capacity of the EU remains well short of any nation-state, relying as it does on a very limited budget and on the national implementation of European legislation. At the same time, we have seen how the pressure of economic integration has led to the continuing expansion of the scope of the EU's policy remit, from policies directly related to market-building, to market-correcting and then market-cushioning. The current Eurozone crisis might well continue this pattern, and European economic governance might well come out of it much more integrated than it was only a few years previously.

DISCUSSION QUESTIONS

1. Why has the EU privileged economic policies over social welfare policies?

2. Why is the EU budget so much smaller than that of its major member states?

3. What implications does a single monetary policy have for the development of other types of policies within the EU?

4. What obstacles to the execution of EU policies exist that do not exist at the national level?

5. The CAP (common agricultural policy) is often criticized on efficiency grounds. What environmental or social considerations can be brought to bear to support the CAP?

6. How has enlargement affected the EU's economic policies?

FURTHER READING

For an in-depth analysis of the EU's major policy areas, including those discussed in this chapter, see Wallace et al. (2015). Another excellent, but more succinct review of policy-making in the EU is Nugent (2010). Quaglia (2010) analyses the governance of the financial services industry, and Baun and Marek (2008) and Bachtler et al. (2013) focus on cohesion policy. A comprehensive overview of environmental policy is Knill and Liefferink (2007), while Wurzel et al. (2013) provide detailed coverage of recent developments in environmental policy in the EU and several member states. Jabko (2006) offers a provocative interpretation of the process of economic integration as a consistent strategy to achieve broader integration goals. Falkner et al. (2008) tackle the question of the (lack of) implementation of EU legislation by the member states. A detailed account of how individual member states have contributed to the creation of the EMU is in Dyson and Featherstone (1999). For a critical assessment of the impact of the EMU see Hancke (2013). Quaglia (2007) describes central banking in Europe after the creation of EMU. A very clear explanation of the economics of the EMU is in De Grauwe (2012).

Bachtler, J., Mendez, C., and Wishlade, F. (2013), *EU Cohesion Policy and European Integration* (Farnham: Ashgate).

Baun, M. and Marek, D. (2008), *EU Cohesion Policy after Enlargement* (Basingstoke: Palgrave Macmillan).

De Grauwe, P. (2012), *Economics of Monetary Union*, 10th edn. (Oxford: Oxford University Press).

Dyson, K., and Featherstone, K. (1999), *The Road to Maastricht: Negotiating Economic and Monetary Union* (Oxford: Oxford University Press).

Falkner, G., Treib, O., and Holzleithner, E. (2008), *Compliance in the Enlarged European Union* (Aldershot: Ashgate).

Hancke, B. (2013), *Unions, Central Banks, and EMU: Labour Market Institutions and Monetary Integration in Europe* (Oxford: Oxford University Press).

Jabko, N. (2006), *Playing the Market* (Ithaca, NY: Cornell University Press).

Knill, C. and Liefferink, D. (2007), *Environmental Politics in the European Union* (Manchester: Manchester University Press).

Nugent, N. (2010), *The Government and Politics of the European Union*, 7th edn. (London: Palgrave Macmillan).

Quaglia, L. (2007), *Central Banking Governance in the European Union* (London and New York: Routledge).

Quaglia, L. (2010), *Governing Financial Services in the European Union* (London and New York: Routledge).

Wallace, H., Pollack, M., and Young, A. (eds) (2015), *Policy-Making in the European Union*, 8th edn. (Oxford: Oxford University Press).

Wurzel, R., Zito, A., and Jordan, A. (2013), *Environmental Governance in Europe: A Comparative Analysis of New Environmental Policy Instruments* (Cheltenham, UK: Edward Elgar Publishing).

WEB LINKS

To locate EU publications covering policy, try the EU portal EUR-Lex at: **www.europa.eu.int/eur-lex/** It is bibliographical in nature, but contains links to many full-text documents. For a record of EU legislation, search this site from the European Parliament: **www.europa.eu/eu-law/legislation/index_en.htm** For full-text, non-EU documents, see the websites 'European Integration Online Papers' at: **www.eiop.or.at/eiop/** and 'European Research Papers Archive' at: **www.eiop.or.at/erpa/erpaframe.html**

Visit the Online Resource Centre that accompanies this book for additional material: **www.oxfordtextbooks.co.uk/orc/kenealy4e/**

How Policies Are Made

Fiona Hayes-Renshaw

▌ Summary

EU policies have a direct effect on the daily lives of ordinary people, and it is important to understand how they are made and who is involved in the process. Most EU legislation is now adopted according to the **Ordinary Legislative Procedure**, under which the Council and the European Parliament have equal powers. The basic policy-making rules laid down in the Treaties have been supplemented over the years by formal agreements and informal understandings between the main actors in the decision-making institutions. The result is a highly complex process, involving large numbers of participants in a constant cycle of communication and negotiation at all levels. The process is followed closely by the international media and by interest representatives, who frequently try to influence the outcome. EU policy-making is open to criticism on grounds of democracy, **transparency**, and efficiency, but it continues to deliver an impressive amount and array of policy outcomes.

Introduction

The EU has an impact on the daily lives of citizens in Europe and beyond. It is responsible for the format and content of the labels on breakfast cereal, permitted pollution levels of modes of transport and the cost of roaming charges for mobile communications. On a daily basis, individuals are speaking on Europe's behalf about nuclear security in international forums, imposing sanctions in Europe's name on foreign individuals or states and placing tariffs on the goods Europe imports. EU money is used to fund the building of roads and bridges in various parts of the Union and to assist development in far-flung parts of the world, such as Palestine and many countries in Africa. Yet the ways in which polices are devised, formulated and adopted remain a mystery to most EU citizens, many of whom—understandably—feel a helpless sense of alienation from the process.

There is a tendency in the member states to view EU policy-making as something that happens 'over there' in Brussels. 'There' is seen as a distant, unfamiliar, even threatening place, populated by antagonistic foreigners with different interests and goals. People directly involved in the process are not always necessarily interested in revealing exactly how the policies are made in practice. It may be convenient, if the final policy outcome is unwelcome, to blame it on 'the EU' or 'Brussels'. On the other hand, if the policy outcome is likely to be popular within a certain community, many will rush to take credit for it. In particular, if the outcome is 'bad' for a given member state, the EU gets the blame. If the outcome is 'good', the member government claims responsibility.

How can we find out how policies are made? Since the EU is a law-based organization, the first place to look is in its constituent Treaties, now thankfully consolidated in the 2007 Treaty of Lisbon. The basic policy-making rules can all be found there. But decades of decision-making at EU level have given rise to a range of conventions or accepted ways of doing things that have evolved through practice (see Box 6.1). Such conventions have been embraced as a means for increasing efficiency, transparency or decision-making speed. Some are formalized in written texts, such as inter-institutional agreements or codes of conduct, thereby adding flesh to the bones of the basic rules. Other informal ways of doing things have not been codified but nonetheless need to be understood in order to gain a realistic picture of how EU decision-making operates in practice.

How it Works Formally

If opponents of European integration are to be believed, intrusive laws made by faceless bureaucrats in Brussels increasingly and adversely affect the lives of EU citizens. However, the powers of the EU's institutions and members have been formally agreed by each of the member states and are clearly stated in the Treaties. Even a quick read

BOX 6.1	Key concepts and terms

Civil society refers to the broad collection of associations and groups (including private firms, trades unions, community groups, and non-governmental organizations) active between the level of the individual and the state. These groups generally operate independently of direct governmental control.

A **European Citizens' Initiative** is a request addressed to the European Commission from at least one million EU citizens drawn from at least 7 of the 28 member states to propose a specific piece of legislation in a policy area where the EU has competence to legislate.

Fonctionnaires or EU officials are international civil servants, who have successfully passed an entrance exam known as the 'concours', and who work for the EU's institutions.

The **legal basis** of an EU law is the Treaty article or articles (cited in the legislation) which give(s) the EU authority to act in that area and lay(s) down the decision-making rules that apply.

Lobbying is an attempt to influence policy-makers to adopt a course of action advantageous, or not detrimental, to a particular group or interest. A lobbyist is a person employed by a group, firm, organization, region or country to carry out lobbying. Lobbyists in Brussels are increasingly referred to as interest representatives.

A **Rapporteur** is a Member of the European Parliament who has been given responsibility for preparing a report of one of the Parliament's committees on behalf of the rest of its members.

Transparency refers to the process of making EU documents and decision-making processes more open and accessible to the public.

Trilogues (known as *trialogues* in French) are three-way meetings between key representatives of the Commission, the Council, and the European Parliament, designed to advance negotiations and speed-up budgetary and legislative decision-making.

over these formal rules casts doubt on the Eurosceptics' claims. Yes, decisions are now taken at European level in a large number of policy areas. But the EU and its institutions are not involved to the same extent in each. Rather than faceless bureaucrats, these institutions are made up of individuals from each of the member states, usually very talented and often very committed ones. In fulfilling their respective roles in the legislative process, these individuals must follow strict rules and procedures that are open to scrutiny by a variety of observers.

The basic rules

The EU cannot unilaterally decide to get involved in a particular policy area. There are plenty of checks and balances to ensure that it does not over-step its assigned policy-making role. The first constraint is that the EU can only intervene in a given policy area if the member states have empowered it to do so: the Union can act only to the extent and following the rules laid down in the Treaties. Policy competence may lie exclusively with the EU (as in external trade policy), or primarily with the member states (as in development cooperation). Sometimes, it is shared between the member states and the EU (as in transport policy). Every piece of EU legislation refers to one or more Treaty articles as the authority for its involvement in that policy area: the so-called 'legal basis'.

Secondly, the EU must respect two fundamental principles when it makes policy. The first is subsidiarity, meaning that the EU should only act in circumstances where its intervention is likely to be more effective than that undertaken by the member states individually. So the Union has competence in environmental policy where collective European action is required. But subsidiarity means that the EU is not involved in rubbish collection (although it may regulate landfills because of its environmental policy competence).

The second fundamental principle is proportionality. The EU's involvement is limited only to what is required to fulfill the objectives outlined in the Treaties. Thus, it can be argued (albeit controversially) that the declared aim of consumer protection could be adequately achieved by providing information and advice to EU citizens rather than by imposing an outright ban on the use of all hormones in livestock farming.

Even clearing these initial hurdles does not imply a successful outcome for a proposal. Usually, a third basic rule is shared legislative authority. Policy-making in the EU allows for input from a wide variety of actors, many of whom have competing interests. Under the Ordinary Legislative Procedure, the European Commission—a body representing the general interest of the EU—proposes draft legislation. Two other institutions, composed of the representatives of the EU's citizens—the European Parliament—and representatives of the governments of the member states—the Council of Ministers—are designated as co-legislators. This means that a new piece of legislation can only be adopted if both the EP and the Council agree to its content. Put another way, each institution has the power to ensure that a draft piece of legislation with which it disagrees cannot be enacted.

The principal actors

The Treaty of Lisbon describes the basic composition and powers of the main institutions and bodies that are directly involved in the EU's policy-making process (see Chapter 3). The European Commission—headed by a President who together with his fellow Commissioners forms a 28-person college—enjoys an almost exclusive right to initiate legislative proposals. The College decides and acts collectively, formally by simple majority but usually by consensus.

The 751 Members of the European Parliament (MEPs) are directly elected by EU citizens, whose interests they represent. They have the power to adopt, amend, or reject the Commission's legislative proposals, working in conjunction with the Council and reaching agreement by majority. The Council is composed of ministers from each of the member states and exists to represent their interests. Like the EP, and in conjunction with it, a majority of the Council's members may decide to adopt, amend, or reject draft legislation put forward by the Commission.

The Treaty of Lisbon also mentions the Economic and Social Committee (comprising economic and social actors from each of the member states) and the Committee of the Regions (bringing together representatives of EU-wide regional and local governments), which are consulted for their specialist views in policy areas within their remit. A far more weighty and powerful institution is the European Council: the heads of state or government from each of the member states. It sometimes becomes involved in the policy-making process, either at the beginning, when it may define political directions or priorities, or towards the end, if sensitive political issues are at stake. But the European Council—despite bringing together Europe's most powerful political leaders—does not have the power to take actual legislative decisions.

A casual observer might be aware, through media reports, of a new proposal being presented by a Commissioner. Many months, or even years, later, announcements by representatives of the EP or of the Council to the effect that they have reached agreement on the final piece of legislation might make the evening news. In the interim, the ordinary citizen might be conscious, again via media reports, of debates between stakeholders as to the merits and demerits of what is being proposed. They might even hear of protests organized locally, or in Brussels, by those likely to be directly affected by the future law. However, for most EU citizens, the discussions and events leading up to the final adoption of a new piece of EU legislation either remain a mystery or appear too confusing to decipher.

The key stages

Each chapter of the Treaty of Lisbon dealing with a specific policy area lays down the procedure according to which policy decisions are made. In most cases today, the legislative procedure in question is the Ordinary Legislative Procedure. On the face of it, the procedure is very simple:

- The Commission produces a draft piece of legislation and sends it to the EP and the Council for their views.
- The Parliament and Council discuss the draft separately in the course of one or two readings, and may propose amendments to the text.
- If a specified majority in each institution reaches agreement on a mutually acceptable text, it is adopted as a legislative act.
- If after two readings agreement has still not been reached between the Council and EP, a joint conciliation committee is convened to try to find a compromise.
- If no agreement can be reached at this stage, the proposal is not adopted.

The Treaty's description of the Ordinary Legislative Procedure demonstrates that it follows three key stages of policy-making:

1. Identifying specific goals in a given policy area (agenda-setting),
2. Discussing alternative ways of achieving them (negotiation),
3. Reaching agreement on the end product (final decision).

By way of comparison, the UK government and civil service set the agenda by tabling draft legislation, which is examined, debated and amended by the House of Commons and the House of Lords, who then decide whether to approve or reject it. In the EU, the agenda-setting role is attributed mainly to the Commission, while the EP and the Council are the principal players in the second and third stages (negotiation and final decision).

What Happens in Practice

The Treaty of Lisbon's provisions on policy-making provide us with a broad-brush understanding of the process as a whole. However, a more in-depth examination of what happens in practice adds finer detail that in many cases can change the overall picture. For example, the Treaty suggests that the EU's three main legislative institutions—the Commission, the Council and EP—operate as a triangle, each one directly connected to the other two. The reality is that they can more correctly be visualized as three icebergs, whose tips are inhabited respectively by Commissioners, ministers, and MEPs. However, the (somewhat crowded!) iceberg tips are only the smallest, most publicized and visible part of far larger masses, which prove to be much more inter-connected and closer together beneath the surface of the water than above it. Exploring the less visible parts of the icebergs can help to identify the pivotal actors and key stages that are of paramount importance to those attempting to follow or influence the process.

The EU's policy-making remit has been subject to an impressive amount of expansion over the years, as has the membership of the Union. As a result, the institutions and other actors in the process have had to adapt to many new rules, roles, and procedures. Today, the connections between the large numbers of legislative actors at EU level are extensive, very complex and shape much of what happens on a day-to-day basis.

The adapted rules

The Ordinary Legislative Procedure (see Box 6.2) requires a high level of agreement among the main institutional actors in order for new legislation to be adopted. Many different interests have to be reconciled at all stages of the procedure. The result is that a constant search for compromise has emerged as an important feature of the policy-making process, both within and between the institutions. This fact is evident in the ways in which the institutions now organize themselves and their respective work programmes in order to fulfill their legislative responsibilities. Written agreements co-exist with a number of tacit understandings about 'how things should be done' in order to ensure a harmonious working environment that encourages cooperation and facilitates agreement.

Inter-institutional cooperation and transparency are the first prerequisites for an efficient policy-making process based on compromise and consensus. In the 1990s, early experience with the pre-Lisbon precursor to the Ordinary Legislative Procedure—the co-decision procedure—made it clear that, if agreement was to be reached within a reasonable amount of time, inter-institutional discussions and negotiations needed to get underway sooner rather than later, once the Commission had presented its proposal. Regular meetings, known as trilogues (or *trialogues* in French), were therefore scheduled between the key players in each of the three institutions, with the aim of keeping one another informed about the progress of the discussions on dossiers going on in parallel within the Council and EP and to assist in the search for compromises. Over time, trilogues proved to be a useful behind-the-scenes means of identifying the most contentious issues for each institution. Similarly, they constituted a relatively 'safe' forum for assessing the potential degree of support for proposed amendments before they were officially put to a vote.

An inter-institutional agreement on better law-making, published in 2003, made public the intention of the Commission, Council and EP to further improve the coordination of their individual and joint legislative activities under co-decision. They agreed to keep one another permanently informed about their work throughout the legislative process and to synchronize the handling of dossiers by their respective preparatory bodies. They also undertook to keep the public better informed at every stage, including by broadcasting political debates and votes on legislative proposals and publishing the results of their deliberations. This latter commitment entailed a significant cultural shift for the Council, which had a history of conducting its negotiations behind closed doors and avoiding votes where possible, preferring to adopt its positions by means of consensus.

One rather controversial feature of EU policy-making concerns how interested parties can have input, whether in the form of consultation or lobbying. It is generally accepted that the Commission should be open to input from interested parties. To this end, it engages in widespread consultations in order to ensure that its proposed legislation will be both fit for purpose and likely to be acceptable to a majority of stakeholders. There is little point in the Commission spending time producing a draft piece of legislation that fails to achieve the necessary majorities in the EP and the Council. The same goes for legislation that proves either difficult to implement or incapable of dealing with the problems it has been designed to address. Similarly, MEPs and national government officials may consult interested parties when determining what position to take on a new Commission proposal.

| BOX 6.2 | A plethora of policies, processes, and procedures |

The EU has much broader policy responsibilities than the original European Communities. Today, it is involved not only in trade, agriculture, and energy, but also foreign affairs, citizens' rights, and monetary policy, among other policy areas.

However, the EU is not involved to the same extent in every area, because the ways in which it makes policy differ between policy areas, depending on where policy competence lies. In some policy areas, such as competition and external trade, most major policy decisions are taken at EU level, whereas in others, such as consumer protection or the environment, responsibility for major policy decisions is shared between the EU and national levels.

The majority of EU policy processes result in detailed legislation, but others produce such outcomes as an agreed budget or threshold (for example, the annual EU budget or total allowable catches in fisheries policy), rules set by the EU's institutions (such as the Commission's merger policy decisions) or coordinated national positions (such as the details of the Stability and Growth Pact or a joint statement on the crisis in Ukraine).

Most EU legislation is adopted by means of the **Ordinary Legislative Procedure**, under which the Council and the European Parliament have equal powers to accept, reject, or amend legislation proposed by the Commission. The Treaty of Lisbon extended its scope and it now applies to 85 policy areas. The European Parliament has more restricted rights under two special legislative procedures: the **Consultation Procedure** (which is used, for example, for certain measures in the Common Foreign and Security Policy) and the **Consent Procedure** (previously known as the Assent Procedure, which applies in a number of fields, including association agreements and the Multiannual Financial Framework). The Consultation and Consent Procedures are also used for the adoption of certain non-legislative international agreements.

It is also possible for a group of like-minded member states (who must number at least one third, currently nine of the 28) to act together in the interests of advanced integration in certain policy areas, using the EU's institutions and procedures. This is known as **Enhanced Cooperation** and has been used most recently in the areas of divorce (15 participating member states) and patents (25 participating member states).

Another more public feature of the Ordinary Legislative Procedure that has developed over the years is inter-institutional signaling to indicate what will or will not be acceptable to the relevant legislative partner. Thus, although the Procedure requires the Council to await the EP's first reading position before it adopts its own Common Position, ministers frequently issue a 'political agreement' to indicate which elements of the Commission's proposal (and the EP's proposed amendments) would or would not be acceptable to the Council. Similarly, the EP might choose to postpone a scheduled plenary vote to establish its first reading position on a Commission proposal in order to signal its readiness to continue to negotiate with the Council.

In line with its overtly democratic nature, voting in the EP has always been public. Decision-making within the Council has historically been more opaque, due to the so-called 'consensual reflex' that lingers throughout its various layers as a consequence (largely) of the EEC's original voting rules based on unanimity (Heisenberg 2005). For many years after majority voting rules were introduced, national officials and ministers continued to try to reach agreements acceptable to as many members of the Council as possible, in an attempt to avoid publicly out-voting one or more of their colleagues. The effect was to discourage active voting, making the officially required production of voting figures problematic. Only since the introduction of co-decision has data on voting at ministerial level been made publicly available. Early analyses of this data demonstrated that the Council only registered negative votes or abstentions around 14 per cent of the time (Hayes-Renshaw and Wallace 2006: 259), rising to about 35 per cent in recent years (Miller 2013). The rest of the time it decides by consensus.

A variety of actors

When explaining the EU's policy-making processes, it is customary to use a kind of institutional shorthand to describe the main actors. As a result, we speak and read about 'the Parliament', 'the Commission', and 'the Council' as though they were single entities with a recognizable face and a given set of attitudes and characteristics. However, each of these institutions is made up of layers of individuals, each of whom possesses their own priorities and interests.

The principal actors are the College of Commissioners, Ministers in the Council, and MEPs meeting in plenary in the EP. But most of the detailed policy-making work actually takes place elsewhere (usually lower down) within each of these institutions. Each Commissioner, Minister, and MEP is assisted by a large number of aides and officials who do the preparatory work on draft legislation, often leaving just a small number of issues to be dealt with directly at formal meetings of the Commission, Council, or EP. This detailed work frequently involves the accommodation of competing interests, with the result that, more often than not, the single 'position' of each institution is only arrived at after a process of intense internal negotiation. In fact, internal debates within the Commission, Council, or EP may well continue after the formal discussions with the other institutions have commenced. The negotiation of the 2011 Eurovignette Directive to regulate the costs to infrastructure, health and the environment of heavy goods vehicles illustrates the point (see Dyrhauge 2014).

The detailed policy-making work in the Commission is carried out by officials (*fonctionnaires*) who are recruited centrally from among the EU's citizens. They are responsible for the detailed drafting of the Commission's proposals and may attend meetings in the EP committees and Council working groups when they are being discussed. Turf battles within the Commission are not unknown, with the result that the 'Commission position' may not be supported with equal enthusiasm by all those bound by it. For example, a proposal to ban or restrict the use of a pesticide may be energetically supported by DG Environment, but only lackadaisically (if at all) by DG Agriculture.

The EP's detailed legislative work is done in its 20 or so specialized permanent committees, and each MEP belongs to one or more of them according to his or her policy interests or expertise. The committees vary in size but each contains representatives of most of the EP's political groups. At committee meetings, the MEPs discuss the Commission's proposal in detail and agree on a report (prepared by a 'rapporteur') that contains those amendments that have attracted the necessary majority. The rapporteur's report is then sent to the EP plenary session, where it is discussed and voted upon by all the MEPs, whereupon it becomes 'the EP's position'.

MEPs are individually accountable to their respective electorates. Thus, they try to ensure that the interests of their constituents are protected when they vote on proposed legislation. However, most MEPs also belong to one of the EP's political groups, whose members try to vote together on draft legislation. The EP's position is therefore normally a compromise between different positions among the MEPs, some of whom will have been out-voted in the committee or the plenary on details of the position of importance to them.

The Council of Ministers meets in ten main configurations and a number of sub-formations, each one dealing with a specific policy area or set of related policy areas. A member of the national government, who is authorized to speak and take decisions on its behalf, represents every member state. The Environment Council consists of national Environmental Ministers, the Foreign Affairs Council brings together Foreign Ministers, and so on. The total ministerial membership of the Council is therefore very large (at least 300 people) and changes as a result of national elections, cabinet reshuffles, or other reallocations of responsibility in the member states. The Council's political approach is also subject to change as left and right wing parties move in and out of power or governing coalitions are formed or reformed at national level. Many different views co-exist in the Council, requiring a constant process of negotiation in order to achieve 'the Council position'. A key figure in finding that position is the Council chair, occupied by the minister from the member state that holds the Council presidency. The presidency rotates every six months except in the Foreign Affairs Council, which is always chaired by the High Representative for Foreign Affairs and Security Policy (see Chapter 3).

The detailed preparatory work for Council meetings takes place first in one or more of its 150 or so specialist technical working groups, composed of officials from the relevant ministries in the member states. They routinely discuss the Commission proposal article by article, registering agreements and disagreements and suggesting amendments. Any provisions that cannot be agreed at working group level (usually the more political aspects of the proposals) are sent up to the more senior Committee of Permanent Representatives (Coreper). There they are agreed or sent back down to the working group or up to the ministers in Council for further discussion and/or agreement. A representative of the Commission attends all meetings in the Council hierarchy when a Commission proposal is being discussed. Officials from the Council Secretariat are also present, to take minutes and advise the presidency. The national civil servants who sit on these preparatory bodies negotiate on behalf of their member governments. But only ministers in the Council can take the final decision, which then constitutes 'the Council's position'.

Members of EU institutions do not operate in a vacuum when engaging in policy-making. The policy outcomes they produce affect countless people who need to be informed about them and who may have valuable contributions to make regarding their design. As a result, large numbers of people are engaged in finding out the state of play on dossiers under discussion and, more controversially, in trying to ensure that particular interests are either protected or are at least unharmed by proposed legislation. A large Brussels-based international press/media corps follows and reports on EU policy-making. It consists of around 1,000 accredited journalists and over 500 accredited media personnel covering 69 nationalities, and thus is only slightly smaller than the media delegations based in Washington or London. Full-time correspondents, freelance journalists and those employed by online services report, analyse, and comment upon the activities of the EU's policy-makers. Equally, of course, they may be sought out by individual policy-makers anxious to present their particular view to a specific group of readers, listeners or viewers.

Another large group trying to influence EU policy-making is interest representatives, commonly known as lobbyists. They work for and speak on behalf of companies, trade associations, NGOs, law firms, think tanks, academic institutions, churches, and local, regional, and municipal authorities. In 2011, in an effort to shed some light on their existence and activities, the Commission and EP amalgamated two previously separate registers and established a common Transparency Register for interest representatives. By October 2014, it had almost 7,000 registrants. However, given that the entries in the register are voluntary, the estimate by the Corporate European Observatory of some 30,000 interest representatives operating in Brussels is probably not wide of the mark.

EU policy-makers are not necessarily averse to approaches from lobbyists. The Commission consults widely when preparing its draft proposals and each of the key policy-makers consults (or is approached by) a number of groups that are likely to be affected by the resulting legislation. The information gathered is of great importance and utility to the policy-makers, who have to be aware of interests that need to be accommodated in any proposed legislation. Some interest representatives even prepare amendments to be presented by MEPs in the EP's committee and plenary sessions. Others target national ministers and officials in an attempt to influence the position they will defend during discussions and votes on draft legislation in the Council. In short, exerting influence on EU policy-makers has become something of an industry. Those who do it best know how to focus their efforts on the most important individuals and stages—which are not necessarily the key ones mentioned in the Treaties.

Fluid stages

The three key stages in the policy-making process—agenda setting, negotiation, and final decision—are not distinct phases but rather overlapping sequences (Pollack 2010). It can be difficult for outsiders to determine or predict the length of the process and also to identify the exact occasion on which key events in the process actually take place. EU policy-making is an intensely political process, and events such as an upcoming national or EP election, a changeover in the Council presidency or the appointment of a new European Commissioner can have important implications for the adoption (or not) of proposed legislation.

The first (agenda-setting) stage can last a very long time, depending on the perceived need for the policy instrument in question and the urgency with which it is required. The Commission enjoys the right of initiative, and the 'power of the text' is an important one. Amending the text is a power possessed by the Commission, or by the Council and the EP but subject to strict majority voting rules. However, the Commission is careful to do its homework before submitting a draft proposal. It holds wide-ranging consultations with a variety of actors (often with competing or even contradictory interests) to determine the best way to deal with an existing situation and to identify possible difficulties of implementation once the legislation has been enacted.

When the Commission publishes its initial proposal, it is sent at the same time to a variety of different bodies—the EP, the Council, and the 28 national parliaments and, where required, the Committee of the Regions and the Economic and Social Committee. Their respective responses are subject to strict time limits. Thus, national parliaments have a period of 8 weeks from the date of receipt of the proposal to indicate whether they think the twin principles of subsidiarity and proportionality have been respected. There is no set time limit for the EP and the Council to complete their respective first readings, but the EP is required to complete its first reading before the Council does, and the Council is expected to take the EP's position into account when determining its own position. Second readings in the EP and the Council are subject to time limits, as is the conciliation process, and failure to abide by them results in the demise of the proposed legislation.

Negotiation (the second stage) occurs throughout the process: between stakeholders and the Commission when the proposal is being drafted, between left-wing and right-wing political groups when the EP is trying to agree its official position, and often between the Council presidency and a group of member states trying to block the adoption of a compromise. A draft piece of legislation is thus subject to intense scrutiny both within and between the institutions. These negotiations can continue for many months, if not years, before any key stages in the process are completed.

However, the (third stage) 'final decision', when it occurs, is often merely the rubber-stamping of agreements reached earlier in other forums. The final adoption of a piece of legislation takes the form of agreement on an agenda point at a ministerial Council meeting. The agenda point is normally passed without discussion and frequently by consensus, on a recommendation from Coreper and following intensive discussions between the three institutions. Knowing when and where to intervene in the process is therefore very important for those trying to affect its outcome.

Assessing the Process

We have seen how the EU policy-making process works in practice. While a detailed examination of the process may enable us to understand why the process works in the way it does, it is worth asking whether the process can be viewed as democratic, transparent and efficient. Since a more detailed account of democracy and transparency in the EU can be found in Chapter 7, the discussion on these two points here is brief. The question of efficiency is considered in somewhat more detail.

Is the process democratic?

It is common to talk of the EU's 'democratic deficit' to indicate a general feeling that those who take the crucial decisions are not in some way answerable for their actions. Our examination of the Ordinary Legislative Procedure and the actors who play the key roles in the process suggests otherwise. The Commission as a body is answerable to the EP, which has, in recent years, become increasingly assertive in wielding its power to appoint and dismiss individual Commissioners. As the only directly-elected actors in the EU's legislative process, the MEPs have frequently claimed a special status among the Union's legislators, although the sheer number, broad spectrum and uneven discipline of the EP's membership has at times tended to diminish its authority. The members of the Council occupy this position *ex officio*, in their individual capacities as the authorized (usually elected) representatives of their respective member states for the policy area under discussion.

   The position of those who operate at lower levels in the system is rather different. The national civil servants who sit in the Council's working groups speak on behalf of, and are answerable to, the members of their respective national governments. EU governments are, of course, in turn answerable to the citizens of that member state. The *fonctionnaires* in the Commission's DGs who draft the legislative proposals report to their respective Commissioners, who are in turn answerable to the EP. While it is true that their democratic accountability is less direct than that of the MEPs, it is wrong to suggest that they somehow operate with no limits to their powers.

   Apart from the official actors, there are also opportunities for other individuals to be heard in the EU's legislative process. The Commission consults widely when drawing up its proposals. Each of the EU's institutions is open to input from stakeholders affected by current and future legislation. Interest groups, whether organized at local, regional, national or pan-European level, can also gain access to the process, although it is a fact of life that those with the greatest resources find it easiest to make their voices heard. However, resource-rich lobby groups do not always achieve their objectives, as the revision of the tobacco products directive demonstrated in 2014. Despite an intensive and well-funded effort by tobacco producers, a new directive was agreed that promised to make smoking less attractive to young people and that regulated electronic cigarettes (see Online Resource Centre).

More generally, anyone with a legitimate message to convey to the official actors in the process can do so by multiple means. One is to sign a European Citizens' Initiative, a device included in the Lisbon Treaty whereby a specified number of citizens in a specified number of member states can invite the Commission to propose legislation in any area of EU competence. Other ways to influence EU policy-making include personally approaching a local public representative or (especially) an MEP, or contributing to a public consultation organized by the Commission.

Is the process transparent?

Concern about the democratic deficit has resulted in a number of measures aimed at making the policy-making process more open to the public. The EP has always tried to be very open about its actions and modes of operation and has embraced the notion of transparency with considerable zeal. The Parliament's committee and plenary sessions are open to the public and are broadcast live. The majority of its parliamentary documents are available in all 24 official languages in electronic format via a register.

Although initially less enthusiastic, the Council has slowly improved access to information about its meetings and its documents. However the Council continues to be divided into a minority pro-transparency coalition and a majority of more sceptical member states, who have managed to slow down the pace of transparency within the Council since 2006 (Hillebrandt et al. 2014). Although video-streaming of parts of Council meetings is now commonplace, the real negotiations continue to take place away from the cameras, lending credence to the view that most deals are still done behind closed doors in the interest of achieving consensus.

Contrasting attitudes towards transparency within the EP and the Council are explained by the different nature of the policy-making process within each institution. In the EP, debates in the committees and plenary are followed by a public vote, on which MEPs can be held to account by their constituents. In the Council, public votes by ministers reflect agreements reached elsewhere following detailed discussions behind closed doors among national officials in the preparatory working groups (see Miller 2013). It is significant that the conciliation process in the Ordinary Legislative Procedure (which brings together representatives of the Commission, the EP and the Council) also takes place behind closed doors. Usually, it is easier to reach agreement on controversial issues if the negotiations take place in private.

Is the process efficient?

Assessing the efficiency of the EU's legislative process has both quantitative and qualitative dimensions. It is relatively easy to produce figures on the number of legis-lative acts adopted each year, the stage in the process at which they are adopted and the average length of time required (see Tables 6.1, 6.2, and 6.3). Undertaking a qualitative assessment is a more difficult exercise, because of the value judgments it is likely to contain about the process as a whole and the content of the output.

TABLE 6.1 Dossiers concluded under the co-decision / Ordinary Legislative Procedure since the entry into force of the Treaty of Amsterdam

Year	Period of year	Presidency Member State	Concluded at 1st Reading	Concluded at 2nd Reading	Concluded after conciliation	Total	Year	Total For Year	Failed after conciliation
1999	July-December	Finland	9	8	5	22	1999 (J-D)	22	
2000	January-June	Portugal	9	16	12	37	2000	72	
	July-December	France	10	16	9	35			
2001	January-June	Sweden	16	15	11	42	2001	73	Takeover directive
	July-December	Belgium	4	19	8	31			
2002	January-June	Spain	11	19	9	39	2002	76	
	July-December	Denmark	6	18	13	37			
2003	January-June	Greece	16	33	4	53	2003	104	Port services directive
	July-December	Italy	23	17	11	51			
2004	January-June	Ireland	42	26	6	74	2004	81	
	July-December	Netherlands	4	3	–	7			
2005	January-June	Luxembourg	28	14	–	42	2005	77	
	July-December	United Kingdom	24	6	5	35			
2006	January-June	Austria	21	6	4	31	2006	94	
	July-December	Finland	53	8	2	63			

Cont. ➤

Cont.

2007	January–June	Germany	52	5	62	2007	113	
	July–December	Portugal	46	4	51			
2008	January–June	Slovenia	62	12	74	2008	147	
	July–December	France	57	10	73			
2009	January–June	Czech Republic	44	12	57	2009	72	Working time directive
	July–December	Sweden	6	7	15			
2010	January–June	Spain	28	5	33	2010	72	
	July–December	Belgium	35	3	39			
2011	January–June	Hungary	25	7	33	2011	74	Novel foods regulation
	July–December	Poland	29	8	41			
2012	January–June	Denmark	39	5	44	2012	84	
	July–December	Cyprus	36	4	40			
2013	January–June	Ireland	59	8	68	2013	160	
	July–December	Lithuania	87	5	92			
2014	January–June	Greece	64	3	67	2014 (J–J)	67	
Total			**945**	**322**	**121**	**1388**	**1388**	

From 1 July 1999 to 30 June 2014—Broken down by Presidency period and calendar year—EP elections took place in 1999, 2004, 2009 and 2014

Source—Council website.

Generally, however, the output of the Ordinary Legislative Procedure is perfectly respectable (an average of 93 legislative acts adopted annually) and compares favourably to the output of many national systems. It is all the more impressive given the diversity of the actors and interests involved and the additional administrative steps required to accommodate the EU's 28 component national systems. It is clear from Table 6.1 that legislative output follows a certain rhythm, which is linked to both the EP's legislative term and the five-year life of each Commission. There are good reasons for this rhythm. A newly-elected European Parliament takes time to get itself organized: to decide on the composition and leadership of the committees and other organizational bodies, to agree on the appointment of *rapporteurs* for specific dossiers, and to get into a sustained tempo of work. Similarly, a newly-appointed Commission must establish its priorities in legislative terms and either continue or set in train a series of consultations and drafting exercises in order to produce proposals for legislative acts. Steering a legislative proposal through the various stages of the process in each of the institutions takes time (a minimum of 12 months). It also requires large amounts of coordination and communication both within and between the institutions.

As a result, the legislative output of the first year or so of the life of a new EP and Commission tends to be rather sparse. In contrast, the final year or 18 months of the

TABLE 6.2	Stage at which agreement has been reached on dossiers concluded under the co-decision / Ordinary Legislative Procedure 1999–2014				
Legislative period	Concluded at 1st Reading	Concluded at 2nd Reading	Concluded after conciliation	No agreement after conciliation	Total
1999–2004 (1 July 1999– 30 June 2004)	146 (34.5%)	187 (44.2%)	88 (20.8%)	2 (0.5%) (Takeovers & Port services directives)	**423**
2004–9 (1 July 2004– 30 June 2009)	391 (78.8%)	80 (16.1%)	24 (4.9%)	1 (0.2%) (Working time directive)	**496**
2009–14 (1 July 2009– 30 June 2014)	408 (86.3%)	55 (11.6%)	9 (1.9%)	1 (0.2%) (Novel foods regulation)	**473**
Total (1 July 1999– 30 June 2014)	**945** (67.9%)	**322** (23.1%)	**121** (8.7%)	4 (0.3%)	**1392**

Broken down by EP legislative terms and corresponding Council Presidency periods
Compiled from statistics available on the Council website

TABLE 6.3	Average length of time required to reach agreement under the co-decision / Ordinary Legislative Procedure		
	1999-2004	**2004-2009**	**2009-2014**
1ˢᵗ Reading	11 months	16 months	17 months
2ⁿᵈ Reading	24 months	29 months	32 months
3ʳᵈ Reading (conciliation)	31 months	43 months	29 months
Total average length	**22 months**	**21 months**	**19 months**

Source: EP Activity Report on Codecision and Conciliation 14 July 2009–30 June 2014

EP's legislative term sees a sustained effort on the part of all the legislative actors to get as many procedures concluded as possible, if only because of uncertainty about their eventual fate in a new, unknown configuration of the EP (and Commission) after the European elections. This political reality explains the increased number of completed dossiers in the six months or so prior to the end of each legislative assembly's term.

Similarly, each Council Presidency period is marked by progress in the discussion and conclusion of procedures or, at least, agreement on the Council's stance on a particular dossier. Normally, agreements on Council positions reach a peak in the last month of the Presidency's term of office. Exit velocity is good for the Presidency's overall balance sheet, with legislative agreement being viewed as one of the hallmarks of 'a good Presidency'. In qualitative terms, however, it is worth questioning the calibre of the legislative acts that are agreed, particularly if there is a suspicion that they were agreed under pressure of time. Sometimes, the EU is accused of producing poor quality legislation or regulations that are difficult, if not impossible, to implement properly.

The procedural stage at which the final decision is reached between the Council and the EP is another means often used to assess the efficiency of the EU's legislative process. Since the introduction of the co-decision procedure there has been a steady increase in the number of dossiers agreed at an early stage in the process, and this increase has become more significant in recent years. At the same time, there has been a corresponding decrease in the number of issues that have been subject to conciliation. At face value, this shift suggests that the institutions are working well together to coordinate their positions in order to reach agreement without having to resort to additional readings. However, it is also likely that at least some of the dossiers included in these rather impressive totals were non-controversial and therefore had an easy passage through the process. It is also possible that the large number of dossiers ending up in conciliation in the early years of the co-decision procedure owed more to a high level of inter-institutional mistrust and the desire of the EP to flex its newly acquired legislative powers than to the divisive nature of the dossiers themselves.

It now takes an average of 17 months to reach agreement on the majority of dossiers adopted under the Ordinary Legislative Procedure. The general desire to avoid conciliation where possible has resulted in certain difficult dossiers now being agreed earlier in the process, thereby accounting for the increase in the average amount of time required for first and second reading agreements since 1999–2004. However, it should be remembered that, while strict time limits apply to the second reading and conciliation (third reading) phases of the procedure, no such limits apply to the first reading. It is therefore possible for either the EP or the Council to continue their internal first reading discussions on the dossier indefinitely with no legal or administrative consequences (apart perhaps from the irritation of those actors wanting an outcome).

More positively, no time limit on the first reading gives the actors the opportunity to iron out difficulties and explore alternative solutions, which could lead to inter-institutional agreement at the end of the first reading. Taking a long time to reach an agreement may also be an indicator of the complexity of the dossier or of the initial distance between the positions of the various actors, which takes time to resolve. Time is often a valuable resource in all senses in EU policy-making. Inevitably, it frequently takes quite a lot of it to reach consensus on a policy result amongst 28 member states, three legislative institutions, and a vast number of affected interests, in Europe and beyond.

Theory and Practice

We have seen how EU policy-making takes place in practice. What light does theory shed? International relations approaches tend to focus on the broad development of European integration, rather than on how the Union makes policies. But neofunctionalists would highlight how the need for common European policy solutions has pushed integration forward via Treaty changes to make collective action easier. For their part, liberal intergovernmentalists would insist that national EU governments still retain essential control—especially through the Council as well as the European Council—of what policies the EU actually produces.

Meanwhile, institutionalists would argue that EU policy-making is now at least as much, if not more, about cooperation and competition between the EU's institutions than between European states. In particular, the EP has been empowered with each revision of the EU Treaties. It has come into its own as a politically and legally equal co-legislator with the Council. Institutions truly matter in EU policy-making, especially because the EP and Commission are so much more powerful than their counterparts in other international organizations.

Public policy scholars stand on strong ground in arguing that European policy-making is dominated by discrete policy networks, especially ones that are policy-specialized. Much of the EU's policy work is highly technical and requires specialist expertise, which creates barriers to entry to all but experts. Even at a more political level, each policy sector has its own Council, Commissioner, Commission DG, and EP committee. EU policies thus may be viewed as mostly a result of bargaining between (usually) a diverse collection of participants in sectoral policy networks.

Similarly, constructivists can claim to shed considerable light on EU policy-making. They find no shortage of evidence that the preferences—even the *interests*—of policy-makers are constructed in the course of bargaining at the EU level, as opposed to defined extrinsically and prior to negotiations in Brussels. The relentless search for compromise and consensus means that even when, say, a member state brings a strong position fixed in their national capital to EU negotiations, it almost inevitably is shaped and 'bent' in ways that make it possible to attract allies to adopt or block a policy decision.

Conclusion

We have surveyed the formal rules that describe how the legislative process works in theory. We have also examined the ways in which these rules have been interpreted and implemented over the years in order to show how EU legislation is actually adopted in practice. Our analysis has highlighted the ways in which formal actors—the members of the EU's institutions—operate alongside and in close collaboration with a host of other participants drawn from a wide range of sectors of civil society. We have noted how the formal stages of the legislative process have been adapted to operate alongside other informal processes that can and do affect the final outcomes. In other words, we have put some flesh on the bones of the process in order to build up a more accurate picture of its actual appearance—and hopefully to dispel a few myths.

No one denies that the EU's policy-making process is complex. A very large number of official actors are involved at every stage of the process, operating in diverse forums, using a variety of languages and following complicated procedures. Their proceedings are monitored closely by a growing number of representatives of European civil society. Its members do their best, both publicly and behind the scenes, to have their interests taken into account when legislation affecting them is being prepared. A large European and international media corps publicizes and comments on the process. Each of the EU's institutions maintains a website with information on its activities in all the policy areas in which it is involved.

There is therefore no dearth of information about what is going on in the EU today. But there is no denying a lack of understanding about how the process actually operates in practice. Our description demonstrates that compromise and consensus are the key features of the process. In order to reach agreement at EU level, bargains must be struck not only between but also within the institutions in an ongoing process of negotiation. Some of these negotiations are played out in public. But the most difficult and sensitive discussions continue to take place behind closed doors. The most visible stages of the decision-making process are only one small part of a long and complex series of exchanges that are open to input from a much greater variety of actors, including ordinary citizens, than is immediately apparent. The process is still not as democratic or as transparent as many would like. But it continues to function and to produce a rather impressive amount of legislation that affects a growing number of aspects of the daily lives of ordinary citizens in Europe and beyond.

DISCUSSION QUESTIONS

1. What are the most important differences between the formal rules for EU policy-making and more informal norms that have sprouted over time?

2. How do we explain the fact that the Council of Ministers takes a formal vote on proposed policy measures around one-third of the time?

3. Does the increasing involvement of outside interests in the EU's decision-making process make for better policy?

4. Is democracy strengthened or undermined by the presence of non-elected interest groups in the EU decision-making process?

FURTHER READING

The definitive guide to policy-making in the EU remains Wallace et al. 7th edn. 2005. Richardson (2006) is also useful. On the European Parliament, including its political groups, see Corbett et al (2011, especially Chapter 10). On the Council of Ministers, see Naurin and Wallace (2008). For a comprehensive overview of analyses of Council voting, see Miller (2013). A special issue of the journal *West European Politics* (2011) contains interesting articles on the effects that changes in inter-institutional decision-making rules have had on politics and behaviour within the institutions. There is a very wide literature on lobbying in the EU. The most recent general text is Coen and Richardson (2009), but Greenwood (2011) also provides a useful, detailed examination of different interest groups. A special issue of the *Journal of European Public Policy* (2007) is devoted specifically to lobbying. Goergen (2006) offers a very comprehensive practical guide to lobbying, and the regularly updated publication, the Stakeholder.EU directory (2012), compiled by the former MEP Frank Schwalba Hoth, offers an overview of the wide range of actors involved.

Coen, D. and Richardson, J. (2009), *Lobbying in the European Union: Institutions, Actors and Issues* (Oxford: Oxford University Press)

Corbett, R., Jacobs, F., and Shackleton, M. (2011), *The European Parliament*, 8th edn. (London: Cartermill)

Goergen, P. (2006), *Lobbying in Brussels: A Practical Guide to the European Union for Cities, Regions, Networks and Enterprises* (Brussels, D&P Services).

Greenwood, J. (2011), *Interest Representation in the European Union*, 3rd edn. (Basingstoke and New York: Palgrave).

Journal of European Public Policy (2007), Special issue on 'Empirical and Theoretical Studies in EU Lobbying', 14/3.

Miller, V. (2013), 'Voting Behaviour in the EU Council', *House of Commons Library Standard Note SN06646*.

Naurin, D. and Wallace, H. (2008), *Unveiling the Council of the European Union* (Basingstoke and New York: Palgrave).

Richardson, J. (2006), *European Union: Power and Policy-Making*, 3rd edn. (London and New York: Routledge).

Stakeholder. EU: The Directory for Brussels, 2nd edn. (2012), (Berlin: Lexxion).

Wallace, H., Pollack, M.A., and Young, A.R. (eds) (2015), *Policy-Making in the European Union*, 7th edn. (Oxford and New York: Oxford University Press).

West European Politics (2011), Special issue on 'Linking Inter- and Intra-Institutional Change in the European Union', 34/1.

WEB LINKS

- Information on the state of play of all dossiers under discussion in the Ordinary Legislative Procedure can be found on the websites of the Commission (**www.ec.europa.eu/prelex**) and the EP (**www.europarl.europa.eu/oeil**), with links to relevant documents available from the Council's register of documents, available on its website (**www.consilium.europa.eu**). The European Parliament's conciliations and co-decision website (**www.europarl.europa.eu/code**) contains much useful and interesting information and statistics on dossiers now subject to the Ordinary Legislative Procedure.

- The Commission's and the European Parliament's Transparency Register, which is constantly being updated, can be viewed at: **www.ec.europa.eu/transparencyregister** See: **www.lobbyfacts.eu** for further information about interest representation in the EU and specifically about groups who have signed up for the Transparency Register. The web-site of stakeholder.eu is: **http://www.stakeholder.eu/**

- For the public register of expert groups advising the Commission, see: **www.ec.europa. eu./transparency/regexpert/index.cfm** for details of recipients of EU grants, see: **www.ec.europa.eu/grants/beneficiaries_en.htm** and for beneficiaries of EU public contracts, see: **www.ec.europa.eu./public_contracts/beneficiaries_en.htm** To see the rules on European Citizens' Initiatives, see: **http://ec.europa.eu/citizens-initiative/public/basic-facts**

- This **'world newspapers'** site provides links to newspapers from all over the world, including pan-European newspapers and links: **http://www.world-newspapers.com/europe.html** For detailed information on the Brussels press corps, see: **http://gareth-harding.com/the-myth-of-the-shrinking-eu-press-corps/**
- The websites of the main Brussels-focused think tanks include the Centre for European Policy Studies (**www.ceps.be**); the European Policy Centre (**www.theepc.be**); the Centre for European Reform (**www.cer.org.uk**); and the Trans European Policy Studies Association (**www.tepsa.be**).
- The website of the EUI Observatory on Institutional Change and Reforms contains links to the main documents introducing changes to the co-decision procedure (**www.eui.eu/Projects/EUDO-Institutions/DocumentsonLegislation.aspx**).
- The European Parliament's activity reports on co-decision and conciliation can be found at (**www.europarl.europa.eu/code**).

Visit the Online Resource Centre for this volume (see the following link) which includes a case study on the revision of the tobacco products directive. **www.oxfordtextbooks.co.uk/orc/kenealy4e/**

CHAPTER 7

Democracy in the European Union

Richard Corbett

▌ Summary

With so many decisions taken at EU level, what are the implications for democracy? All EU member states are (indeed, have to be, as a condition for membership) democratic. But when they take collective decisions through European institutions, the individual choices available to national democracies are naturally constrained. To what extent do democratic procedures at the European level compensate for this narrowing of choices at national level? Is there a 'democratic deficit'? How, anyway, do we measure 'democracy'? National democratic systems are diverse, but do have some common features: can we evaluate the EU using them as a yardstick?

Democracy Beyond the State?

Economic, environmental, and other forms of interdependence mean that national authorities alone cannot adequately deal with a growing number of problems. Many require concerted international action at various levels. But traditional methods of international cooperation are slow, cumbersome, and frequently opaque. They involve negotiations among ministers (and, in practice, mainly officials) representing their countries. In most cases, nothing can be agreed without consensus—thus creating a bias towards weak, lowest common denominator agreements. When an agreement is reached, it is submitted, if at all, as a *fait accompli* to national parliaments on a take-it-or-leave-it basis. The quality of democracy on such issues is low. Such are the working methods of the World Trade Organization (WTO), the International Monetary Fund (IMF), the World Bank, the United Nations (UN, including on climate change), NATO, and regular summits such as the Groups of 8 or 20 (G8 and G20) and countless other structures.

The EU purports to be different. It is not (always) in hock to the lowest common denominator. It has an elected multinational Parliament, directly representing citizens and bringing into the process representatives of both governing and opposition parties in each country. Decisions on legislation are taken in public. It has an independent executive, the European Commission, headed by Commissioners who are politically accountable to the Parliament. It has a common Court to ensure uniform interpretation of what has been agreed. It has safeguards to ensure that it respects fundamental rights. It has more developed mechanisms than any other international organization for informing, and sometimes involving, national parliaments. So, can we say that 'the EU not only forms a Union of sovereign democratic states, but also constitutes a democracy of its own' (Hoeksma 2010)? Can democracy work at all on an international basis?

Some argue that democracy can only work when there is a demos, that is, a common feeling of belonging to the same community (see Moravcsik 2002). A demos is usually held to involve speaking the same language and having a shared past and similar expectations about behaviour and values. Others argue that this view of democracy is tribalist and point out that if speaking a common language is a requirement, then Switzerland, India, Canada, South Africa, and many others cannot be categorized as democratic. Debates around 'demos' and decision-making will continue, but most agree that, as some decisions *are* taken at European level, it should be in as transparent, accountable, and democratic a way as possible.

The EU's basic rulebook is set out in the Treaties. They lay down its field of competences, the powers of its institutions, how to elect or appoint people to those institutions, and the details of its decision-making procedures. Some scholars argue that the Treaties can therefore be described as a *de facto* constitution (see Weiler 1999; Box 11.1). But, an attempt to rewrite those Treaties and formally label them as a 'constitution' failed in part because of reticence in some countries to the idea of the EU being a state-like federation. Opinions diverge as to what the nature of the EU should be and how far its democratic accountability should flow through democratically chosen governments in each county or, alternatively, through the directly elected Parliament. Or perhaps it should flow through both, with a dual democratic legitimacy, represented by its bicameral legislature: the Council representing the governments of the member states, whose democratic legitimacy is conferred on the national level, and the European Parliament, directly elected by citizens. It is not a question of whether national governments *or* the European Parliament best represent EU citizens: both are needed to sustain the EU's claim to be democratic.

Caveats, however, apply. First, the EU does not operate by simple majoritarian rule. The adoption of legislation by a qualified majority vote in the Council may indeed achieve more than the lowest common denominator consensus that applies in traditional international organizations. But it still requires a hefty majority: as we saw in Chapter 3, a qualified majority must comprise at least 65 per cent of the represented population in the Council. And in the Parliament, MEPs do not represent citizens equally, as the ratio of member to population is considerably lower in the smaller member states. This point was highlighted by the German Constitutional Court in its 2009 ruling on the Lisbon Treaty in which it held that, for that very reason, the EP could not be compared to a parliament representing a single people. Second, democratic choice of the executive is not as visible in the way that citizens are used to in a national context (see Hix 2008; Chevenal and Schimmelfennig 2013; Hurrelmann 2014). Neither by direct election nor through parliamentary elections does the electorate determine the political composition of the executive—or at best, only for its President (and for the others, in national segments). Do these caveats render the EU undemocratic? Is there a democratic deficit in the EU? (See Box 7.1.)

To shed more light on this discussion, we evaluate the democratic credentials of the EU by asking whether it matches some key features common to many modern democratic systems:

1. representation: is legislation adopted by representative assemblies?
2. are powers separated?
3. is the executive democratically accountable?
4. are fundamental rights guaranteed? and
5. do competing political parties offer voters genuine choice?

Legislating through Representative Assemblies

Under the Union's 'Ordinary Legislative Procedure', proposals need to be approved by directly elected representatives in the Parliament and indirectly elected representatives in the Council. The budget is similarly subject to the approval of both, as are almost all international agreements entered into by the Union. This dual requirement involves a scale of parliamentary scrutiny not found elsewhere beyond the level of the

> **BOX 7.1**   **Key concepts and terms**
>
> **Bicameralism:** from Latin *bi*, two + *camera*, chamber. When a legislature comprises two chambers, usually chosen by different methods or electoral systems.
>
> **Democratic deficit:** was a term initially used to denote the loss of democratic account-ability inherent in national parliaments transferring their right to legislate to ministers meeting in the Council. It was considered that this transfer of power should be compen-sated for by giving the EP the right to approve or reject EU legislation. Now that the EP has such powers (in most policy areas), the term has taken on a less precise meaning, often linked to the distance between EU institutions and voters.
>
> **European Convention on Human Rights:** (ECHR) is completely separate from the EU and its Court of Justice. It is an international treaty drafted in 1950 by the then newly formed **Council of Europe**. All (the now 48) Council of Europe member states are party to the Convention. Any person who feels his or her rights, as defined in the Charter, have been violated by a state can appeal to the **European Court of Human Rights**. Judg-ments finding violations are binding on the state(s) concerned.
>
> **Charter of Fundamental Rights of the European Union:** the EU has its own Charter of Rights that binds the EU institutions and EU law. Adopted initially as a political declara-tion by the EU institutions in 2000, it was given treaty status by the Treaty of Lisbon. It obliges EU institutions to respect the rights contained in the ECHR and others.

nation state. And, as we saw in Chapter 3, the EP is not a rubber stamp, subservient to the executive through a governing majority party or a coalition. It has been described as one of the most powerful legislatures in the world. We also saw (in Chapter 2) that it has not always been thus. Originally, the EP was merely a consultative body of seconded national parliamentarians, with final decisions being taken behind closed doors in the Council. After the first direct elections in 1979, it took three decades and successive revisions of the Treaty to change this state of affairs. Public perceptions have lagged behind, and the Parliament is still seen by many as a toothless tiger.

The EP is also sometimes held to be inadequate in another respect. It is not just the approval of legislation, but also the right to initiate it, which is held to be an important democratic criterion. After all, people are elected to parliaments having made promises to their voters: at least some of those promises require initiating or repealing legislation. But in the EU, there is a gap insofar as the EP cannot (except in a few specific cases) itself table proposals for adoption.

Yet this difference must be nuanced. Parliament and Council both have the right to request the Commission to put forward a legislative proposal. If it does not, both have ways and means to make life difficult for the Commission. Conversely, in national parliaments, which in most (but by no means all) cases do enjoy a right of legislative initiative, it is almost invariably the government that initiates proposals. It is in the give-and-take of debate and discussion between the legislature and the executive that ideas and initiatives emerge. This dynamic is not so different at EU level.

How representative are the Parliament and the Council?

Where the *Parliament* is concerned, the question of representation is often linked to electoral turnout. Turnout in the most recent EP elections has been around 43 per cent, or about the same as for mid-term US Congress elections (that is, when there is no Presidential election). By one view, it is normal that turnout is lower than for national parliamentary elections in European countries—less is at stake. But turnout for EP elections has also fallen—by nearly 20 percentage points over a 30-year period. This decline (accentuated by the accession of new member states, several of whom have a low turnout in all elections) is not actually less than the decline in turnout in national parliamentary elections in most countries. Declining participation is a challenge for democracy at all levels, not peculiar to the European level, even if the latter does have special features (see also Box 7.2).

BOX 7.2   **Compared to what?**

Referenda in EU member states

An alternative to representative democracy is direct democracy: the organizing of referenda to settle issues. National traditions diverge enormously, with referenda being (almost) unknown in most member states, or at least reserved only for constitutional changes. There is no provision under the Treaties to allow for EU-wide referenda, even on 'constitutional' changes to the EU system. Occasional proposals to introduce them come up against the opposition of countries that do not have referenda as part of their national traditions. Even if member states did agree, the question remains: of what majority decisions should be taken? Just a simple majority of those voting, or also a majority (or more) of states as well?

Some member states have organized national referenda on European issues. Most countries acceding to the EU did so, with only Norway deciding not to join. Some have had referenda on Treaty changes: two frequently (Ireland and Denmark, because of national constitutional requirements) and four (France, Luxembourg, the Netherlands, and Spain) occasionally. The UK coalition government in 2010 introduced legislation to require a national referendum for any future Treaty change that transfers powers or competences from the UK to the EU. In 2013, David Cameron, as the leader of the Conservative party, said that, if his party secured a majority at the 2015 general election, they would hold a referendum on UK membership (after the UK government renegotiated the terms of British membership) in 2017.

Debate on the merits of referenda on Treaties reached a crescendo during the ratification stage of the proposed Constitution in 2005. Most member states considered that it required detailed scrutiny and a vote by their national parliament. Four held national referenda: two approving it (Spain and Luxembourg) and two rejecting it (France and Netherlands). Although the grand total of the votes in the four countries showed a majority in favour—and every parliamentary vote approved it—the need for every single member state to ratify individually caused the Constitutional Treaty to fall.

Even on a low turnout, European elections do result in all the main strands of public opinion being represented in the EP. A transnational parliament highlights that most policy choices at European level have political, not national, dividing lines, with the different sides of an argument present in every member state. MEPs come from parties of the left and of the right and even some parties who are opposed to the very existence of the EU. Because EP elections frequently fall mid-term in national political cycles, they often result in a larger share of the seats going to opposition parties and smaller parties than would be the case in most national elections. EP elections thus can perhaps be dismissed as little more than a protest vote, but the results matter: they elect a wide variety of parties and thus have the effect of balancing the Council, whose members come exclusively from governing parties. The Parliament thus enhances pluralism and ensures that EU decisions are not left exclusively to ministers, diplomats and bureaucrats.

In the *Council*, member states' representatives (ministers) cast a number of votes related to their size, unlike in many federal systems where the 'chamber of states' often gives equal representation to all states irrespective of size. This proportionality can be seen as making the Council more representative of citizens. Yet, the fact that Council representatives must cast all their votes on behalf of their member state as a bloc could be viewed as distorting the representation of the people. However it is viewed, the weighted bloc vote is a feature that Council shares with the German Bundesrat, with which it also shares a number of other structural similarities (see Table 7.1).

TABLE 7.1	Compared to what? The Council and the German Bundesrat	
	Council	**Bundesrat**
Composition	Ministers from member state governments. Preparatory meetings by Permanent Representatives (Ambassadors) of member states in Brussels	Ministers from State (*Länder*) governments. Preparatory meetings by Permanent Representatives of States in Berlin
Voting	Each member state's vote weighted by size and cast as a bloc	Each State's (*Land*) vote weighted by size and cast as a bloc
Majorities required	Usually, threshold higher than simple majority (qualified majority or unanimity)	To disagree with Bundestag, threshold usually higher than simple majority (absolute majority)
Reconciliation with elected chamber	Conciliation Committee with EP	Conciliation Committee with Bundestag

As we saw in Chapter 3, what had originally been the key aspect of this weighted bloc vote, namely a fixed number of votes, disappeared in 2014 (though member states still have a right to call for a vote under the old system until 2017). The new system features a double majority based on one vote per state on the one hand, and a vote weighted by population (still cast as a bloc) on the other. Thus, the two traditional representational features found in bicameral federal systems—equality of states in one chamber and equality of citizens in the other—will both be found in a single chamber in the EU: the Council. Meanwhile, representation in the Parliament will over-represent smaller states.

Nonetheless, the Parliament and Council between them can test the acceptability of proposals from the point of view of both a majority of component states and the majority of the component population, with states represented as such in one chamber, and citizens in the other. They perform these functions in the context of a consensual, rather than an adversarial, style of political system. High thresholds are needed, notably in the Council, to adopt any legislation, budget or policy. All in all, the EU system involves a greater number of representative channels than can be found anywhere else in the world above the level of the nation state.

Involving national parliaments

Also unique are the Union's provisions for helping *national parliaments* scrutinize the participation of their government in EU institutions. In certain cases, national parliaments may intervene directly themselves independently of their national government. The Treaty lists a number of ways in which national parliaments 'contribute actively to the good functioning of the Union'.

One notable innovation in the Lisbon Treaty is a Protocol 'on the Application of the Principles of Subsidiarity and Proportionality'. It contains a new procedure allowing national parliaments to send, within eight weeks of receiving a legislative proposal, a reasoned opinion to the EU institutions stating why they consider that the draft does not comply with the principle of subsidiarity (that is, it goes beyond the remit of the EU). If such reasoned opinions come from enough national parliaments (roughly one-third), then the Commission must review the draft. It must then justify its decision to maintain, amend, or withdraw its proposal. Employing a football analogy, this procedure is known as the *'Yellow card'*. Alternatively, if such reasoned opinions come from more than half of EU parliaments, then a special vote must take place in the Council and in the EP, either of which can immediately kill off the proposal (by a simple majority in the EP or by a majority of 55 per cent of the members of the Council). This is known as the *'Orange card* procedure', as it was proposed by the Dutch (whose football team wears orange), and is not quite a red card. These procedures are an important safeguard to prevent over-centralization of powers, even if they are rarely needed: in the first five years of operation of the procedures, only two proposals triggered even a yellow card.

But the very existence of these procedures means that more national parliaments are paying close attention to European legislation —and in practice to its substance, rather than just checking subsidiarity. More may start holding committee hearings of their country's minister before Council meetings, as is already standard practice in the Nordic countries, or send comments on the substance of proposals directly to the Commission (there are currently some 200 such submissions per year). Also, parliaments confer among themselves, exchanging documents through an electronic exchange system, or meeting together at committee level or in interparliamentary conferences.

National parliaments are also involved in the process of future Treaty change. Any intergovernmental conference to revise the Treaty must (unless the EP decides otherwise) be preceded by a Convention composed of members of national parliaments, the EP, the Commission, and a representative of each government. And, of course, in most member states, national parliaments must ultimately ratify such Treaty changes.

The Treaty provisions involving national parliaments are thus quite numerous. In truth, most national parliaments have little time to devote to the fine-grained detail of EU issues. Unlike the EP, most are in a classic government/opposition structure where governing majorities mean that there is, in practice, little scope to amend government texts or reverse their policies. National parliaments also have less time, expertise, and staff to devote to European matters than does the EP, which works full time on EU affairs. National parliamentary procedures, practices, and timetables all diverge. Nonetheless, national parliaments are able to scrutinize and sometimes take part in EU decision-taking to a degree that simply does not exist in other international organizations. In sum, the involvement in the adoption of legislation of both a dedicated European parliament, and national parliaments, means that the EU's credentials measured against this particular yardstick of democracy are substantial.

Separation of Powers

Most democracies operate a separation of powers, although the separation of the legislative, executive, and judicial functions is not always clear. Indeed, many speak of a 'sharing' of powers across institutions, with checks and balances, rather than a separation of powers (Neustadt 1991). In particular, the executive and the legislative functions have tended to merge in most European democratic systems (although they remain more distinct in presidential systems, notably in the Americas).

Some European countries blur this distinction completely. The UK and Ireland, for instance, actually require members of the government to be simultaneously members of the legislature (even if this sometimes just means appointment to the UK House of Lords or the Irish Senate). By contrast, in France, a parliamentarian who becomes a minister must resign his/her seat for the duration of his/her ministerial mandate. Either way, it is the norm in most European countries for the executive to have a majority in Parliament, which, through the party system and other mechanisms, is usually compliant to the wishes of the executive. The separation between these two branches thus becomes less than clear. Only the judicial function remains clearly separate.

In the EU, the separation between the executive and the legislature is in some ways more distinct. Commissioners may not simultaneously be MEPs. In the EP there is no compliant governing majority for the executive. Thus, in adopting legislation, a majority has to be built anew for each item through explanation, persuasion, and negotiation. The EP's role is thus more proactive than that of most national parliaments in Europe.

The Council (of ministers) is the institution that muddies the waters. It is, of course, a co-legislator with the EP. However, it is also empowered to act as an executive in specific cases. When acting on macroeconomic policy or foreign affairs, it is fulfilling an executive rather than a legislative function, albeit one that consists largely of coordinating national executives rather than constituting a European one.

The European Council (of heads of state and government) does not directly act as an executive, nor as a legislature (indeed it is precluded from exercising a formal legislative role by the Treaty). Yet it influences both. Formally, it is the strategic body, charged with defining the 'the general political directions and priorities' of the Union. Informally, as a meeting of the most powerful political figures of the member states and the Union, it is often called upon to settle thorny political questions that can be of an executive, legislative, or constitutional nature. It also nominates or appoints a number of key posts in the Union. Its own President has a representational role in addition to his main task of preparing and building consensus. The European Council could be considered as a sort of collective 'head of state' of the Union in that its political role is similar to that of heads of state in national semi-presidential systems.

As for the judicial function, the European Court of Justice (ECJ) is composed of judges 'chosen from persons whose independence is beyond doubt'. They must take an oath to 'perform their duties impartially and conscientiously'. The deliberations of the Court are secret, so individual judges cannot be pressurized about judgments. We never know how any judge voted on any case unless they reveal how they voted in their memoirs.

Interestingly, the Court's members are appointed neither by the EU's executive nor by its legislature. Instead, they are appointed by the member states. The Court thus differs from the US Supreme Court, whose justices are appointed by federal authorities (President and Senate), not by the states. The only common European element in the appointment procedure of the members of the ECJ was introduced in the Lisbon Treaty. Appointees are now scrutinized by a panel chosen by the Council and consisting of seven former judges of the Court (or of national supreme courts) or eminent lawyers.

The appointment of individual judges therefore depends more on the government of the member state from which they originate than on the European executive or legislature. If there is any political consideration in their appointment, it is at the member state level and diffuse: each national government nominates only one judge. Another method used in many democracies to lessen political pressure on judges is to appoint them for a lengthy term of office, or even for life, as in the US Supreme Court. Judges in the ECJ are appointed for a (renewable) six-year term of office.

The Court has exercised an important independent function, ensuring that the institutions respect the law, though it can only do so when a matter is referred to it. The independence of the judiciary is clear. It has both struck down acts of the Union's political institutions and ruled against member states when they have failed to apply European law. Overall, the Union system is characterized by a separation, or sharing, of powers, which is at least as distinct as is the case in most of its member states.

Executive Accountability

The relationship between the outcome of European parliamentary elections and the composition of the executive is not as visible as it is in most European national parliamentary elections. But, the view that the Commission is 'unelected', unlike national governments that are, is simplistic. For example, the people do not elect the UK government: technically, the head of state (an unelected one at that) appoints a government but crucially the government must enjoy the confidence of the directly elected House of Commons. Similarly, the European Commission must enjoy the confidence of the European Parliament. The EP has always had the right to dismiss the Commission. It recently acquired the right to approve the appointment of the Commission, and indeed to elect its President. In fact the EP took such votes even before such procedures were laid down formally in the Treaties (see Table 7.2). The grilling that candidate Commissioners receive from EP committees at their confirmation hearings prior to their confirmation goes well beyond what ministers have to face in most European countries.

Despite all this, few citizens would consider the Commission to have an elected mandate. They might if the college of Commissioners were composed to reflect a majority party or, more likely, a majority coalition, in the EP. Yet a Commission thus composed is unlikely to emerge in the short to medium term: most governments want to nominate as the Commissioner from their country a member of their own political 'family'. What *has* begun to change is that the vote on the President of the Commission is becoming more political and linked to the outcome of elections. That vote is increasingly important, as the President's pre-eminence within the Commission has grown.

The change to the Treaties brought in by Lisbon refers to the 'election' of the President of the Commission by the Parliament. This vote is, as before, on a proposal of the European Council but the latter must now 'take into account the results of the European elections' in making its nomination. This provision potentially makes the

TABLE 7.2	Election of Commission President by the European Parliament	
	Incoming Commission Presidents	**Parliamentary Votes**
July 1992	Jacques Delors (third term)	278 votes for, 9 against
July 1994	Jacques Santer	260 votes for, 238 against (23 abstentions)
May 1999	Romano Prodi (for unfilled portion of Santer term)	392 in favour, 72 against, (41 abstentions)
September 1999	Romano Prodi (full 2000–5 term)	426 in favour to 134 against (32 abstentions)
July 2004	Jose Manuel Barroso (first term)	431 in favour to 251 against (44 abstentions)
September 2009	Jose Manuel Barroso (second term)	382 in favour to 219 against (117 abstentions)
July 2014	Jean Claude Juncker	422 in favour to 250 against (47 abstentions)

nomination similar to that of a head of state choosing a candidate Prime Minister who is capable of enjoying a parliamentary majority (see Box 7.3).

As a result, European political parties have started nominating their candidates for Commission President ahead of European elections. Even before Lisbon, ahead of the 2009 elections, the European People's Party (centre-right) was very clear that, in the event of it having the largest number of seats in the EP, it would expect the nominee for Commission President to come from its ranks. The Greens actually nominated Daniel Cohn-Bendit as their candidate, in the unlikely event that they would obtain a parliamentary majority. This momentum continued in 2014, with all the main European political parties naming their candidates for Commission President ahead of the elections, and televised debates held between these candidates ahead of the elections. The public attention this generated, however, varied from country to country.

In practice, no single party ever wins a majority of seats in the EP. Some bargaining and coalition forming is inevitable. But this kind of negotiation also occurs in most member states. The spectacularly direct link between the outcome of a parliamentary election and the designation of a prime minister seen (usually) in the UK is the exception rather than the norm. But the outcome even in, say, the Netherlands is that

---

BOX 7.3   **Compared to what?**

How are heads of executive chosen?

Commission President: elected by EP by an absolute majority on a proposal of the European Council, which must take account of the results of European Parliamentary elections.

German Chancellor: elected by the Bundestag by an absolute majority on a proposal of the Federal President.

UK Prime Minister: appointed by the Queen in light of advice as to who can secure a parliamentary majority in the lower chamber (House of Commons), but with no formal vote in parliament.

US President: chosen by an electoral college, whose members are elected in each state, normally as a function of which presidential candidate they support.

French Prime Minister: chosen by the directly elected President, without requiring a vote by parliament. However, the lower chamber (*Assemblée*) may dismiss the government by an absolute majority.

Swiss government: college of seven (with annual rotation of President among them), elected by the two chambers of the parliament (and comprising members of all major parties).

Swedish Prime Minister: nominated by Speaker of the parliament and serves unless opposed by an absolute majority of (single chamber) parliament.

Italian Prime Minister: nominated by President. His cabinet then requires approval by both chambers of the parliament (simple majority).

---

the public sees that the executive—usually consisting of a coalition of parties—that emerges is connected to an election and reflects its pattern of votes.

If this pattern becomes established practice at the EU level, it will happen only as regards the *head* of the EU's day-to-day executive: the Commission President. Does this 'halfway house' mean the Union is not comparable to a national democracy and can never be? Not necessarily. Take the case of Switzerland, which for over half a century has been governed by a coalition of the four largest parties, with an annually rotating President. Is such a collegiate system undemocratic? Does the lack of a direct relationship between the outcome of the parliamentary elections and the governing coalition render elections meaningless? Most Swiss would seriously object to their country being described as undemocratic. Yet the composition of the European Commission too is always (in political terms) a coalition of at least the three main political parties in Europe (the second Barroso Commission contained 13 Christian Democrats, 6 Socialists and 8 Liberals). The Commission would appear to be edging towards a hybrid of Swiss-style collegiality in its overall composition, but with a more majoritarian approach to designating its President.

If so, it is part of a long-term trend. Before 1994, Commissioners were simply designated by the member states to serve a four-year period without further ado. The

Maastricht Treaty changed the term of office to five years to coincide with the cycle of European Parliamentary elections, and provided for a vote of confidence by Parliament on the Commission as a whole. From 1999, the Amsterdam Treaty required a decisive Parliamentary vote on the designation of the President. The Lisbon Treaty characterized this vote as an election and required the European Council to make its nomination in function of the elections—further implying that the parliamentary majority is what will be decisive.

What of the President of the European Council? From December 2009 this post became a full-time and longer-term position, and thus vital for the dynamics of the European Council. The President's role as a facilitator and broker of deals at the highest political level is crucial, but he has no formal powers to take decisions as an individual, other than setting the agenda and convening meetings.

Certainly, it can be a confusing post for the public to understand. The press sometimes uses the term 'President of Europe' in some cases (and in some countries) for the President of the European Council and in other cases (and other countries) for the President of the Commission. With one chairing the day-to-day executive with a right of initiative, and the other chairing the strategic body laying down the Union's priorities and settling key issues, the difference between the two Presidents will not always be clear to average Europeans. Nor indeed for third countries: both Presidents represent the Union at external summit meetings.

But above all, the two Presidents have quite different forms of democratic legitimacy. That of the Commission President (elected by the EP and linked to majorities resulting from its elections) is likely to be more visible than that of the President of the European Council (elected by the heads of state or government of the member states). Suggestions that one or both should be directly elected are unlikely to get very far and would in any case likely cause further problems in the relationship between the two. Even with the best will in the world, some degree of uncertainty about these respective 'presidential' roles is likely to continue for years to come. The possibility of merging them, as has been done at the level of the High Representative (who is both a Vice-President of the Commission and chair of the Council (of Foreign Ministers), may return to the agenda. But it is unclear that it would ever gain sufficient support.

Finally, to the extent that the Council has an executive role, to whom is it accountable? Collectively, to no one—though most decisions require EP approval. But individually each of its members is accountable through a national government to a national parliament. Given that the Council's main 'executive' tasks are essentially about coordinating national policies (foreign policy, defence, macroeconomic coordination), this member state-based accountability may be considered appropriate. In any event, the Council must additionally justify itself in EP debates and answer parliamentary questions.

To sum up, accountability of the executive is present in the EU even if it is complex. For the main executive body (the Commission), a system close to what is found in most national contexts—that is, accountability to a Parliament—has been established. However, the system is not well known to citizens and the link between the results of parliamentary elections and the composition of the executive is not very visible. As for executive functions exercised elsewhere, they are either in an institution that is deliberately independent (the Central Bank), or else through institutions (Council and European Council) whose members are accountable individually to separate parliaments.

Respecting Fundamental Rights

Democracy is frequently defined as rule by the majority. But in modern times, it is increasingly seen as going hand-in-hand with respect for minorities and for the rights of individuals. Governments and even elected parliaments can be challenged in the courts should they fail to respect fundamental rights.

This feature can also be found in the EU. Initially it was exercised via case law: the ECJ acknowledged that the Union had to respect the fundamental rights that are common to the constitutional traditions of the member states. The Court recognized that all member states had signed the ECHR (the European Convention on Human Rights of the Council of Europe) and that it should be a source of law for its own deliberations. The Maastricht Treaty after 1992 entrenched this case law in the Treaty itself.

With the Lisbon Treaty, the Union obtained its own Charter of Rights (see Box 7.1), intended both to make those rights already contained in the ECHR visibly applicable to the Union but also to complement them with other rights. The Charter was framed in such a way as to be binding in the field of EU law. In other words, it binds the EU institutions, and member states when applying European law. It means that decisions or acts of the Union can be struck down by the Court should they fail to respect the rights contained in the Charter.

Furthermore, the Lisbon Treaty provided for the Union itself to accede to the ECHR. This will give plaintiffs the right to appeal to the European Court of Human Rights should they fail to gain satisfaction from the ECJ, much in the same way as in member states an appeal can be made against the final judgment of a national court. In other words, the EU's legal system will be subject to the same external yardstick as member states' legal systems. Thus, in relation to the formal criterion of respecting fundamental rights, the EU system and procedures measure up well.

Political Parties

Besides the constitutional requirements for democracy to function effectively, a functioning system of political parties is a practical need. As we have seen, the EP provides a pluralistic forum, with over 150 national political parties converging into political groupings. But to offer choice to the electorate in elections, and to channel and aggregate policy demands into workable programmes, party structures beyond Parliament are needed. One of the main points of debate about democracy in the EU is about whether pan-European democracy is impossible in the absence of pan-European parties (see Lindberg et al. 2008). In the European context, such parties have evolved as federations of national parties, but they are looser groupings than are parties in most national European contexts (see Box 7.4).

BOX 7.4   European political parties

European political parties are cross-national and reach beyond the EU. They are linked to but distinct from the political groups in the European Parliament. Three existed before the first direct elections to the EP:

- the Party of European Socialists (PES), comprising parties affiliated to the Socialist International;
- the European People's Party (EPP), comprising Christian Democrats and other centre-right or conservative parties; and
- the Alliance of Liberals & Democrats for Europe (ALDE), previously the European Liberal, Democratic and Reformist Party (ELDR), comprising a variety of liberal and allied parties.

Two more emerged between 1979 and 2004 (and MEPs from these two parties currently sit in the same Group in the Parliament):

- the European Green Party;
- the European Free Alliance, comprising regionalist and nationalist parties such as the Scottish, Flemish, Basque, Corsican, Sardinian, Catalan, and Welsh nationalists.

A number of other (smaller) European political parties were created following the adoption of a system for financing such parties in 2004. Some on the right or far right have been through several configurations, and regroupings, as alliances have shifted. As they stand in 2014:

- the European Left (which includes a number of Communist or former Communist parties);
- the European Democratic Party (which describes itself as a 'centrist political party in favour of European integration');
- the Alliance of European Conservatives and Reformists (AECR, including notably the UK Conservatives);
- Movement for a Europe of Liberties and Democracy (Eurosceptic national conservatives);
- the European Alliance for Freedom (EAF) (far right, ultra nationalists);
- the Alliance of European National Movements (far right, ultra-nationalist);
- Europeans United for Democracy (formerly EU Democrats) (Eurosceptic);
- the European Christian Political Movement (socially conservative)

The recognition and the development of these parties have been incremental. The Treaty of Maastricht introduced a new article referring to the importance of European political parties. Later, they were granted legal personality and—crucially—access to funding, provided certain conditions are met, such as being represented in a sufficient number of member states (at least one quarter) and respecting the principles of the EU (such as liberty, human rights, and so on), although they do not have to support the existence of the Union itself. They also must publish their accounts and have them independently audited, as well as publish the names of any donors contributing more than €500. Parties may not accept donations of more than €12,000 from any single donor, nor accept anonymous donations. The money provided from the EU budget is for European parties; it may not be passed on to national parties.

The main parties are active in a growing number of areas. They organize regular congresses, composed of delegates from the respective national parties and involving their EP Group. Their leaders can hold 'summits' (often prior to European Council meetings) with fellow party members in the Commission, EP, and heads of government. They adopt common manifestos for European elections. Their decision-making tends in practice to be by consensus among the national member parties, which means that the content of their policies tends towards the lowest common denominator. However, the incentive to achieve convergence can shape the positions of individual national parties.

What is the real impact of these parties? They are generally unknown to the public, except in the broadest sense that—for the Socialists, Liberals, Greens, and Christian Democrats—their national voters may be aware that they are part of a larger European grouping and that they work together in the EP. Only a sophisticated minority of voters will actually be aware of the common manifestos on which they stand in European elections. However, even without such awareness, the elaboration of such manifestos can lead to a degree of convergence around common positions of corresponding parties. The parties do certainly play a role in the 'division of spoils' in terms of securing prominent positions at European level, and not just within the EP. For example, it was quite clear at the time of the choice of President of the European Council and High Representative in 2009, and again in 2014, that these posts were to be shared between the EPP and the Socialists.

Parties also play a role in the choice of President of the Commission, as we have seen earlier in the chapter. The further development of this role provides an opportunity for European political parties to become more visible, as well as offering the electorate a choice of personalities and not just of policies.

In short, European political parties do play a role, not just in representation but also in policy formation and in the choice of key political office holders. That role remains limited and rather invisible to the bulk of the electorate. However, it has been developing and expanding, even if the process has been slow and very gradual.

Conclusion

The EU requires that its member states be democratic and respect fundamental rights (and even has a procedure for suspending a member state that ceases to fulfil this requirement). Whether the EU itself fulfils these criteria is a more complex question. It has given rise not only to much debate, but also to many of the Treaty amendments of the last 30 years.

We have seen that the EU system does fulfil fundamental democratic norms, but in a way that is more complex and less visible to the public than is the case at national level. Like any political system, it has its own idiosyncrasies. Inevitably, its detailed functioning is different from what people are familiar with within their national system (themselves diverse). Those differences and complexity give rise to misunderstandings amongst concerned citizens, and can also be exploited by its opponents.

Nonetheless, the EU is unique in how far it goes to try to apply democratic principles at a level above the nation state. How successful it is, remains open to debate (see Habermas 2008). Nevertheless, there is no doubt that the debate itself is one of the features of the EU that make it so fascinating.

DISCUSSION QUESTIONS

1. How can democratic accountability be assured for those matters dealt with at European level? Should it be via national parliamentary scrutiny over their own government's negotiating position, or via the European Parliament, or both?

2. Does the relatively low turnout in European elections matter?

3. Are fundamental rights sufficiently protected at European level?

4. Should the European Commission emanate from a parliamentary majority in the EP?

5. Are referenda in individual member states an appropriate way to ratify EU Treaties?

FURTHER READING

For detailed accounts of the EP, see Corbett et al. (2011) and Judge and Earnshaw (2008). Internal cleavages and voting patterns in the Parliament are covered by Hix et al. (2007) and Hix (2009), who also (2008) offers a comprehensive programme for democratic reform of the EU. For a critical appraisal of the EP's links with the public, see Hug (2010). For different evaluations of the democratic credentials of the EU and the challenges of transnational democracy, see Pinder (1999), Moravscik (2002), Siedentop (2002), Bogdanor (2007), and Hoeksma (2010). For an interesting argument that the EU should be evaluated not as a democracy but rather as a 'demoicracy'; that is a polity of multiple, distinct peoples, see

Nicolaidis (2012, 2013) and *Journal of European Public Policy* (2015). Glencross (2011) offers interesting insights on ways to legitimize the EU. Corbett (2002) assesses the impact of having an elected parliament on the process of integration. For an interesting examination of alternative futures by a leading European intellectual, see Habermas (2008).

Bogdanor, V. (2007), *Democracy, Accountability and Legitimacy in the European Union* (London: Federal Trust for Education and Research).

Corbett, R. (2002), *The European Parliament's Role in Closer EU Integration* (Basingstoke and New York: Macmillan).

Corbett, R., Jacobs, J., and Shackleton, M. (2011), *The European Parliament*, 8th edn. (London: John Harper Publishing).

Glencross, A. (2011), 'A Post-National EU? The Problem of Legitimising the EU without the Nation and National Representation', *Political Studies*, 59/2: 348–67.

Habermas, J. (2008), *Europe: The Faltering Project* (Cambridge and Malden, MA: Polity).

Hix, S. (2008), *What's Wrong with the European Union and How to Fix It* (London: Polity).

Hix, S. (2009), *What to Expect in the 2009–14 European Parliament: Return of the Grand Coalition?* (Stockholm: Swedish Institute for European Policy Analysis).

Hix, S., Noury, A., and Roland, G. (2007), *Democratic Politics in the European Parliament* (Cambridge and New York: Cambridge University Press).

Hoeksma, J. (2010), *A Polity called EU: The European as a Transnational Democracy* (Amsterdam: Europe's World).

Hug, A. (2010), *Reconnecting the European Parliament and its People* (London: Foreign Policy Centre).

Journal of European Public Policy (2015), Special Issue on Demoicracy in the European Union, 22/1.

Judge, D., and Earnshaw, D. (2008), *The European Parliament*, 2nd edn. (London: Palgrave Macmillan).

Moravcsik, A. (2002), 'Reassessing Legitimacy in the European Union', *Journal of Common Market Studies*, 40/4: 603–24.

Nicolaidis, K. (2012), The Idea of European Demoicracy, in J. Dickson and P. Eleftheriadis (eds), *Philosophical Foundations of European Union Law* (Oxford and New York: Oxford University Press).

Nicolaidis, K. (2013), 'European Demoicracy and Its Critics', *Journal of Common Market Studies*, 51/2: 351–69.

Pinder, J. (1999), *Foundations of Democracy in the European Union* (Basingstoke and New York: Macmillan and St. Martin's Press).

Siedentop, L. (2002), *Democracy in Europe* (Harmondsworth: Penguin).

 WEB LINKS

- Websites of the institutions: see Chapter 3.
- Voting Behaviour in the European Parliament: **http://www.votewatch.eu/**
- European People's Party: **http://www.epp.eu/**

- Party of European Socialists: **http://www.pes.org/**
- European Liberal Democrats: **http://www.aldeparty.eu/en**
- European Green Party: **http://europeangreens.eu/**
- COSAC: **http://www.cosac.eu/en/cosac/**

 Visit the Online Resource Centre that accompanies this book for additional material: **www.oxfordtextbooks.co.uk/orc/kenealy4e/**

PART IV

The EU and
The Wider World

CHAPTER 8

EU Expansion and Wider Europe

Graham Avery

▌ Summary

The European Union (EU) has expanded many times, and its widening continues. Enlargement illustrates the success of the European model of integration. But it also poses fundamental questions. Enlargement has implications both for how the EU works (its structure and institutions) and for what it does (its policies). The expansion to include countries of Central and Eastern Europe showed how the EU's transformative power can promote stability, prosperity, and security. The EU has extended the prospect of membership to countries in the Balkans and Turkey. It has developed a 'neighbourhood' policy towards other countries, some of which may want to join in future. Where will the EU's final frontiers lie?

Introduction

The EU's process of expansion goes to the heart of important questions about the nature and functioning of the Union. Why do countries wish to join? How does the EU decide its future shape and size? How should it interact with its neighbours? Enlargement is also ongoing: the EU is committed to further expansion, so past experience can help to guide future policy.

It is often said that enlargement is the EU's most successful foreign policy. It has indeed extended prosperity, stability, and good governance to neighbouring countries by means of its membership criteria, and this success gives enlargement a special place among the EU's external policies. But enlargement is much more than foreign policy: it is the process whereby the external becomes internal. It is about how non-member countries become members, and shape the development of the EU itself. In accepting new partners, and deciding the conditions under which they join, existing members define the EU's future composition and collective identity. In that sense, enlargement could better be described as 'existential' policy: when the EU makes choices of new members, it determines its own future.

Widening versus deepening

The prospect of enlargement poses basic questions both for applicant countries and existing members. Before applying, countries need to analyse how membership will affect them. What will accession (see Box 8.1) mean in political and economic terms? What will be the costs and benefits? What should be the country's long-term aims as a member? This kind of reflection raises questions of national strategy and identity.

A recurrent theme in the development of the EU has been the tension between the 'widening' of its membership and the 'deepening' of integration between its members. Each time the EU contemplates a further expansion, its members are compelled to address fundamental questions that do not present themselves to policy-makers in the normal course of events.

When considering who should be new members, the EU has to reflect on what it should do with them (what set of common policies?) and how to do it (with what institutional set-up?). Debates on the future of European integration regularly accompany enlargement, although for countries trying to join the EU the 'widening versus deepening' debate can seem introspective. But the potential impact of enlargement on the Union's capacity to take decisions is an important question. Non-members apply to join the EU because it is attractive, and one of the reasons why it is attractive is that the Union is effective in taking decisions and developing policies. To expand without safeguarding its effectiveness would be an error. Enlargement policy is thus linked with wider debates on European integration. In fact, the accession of new members often provides an occasion for institutional reform.

> **BOX 8.1   Key concepts and terms**
>
> **Absorption capacity** refers to the EU's ability to integrate new members into its system.
>
> **Accession** is the process whereby a country joins the EU and becomes a member state.
>
> **Benchmarks** in accession negotiations are conditions for opening and closing 'chapters' related to specific EU policies
>
> **Candidate** refers to a country whose application for membership the EU has confirmed, but which is not yet a member.
>
> **Conditionality** refers to the fact that accession is conditional on a country fulfilling the criteria for membership.
>
> **European Economic Area** (EEA) is an arrangement that extends the EU's single market to Norway, Iceland, and Liechtenstein.
>
> **Screening** occurs at the start of negotiations when the applicant and the Commission examine the *acquis* to see if there are particular problems to be resolved.
>
> **Variable geometry**, also known as multi-speed Europe, is the idea that not all EU member states should take part in every field of policy.

Have successive enlargements weakened the EU? Although the arrival of new members requires a period of 'settling in', it is often followed by the development of new policies and the strengthening of the institutional framework. For example, the EU's structural funds and a more ambitious cohesion policy resulted from the accession of Greece, Portugal, and Spain, poorer countries needing financial aid. Later it was feared that the accession of Austria, Sweden, and Finland, countries that had pursued neutrality or non-alliance, would put a stop to the EU's Common Foreign and Security Policy (CFSP). But in practice these countries have viewed the CFSP's development more favourably than some of the older members.

From time to time older members complain that it was easier to take decisions when the EU was smaller. That may be true (though crises were a regular feature of the EU in its early days). But nevertheless it is arguable that successive increases in size have allowed the EU to develop more substantial and effective policies, internally and externally, than would have been possible with a smaller group. The process of widening has often accompanied or driven deepening: 'more' has not led to 'less'.

Enlargement as soft power

The success of enlargement in helping to drive political and economic change in Central and East European countries offers a good illustration of the EU's 'soft power'—its capacity to persuade others to want for themselves what the Union wants for them (Nye 2004; Grabbe 2006). The conditionality (see Box 8.1) or leverage of prospective membership encouraged policy-makers in those countries to pursue basic reforms, and this external pressure from the EU was a powerful transformative factor in the pre-accession period. As countries in transition, they were in search of western political and economic models, and needed sustained external assistance.

Conditionality was not employed in earlier enlargements. When the Commission proposed in 1975 that Greece's membership should be preceded by a period of preparation, the EU's leaders rejected the idea. Later, Austria, Sweden, and Finland were able to join within two or three years of applying for membership. The principle of conditionality was developed for the countries of Central and Eastern Europe because the existing members were apprehensive that taking in so many new countries without adequate preparation could impair the EU. It was enlightened self-interest, rather than altruism, that led the Union in 1993 to define the membership criteria for the countries of Central and Eastern Europe.

These membership requirements (referred to as the Copenhagen criteria, see Box 8.2) have become the standard template for enlargement. They require a

---

BOX 8.2   **Criteria for membership**

TREATY PROVISIONS

The Treaty on European Union states:

Article 49:
Any European state which respects the values referred to in Article 2 and is committed to promoting them may apply to become a member of the Union.

Article 2:
The Union is founded on the values of respect for human dignity, freedom, democracy, equality, the rule of law, and respect for human rights, including the rights of persons belonging to minorities. These values are common to the Member States in a society in which pluralism, non-discrimination, tolerance, justice, solidarity, and equality between women and men prevail.

COPENHAGEN CRITERIA

The European Council at Copenhagen (1993) stated in its conclusions that membership requires:

- that the candidate country has achieved stability of institutions guaranteeing democracy, the rule of law, human rights, and respect for and protection of minorities;
- the existence of a functioning market economy as well as the capacity to cope with competitive pressure and market forces within the Union;
- the ability to take on the obligations of membership including adherence to the aims of political, economic, and monetary union.

It added another criterion for enlargement:

- The Union's capacity to absorb new members, while maintaining the momentum of European integration, is also an important consideration in the general interest of both the Union and the candidate countries.

wide-ranging assessment of a country's political, economic, and administrative standards that goes further than any examination made by the EU of its existing members (although member states can be sanctioned for failure to respect the Union's basic principles). The membership criteria are asymmetric: the Union demands higher standards of new members than it does of itself. Also, the leverage of membership is effective only in the pre-accession period. After joining, an applicant country becomes a member like others.

An institutional paradox

The enlargement process casts interesting light on the functioning of the EU's institutions.

The mode of operation for enlargement is essentially intergovernmental. The Council adopts all decisions on enlargement by unanimity. While majority voting in EU decision-making has been extended in many areas, no one has ever suggested extending it to enlargement. Accession negotiations take place in an intergovernmental conference organized between the member states and the applicant state. The result is an Accession Treaty, signed and ratified by sovereign states.

The roles of the European Parliament and the Commission in the process of enlargement are limited. The Parliament has the right to approve or reject enlargement, but only at the end of the negotiation process, when it votes on a yes/no basis without being able to modify the Accession Treaty. During accession negotiations, Parliament is informed regularly, but has no seat at the table.

The Commission's status in accession negotiations is not the same as in external negotiations where it acts as spokesperson. In accession conferences the Council presidency, rather than the Commission, presents EU positions, even on matters where the Commission has competence. Formally the Commission is not the EU's negotiator, although it may be mandated by the Council to 'seek solutions' with applicants. Nevertheless, in practice the Commission plays an extremely influential role in the process of enlargement. In fact, it exercises more influence over applicant countries than after they become members. The Commission is better equipped technically than member states to monitor the progress of applicant countries in respect of the criteria for EU membership, and its regular reports on each country provide the benchmarks for decisions on the conduct of enlargement. It is the Commission that presents proposals to the Council for 'common positions' to be taken by the EU side, and it is thus in a position to act as an intermediary with the applicant countries. It can (and should) take account of the future interests of the EU by making proposals that reflect the views of the future members as well as existing ones.

Within the Council, enlargement is handled in the General Affairs Council, not the Foreign Affairs Council. One upshot is that the EU's High Representative for foreign and security policy has no role in accession negotiations. The fact that the Commission, not the European External Action Service, manages Enlargement policy shows that it is not considered primarily foreign policy.

How the EU has Expanded

The first applications for membership were made by the United Kingdom (UK), Denmark, and Ireland in 1961, soon after the European Communities came into existence. Although that first attempt was stopped when France said 'No' (twice), the three tried again, and joined in 1973. This first enlargement was followed by others (see Box 8.3) and more are in prospect (see Box 8.4). Over time the number of EU member states has quadrupled, its population has tripled, and its official languages have increased from four to 24. In fact there have been few periods in the life of the EU when it was not engaged in discussions with prospective members.

BOX 8.3	Chronology of enlargement		
	Application for Membership	Opening of negotiations	Accession
United Kingdom	1967	1970	1973
Denmark	1967	1970	1973
Ireland	1967	1970	1973
Greece	1975	1976	1981
Portugal	1977	1978	1986
Spain	1977	1979	1986
Austria	1989	1993	1995
Sweden	1991	1993	1995
Finland	1992	1993	1995
Hungary	1994	1998	2004
Poland	1994	1998	2004
Slovakia	1995	2000	2004
Latvia	1995	2000	2004
Estonia	1995	1998	2004
Lithuania	1995	2000	2004
Czech Republic	1996	1998	2004
Slovenia	1996	1998	2004
Cyprus	1990	1998	2004
Malta	1990	2000	2004

Cont. ➤

Cont.

Romania	1995	2000	2007
Bulgaria	1995	2000	2007
Croatia	2003	2004	2013

Notes:

The UK, Denmark, and Ireland first applied in 1961, but negotiations ended in 1963 after France vetoed their admission.

Norway applied twice (1967, 1992) and completed negotiations (begun in 1970, 1993), but Norwegians twice said 'No' in referenda (1972, 1994).

Switzerland made an application in 1992 but suspended it in the same year after a 'No' in a referendum on the EEA.

Iceland made an application in 2009 and negotiations began in 2010, but were suspended in 2013 by its government.

In 1990 enlargement took place without accession when East Germany joined the German Federal Republic.

In response to Morocco's approach in 1987—not a formal application—the EC deemed that the country was not European.

But for countries wishing to join, the path to membership is not easy. Negotiations for accession are arduous (see Boxes 8.5 and 8.7): there is no guarantee that they will end in agreement, or by a certain date, and the bargaining is one-sided. The EU insists that applicant countries accept all its rules (known as the *acquis*), and allows delays of application (transitional periods, see Box 8.1) only in exceptional cases. Meanwhile, as the EU's policies have expanded over the years, the 'bar' for applicants to cross has been raised to a higher level. But after all, they applied to join the EU, not vice versa. The EU has never invited others to join its club—in fact it has tended to discourage them. In this sense, the EU's strategy for enlargement has been reactive rather than proactive. The Union has grown because of its magnetism for neighbouring countries, not as a result of expansionist ambition.

Why countries want to join

Countries apply to join the EU because they consider that membership is in their political and economic interest. While opinions have differed, according to the applicant state, on whether economics or politics were the most important factor, both have always counted. In the case of the UK, its application was motivated by the prospective benefits of the common market for its trade and economic growth. But its leaders also realized that the original six members were on the way to creating a European system from which the UK could not afford politically to be excluded. It

BOX 8.4	Prospective members			
		Application for membership	Candidate status	Opening of negotiations
Turkey		1987	1999	2005
Macedonia (FYROM)		2004	2005	
Montenegro		2008	2010	2012
Albania		2009		
Serbia		2009	2012	2014
Bosnia-Herzegovina				
Kosovo				

Notes:

This list includes all countries currently considered by the EU to be in the accession process.

When the EU decides that an applicant country has made sufficient progress, it may award it the status of 'candidate'. Until then, it has the status of 'potential candidate'.

Kosovo is not recognized as a state by some EU members.

was natural for Ireland and Denmark, having close economic relations with the UK, to apply at the same time.

The applications from Greece, Portugal, and Spain were made in different circumstances. After getting rid of totalitarian regimes, these countries wanted membership as a confirmation (and guarantee) of their return to democracy. The sense of being accepted back into the European family was as important to them as the prospect of access to the common market and the budget. Austria, Sweden, and Finland applied for membership because their access to the common market through the European Economic Area (EEA; see Box 8.1) obliged them to accept EU rules without having a say in deciding them. They also realized that the collapse of the Soviet Union created a new political situation in Europe in which their traditional neutrality was less appropriate.

When the 10 countries of Central and Eastern Europe made the change from communism and Soviet domination, they turned to the EU for economic assistance and for membership. Like Greece, Spain, and Portugal, they wanted to rejoin the European family, and to consolidate their return to democracy. For their transition from central planning to market economy, the EU's standards offered a convenient 'template'. Uncertain of Russia's future role, they wanted EU membership for security as a back up to NATO membership, which they pursued at the same time (see Box 8.6).

| BOX 8.5 | The path to membership |

Start. A country submits an application for membership to the Council of the European Union

1. The Council considers whether the country satisfies the conditions of Article 49 (see Box 8.2)

2. The Council asks the Commission for an Opinion.

3. The Commission delivers its Opinion to the Council.

4. The Council confirms the applicant country's status as a candidate.

5. The Council decides to open accession negotiations, conducted in an intergovernmental conference between the EU member states and each applicant individually.

6. The Commission screens (see Box 8.1) the 34 chapters of the acquis with the applicant

7. Individual chapters in the negotiations are opened when the Council decides that the applicant has met the relevant benchmarks (see Box 8.1).

8. The applicant presents its position for that chapter; the Commission proposes a 'common position' of the EU, the Council approves it, and presents it to the applicant.

9. After agreement is reached on each chapter, it is closed when the EU decides that the applicant has met the relevant benchmarks.

10. When all chapters are closed, the EU and the applicant agree on a draft Treaty of Accession (which may include other applicants).

11. The Commission issues an Opinion on the Treaty.

12. The European Parliament gives its consent.

13. The member states and the applicant(s) sign the Treaty.

14. The signatory states ratify the Treaty according to their national procedures, which may include a referendum.

Finish. The Treaty comes into force, and the applicant country becomes a member state.

> **BOX 8.6** **Compared to what?**
>
> **EU and NATO—a double race to membership**
>
> After the end of the Cold War, most of the countries of Central and Eastern Europe wanted to join the North Atlantic Treaty Organization (NATO) as well as the EU. NATO is a transatlantic alliance created in 1949 in face of a perceived threat from the Soviet Union. Its members are committed to mutual assistance under Article 5 of the NATO Treaty, which says that 'an armed attack against one or more of them in Europe or North America shall be considered an attack against them all'. NATO now has 28 members:
>
> - US, Canada,
> - 22 EU states (all except Austria, Cyprus, Finland, Ireland, Malta, Sweden),
> - Norway, Iceland, Turkey, Albania.
>
> Most other European states, including Russia, have an association with NATO but are not full members.
>
> For the countries of Central and Eastern Europe, concerned about Russia's future intentions, NATO offers hard security in the military sense, including its nuclear 'umbrella'. In contrast, the EU offers soft security in the sense of membership of its political and economic union. For these countries NATO was easier to join than the EU because:
>
> - NATO has less demanding membership requirements, mainly concerning the organization and equipment of troops,
> - NATO's leading member, the US, pressed for its enlargement.
>
> The result of the double enlargement is that the membership of the two organizations now largely overlaps, which makes it easier for them to work together. But the NATO/EU relationship is not simple, and there remains a basic asymmetry. NATO, unlike the EU, includes the US. NATO has the military tools to deal with the results of insecurity, while the EU has the civilian tools to deal with its causes, by promoting integration and good governance.

Recent enlargements

The disintegration of the Soviet bloc in 1989 was a seismic shock, creating risks of instability in Europe. Civil war broke out in ex-Yugoslavia, and this strife could have occurred elsewhere if events had unfolded differently. But the countries of Central and Eastern Europe succeeded in charting a route to democracy, stability, and prosperity by making far-reaching economic, social, and political reforms. The prospect of EU membership served to guide them in a peaceful 'regime change' in which the process of Europeanization (adapting domestic politics to the EU's rules, norms, and policies) played a key role (see Chapter 4 and Grabbe 2006).

Faced in the early 1990s by many new aspirants for membership, the EU responded cautiously. At first, 'Europe Agreements' on aid, trade, and political links

---

BOX 8.7   **How it really works**

Joining the EU singly or together

The EU says it treats all applicant countries on their merits, according to the principle of 'differentiation': this means that the path to membership depends on individual progress in meeting the criteria, with no linkage between applicants. That is why the EU conducts accession negotiations with each applicant separately. Differentiation also allows it to play them off against each other ('divide and rule').

By creating competition between applicant countries the EU brings the market into the enlargement process. The wish to emulate others, and the fear of being left behind, helped to push the Central and East European countries forward to membership together in 2004.

Although each accession negotiation is separate, and a country can join singly (as did Greece and Croatia) there have usually been groups or waves of accession in the past.

Applicants often demand a target date for membership. But the EU does not concede that until the end of negotiations, since the promise of a date weakens the conditionality of the process.

Accession negotiations are 'asymmetric': the EU is in a far stronger bargaining position.

---

were negotiated with countries of Central and Eastern Europe, to which the EU initially refused to promise membership. But at the Copenhagen summit in 1993, the Union accepted that these countries could join when they fulfilled the criteria for membership, which were defined there and became known as the 'Copenhagen criteria' (Box 8.2).

In the accession negotiations, which opened with six countries in 1998 and six more in 2000, the main problems were:

- free movement of labour: the EU allowed old members to maintain restrictions on workers from new member states for up to seven years;

- agricultural policy: the EU insisted on a period of 12 years for introducing direct payments to farmers in the new member states; and

- the EU budget: the level of payments to new, much poorer members was a difficult issue (see Avery 2004).

Meanwhile the 'conditionality' of the process created a framework in which the Central and East European countries were able to make the transition to democracy and market economy peacefully and on a durable basis. The economic consequences of enlargement were positive for both old and new member states, and created conditions for the European economy to face increased global competition. However, the influx of migrants from the new members caused social problems in some countries, and the persistence of bad governance (corruption, maladministration, weak judiciary) in some countries led to the realization that the accession criteria should be applied more rigorously. As a result, the EU adopted a 'New Approach' to accession negotiations in 2012, under which the chapters on fundamental rights, justice, freedom, and security are treated as a priority.

Nevertheless the enlargement to Central and Eastern Europe was an extraordinary episode in the history of European integration, and it shifted the EU's scale of activity to a continental level. Previous enlargements took place in a Europe divided between East and West, while this enlargement helped to unite it. In awarding the Peace Prize to the EU in 2012 the Norwegian Nobel Committee cited enlargement, declaring that it had 'helped to transform most of Europe from a continent of war to a continent of peace'.

The admission of the countries of Central and Eastern Europe has led to an interesting debate among political scientists. According to liberal intergovernmentalism, the EU-15 should have been guided in their decision to enlarge by the expected costs and benefits, and since enlargement proceeds by unanimity all member states must have reckoned that it was advantageous to them. But was that really so? In fact, some members were quite reluctant. According to the constructivist approach, which emphasizes the role of principles and values, it was the historic promise of peace and unity, rather than the material prospects, which led to a 'rhetorical entrapment' of the EU's member states in the process of enlargement (see Schimmelfennig and Sedelmeier 2005).

Another thesis is that the EU's policy towards its neighbourhood has been an exercise in empire-building (Zielonka 2007). In this analysis, enlargement has been an imperial policy of the EU, designed to assert political and economic control over the impoverished Eastern part of the continent and to fill the power vacuum left by the demise of the Soviet Union. But 'empire' is hardly an accurate description of the Union, which has no ruler or ruling state, and although it exercises strong pressure on applicant countries to accept its rules and values, it offers in return the prospect of accession with full rights of membership.

Leaving and Joining

States may leave the EU, as well as join it. The procedure in Article 50 of the EU Treaty provides for two years of negotiation with the departing state; if that does not lead to agreement, it is free to leave. No EU member has invoked this procedure, although Eurosceptic parties in several countries seek withdrawal from the EU. In the UK, demand has grown for a referendum on EU membership.

The frontiers of the EU have changed from time to time for reasons other than accession. Parts of the territories of member states have gained independence—Algeria from France in 1962, Greenland from Denmark in the 1980s—but chose not to remain within the EC. In 1990, when East Germany (not a member state of the EU) and West Germany (a founding member state) reunified, 16 million East Germans joined the EU.

National independence movements, which have gained popularity in Scotland, Catalonia, Flanders and elsewhere, pose a question for which the EU has no precedent: the division of one of its member states into two states, both of which wish to remain within the EU. The EU Treaty is silent on this question, and the Union itself has no explicit policy on independentism other than to respect the constitutional arrangements of its member states. However, it is clear that EU membership would not be automatic for a newly independent state: amendment of the Treaty, requiring unanimity, would be needed (Avery 2014a, 2014b; Kenealy 2014; Kenealy and MacLennan 2014).

Prospective Members

The EU considers: Turkey, the Western Balkan countries as prospective members (see Box 8.4). Others—Norway, Iceland, and Switzerland—have applied for membership in the past. Although the Treaty says that any European state may apply to become a member (see Box 8.2), other countries are at present discouraged from applying, including those subject to the EU's Neighbourhood Policy (see later).

Balkan countries

In South-east Europe about 20 million people remain outside the EU:

- Albania: 3.6 million
- Bosnia-Herzegovina: 4.5 million
- Former Yugoslav Republic of Macedonia (FYROM): 2.1 million
- Kosovo: 1.8 million
- Montenegro: 0.7 million
- Serbia: 7.3 million.

A glance at the map (Figure 8.1) shows that the EU surrounds these countries—known as the Western Balkans. They are trying to make the political and economic reforms necessary to join the EU, but have a difficult legacy of ethnic, social, and religious conflict. For most of the twentieth century the region was united in Yugoslavia, but the disintegration of that federation in the 1990s led to civil war and the intervention of the UN and NATO.

Ancient rivalries and fears lie just below the surface, and problems of frontiers and statehood persist. The question of Kosovo's international status is not fully resolved (its independence from Serbia is not recognized by all EU members), and its government is supervised by a European Union Rule of Law Mission (EULEX). Bosnia is still under external tutelage: a UN High Representative, who is also an EU Special Representative, supervises it. Coupled with problems of poor governance,

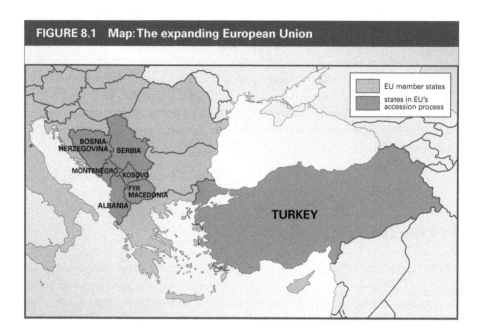

FIGURE 8.1   Map: The expanding European Union

corruption, and criminality, the region suffers from a syndrome of political dependency on external actors. But reforms, and EU membership itself, require autonomy and a functioning democracy.

These Balkan countries are at different stages on the way to EU membership (see Box 8.4). Although the United States and Russia have influence in the region, the international community sees it as Europe's main responsibility. At a summit at Thessaloniki in 2003, the EU's leaders recognized all the countries of the Western Balkans as prospective members, and the Union now provides financial and technical help through its pre-accession programmes.

The region poses the biggest test yet of the EU's transformative power. Can conditionality and pre-accession instruments be used as successfully as they were in Central Europe? Can European integration provide a basis for the region's stability and prosperity by encouraging good governance and reconciliation between communities? The fact that Croatia succeeded in joining the EU in 2013, and that Serbia has begun to normalize its relations with Kosovo, are encouraging signs. But many problems remain to be solved.

Turkey

Turkey's 'European vocation' was avowed as early as 1964 in its Association Agreement with the EC. Its application for membership dates from 1987. But as Redmond (2007) recounts, the path towards membership has been long, and remains difficult. Despite the fact that accession negotiations opened in 2005, Turkey's future membership is by no means assured.

Many of the arguments that were valid for preceding enlargements apply to Turkey. As Barysch et al. (2005) explain, its growing economy and young labour force would bring benefits for the single market. Although there would be costs for the EU's budget in the fields of agriculture and cohesion policy, the overall economic impact of Turkey's accession should be positive. Turkey has a big population: 78 million now, expected to grow to 90 million or more in future. In terms of income per head, it is poorer than the EU average, although its economic growth in recent years has been impressive. Its position on Europe's southeastern flank gives it geostrategic importance in relation to the Middle East and the Black Sea region; being in NATO, and with the biggest army of NATO's European members, it has a key role in European security (see Tocci 2011). The majority of Turkey's population is Islamic, but it has been a secular state since the 1930s. Its efforts to conform to European standards of democracy, human rights, and rule of law are monitored closely by the EU. Progress has been made towards meeting the Copenhagen criteria, but more needs to be done. The main problems include Turkey's treatment of its Kurdish minority, its restrictions on freedom of expression, and the political role of its military.

Some argue that by admitting Turkey, the EU would give a signal to other countries that it accepts Islam. To refuse Turkey would show that Europe is culturally prejudiced, and might lead to a reversal of Turkey's reforms, or even turn it against the West. Others reject this argument: just as religion is not a reason to say 'No' to Turkey, it is not a reason to say 'Yes'. Although Turkey's membership offers benefits for the EU in terms of foreign policy, it would bring new problems and risks. With Turkey's accession, the EU's external frontiers would extend to Azerbaijan, Armenia, Iran, Iraq, and Syria, bringing it into direct contact with regions of instability.

Public opinion in the EU is influenced by fear of an influx of Turkish migrant workers, and the idea that Turkey is different—that it is not part of Europe in geographical or cultural terms. As a result mainstream political parties in France, Germany, and Austria (amongst others) oppose Turkish membership. It is also argued that the EU's decision-making system would have difficulty in coping with Turkey, which would be the biggest member state by the time it joined. Cyprus is a further bone of contention. Since Turkey intervened militarily in 1974, the Turkish Republic of Northern Cyprus—not recognized by the rest of the international community—has been separated from the south. Hopes of reuniting the two parts of the island were dashed in 2003 when the Greek Cypriots in the south said 'No' to a UN plan that was accepted by the north. As a result, the EU's enlargement of 2004 brought in a divided island.

All these problems put a question mark over Turkey's bid for EU membership. Some argue that, even if it does not finally become a member, Turkey has an interest in continued modernization in line with European criteria. But with an uncertain prospect of membership, the leverage for change in Turkey is less effective. There is a growing risk of crisis with Turkey in the accession negotiations, where progress has been slow and several chapters are blocked by objections from France and Cyprus.

Norway, Switzerland, and Iceland

It is sometimes forgotten that membership applications have been made by Norway, Switzerland and Iceland (see Box 8.3). Oil-rich Norway negotiated and signed two Accession Treaties, but did not join after its people said 'No' twice in referenda. This divisive experience has made its politicians reluctant to reopen the question of EU membership. As a member of the EEA (Box 8.1) it has access to the common market and participates in other EU policies. In fact, the EEA is the closest form of relationship that the Union has ever made with non-member countries.

Switzerland's application for EU membership was suspended when its citizens voted 'No' in a referendum on the EEA, and since then it has pursued its interests through bilateral agreements with the EU. While the French-speaking part of the population is broadly in favour of the EU, a majority of German-speakers are

FIGURE 8.2   Map: The European Union's Neighbourhood Policy

opposed. Switzerland's 'direct democracy' with frequent use of referenda could pose problems for its membership.

Iceland, as a member of the EEA, decided to apply for EU membership in 2009 after a banking crisis showed its vulnerability as a small country (see Avery et al. 2011). Accession negotiations began in 2010, but were suspended by Iceland's new government in 2013, before discussions began on the EU's common fisheries policy, the main obstacle to membership for Iceland.

However, small, rich countries like these easily fulfil the conditions for membership and are thus ideal applicants for the EU. If they decided to apply again, they would be accepted readily as candidates.

Wider Europe

European Neighbourhood Policy

With its expansion to Central and Eastern Europe, the EU encountered a series of new neighbours to the east. It already had a Euro-Mediterranean Partnership with countries to the south, and now was obliged to rethink relations with the countries of Eastern Europe that were formerly in the Soviet Union. New EU members such as Poland and Hungary did not want to see their accession lead to the erection of new barriers to countries with which they have cultural, social, and economic links. The result was the development of the European Neighbourhood Policy (ENP) covering 16 countries: Morocco, Algeria, Tunisia, Libya, Egypt, Israel, Jordan, the Palestinian Authority, Lebanon, Syria, Armenia, Azerbaijan, Georgia, Moldova, Ukraine, and Belarus (see Figure 8.1). Its aim is to extend stability, prosperity, and security, and create a 'ring of friends' by developing political links and economic integration with the EU. Its main instrument is a series of Action Plans negotiated with each partner country and backed by financial and technical assistance. These plans cover political dialogue, economic and social reform, trade, cooperation in justice and security affairs, transport, energy, environment, education, and so on. They require the neighbours to take on European regulation and a large part of the acquis: the system is modelled, in fact, on the EU's Accession Partnerships with future members.

But the ENP lacks the big incentive of the enlargement process—the 'golden carrot' of accession. Its message is 'be like us' not 'be one of us'. For Eastern Europeans such as Ukraine, the fact that the policy is 'accession-neutral' has been a disappointment. Although it offers financial aid and long-term benefits, it demands reforms that are difficult and costly.

The policy has been diversified to take account of the different situations and interests of the countries concerned. On the initiative of France, relations with the countries of the EU's Southern neighbourhood were deepened through the creation in 2008 of the 'Union for the Mediterranean'. An initiative from Poland and Sweden led to the creation in 2009 of the 'Eastern Partnership' with six East European countries (Armenia, Azerbaijan, Belarus, Georgia, Moldova, and Ukraine). Although the Partnership remains accession-neutral, it offers improved political cooperation, further economic integration, and increased financial assistance, and is now leading to the conclusion of Association Agreements, which in the past have been precursors to the accession process.

However, despite the ENP's declared aims, it has had limited success in promoting democracy, good governance and prosperity. The Union for the Mediterranean has been largely ineffective; in the EU's Southern neighbourhood peoples overthrew autocratic regimes in the 'Arab spring' of 2011. Syria has suffered a traumatic civil war. In Eastern Europe, Belarus still has an autocratic regime, while Ukraine has experienced a series of political and economic crises. Nevertheless, the EU continues to be attractive: the decision of Ukraine's President in 2013 to pursue closer ties with Russia, rather than an Association Agreement with the EU, led to popular protests and the fall of his government. Russia's response, with its annexation of Crimea and support of dissidents in Eastern Ukraine, has caused Ukraine to ask for support from the West and seek membership of the EU and NATO.

The EU offered to extend its European Neighbourhood Policy to Russia, but the invitation was rejected. The hope of European policy-makers for cooperation with Russia in other countries of the region has been disappointed. Russia considers former Soviet countries such as Ukraine to be part of its zone of influence. It fears that closer relations with the EU may lead to them joining NATO, and adoption of European standards of governance may pose a threat to Russia's own political and economic system. Russia's invasion of Georgia in 2008 and its actions in Ukraine since 2014 have shown that it is prepared to use force to control its neighbours and redraw frontiers.

What Limits for the EU?

The EU has used the prospect of membership successfully to extend stability and prosperity to neighbouring countries. But is it realistic to continue without predetermined limits? Logically, the EU cannot expand indefinitely: it was not designed to be a world system of government, but an 'ever-closer union among the peoples of Europe'. How far can the European Union's expansion continue? Where will its final frontiers lie?

The EU can have different frontiers for different policies. This is already the case for the euro and Schengen. In this sense, the EU is already a multi-frontier system. But problems arise when its multi-tier potential is perceived as leading to a 'core-group', with some states having more rights than others. All members, and all applicants, want full rights in decision-making; there is no market for 'second-class' membership.

What is Europe?

The founding EU Treaties said 'any European state may apply to become a member' and subsequent Treaties have added a reference to values (see Box 8.2). It is sometimes suggested that the EU is based on shared values rather than geography. But if this argument were correct we would expect like-minded states in distant parts of the world—such as New Zealand—to be considered as future members. In fact geographic contiguity or proximity is a precondition for membership. An exception, which proves the rule, is France's overseas departments (such as Guadeloupe or Martinique), which are in the EU because they are part of French territory.

What are the geographical limits of the European continent? To the North, West, and South, seas and oceans define it, but to the East there is no clear boundary. Although the Ural Mountains and the Caspian Sea are often invoked as natural frontiers, some geographers consider Europe as the western peninsula of the Asian landmass - a subcontinent rather than a continent.

In any case, different geographical, political, and cultural concepts of Europe have prevailed at different times. Asia Minor and Northern Africa were within the political and economic area of the Roman Empire, but much of today's EU was outside it. Other historical periods are cited as characterizing Europe in cultural terms, such as the experience of the Renaissance or the Enlightenment. For some, Christianity is a defining element of European identity. Such examples show how difficult it is to arrive at an agreed definition. The European Commission (1992) has taken the view that:

The term 'European' has not been officially defined. It combines geographical, historical and cultural elements which all contribute to the European identity. The shared experience of proximity, ideas, values and historical interaction cannot be condensed into a simple formula, and is subject to review by each succeeding generation. It is neither possible nor opportune to establish now the frontiers of the European Union, whose contours will be shaped over many years to come.

But is it so difficult to know which countries are considered European today? Another European organization, founded in 1949 before the creation of the European Communities, is the Council of Europe. It has a wider membership than the EU (see Box 8.8) and thus provides an indication of the limits of Europe as recognized internationally. All EU members are members of the Council of Europe, and can hardly refuse to consider other signatories as 'European'. This suggests the following list of potential members of the EU:

- Albania, Bosnia-Herzegovina, Kosovo, Macedonia, Montenegro, Serbia
- Turkey
- Iceland, Norway, Switzerland
- Armenia, Azerbaijan, Belarus, Georgia, Moldova, Ukraine
- Russia.

BOX 8.8	**Other Europeans**

Not all European states are in the EU. The other main intergovernmental organization in Europe is the Council of Europe, which is mainly concerned with human rights, social and legal affairs, and culture. It has 47 members:

- 28 EU states,
- Albania, Bosnia-Herzegovina, Macedonia (FYROM), Montenegro, Serbia,
- Turkey,
- Iceland, Norway, Switzerland,
- Armenia, Azerbaijan, Georgia, Moldova, Russian Federation, Ukraine,
- Andorra, Liechtenstein, Monaco, San Marino.

We should add two potential members: Belarus, which would be accepted as a member of the Council of Europe if it became more democratic, and Kosovo, which would be accepted if the problem of its international recognition was solved.

Looking at the list in relation to membership of the EU, we should leave aside the last four, which as mini-states have little interest in joining. So we have a total of 17 states that are in the Council of Europe but not in the EU.

Of this list of 17, the EU already considers some as potential members. Could it eventually embrace all the others? Will the final limits of the EU be set at 45 countries?

That's unlikely: no state is obliged to apply, and the EU is not obliged to accept applicants. Meanwhile states may leave the EU, and new states may be created. In any case, an attempt by the EU institutions to decide the ultimate limits in advance would not give a clear answer. Such a decision would require unanimity, and existing member states have differing views on future membership. Those sharing borders with non-members often wish to bring them into the EU for reasons of stability and security. Poland, for example, wants its neighbour Ukraine to be a member of the EU. But others such as France are more restrictive, especially on the inclusion of Turkey. In fact, a discussion of the 'limits of Europe' can easily become a debate on 'should Turkey join?'

What are the prospects for countries such as Ukraine, which are presently in the framework of the EU's European Neighbourhood Policy? They are far from meeting the Copenhagen criteria, and EU membership is unrealistic for them for many years. But Russia's actions in Ukraine have driven it towards the West for political support and financial assistance. Such actions have also strengthened the case for using the leverage of prospective EU membership to encourage the long-term reforms needed to rebuild the Ukrainian state and economy.

Prudence argues for keeping open the prospect of EU enlargement to all European states. Aspirant countries can modify their behaviour significantly in the hope of obtaining membership. To define the EU's ultimate borders now would demotivate those excluded, and diminish the leverage for those included. Thus a strategy of 'constructive ambiguity' is likely to prevail in the EU's enlargement policy.

Finally, what of Russia? It too is a European country, but its geographic expanse and population of 140 million mean that Russia joining the EU would be more like the EU joining Russia. With its self-identity as a great power could Russia ever accept the EU's rules and policies? Its political trajectory in recent years has moved it away from European values, not towards them.

Evaluating Enlargement

The pace of enlargement depends not only on the applicant countries but also on the attitude of the public and politicians in the EU. With the enlargements of 2004 and 2007 and the financial crisis of 2008, the question of absorption capacity (see Box 8.1) has become an element in the debate. This notion, introduced at Copenhagen in 1993 (see Box 8.2), refers to the need to 'maintain the momentum of European integration'. It thus links future enlargement to the development of the EU's institutions, policies, and budget.

This brings us to the question: what is the purpose of enlargement? At the beginning of this chapter we saw that enlargement is not only foreign policy, but also a kind of existential policy, in the sense that each successive accession reconfigures the EU's composition. So what are the criteria for evaluating the success of enlargement policy? One cannot evaluate it simply by reference to the number of countries joining, or the speed of their accession. The correct approach for evaluation is twofold: a first group of criteria applying to the period before enlargement—the 'pre-accession' period—and a second group to the period after accession, when applicant countries have become members of the EU.

The criteria for the pre-accession period are similar to those for foreign policy: enlargement policy is successful if it enhances security, stability, and prosperity both for the EU and for the neighbouring countries concerned. But a more important test of enlargement policy concerns the period after accession. Here the conditions for a successful result may be defined as the harmonious integration of new members (without disrupting existing members, or the functioning of the EU's institutions and policies) and the satisfactory continuation of the EU's development. Since there is no general agreement on the last criterion (what is a satisfactory development of the EU?) it is not surprising that opinions differ on the merits of enlargement. According to some, the supporters of expansion (typically, the British) want to weaken the EU, while according to others the opponents of expansion (typically, the French) want to safeguard acquired positions and advantages. Although these caricatures are both false, they show how attitudes to enlargement policy can differ widely within the EU (see Sjursen 2008).

What was the result of the increase from 15 to 28? It has not, as some feared, paralysed the EU's decision-making, which seems to work as well, or as badly, as it did in the past (Best et al. 2008). Nor has it led to an increase in 'variable geometry' within the EU, with more fields of policy having different memberships, as some commentators predicted. Most of the new members, unlike some old members, have joined the Schengen system, and many of them have joined the euro.

But in recent years 'enlargement fatigue' has become a factor: public opinion in the EU, particularly among the older member states, is more resistant to enlargement, which is often blamed for problems arising from other causes such as globalization or the economic situation. Accessions may in future be subject more often to referenda in existing member states. Consequently the EU will be rigorous in applying its conditions for potential members, and cautious in making promises.

Conclusion

The expansion of the EU has been remarkable in its pace and impact. But after increasing its membership from 12 to 28 states and its population by a third in the period from 1995 to 2013, the EU will expand more slowly in future. In the medium term, it will limit its expansion to the countries of the Balkans, and possibly to Turkey, whose accession is uncertain and in any case will not take place for many years. In the longer term the EU may eventually accept other East European countries such as Ukraine. But in the meantime they remain in the framework of its Neighbourhood Policy. The final limits of the Union are likely to result from the course of events and successive political decisions, rather than from a strategic choice made in advance.

DISCUSSION QUESTIONS

1. Has the EU's enlargement to 28 members weakened its capacity for effective action? Has the 'widening' stopped the 'deepening'?

2. Turkey's application for membership dates from 1987: why is it so difficult for the EU to handle? Will Turkey ever succeed in joining?

3. The EU's basic Treaty says 'any European state may apply for membership'. Should the Union try to decide where its frontiers would ultimately lie?

4. The EU's Neighbourhood Policy aims at creating a 'ring of friendly countries.' Can it ever be a substitute for joining the EU?

FURTHER READING

The enlargements of 2004 and 2007 are the subject of a voluminous literature, particularly on EU conditionality and reform in Central and Eastern Europe. The early stages of the process are covered in Mayhew (1998) and Torreblanca (2001), while the accession negotiations are described in Avery (2004). Schimmelfennig (2003) examines the expansion of NATO as well as the EU. Analyses of the theoretical aspects of enlargement can be found in Schimmelfennig and Sedelmeier (2005) while Sjursen (2006) comments on the EU's motives, Vachudova (2005) presents the 'realist' view, and Schneider (2008) analyses the role of transitional periods. For conditionality and 'Europeanization', see Grabbe (2006) and Epstein and Sedelmeier (2009); for a critique of the EU's handling of Romania, see Gallagher (2009), and for problems of corruption in new member states see Vachudova (2009). On neighbourhood policy see Hillion (2008) and Cardwell (2011). Copsey et al. (2014) describes Poland's role in creating the Eastern Partnership. A good summary of developments, updated annually, can be found in the chapter on enlargement and neighbourhood policy in the JCMS Annual Review of the European Union.

Avery, G. (2004), *The Enlargement Negotiations*, in F. Cameron (ed), *The Future of Europe, Integration and Enlargement* (London: Routledge): 35–62.

Cardwell, P. J. (2011), 'Euromed, European Neighbourhood Policy and the Union for the Mediterranean: Overlapping Policy Frames in the EU's Governance of the Mediterranean', *Journal of Common Market Studies*, 49/2: 219–41.

Copsey, N. and Pomorska, K. (2014), 'The Influence of the Newer Member States in the European Union: The Case of Poland and the Eastern Partnership', *Europe-Asia Studies*, 66/3: 421–43.

Epstein, R. and Sedelmeier, U. (eds) (2009), *International Influence beyond Conditionality: Postcommunist Europe after EU Enlargement* (London: Routledge).

Gallagher, T. (2009), *Romania and the European Union: How the Weak Vanquished the Strong* (Manchester: Manchester University Press).

Grabbe, H. (2006), *The EU's Transformative Power: Europeanization through Conditionality in Central and Eastern Europe* (Basingstoke: Palgrave Macmillan).

Hillion, C. (2008), The EU's Neighbourhood Policy towards Eastern Europe, in Dashwood A., Maresceau M. (eds), *Law and Practice of EU External Relations: Salient Features of a Changing Landscape* (Cambridge: Cambridge University Press): 309–33.

Mayhew, A. (1998), *Recreating Europe: The European Union's Policy towards Central and Eastern Europe* (Cambridge: Cambridge University Press).

Schimmelfennig, F. (2003), *The EU, NATO and the Integration of Europe* (Cambridge: Cambridge University Press).

Schimmelfennig, F., and Sedelmeier, U. (eds) (2005), *The Politics of European Union Enlargement: Theoretical Approaches* (London: Routledge).

Schneider C. J. (2008), *Conflict, Negotiation and European Union Enlargement* (Cambridge: Cambridge University Press).

Sjursen, H. (ed.) (2006), *Questioning EU enlargement: Europe in search of identity* (London: Routledge).

Torreblanca, J. I. (2001), *The Reuniting of Europe: Promises, Negotiations and Compromises* (Aldershot: Ashgate).

Vachudova, M. (2005), *Europe Undivided: Democracy, Leverage, and Integration after Communism* (Oxford: Oxford University Press).

Vachudova, M. (2009), Corruption and Compliance in the EU's Post-Communist Members and Candidates, *JCMS Annual Review of the European Union in 2008*: 43–62.

WEB LINKS

- The European Commission provides information and official documents on Enlargement at: **http://ec.europa.eu/enlargement/index_en.htm**
- The European External Action Service provides information and official documents on Neighbourhood Policy at: **http://www.eeas.europa.eu/enp/**

Visit the Online Resource Centre that accompanies this book for additional material: **www.oxfordtextbooks.co.uk/orc/kenealy4e/**

CHAPTER 9

The EU as a Security Actor

John Peterson and Andrew Geddes

▌ Summary

At first glance, EU security policy seems limited by three powerful constraints. First, it is exclusively concerned with 'soft' security issues, such as immigration, transnational crime, and drug trafficking. Second, policy-making is dominated by sovereignty-conscious EU member states and national capitals. Third, security is not a major driver of European integration. We challenge all three of these assumptions. The EU is now involved in 'hard' security, especially counterterrorism but also military operations. Second, security policy-making is increasingly Brussels-centred. Third, while European integration has been driven primarily by economic cooperation, the safeguarding of Europe's (especially internal) security has emerged as a major *raison d'être* of the integration project.

Introducing European Security Policy

When we think about international security—questions of war and peace or conflict and cooperation—we tend to assume that the major actors are inevitably states or security alliances, such as NATO (the North Atlantic Treaty Organization). But the EU has assumed a more important security role over time, especially on matters concerning its own internal security. EU policy on security within its borders has been one of the busiest areas of European policy-making and legislation for most of the twenty-first century. Today, there are very few areas of security policy where the EU does not play a role, often working alongside other organizations. While traditionally and still primarily viewed as an economic actor, the European Union is very much in the security business.

EU activities that seek to promote security are diverse and spread between different policy areas. It is difficult to generalize about them. In fact, few in Brussels would recognize or understand what was meant by 'EU security policy'. More familiar would be the designations **Common Foreign and Security Policy (CFSP)**, **Common Security and Defence Policy (CSDP**; formerly known as the European Security and Defence Policy), and what is officially known today as **Police and Judicial Cooperation in Criminal Matters**. But EU security policy also extends to issues related to free movement, migration and asylum: that is, *internal* security, which seeks to defuse or counter threats to security within the Union's own borders. Instead of security policy, scholars tend to focus on EU security 'governance' since it takes place without a single authority. The governance approach portrays the Union as an 'evolving, yet fairly stable policy-making system' (Norheim-Martinsen 2010: 1360; see also Christou and Croft 2012).

The CFSP, created by the Maastricht Treaty in 1992, is meant to cover 'all aspects of foreign and security policy'. As we will see (in Chapter 10), it has often been criticized for its failure to be comprehensive or coherent. The CFSP certainly has not replaced national foreign or security policies in Europe or made them obsolete, even if they are shaped increasingly by Brussels-based cooperation. The EU plays no role in territorial defence and the CSDP is central to no EU member state's national defence policy (Cooper 2004b: 189). It is safe to assume that no European army, marching under an EU flag, will ever be sent to fight on one side of any inter-state war in the lifetime of any reader of this book. Command of the spring 2011 military action to protect civilians in Libya from forces loyal to Moammar Qaddafi was controlled by NATO with the EU active only on the civilian front (for instance, by freezing Libyan assets). Despite the Union offering Ukraine a trade agreement, and thus playing a role in the 2014 overthrow of a Russian-oriented Ukrainian government, there was no EU defence force to deter Russia's subsequent annexation of Crimea or its stirring up of separatism in eastern Ukraine.

The EU thus is mostly a supplier of 'soft security' through non-military policies that seek to defuse or prevent conflict. It is accepted wisdom that the Union is not in the 'hard' security business: defence of the state via military power. But in an era when it is often argued that a 'new security agenda' has emerged (Cottey 2013: 34–62: see also Dannreuther 2007; Coker 2009), with threats that are more diverse and not always state-based, the EU is a policy factory. It is active in areas such as civilian and military crisis management, climate change, energy security, cybersecurity and counterterrorism: all issues on which security policies have become more focused in general.

Meanwhile, internal security policy is the single policy area where the EU—perhaps ironically—has been most active since the mid-90s. The irony stems from the stubborn refusal of member states over the course of years to subject internal security policy to the Community method, whereby the Commission has a monopoly on the right to propose legislation, the European Parliament (EP) has the right to co-decide legislation or propose amendments, and the Council usually acts by a qualified majority. Under the post-1992 'pillar system', internal security policy—as well as the CFSP—was mostly subject to intergovernmental decision-making, not requiring a Commission proposal nor agreement of the Parliament, with nearly all decisions requiring the unanimity of all member states. Such cumbersome arrangements, however, proved inadequate to deal with policy problems arising from the abolition of checks at internal borders, including organized crime, drug and people trafficking, asylum-seeking and irregular migration. Over the course of a decade and a half, the EU spent far more time and effort debating internal security than on producing policy output.

The Lisbon Treaty abolished the pillar system. Qualified majority voting (QMV) was applied to key internal security policies, including police and judicial cooperation, with the EP given co-decision rights in many. Unanimity persists as the decision rule for most EU foreign and external security policy decisions. But hopes for a more coherent and effective CSDP were boosted by Lisbon's creation of a new High Representative, initially in the person of Catherine Ashton, whose (impossibly?) busy job description included 'steering . . . [the] common defence policy' (Council 2009: 2), chairing meetings of European Defence Ministers (twice a year formally), and heading the European Defence Agency. Despite Ashton's disappointing start as the first post-Lisbon High Representative (see Helwig 2013), there remained hope that her successor(s)—starting with Frederica Mogherini—would be able to steer the EU towards a more consistent and successful defence policy. In any event, the EU has become a far more active security actor in recent years. Most signs point towards it becoming still more active in the post-Lisbon era.

How it developed

In a sense, security was the most important objective of the first steps in post-war European institution-building (see Weiler 1998). The European Coal and Steel Community, and later the EEC, were created above all to cure Europe of its bad habit of going to war every 35 years or so. Specifically, they sought to combine the economies—especially the war-making industries—of France and (then West) Germany. An early attempt to integrate European militaries—the European Defence Community—proved a step too far and was buried by France in 1954 (see Chapter 2). Thus, it took several decades before what became the EU was given any security policy role. Meanwhile, NATO became the main forum for military cooperation during the Cold War. Nevertheless, security has always been a fundamental goal of European integration.

Policy cooperation on internal security is rooted primarily in two intergovernmental frameworks initially created outside the (then) European Community: the 1976 Trevi framework to fight terrorism and drug trafficking and the 1985 Schengen Agreement that sought to lift internal border controls. These two domains were linked and brought into the newly-created European Union under the 1992 Maastricht Treaty. In defiance of proposals by the 1992 Dutch Council Presidency, internal security policy was not inserted into the Community pillar but instead formed a new intergovernmental 'third pillar' on Justice and Home Affairs (JHA). Given this awkward institutional structure, and the tendency of internal security ministry officials (unlike diplomats) to shun cooperation and guard jealously their national legal systems, the 1990s saw only a handful of specific actions agreed within the third pillar. As a partial solution, the 1997 Amsterdam Treaty mandated that migration and asylum policy would be made within the Community pillar, and that border controls, immigration, asylum, visas, as well as judicial cooperation in civil law matters could gradually become subject to Community rules with the possibility of applying QMV within five years. Institutional compromises, such as absorbing the Schengen Agreement into the EU's Treaties but with opt-outs for the UK, Denmark, and Ireland, led to institutional complexity, but also had the advantage of making it easier for participating member states to move ahead if they so wished. The Amsterdam Treaty's section on internal security was widely-thought to be one of the most complex treaties ever agreed.

In constructing its cooperative framework for internal security, as in building the EU's defence policy, formal Treaty reforms often have mattered less than informal learning by doing. Maastricht's pillar III (the pillar for JHA) gave an EU home to practical cooperation designed to open European borders but also to respond to concerns that the main beneficiaries could be terrorists or criminals by, inter alia, reinforcing the Union's external borders. The Amsterdam Treaty's (enormously complex) provisions for JHA sought to provide a stronger institutional base and also embraced the idea of making the EU an 'Area of Freedom, Justice, and Security'. Yet, this grand declaration by EU leaders did less to hasten new policies than pragmatic, ongoing cooperation on practical matters such as coping with different national laws on the prosecution of suspected criminals or seeking to control irregular migration.

Similarly, the EU's external defence policy emerged mainly out of practical cooperation. On one hand, when it committed itself to (what became) the Common Security and Defence Policy, the Union still had yet to take on an independent military operation. The EU's failure to manage peacefully the break-up of Yugoslavia after 1991 led to broad consensus on the need for the Union to develop a military capability. The Maastricht Treaty, agreed as the Balkans burst into flames, contained vague language committing the EU to a 'common defence policy that might, in time, lead to a common defence'. However, a bilateral agreement preceded by ad hoc, practical, cooperation between Europe's two major military powers—France and the United Kingdom (UK)—kick-started EU military cooperation. The Anglo-French St. Malo Declaration in 1998 followed extensive operational cooperation between the French and UK militaries on the ground in the former Yugoslavia. With the Bosnian crisis a recent memory, and the Kosovo crisis still to come, EU Heads of State and Government formally launched (what became) CSDP at the 1999 Cologne summit.

Later the same year, two EU summits under the Council presidency of Finland marked turning points. Meeting in Tampere, European leaders tried to rekindle the Area of Freedom, Security and Justice. Tampere produced agreement on new criteria by which to measure progress and new institutions such as a European Police College and an agency responsible for co-ordination of member states' efforts to control their borders: Frontex. It also extended the powers of Europol, established in 1995 to facilitate the exchange of intelligence and coordination of criminal investigations between national police forces. A subsequent European Council in Helsinki was hailed as marking the moment when the EU finally 'came of age' as an international actor (Taylor 1999). Besides major decisions on enlargement and Turkey, the Helsinki summit also yielded decisive steps towards giving the EU an independent military capability, as well as civilian resources, to deal with crises on or near its borders. Helsinki was the moment when the Union went beyond conflict prevention amongst its own member states to take responsibility for crisis management in its neighbourhood.

The 2001 Treaty of Nice was mainly concerned with preparing the EU for its next enlargement. It did little to advance internal or external security policy. However, the 2002–3 Convention on the Future of Europe agreed wide-ranging reforms of both security policy institutions and decision rules, most of which were accepted in the Constitutional Treaty. Its rejection by French and Dutch voters in 2005 referendums eventually led to the new model Lisbon Treaty, with its multiple provisions to try to make both EU internal and external security policy more coherent and effective. Lisbon reasserted the fundamental security vocation of European integration by placing the target of an 'Area of Freedom, Security and Justice' second in a list of fundamental EU goals in Article 3 of the Treaty, just after a general commitment to peace and welfare, and preceding the goals of the single market or economic and monetary union. After Lisbon came into force, the key question became: could the EU finally deliver on its—still largely unfulfilled—potential as a security actor?

The basics

The EU's emergence as a security actor has mostly been a post-Cold War phenomenon. Although the freeing of the internal market prompted intergovernmental cooperation on internal security in the 1980s (and even before), EU policy prior to the fall of the Berlin Wall and collapse of the Soviet Union focused overwhelmingly on economics—not security. Forty years of European integration did, of course, accomplish the primordial goal of eliminating the possibility of any future war between

France and Germany. Only later did post-Cold War geopolitical conditions enable the Union to achieve the same sort of rapprochement between Germany and Poland, an often-neglected but historically remarkable feat (Cottey 2013: 17). The EU thus is a fundamentally different kind of security actor than the US or China or Russia. Its primary contribution historically has been as a 'peace project' confined mostly to the European continent (Smith 2014: 171). Still, as a core area of a 'security community' (Deutsch et al. 1969) that extends to other modern democracies including the US and Japan, and between whom war is unimaginable, the EU has made an important contribution to security ever since its origins.

The Union's post-Cold War transformation into a supplier of security has involved a gradual strengthening of powers, resources and institutions in two quite distinct policy domains. Its *external* security role is focused, above all, on preventing or managing crises on the EU's doorstep as well as reconstructing conflict-ridden regions (or 'nation-building'). Unlike other international organizations that are similarly tasked with conflict prevention such as the United Nations or OSCE (Organization for Security and Cooperation in Europe), the EU has both 'a considerable toolbox of policy instruments and, crucially, its own unique legacy as a successful exercise in conflict prevention' (Smith 2014: 170). Inside the toolbox are trade privileges (or sanctions), aid and various forms of political dialogue. When conflicts cannot be prevented, and turn into outright crises, the EU now has considerable resources for crisis management, including disaster relief, reconstruction aid, and even military force. Whether Lisbon's new and stronger machinery for foreign and security policy will make the Union a more effective external security actor is an open question. The tools are there, but they must be wielded more coherently for the EU to be an effective security actor.

The EU's *internal* security regime involves a very different and very heterogeneous set of actors and institutions. Initially framed as a form of compensation—safeguarding internal security after the abolition of internal border controls—EU Justice and Home Affairs policies historically have linked very disparate issues such as asylum, migration, and organized crime. The primary impetus for this cooperation has been upgrading the EU's capacity to respond to asylum-seeking migration, irregular migration and transboundary crime. However, questions relating to the rights of migrants and refugees as well as, to a lesser extent, criminal suspects, have gained more attention over time. The empowering of the EU's supranational institutions, in particular the Commission, the Parliament and, especially after Lisbon, the ECJ, has been key in this development (Lavenex 2006; Geddes 2008; Acosta and Geddes 2013).

In parallel to this internal evolution, cooperation on the external dimension of migration and organized crime has developed over time. Paradoxically, while policy substance has become blurred in terms of the distinction between 'internal' and 'external' security policy (Rees 2008), structures for making policies remain rigidly compartmentalized. The Union's external and internal security policies sometimes seem to be made on two islands between which there is little exchange or coherence.

Yet, an increasingly important international task for the EU is reconciling its internal security policies with its external obligations. What were previously deemed 'soft' security issues, such as irregular migration and transnational crime, have risen to the top of the policy agenda and become infused with new urgency. The link between internal and external security cooperation became especially salient after the terrorist attacks in the US, Madrid, and London of 2001–5, and again in the context of the migration flows unleashed by the Arab Revolutions of 2011. These events acted as external shocks prompting a new impetus to European cooperation. To the surprise of many, the EU managed rapidly to reach ambitious agreements on a common definition of terrorism and a European arrest warrant in the immediate aftermath of 11 September 2001. Events in the southern Mediterranean, especially in Arab states, in early 2011 stimulated a strengthening of the Union's external borders agency Frontex (see later) and intensified calls for greater solidarity and burden-sharing between member states.

Yet, the EU's potential for policy cooperation often goes unrealized due to a lack of solidarity. In October 2013, the Italian government established the *Mare Nostrum* operation to rescue migrants seeking to cross the Mediterranean, often in barely seaworthy vessels operated by people-smugglers, following the death of 366 people off the coast of Italy when their boat capsized near Lampedusa. The effect of the Italian operation may have been to encourage even more refugees to risk their lives trying to reach Europe: in the first 9 months of 2014, more than 3,000 migrants died at sea, more than double the annual average, even as *Mare Nostrum* saved an estimated 150,000 lives over the course of a year. Finally, however, the Italian government ended the operation, citing a lack of support from other EU member states and monthly costs of around £9 million.

The EU stepped into the breach with Operation Triton, but with only one-third of the funding of *Mare Nostrum* and strict rules restricting Frontex to operations in European territorial waters and prohibiting search and rescue operations beyond them, as the Italians had done. After they came into force in 2009, the Lisbon Treaty's revised provisions for decision-making on internal security, and its abolition of the pillar system, seemed to hold out the prospect of more effective, coherent, and timely internal security policies. But in the case of Operation Triton, the leading UK politician Paddy Ashdown spoke for many in declaring that 'the policy the EU proposes . . . apart from being inhuman, immoral and potentially illegal, will also not work' (*Financial Times*, 31 October 2014).

The EU and International Security

The EU's role in international security has expanded over time. By early 2014 it had engaged in some 30 missions on three different continents. Most—around two-thirds—were purely civilian missions, which channeled development aid or sent law enforcement officers or advisors to troubled regions, as opposed to military forces. An example trumpeted by the EU as a success has been one of its largest CSDP civilian missions: EULEX in Kosovo, which sent more than 2700 judges, prosecutors and police to fight corruption, organized crime, and investigate war crimes between 2008–12. Working under the general framework of a United Nations Security Council Resolution, EULEX was EU-led but included contributions from Norway, Switzerland, Turkey, Canada, and the United States.

Other EU missions have involved sending military forces together with civilian delegations. Such mixed missions have not been without critics. Smith (2014: 179–82) goes as far as to argue that '[c]onflict-prevention policy exposes the weaknesses of the EU foreign policy system' since 'coordination between the military and civilian crisis management institutions within the Council . . . [is] poor', with the civilian side 'comparatively underdeveloped'. Over time, the CSDP has evolved from a focus on military crisis management to investment in civilian stabilization, including counter-terrorism and preventing the proliferation of weapons of mass destruction. To illustrate, Bickerton et al. (2011: 5) note an 'absence of real failure' in any CSDP mission with most demonstrably having a 'beneficial impact'. The EU possesses more earmarked resources to promote security in troubled regions than any other international organization (see Box 9.1). Still, there is no question that EU missions often lack coherence.

BOX 9.1	Compared to what?

The EU as an international security actor

The EU is an alliance of states, so it naturally is a different kind of security actor than are other great powers. First and foremost, it has no role in territorial defence and no standing army. It would never enter into a security pact with non-EU states as, say, the US has done with Japan and the antipodean states (through ANZUS—the Australia, New Zealand, US—Treaty). Most (not all) EU member states are active members of NATO. In fact, most EU military operations have required cooperation with NATO and use of its military assets.

Second, the Union is often portrayed as a 'civilian' power (see Chapter 10), which favours persuasion over coercion and primarily uses its economic and aid policies to try to achieve international peace and security. Other major international players—such as the US, China, and Russia—rely far more on their military power (or at least the threat of using it) to achieve their international objectives. In recent years, Manners (2002, 2008) has portrayed the EU as a 'normative power': that is, one with an active foreign and security policy that nonetheless influences international relations (IR) more because of what it is—a peaceful sub-system of IR—than what it does. Sometimes what it does makes a real difference, as in the case of the French-led EU mission to mediate an end to the Russo-Georgian war in 2008. But, in illustrating the Union's limits, van Middelaar (2013: 209) shows considerable foresight in noting that the EU was always going to have

Cont. ➤

Cont.

to be 'a good deal less ambitious than—imagine!—trying to keep the Ukrainian Crimea out of the clutches of Russia by dispatching European troops or gunboats', as was illustrated in 2014. Faced with any kind of conflict, the Union inevitably favours negotiated settlements over the use of force. Toje (2011) characterizes the EU as a 'small power' in its dependence on great powers (such as the US), preference for multilateralism, and risk-aversion, while Laïdi (2008) claims that the Union not only avoids power politics, it avoids *power* itself.

Third and finally, the EU's external security interventions would be viewed by most students of international relations as modest and insignificant compared to those undertaken by other Great Powers. Security policy specialists tend to scoff at the notion of 'soft power'—the ability to get others to do what one wants them to do without coercion (see Nye 2004)—as a chimera in the hard-nosed, Hobbesian world of international politics. Whether or not they are right, none of the twenty-first century's Great Powers, the US, China, or Russia, would consider it a major security policy success story to have launched (say) a small, if successful, civilian mission in the troubled Indonesian province of Aceh.

The EU's contribution to international security also raises questions about whether the Union is truly a global actor (see Chapter 10) or merely one whose influence and activities are mostly confined to the European continent or its near-abroad. In a purely European context, the EU again shows itself to be as or more important for what it is than what it does. Neutral or non-aligned European states find the EU provides them with a forum for security cooperation without requiring them to sign on to a mutual defence pact, as NATO does. In particular, Sweden, Finland, and Austria all have made significant contributions to EU security missions that would not have been politically possible if they were NATO missions (see Bergman and Peterson 2006). Still, with some exceptions, such as its widely-praised contribution to anti-piracy efforts on the east coast of Africa (see Box 9.2), the EU's international security operations in Africa, the Palestinian territories, Iraq, Afghanistan, Indonesia, and Libya have been relatively small and incidental to much larger operations under the auspices of the UN, NATO, or the US.

The Common Security and Defence Policy

Given the CFSP's mixed record, as well as Europe's claims to be a civilian power, it might seem paradoxical to extend the EU system into the realm of defence. Most EU states have long accepted the supremacy of NATO on defence matters. Yet, the Union has taken small but decisive steps in recent years towards creating a CSDP. The 1999 crisis in Kosovo marked a turning point. Again, the EU at first appeared timid and weak as it had earlier in Bosnia. NATO took the lead in pushing both crises towards resolution, and the US military contributions dwarfed those of Europe. Thus, the EU responded with firmer Treaty commitments to security cooperation first in Amsterdam but especially at Nice. In particular, the Treaty of Nice marked out the so-called Petersberg tasks—humanitarian and rescue missions, peacekeeping, and crisis management, including 'peacemaking' (the latter never clearly defined)—as basic EU foreign policy goals. A new Political and Security Committee (known by its French acronym COPS) of senior national officials was created and designated the linchpin linking CSDP to the CFSP. The EU was also given its own Military Committee and crisis management unit. Plans were agreed to enable deployment of a EU Rapid Reaction Force of up to 60,000 troops. After 2001, for the first time military officers were seen at work in the EU's Council building.

Sceptics argued that the real problem lay not with Treaty language or institutions but with Europe's weak and under-funded militaries. Military spending in most EU states declined sharply after the Cold War, leaving the US to extend its lead in the application of new technologies to military hardware. The target date for declaring the EU Rapid Reaction Force operational was delayed and then fudged. The US administration under George W. Bush initially refused European offers to contribute troops to the war in Afghanistan in 2001, in large part because there was almost nothing that US forces could not do more effectively on their own.

The CSDP has thus been restricted to modest missions. Its supporters insist that it has produced tangible achievements, such as the 2002 military intervention in the Bunia region of Congo (see Box 9.2). Similarly, the EU claimed success in taking over from NATO command of a large peacekeeping force in Bosnia from 2004–12, but also was criticized for perpetuating a culture of 'dependency, helplessness, and disillusionment' in Bosnia and failing to 'coordinate complex civil and military matters' (see Manners 2006: 190–1). More recently, the EU has become heavily involved in Africa, launching multiple CSDP missions in Niger, South Sudan and (in particular) the Horn of Africa (to combat piracy; see Box 9.2).

| **BOX 9.2** | **Bunia and Somalia** |

Throughout its first decade, supporters of the CSDP tended to point to the French-led 2002 intervention in Bunia (Congo), which came in response to a UN request, and was claimed to have prevented a humanitarian disaster from escalating. However, Bunia became a source of considerable debate amongst students of CSDP who in retrospect found its scope very limited and benefits questionable (see Manners 2006; Howorth 2007: 236–7).

A more recent (and probably clearer) case of the CSDP fulfilling its promise was the EU's first naval mission, Operation Atalanta, designed to counter piracy and deliver humanitarian aid to the Horn of Africa, alongside separate missions to assist African Union forces in

Cont. ➤

Cont.

regaining control of Somalia from warlords, training Somali troops, and building maritime capacity in the region. Somali pirates were estimated to have collected $160 million in ransoms in 2011, the year before Operation Atalanta was launched, by taking hostages but also (more often) goods seized from shipping lanes along the east African coast, through which more than one-third of the world's traded goods travelled. The EU's anti-piracy effort had somehow to be integrated with others mounted by the UN, France, the UK and (especially) NATO. In a test of EU-NATO cooperation, formal arrangements were found to be so unworkable that naval forces on either side found themselves hiding their operational collaboration from their political masters and even communicating with each other via Yahoo Messenger (Gebhard and Smith 2014). But Operation Atalanta together with the other CSDP missions (and nearly €200 in EU humanitarian aid) was governed by a new 'comprehensive approach', described as a new trademark for the Union's external action, that sought to use the full range of European policy tools to deal with a specific target or problem; in this case, Somalia's status as a rogue state. While Somalia remained enormously fragile, it 'moved from an impending food crisis and a failed government to tackling justice reform' in 2013, a result that was 'credibly due in part to the EU's sufficiently comprehensive and necessarily sustained engagement in the region' (Hadfield and Fiott 2013: 175).

To its critics, CSDP has been viewed as a way for NATO's reluctant European members—especially the French—to create an alternative security alliance that distances the EU from the United States, and seeks to 'balance' against American hegemony. One leading scholar argues that CSDP 'is not quite a balancing project, but certainly an effort by Europeans . . . to develop an alternative security supplier' (Posen 2004:12). Critics are often quick to add that the 'caveats' that have limited the capacity of European forces to contribute to the NATO effort in Afghanistan (for instance, giving some no more than the right to self-defence) or Libya (when Europe's efforts were heavily dependent on US resources and weaponry) have shown how weakly committed many EU states are to NATO.

However, the CSDP's detractors cannot deny that several developments in the twenty-first century cut against the grain of their argument. First, for the first time since the days of DeGaulle, France is now a full member of NATO's military command. Second, almost no one in EU security policy circles now imagines that CSDP will morph into a collective security framework that replaces NATO. Third, multiple EU member states—particularly the UK but also France and Italy—have suffered significant casualties and loss of lives from their commitment of forces to Afghanistan, itself the scene of a conflict that few in Europe wanted when launched by the US in 2001. The Afghan conflict remained unresolved for many years and ended up being the longest western military intervention since World War II—not least because of American neglect and the distraction of Iraq after 2003. The shift in the CSDP's focus from military to civilian reconstruction efforts led Smith (2014: 161) to observe that 'Americans are simply not very good at the kinds of security problems facing many populations, particularly in the developing world; in other words, America is not very effective as a "state builder"'. One upshot is to allow space for the EU to emerge as a more important and effective security actor because of its focus and expertise in nation-building.

Despite its shift in focus to more civilian tasks, the CSDP also has become a framework for combining European military assets at the 'hard' end of capabilities, through the so-called European battle groups, in specialized areas such as jungle or desert fighting or coping with a chemical weapons attack (see Peterson et al. 2012). Each battle group includes at least 1500 combat troops drawn from multiple EU member states but with one designated as the 'lead nation'. A total of 18 battle groups were operational by 2014. Interestingly, a Nordic battle group initially formed by Sweden and Finland included troops contributed by Norway, despite its non-membership of the Union.

Meanwhile, the European Defence Agency (EDA) has sought to coax sorely needed cooperation between European defence ministries and arms makers, quietly but gradually, since its launch in 2004 (see Box 9.3). If there is one European economic sector where the internal market does *not* exist, at enormous cost to European taxpayers, it is the arms sector. The EDA explicitly seeks to sustain the CSDP. Making the post-Lisbon High Representative the chair of its Steering Board, itself consisting of EU defence ministers, reflected determination to subject cooperation in defence production and spending to a new, higher level of political control. Defence cooperation was embraced to an extent previously unseen in Europe in response to post-recession cuts in public spending. Unprecedented operational military cooperation was embraced by Europe's two largest military powers, France and the UK, after the latter undertook large public expenditure cuts in 2010. The December 2013 European Council focused almost exclusively on enhancing Europe's shared capacity for defence capabilities. More generally, CSDP remains an area with a large gap between ambitions and achievements, but it is also a continuing growth area for European integration.

Internal Security

EU internal security has been an even more buoyant growth area, although the pace has been uneven across the issues that fall under this broad heading. It is now possible to identify a common migration and asylum policy covering some but (importantly) not all aspects of policy. Developments in other areas such as judicial and police co-operation has been significant, but slower. One way to think about EU internal security policy is that it has developed in response to the vast disparity between political and legal integration in Europe. To illustrate the point, the Franco-German alliance has historically been viewed as one of the closest bilateral

BOX 9.3	**Key concepts and terms**

Battle groups combine national military resources at the 'hard end' of European capabilities in specialized areas. The EU decided in 2004 to create 20 Battle Groups of 1,500 troops each, which would be deployable at short notice for limited deployments. Ten years after they were created, none had ever been deployed.

CSDP stands for the Common Security and Defence Policy (formerly known as ESDP: the European Security and Defence Policy). It was created in 1999 to engage in the so-called 'Petersberg tasks' (named after a German castle where an earlier summit devoted to defence was held): humanitarian and rescue missions, peacekeeping, crisis management, and the vaguely-specified task of 'peacemaking'.

European Defence Agency (EDA) was created in 2004 'to support the member states and the Council in their effort to improve European defence capabilities [particularly] in the field of crisis management and to sustain' the ESDP. It aims to move the EU towards more cooperation in arms production and procurement.

Frontex is the EU's agency for the management of its external border. It was created in 2005 to coordinate member states' operational cooperation in external border controls, provide training to national border guards, carry out risk analyses, organize joint control operations, and assist member states in migrant return operations.

Schengen or the 'Schengen Acquis' refers to two intergovernmental treaties concluded in 1985 and 1990 as well as the work of the Schengen Executive Committee, which provides for the abolition of controls at the internal borders of Schengen members. With the Amsterdam Treaty, the Schengen Acquis was integrated into EU. Not all EU states are members—the UK and Ireland have opt-outs—and the Schengen area includes Norway, Switzerland and Iceland. Schengen is the village at the meeting-point of France, Germany and Benelux where those countries initially agreed to end border controls.

Soft security is a post-Cold War concept that refers to security that is obtained through non-military policy instruments (except in cases of peacekeeping) and does not involve territorial defence of the state. It is related to the ideas of 'human security'—defence of the citizen, as opposed to the state—and 'homeland security', obtained via policies designed to eliminate internal security threats.

relationships between any two EU member states, and it has given considerable pulse to the European project. Yet, until recently, legal barriers complicated or even prevented cooperation on internal security policy between even these two closest of allies. When German prosecutors brought to trial four German residents who had planned to blow up a Christmas market in Strasbourg in late 2000, they had to drop a number of the charges, including those of belonging to a terrorist organization (of which these four people clearly were members), partly because it was so hard to bring evidence and witnesses from France. It is possible, of course, to walk from the city centre of Strasbourg to Germany in about 15 minutes.

A recurrent feature of EU internal security policy has been a preference for forms of cooperation that rely on coordination of national law enforcement systems and which do not directly impinge on member states' sovereignty. Since the Amsterdam Treaty of 1997 there has been significant ceding of authority for free movement, migration and asylum that are linked together in Chapter 4 of the Treaty. Since the early 2000s, EU laws have been agreed covering asylum, irregular migration, family migration and the rights of migrants who are long-term residents. Member states also agreed to co-ordination of measures on some forms of labour migration, although the numbers of migrants to be admitted is very clearly identified in the Treaty as a matter for the member states to decide.

While there has been a formal competence shift, member states continue to favour more informal forms of integration via the networking of their domestic authorities in addition to creating new supranational competences. Europol illustrates the point (see Box 9.4), as does Frontex. Established in 2005, Frontex primarily coordinates national border guards with the aim of ensuring that the EU's tight border security standards are implemented evenly throughout the Union. Given the uneven burden carried by those (southern and eastern) member states that lie on the main migration routes to Europe, Frontex has been charged with the coordination of joint operations in which member states share personnel and equipment in the patrolling of a particular border area.

BOX 9.4	Compared to what?

Europol

Europol is short-hand for the European Law Enforcement Agency. Some of Europol's founding fathers, in particular the former German Chancellor Helmut Kohl, hoped that Europol would develop into a European analogue to the US Federal Bureau of Investigation. In reality, this comparison fails to stand up. Europol has no operational capacities of its own. Its officers have no direct powers of arrest. Europol is not a supranational policy force. Rather, it is a coordination structure for national police forces in preventing and combating terrorism, drug trafficking, and other forms of organized crime. Over time, it has grown in size to the point where its staff included nearly 700 senior national EU police officers by 2011.

Its precursor, the European Drugs Unit (EDU), was created in the mid-1990s to fight the drugs trade, the trafficking of radioactive and nuclear substances, as well as vehicles and human beings. Europol was established by a Convention in 1995, although disagreements about the role of the European Court (ECJ) and the immunity of its staff delayed its entry into force for another three years. This legal basis, which placed Europol outside the Community framework and outside the control of the European Parliament, was much debated. In 2010, Europol was reformed as a full EU agency, which gave the EP more control over its activities and budget.

Cont. ➤

Cont.

Europol's main task is to support national law enforcement agencies by gathering, analysing and disseminating information and coordinating operations in the fight against organized international crime. Europol's remit now extends to the fight against the forgery of money and terrorism. In 2002, and with 9.11 still a fresh memory, Europol was granted a limited operational role with the option of launching joint investigation teams in which member state officials conducted, together with Europol staff, joint operations. Contact with the national counterparts is primarily secured through the deployment of national liaison officers at the Europol headquarters in The Hague, including officers from associated third countries such as Australia, Canada, Columbia, Iceland, Norway, Russia, Switzerland, and the US. Despite the existence of this network of now 124 liaison officers, member states have remained reluctant to share their criminal intelligence via Europol and its data bases. Therefore, Europol's contribution to the fight against international organized crime is generally seen to have failed to meet expectations.

To its critics, Europol is neither transparent nor sufficiently accountable, and illustrative of how internal security policy has become gradually institutionalized over time (see Kostakopoulou 2006). Compared to its national counterparts, Europol does seem to operate in a legal grey area with (for example) its officers enjoying a very strong form of legal immunity. However, it is probably easy to overestimate its reach and powers, particularly since it has been portrayed (often very inaccurately) in so many films, TV series and books—as is noted on Europol's own web-site. To its supporters, Europol is an important weapon in Europe's counterterrorism efforts: its investigations have led to the arrest of numerous individuals with links to Al Qaeda and other terrorist organizations since 2001.

In sum, Europol illustrates the choice by the member states to seek better coordination of national law enforcement systems rather than replacing them with new supranational structures that could resemble a European FBI. This coordination is backed by joint professional training for national police officers, such as the joint curricula developed by the European Police College (CEPOL). As the problem of inadequate information-sharing via Europol shows, these bottom-up structures need time to develop, and require a strong degree of mutual trust between national law enforcement agencies.

As in the case of Europol, Frontex has been hampered by a lack of commitment and cooperation from member states, as well as by the scale of movement. In its 2014 Annual Risk Assessment, Frontex reported a steep growth in detections of people making illegal border-crossings from around 72,500 in 2012 to 107,000 in 2013. The increase was strongly driven by conflict in the Middle East with, for example, 25,500 Syrians detected. Across the EU more than a further 50,000 people from Syria made a claim for protection using asylum and refugee provisions. Putting these numbers in perspective, by mid–2014, more than one million Syrians had fled to neighbouring

Lebanon, which shows that far greater numbers of people fled to neighbouring states in the Middle East rather than to the EU.

Member states have actively sought co-operation but have been less willing to share responsibility in the form of actually taking in new migrants. Still, irregular migration is clearly a shared European problem and several initiatives have been launched to render Frontex more operational. They include joint operations at land and sea borders and efforts to develop new technologies of border control and surveillance. In 2014, Frontex identified its priorities as further development of the Eurosur border surveillance system, reinforcing operational capacity in Greece and Italy, and developing new structures to reinforce co-operation such as European Border Guard Teams. An important question is whether these operations only serve to divert migration flows to new routes and travel itineraries that are increasingly dangerous for migrants.

Greece became an illustrative case in 2010–11. It became a weak link in the EU's border controls after other entry points, such as Mediterranean sea routes, became more dangerous and difficult. Frontex estimated that 90 per cent of irregular entrants to the EU crossed the Greek-Turkish border by this route, with 45,000 arriving in the first half of 2010 alone. Yet, in an illustration of how national capitals often flout EU rules, Greece's record of dealing with asylum-seekers was so suspect that in early 2011 the European Court of Justice upheld the claim of an asylum applicant in Belgium that Greece did not offer adequate protection and that return to Greece would breach the standards set out in the EU's Common European Asylum System. The consequence of this ruling was that EU states could not return asylum applicants to Greece who had first entered the Union by crossing the Turkish border, even though the 2003 Dublin Regulation required asylum seekers to request refugee status in their first country of entry (so as to avoid multiple asylum requests). As one EU diplomat put it, 'Most interior ministries, given the chance, will take up any opportunity to rid themselves of potential refugees, especially if they can do so within European rules. That they would stop sending [asylum seekers] back to Greece just highlights how concerned they are' (*Financial Times*, 26 October 2010). This attitude became salient again in Europe's response to increasing immigration pressure following the 2011 revolutions in the Arab world, with calls by Italy and Malta for a redistribution of migrants seeking protection among the EU member states falling on mostly deaf ears.

Member states' reluctance to pool internal security resources has been accompanied by a tendency to limit the scope of supranational legislation. This point was illustrated by the adoption, at the 1999 Tampere European Council, of the principle of mutual recognition in the area of criminal law (see Box 9.5) as opposed to new EU legislation. In short, the pressures for policy cooperation on internal security have intensified. But the hesitancy of member states to create truly common policies using traditional EU methods has remained mostly undiminished.

BOX 9.5	**Does law enforcement trump human rights?**

In contrast to operational cooperation between police forces and border guards, coop-eration in the judicial sphere was initially slow to develop. Yet, since the 1999 Tampere European Council, it has been one of the most dynamic areas of JHA cooperation. The cornerstone of this cooperation is the principle of mutual recognition of national laws and judicial procedures in contrast to harmonization via supranational law. The flagship exam-ple is the European Arrest Warrant (EAW), adopted just a few months after the terrorist attacks of 9.11.2001. Under the EAW, national law enforcement authorities agree to arrest and transfer a criminal suspect or sentenced person to another member state on the basis of an arrest warrant issued by a judicial authority in that other state. Member states thus began to recognize the judicial decisions of another member state, based on the criminal law of that state, as mutually compatible with their own judicial system. Significant national differences in the exact definition of certain crimes or sentences made clear the need for some form of harmonization early on. However, attempts to approximate laws on criminal proceedings and the rights of suspects ranged from difficult to impossible due to member states' reluctance to accept European legislation in core areas of sovereignty. The EAW thus illustrates the 'tension between security and freedom . . . constitutive of any liberal democracy' (Lavenex and Wagner 2007: 225). In the EU's case, criminal law cooperation has tended to favour law enforcement at the expense of the rights of individual citizens. This result may be partly due to the intergovernmental procedures by which these European rules have been adopted. As MacCormick (2008: 172) observed:

. . . no parliament had any real say about the rules adopted in the [EAW] framework decision—not the EP, which was only consulted, and not the national parliaments, which did not even have to be consulted. The principle that a citizen's liberty should be limitable only under laws agreed by his or her elected representatives had gone out of the window. It could be argued that the EAW illustrates clearly that there was a democratic deficit in the former intergovernmental pillar of JHA.

Theorizing European Security Policy

The theoretical perspectives applied throughout this book all shed light, albeit of different hues, on EU security policy. Neofunctionalists could point to how func-tional pressures for cooperation have led both internal and external security policies to become more Brussels-based over time. In particular, the abolition of controls at the EU's internal borders, which was mainly economically motivated, engendered a wide range of cooperation. It now extends to migration and police and judicial cooperation deemed necessary for safeguarding internal security. Moreover, the Lisbon Treaty makes a serious move towards more qualified voting in this policy area. Neofunctionalists would see the move as evidence that economic integration has 'spilled over' and led to supranational policies and processes in areas outside of economic policy per se.

For their part, liberal intergovernmentalists would argue that the dominant actors in both internal and external security policy remain national actors. To be sure, the EU has witnessed more security policy cooperation over time. But that cooperation is overwhelmingly between national officials and other kinds of actor—soldiers, police officers or judicial experts—whose primary affiliation is to an EU member state. One study finds that national representatives to COPS are dominant in decision-making on the CSDP (Mérand et al. 2011). Intergovernmentalism also endures within (say) Europol or the EU battle groups. One EU insider (with no obvious theoretical affiliation) notes that the successful mediation of the European Council President (at the time), France's Nicolas Sarkozy, in the Russo-Georgian war of 2008 'was beginning to look like European high politics'; that is: '[t]he Union had acted as a mediator in a matter of war and peace, with member states turning a war in their backyard into a joint responsibility' (van Middelaar 2013: 208). But it went without saying that it was the EU's member states that brokered the ceasefire, as opposed to its common institutions, with one of its most powerful in the lead: things might well have been very different if (say) Slovenia or Cyprus had held the (then rotating) Council Presidency.

In contrast, institutionalists would note how purely intergovernmental cooperation has become increasingly institutionalized over time, with new institutions such as the Political and Security Committee or Europol being created in recent decades. Path dependency is clearly visible in past choices on (say) the Petersberg tasks or the Amsterdam Treaty's enormously complex section on internal security. More specifically, these choices either shaped subsequent policies—such as the CSDP in the case of the Petersberg tasks—or were viewed as requiring repair, as Lisbon did in its 'clean up' of Amsterdam's internal security policy provisions.

Constructivists would highlight how constant interactions between both internal and external policy elites over the course of years has created both a new spirit and practice of cooperation amongst some of the most inward-looking and least predisposed officials to international collaboration. The steady pace of the Communitarization of internal security policy has culminated in the Lisbon Treaty's provisions to subject most EU policies to the Community method. Meanwhile, constructivists would consider the development of the CSDP as evidence of how much policy cooperation is possible when governments and officials begin to seek common goals, such as the resolution of ethnic conflicts in Africa and the Balkans, because they share common ideas about the virtues of harmonious multiculturalism.

Finally, public policy specialists would note that EU security policy is highly technocratic, dominated by experts, and mostly made within specialized policy networks. Policy analysis that seeks to understand how policies emerge from interactions within networks that bringing together security officials and law enforcement specialists operating from different levels of a multi-level system—incorporating the EU, national capitals, and other international organizations—is central to the 'governance' approach to EU security policy and European integration more generally. Governance via policy networks can lack transparency: EU internal security policies in particular have mostly been made in a process of shadowy bargaining between national officials that has often been considerably less than transparent. But both external and internal security policy networks have expanded to include more different types of actor over time. To illustrate, making internal security policies post-Lisbon will necessitate bargaining with members of the European Parliament, given their new powers to co-legislate with the Council, and therefore through more transparent procedures affording opportunities for NGOs to make their points. And soldiers now rub shoulders with diplomats in the Council building on Rue de la Loi in Brussels, as they never did in the past, with the EU's own Military Committee playing a key role in determining the scope and objectives of the EU's external security missions.

Conclusion

We have covered some very broad terrain in this chapter. Again, few officials in Brussels would recognize the designation 'security policy' as a EU policy area. But all the actions we have discussed, say, to cut down on illegal immigration into the Union, stamp out corruption in Kosovo, or deliver humanitarian aid to Libya have something in common: they seek to ensure security. Moreover, as we have seen, recent years have witnessed a blurring of the boundaries between internal and external security, even if the policy-makers responsible for Police and Judicial Cooperation on one hand and CSDP on the other have little to do with one another.

We also have seen that commonly accepted wisdoms about EU security policies have increasingly come into question. First, it has become more difficult to argue that the Union is exclusively concerned with soft security issues: it has sent soldiers to multiple continents to try to keep or even 'make' peace, and its counterterrorism policy agenda is buoyant. Second, policy-making may still be dominated by the EU's member states and national actors more than in other areas of policy. But both external and internal security policies have become increasingly Brussels-centred. The policy areas covered in this chapter have been among those where European integration has proceeded the fastest and furthest in the two decades or so since the Maastricht Treaty gave birth to what we now know as the European Union. Third, these developments have re-emphasized the centrality of security in the general purpose of the European integration project. Police and judicial cooperation in the fight against irregular migration and transnational crime have progressed faster than the harmonization of judicial procedures or individual freedoms. The Union's CSDP may lack coherence, but the EU has, again arguably, reacted as best it could to the brutal wars of the 1990s in the Balkans or 2000s in Africa. The former German

Foreign Minister, Joshka Fischer, has commented on the CSDP: 'It's quite something compared to the past. Compared to what's needed, it's nothing' (quoted in van Middelaar 2013: 209). Nevertheless, the Union has grown into a vigorous security actor. It shows no sign of becoming any less so.

DISCUSSION QUESTIONS

1. When what is now the EU was originally created, it was given no security role. Now the EU is very much in the security business. Why?

2. What have been the main events that have encouraged or required the EU to develop new security policies?

3. Explain why the creation of the internal market and lifting of internal border controls within the EU gave impetus to create new internal security policies.

4. In what ways does EU internal security policy illustrate how concerns about national sovereignty limit the willingness of EU member states to create new common policies?

FURTHER READING

For a sharp, incisive treatment of twenty-first century security debates, see Dannreuther (2007). Cottey (2013) links these debates to European and EU security more specifically and Bickerton et al. (2011) offer a theory-driven and comprehensive treatment of CSDP. Smith's (2014) volume on EU foreign policy has good sections on the Union's policy instruments, its conflict prevention efforts, and its fight against international crime. For an up-to-date treatment of internal security policy, see Lavenex (2010). Comprehensive analyses of EU asylum and immigration policies include Geddes (2008) and Geddes and Boswell (2011). Kaunert (2011) gives a timely account of the dynamics towards supranational governance in JHA.

Bickerton, Chris J., Irondelle, Bastien, and Menon, Anand (2011), (eds) (special issue on ESDP), *Journal of Common Market Studies* 49 (1): 1–21.

Cottey, A. (2013), *Security in the 21st Century Europe*, 2nd edn. (Basingstoke and New York: Palgrave).

Dannreuther, R. (2007), *International Security the Contemporary Agenda* (Cambridge and Malden MA: Polity).

Geddes, A. (2008), *Immigration and European Integration: Towards Fortress Europe*, 2nd edn. (Manchester: Manchester University Press).

Geddes, A. and Boswell, C. (2011), *Migration and Mobility in the European Union* (Basingstoke and New York: Palgrave).

Kaunert, Christian (2011), *European Internal Security: Towards Supranational Governance in the Area of Freedom, Security, and Justice* (Manchester: Manchester University Press).

Lavenex, S. (2014), 'Justice and Home Affairs: Communitarization with Hesitation', in H. Wallace., M.A. Pollack and A.R. Young (eds), *Policy-Making in the European Union*, 7th edn. (Oxford and New York: Oxford University Press).

Smith, K. E. (2014), *European Union Foreign Policy in a Changing World*, 3rd edn. (Cambridge and Malden MA: Polity).

WEB LINKS

The best and most useful website for current research related to CSDP is that of the Paris-based Institute for Security Studies (**http://www.iss.europa.eu**), which formally became an autonomous European Agency in 2002. The EU External Action Service also maintains a comprehensive site on the CSDP at: **http://www.eeas.europa.eu/csdp/** The European Defence Agency has its own website at: **http://www.eda.europa.eu** so do Frontex at: **http://www.frontex.europa.eu** and Europol at: **http://www.europol.eu** (a somewhat humorous list of portrayals of Europol in films and novels is available at: **http://www.europol.europa.eu/content/page/tv-films-and-books-195**). A comprehensive and critical databank on EU internal security cooperation is provided on: **www.statewatch.org** To see where the EU has ongoing CSDP missions, visit: **http://eeas.europa.eu/csdp/missions-and-operations/index_en.htm**

Visit the Online Resource Centre that accompanies this book for additional material: **www.oxfordtextbooks.co.uk/orc/kenealy4e/**

CHAPTER 10

The EU as a Global Actor

John Peterson and Marlene Gottwald

▌ Summary

The European Union's ambitions to be a global power are a surprising by-product of European integration. Students of European foreign policy mostly focus on EU trade, aid, and the **Common Foreign and Security Policy (CFSP)**, but cannot neglect the extensive national foreign policy activities of its member states. On most economic issues, the EU is able to speak with a genuinely single voice. It has more difficulty showing solidarity on aid policy, but is powerful when it does. The Union's external policy aspirations now extend to traditional foreign and security policy. But distinct national policies persist and the EU suffers from weak or fragmented leadership. Debates about European foreign policy tend to be about whether the glass is half-full—with the EU more active globally than ever before—or half-empty, and mainly about disappointed expectations.

Introducing European Foreign Policy

One of the founders of what is now the EU, Jean Monnet, once described European integration as a 'key step towards the organization of tomorrow's world' (quoted in Jørgensen 2006: 521). Nevertheless, Monnet and the other founders of the original European Economic Community (EEC) had little ambition to create a new kind of international power. In fact, the EEC was initially given explicit external powers only to assist former European colonies in Africa and conduct international trade negotiations, since a common market could not, by definition, exist without a common trade policy. Yet both policies produced considerable political spillover. A narrow commitment (demanded by France) in the Treaty of Rome to offer a small amount of foreign aid and work towards a free trade area with sub-Saharan African states evolved into a full-blown political 'partnership' with no fewer than 46 African, Caribbean and Pacific (ACP) states by 1975. As for trade policy, spirited policy debates ensued almost immediately: trade agreements with whom? What about sanctions against oppressive or aggressive states? Member states soon felt the need to complement trade policy (and the external aspects of other EC policies) with political criteria laid down in what was at first a separate, informal framework of 'political cooperation' and then later became a formal Treaty objective of a common foreign and security policy.

The EU now aspires to be a global power: that is, a major international actor that can, like the United States (US) or China, influence developments anywhere in the world, and draw on its full range of economic, political, and security instruments. It can be argued that 'foreign policy has been one of the areas in which European integration has made the most dynamic advances' (Tonra and Christiansen 2004: 545). Still, the EU is a strange and often ineffective global actor. Distinctive *national* foreign policies endure in Europe and show few signs of disappearing. The notion of 'European foreign policy', comprising all of what the EU and its member states do in world politics, collectively or not, has gained prominence (see Carlsnaes 2006; Hill and Smith 2011).

Debates about European foreign policy tend to be about whether the glass is half-full or half-empty. On one hand, the EU has used enlargement as a tool of foreign policy and dramatically transformed the regions to its east and south (see Chapter 8). The Union is an economic superpower. It has gradually developed its Common Security and Defence Policy (CSDP) for crisis management or humanitarian intervention (see Chapter 9).

On the other hand, the EU suffers from chronic problems of disunity, incoherence, and weak leadership. European foreign policy can be undermined by all manner of rivalries: among its member governments, between EU institutions, and between them and national foreign ministries. The EU was entirely sidelined during the 2003 war in Iraq because it could not come even remotely close to agreeing a common policy (see Peterson 2003/4). The EU remained unable to respond effectively when the Libyan dictator, Muammar al-Gaddafi, threated to instigate a bloodbath against his own people in 2011 (see Box 10.3). And it stood by almost helplessly as Russia annexed the Ukrainian region of Crimea in 2014 (see Box 10.5), adopting sanctions that many considered timid.

Sometimes, the same international event or issue can be used to defend either the half-full or half-empty thesis. Consider the call by the head of a leading non-governmental organization, Human Rights Watch, for the EU to 'fill the leadership void' on human rights post-Iraq, after the US was widely viewed as flaunting them. Here, we might see the Union as a beacon of hope for a more progressive, humane international order. Or, we might share the despair of the issuer of the plea at how the EU continues to 'punch well beneath its weight' on human rights (Roth 2007). The EU frequently fails to meet expectations while never ceasing to develop new ambitions.

How it developed

The EU's international ambitions have their origins in the 1960s. In particular, American disregard for European preferences in Vietnam and the Middle East presented the European countries with incentives to defend their interests collectively, and thus more effectively, in foreign policy. According to a logic known as the 'politics of scale', the whole—the EU speaking and acting as one—is more powerful than the sum of its parts, or member states acting individually (Ginsberg 2001).

By 1970, a loose intergovernmental framework, **European Political Cooperation** (**EPC**), was created to try to coordinate national foreign policies. Linked to the European Community, but independent of it, EPC was very much dominated by national foreign ministers and ministries. Member governments identified where their national interests overlapped, without any pretension to a 'common' foreign policy. The European Commission was little more than an invited guest, and the Parliament largely excluded.

Nonetheless, EPC fostered consensus on difficult issues in the 1970s and 80s, including the Arab–Israeli conflict, apartheid in South Africa, and relations with the Soviet bloc (through what became the Organization for Security and Cooperation in Europe, or **OSCE**; see Box 10.1). Europe was mostly limited to saying things— issuing diplomatic *démarches*—as opposed to doing things via EPC. But increasingly it backed up EPC positions with European Community actions using economic aid or sanctions (which were applied to Argentina during the Falklands War).

EPC's perceived successes led to claims that Europe could become a 'civilian power' (see Galtung 1973). That is, the EC could emerge as an alternative to the two Cold War superpowers, uphold multilateralism, liberalism, and human rights as values, and be an advocate for peaceful conflict resolution. EPC was given Treaty status and formally linked to the activities of the Community in the 1986 Single European Act.

Yet the geopolitical earthquakes that shook Europe beginning in 1989 exposed EPC as weak and unable to foster collective action. The idea of strengthening foreign policy cooperation in a new 'political union' was given impetus by the dramatic transitions

---

BOX 10.1	Key concepts and terms

The **Common Foreign and Security Policy (CFSP)** was created by the 1992 Maastricht Treaty as a successor to the European Political Cooperation mechanism. It has been embellished by successive new Treaties and given (by the Treaty of Nice) a Brussels-based Political and Security Committee to prepare Foreign Ministers' meetings and (by the Treaty of Lisbon) a 'new look' High Representative and the EEAS.

The **Cotonou agreement** was agreed in the African state of Bénin in 2000 and then revised repeatedly (lastly in 2010). It is claimed to be a 'comprehensive partnership' between former European colonies and the EU with the aim of reducing and eventually eradicating poverty, while at the same time promoting sustainable development and the integration of the ACP (African, Caribbean, and Pacific Group of States) countries into global trade.

The **European External Action Service (EEAS)** was established by the Lisbon Treaty and became active in 2010. It works under the authority of the High Representative and brings under one roof EU (Commission and Council) and national diplomats. The EEAS's task is to assist the High Representative in implementing the CFSP and other areas of EU foreign policy.

The **OSCE**—the Organization for Security and Cooperation in Europe—brings together 57 (as of 2014) states from Europe and beyond in what is the world's largest regional security organization. It claims to take a 'comprehensive approach to security', extending especially to human rights. The OSCE works on the basis of unanimity and its decisions are politically, not legally, binding. It thus is criticized as toothless, and failed to defuse the 2014 crisis in the Ukraine (both Russia and Ukraine are OSCE members).

---

in Central and Eastern Europe, the Gulf War, the collapse of the Soviet Union, and war in Yugoslavia. Thus the 1992 Maastricht Treaty grafted a new **Common Foreign and Security Policy** (CFSP, along with a new Justice and Home Affairs (JHA) policy) onto the existing Treaty of Rome, resulting in the EU's then three-pillar structure. There is no question that the EU became far more active internationally in the years that followed. There is considerable debate about whether it also became more effective.

The basics

The EU aspires to international power for two basic reasons. First, even the Union's largest states are medium-sized powers compared to, say, the US or China. All European states, especially smaller ones, seek to use the EU as a 'multiplier' of their power and influence. There is controversy about whether the Union is a truly global, as opposed to a regional, power (Orbie 2008; Krotz 2009). However, its largest member states—France, UK, Germany, and Italy, (the first two being members of the UN Security Council)—give the Union a 'pull towards the global perspective which many of the [other member states] simply do not have as part of their foreign policy traditions' (Hill 2006: 67). EU military and civilian missions in Africa and Afghanistan, as well as the Balkans and Middle East, illustrate the point.

Second, the Union's international weight increases each time it enlarges or expands its policy competence. The 13 countries that joined after 2004 were all (besides Poland) small and (mostly) pro-American states with limited foreign policy ambitions. But EU membership allowed them to distance or defend themselves from the US on issues such as Russia or trade policy, while making the Union a potentially more powerful player on these and other international issues. Meanwhile, the EU has accumulated new foreign policy tools, beginning with its aid programmes for Africa in 1963 and most recently the CSDP (see Chapter 9). It also has created, via the Lisbon Treaty, new figures to represent the Union externally: a 'permanent' European Council President and a **High Representative for Foreign Affairs and Security Policy** who is also a Vice-President of the Commission. Lisbon also gave birth to the **European External Action Service (EEAS)**, potentially a nascent EU foreign ministry. But whatever institutions it creates, the EU is powerful internationally above all because it presides over the world's largest single market (including nearly 500 million consumers, or around 40 per cent more than the US).

Still, European foreign policy is hindered by three basic gaps. One is between task expansion, which has been considerable, and the integration of authority, which has been—at least prior to the Lisbon Treaty—limited. Before the creation of the EEAS, the total number of European diplomatic staff worldwide (EU plus national officials) was more than 40,000 diplomats in 1,500 missions. Yet, no single authority could give orders to this huge collection of officials. No one claimed that the US—with around 15,000 staff in 300 missions— was weaker because it was so outnumbered (Everts 2002: 26). The new High Representative was given authority over the EEAS, which at least promised finally to give the Union a figure who could direct the EU's own diplomatic corps, which often proved impossible in the past because of fragmented institutional structures in Brussels. However, since its establishment in 2010 the EEAS has struggled to 'demonstrate its relevance and added value' (Balfour and Raik 2012: 25). The High Representative has been criticized for providing only weak, sometimes non-existent, leadership (Helwig 2013). Those who see the EU as a global actor glass as (at least) half full tended to urge patience since newly-created institutions—especially in an area as fraught and high-stakes as foreign policy—inevitably need time to establish themselves (see Rüger 2012).

The gap between the EU's economic power and political weakness is a related but separate problem. Europe manages to defend its interests on matters of 'low politics'—economic, trade, and (less often) monetary issues—with a more or less single voice. External trade policy is made via the Community method of decision-making (see Chapter 3), which delegates considerable power to the Union's institutions and sees the Council act by a qualified majority. The EU also has significant resources in aid and development policy, and has emerged as a potentially major power in international environmental diplomacy.

In contrast, the Union often fails to speak as one on matters of traditional diplomacy, or 'high politics', which touch most directly on national sovereignty, prestige, or vital interests, and Council decisions must be unanimous. The CFSP created by the Maastricht Treaty was meant to cover 'all aspects of foreign and security policy'. However, there is no *single* EU foreign policy in the sense of one that replaces or eliminates national policies. In contrast to (say) EU trade policy, the CFSP relies overwhelmingly on intergovernmental consensus. It remains difficult to envisage member states ever delegating power to decide life and death questions, such as whether to contribute military force to a 'hot' war. In short, the gap between the EU's economic power and political weight endures largely because the Community system remains more efficient and decisive than the CFSP system.

A final gap is between the world's expectations of the EU and its capacity to meet them (Hill 1998). In the early days of the post-Cold War period, European foreign policy-makers often oversold the Union's ability to act quickly or resolutely in international affairs. Nearly two decades later, the rhetoric had muted but the EU still struggled to be a truly global, as opposed to a regional, power in its European neighbourhood. Chris Patten (2005: 176), a former Commissioner for External Relations, was frank:

America is a superpower, partly because it is the only country whose will and intentions matter everywhere, and are everywhere decisive to the settlement of the world's problems. Europe can help to solve these problems, but there are only some parts of the world—like the Balkans—where our role (while not necessarily crucial) is as important as, or more important than, that of China in the case of North Korea.

These three gaps—between task expansion and integration, economic unity and political division, and capabilities and expectations—all contribute to a more general mismatch between aspirations and accomplishments. To understand its persistence, we need to unpack European foreign policy and consider it as the product of three distinct but interdependent systems of decision-making (White 2001):

- a national system of foreign policies;
- a Community system focused on economic policy; and
- the CFSP.

These systems remain distinct even if there is considerable overlap between them (see Table 10.1). To illustrate the point, the Lisbon Treaty essentially eliminated the pillar system and put all EU policies under the umbrella of a single institutional system. The 'EU system' now incorporates the CFSP as well as internal security policy. However, as Piris (2010: 260) notes, leaving aside the High Representative, 'the Lisbon Treaty confirms that CFSP remains clearly subject to different rules and procedures from the other activities of the EU. It therefore remains a second pillar as it was before'.

Overlaps between the EU's external policy systems are, however, rife. Europe is the world's largest foreign aid donor, but only when the disparate and largely uncoordinated contributions of the Union and its member states are added together. EU

TABLE 10.1	**European foreign policy: three systems**			
System	**Key characteristic**	**Location (or Treaty basis)**	**Primary actors**	**Policy example**
National	Loose (or no) coordination	Outside EU's structures	National ministers and ministries	War in Iraq
Overlap	*Some coordination of national and EU efforts*	*Coordination with EU with nuances (no funds from EU budget)*	*National ministers and ministries, Commission*	*Cotonou agreement*
Community	EU usually speaks with single voice	Pillar 1*	Commission and Council	Commercial (trade) policy
Overlap	*Turf battles*	*Pillars 1 and 2**	*Council and Commission*	*Economic sanctions policy*
CFSP	'Common, not single' policy	Pillar 2*	High Representative; national ministers and ministries (especially of large states)	Nuclear diplomacy towards Iran

*Pre-Lisbon Treaty

environmental policy is made via the Community method. But it is often unclear who speaks for Europe in international environmental diplomacy, as was revealed—to the Union's cost—at the 2009 Copenhagen summit on climate change when the EU was literally not in the room when the final declaration was drafted. Leadership of the CFSP sometimes falls to sub-groups of member states, as illustrated by the 'EU-3', with France, Germany, and the UK taking the lead on nuclear diplomacy towards Iran, but with the High Representative chairing (a delegation including China, Russia, and the US), in another case of intersecting systems.

Such overlaps reflect how high and low politics often blur together in the twenty-first century. Disputes arising from Europe's dependence on Russia for energy, or the tendency of Chinese exporters to flood European markets, can touch upon vital national interests and preoccupy diplomats and governments at the highest political levels. Meanwhile, the EU now has a considerable track record in security and defence policy, which might be viewed as the ultimate expression of high politics. Blurred boundaries between both policy realms and systems for decision-making make European foreign policy an elusive subject that is far more difficult to 'source' or study than (say) Indian, Mexican, or South African foreign policy.

A national 'system' of foreign policies

Distinctive national foreign policies have not disappeared from Europe, even if the EU has become a more important reference point. France uses the EU to try to enhance its own foreign policy leadership of a Europe that is autonomous from the US. Germany has wrapped its post-war foreign policy in a European cloak in order to rehabilitate itself as an international power. The UK views the EU as useful for organizing pragmatic cooperation on a case-by-case basis. Small states have considerably 'Europeanized' their foreign policies (Tonra 2002; Gross 2009) and rely on the EU to have a voice in debates dominated by large states. But all EU member states conduct their own, individual, *national* foreign policy.

Whether or not national foreign policies in Europe form a true 'system', they are notable for:

- their endurance;
- their continued centrality to European foreign policy; and
- their frequent resistance to coordination.

The last observation points to what makes foreign policy different from other EU policies: the logic of foreign policy coordination differs markedly from the logic of market integration. Integrating markets mostly involves negative integration: sweeping away barriers to trade. Separate national policies can be tolerated as long as they do not impede free movement of goods, services, and people. Market integration typically has clear goals, such as zero tariffs or common standards. Progress can usually be measured and pursued according to timetables.

In contrast, it is plausible to think that a common foreign policy (analogous, for example, to the common agricultural policy (CAP)) requires positive integration: new EU institutions and structures to replace national ones. Foreign policy often has a black or white quality: if all states do not toe the line when the EU condemns a human rights violation or imposes an arms embargo, then the Union cannot be said to have a policy at all. Foreign policy coordination is often difficult to tie to specific goals or timetables. Compare the two main policy projects of the Maastricht Treaty (see Smith 1997). Monetary union had a clear goal—the euro—a timetable for achieving it, and criteria for measuring progress. The CFSP was given no clear goal, nor any timetable or criteria for achieving it.

Defenders of Europe's system of foreign policy coordination, including Chris Patten (2001), concede that Europe lacks a *single* foreign policy. However, they insist that the EU usually has a *common* foreign policy through which its member states and institutions act collectively. Each plays to its strengths and contributes policy resources to a (more or less) common cause. By this view, all member states increasingly tend to respect common EU policies and procedures.

Critics counter-claim that the war in Iraq showed how the EU is easily marginalized on matters of high politics. Decisions on whether to support the war were almost entirely made in national EU capitals, not Brussels. Similarly, in the case of the Libyan crisis in 2011, the decision on a robust response in the form of a military intervention took place mostly outside the EU framework (see Box 10.3). Nation-states have long been primary sources of European foreign policy. They are likely to remain so.

The Community System

The Community system for foreign policy-making consists of three main elements: external trade policy; aid and development policy; and the external dimension of internal policies, not least the internal market.

Commercial (trade) policy

The European Union is a major trading power. It is the world's largest exporter and importer of both goods and services. It accounts for more than one-fifth of all global trade, and claims a higher share than the US. The EU is sometimes portrayed as a purveyor of neoliberalism (which emphasizes the benefits of the free market and limited government interference; see Cafruny and Ryner 2003; Young and Peterson 2014). Yet all trading blocs discriminate against outsiders. More than half of all EU trade is internal trade, crossing European borders within a market that is meant to be borderless. EU member states are sometimes accused of acting like a protectionist club in which each agrees to take in the others' 'high cost washing', or products that are lower in quality or higher in price than goods produced outside Europe, ostensibly to protect European jobs (see Messerlin 2001).

In practice, the EU is a trading power with multiple faces (see Young and Peterson 2014), not least because it blends very different national traditions of political economy. Generally, its southern member states are less imbued with free-market values than those in the north or east. One consequence is that it is sometimes harder for the EU to agree internally than it is to agree deals with its trading partners. The power of the Commission in external trade policy is easy to overestimate (see Box 10.2). However, the EU does a remarkably good job of reconciling Europe's differences on trade. When the EU can agree, international negotiations become far more efficient. There is capacity in the Community system for shaming reluctant states into accepting trade agreements that serve general EU foreign policy interests. For example, in 2001 the Union agreed to offer the world's poorest countries duty-free and quota-free access to the EU's markets for 'everything but arms' (see Faber and Orbie 2009), which France opposed but eventually agreed to accept. The deal was criticized for not doing enough to promote third-world development. But the EU generally claims that it offers the world's poorest countries a better deal than do most industrialized countries.

Europe increasingly finds itself facing fierce economic competition from emerging states such as China, India, and Brazil that have maintained much higher economic growth rates than the EU over recent years. In the circumstances, EU trade policy has been accused of becoming aggressive, reactive, and defensive. The Union also shouldered much of the blame for the breakdown of the Doha Development Round of world trade talks, which floundered in 2008 largely over its (and the US's) agricultural subsidies (although the obduracy of emerging states was at least as much to blame; see Young and Peterson 2014: 94). With multilateral trade negotiations at an impasse, the EU has sought bilateral preferential trade agreements (PTAs). Since the Doha stalemate, the EU has launched bilateral negotiations with the US, Japan, Malaysia, Vietnam, the Latin American MERCOSUR group and others, and agreed PTAs with Canada, Singapore and—controversially—Ukraine (see Box 10.5).

An interesting question for students of European foreign policy is: how often does the EU use its economic power in the pursuit of foreign policy objectives? Agreements after 2010 to apply increasingly severe economic sanctions to Iran in response to its nuclear programme illustrate how the EU occasionally (in this case, after years of US cajoling) uses its economic power for political objectives. The same can be said for the PTAs the Union has agreed with developing countries and states on its borders as part of its Neighbourhood Policy (see Chapter 8).

Still, EU trade policy structures and behaviour challenge the idea of Europe as a 'civilian power'. The Lisbon Treaty states that trade policy 'shall be conducted in the context of the principles and objectives of the Union's external action' (Art. 207). But responsibility is left in the hands of the Commissioner for Trade, not the High Representative. Chad Damro (2010, 2014) characterizes the EU as 'Market Power Europe': an EU that defends its economic interests aggressively in individual trade disputes with little regard for broader foreign policy objectives. An even less charitable portrayal is 'Parochial Global Europe' (Young and Peterson 2014): a trading power whose preoccupation with its own internal politics and policies, involving the staunch defence of its economic interests, hampers the Union's attempts to play a global role.

Aid and development

The EU and its member states spend around €50 billion annually on development aid, or over half of the global total. Aid and access to the Union's huge market are frequently combined, along with other policy instruments, as in the cases of the EU's free trade agreements with Mexico and South Africa or the 2000 Cotonou Agreement agreed with ACP states (see Box 10.1). Market access or aid also may be part of political cooperation agreements designed to promote democracy or human rights. The EU's relations with its most important neighbours—such as Turkey, Ukraine, or Russia (see Box 10.5)—are usually conducted through complex package deals involving trade, aid, and political dialogue.

BOX 10.2	How it really works

Commercial (trade) policy

Trade policy is the most integrated of all EU external policies. The Commission negoti-ates for the EU as a whole in most cases. There is no specific Council of Trade Ministers, and effective oversight by member states (through the so-called Article 207 Committee of national trade officials) seems limited. The EP gained significant new powers from the Lisbon Treaty, with related legislation adopted by co-decision, and its consent now required for all trade agreements. Still, the Commission is clearly the lead institution and, at first sight, its position seems indomitable.

In practice, power is considerably diffused. Member governments defend their eco-nomic interests robustly at all stages: when the Council defines the Commission's man-date for negotiations, during the negotiations themselves, and when the Council ratifies draft deals. The Treaty says that the Council can (with a few limited exceptions) decide by qualified majority (Art. 207 TEU). In practice, important external trade measures almost never pass without unanimity. Moreover, there seems little doubt that the post-Lisbon Parliament will be 'quite ready to make use of its right to reject an agreement', as it did in the case of a US-EU counterterrorism agreement in 2010 (Piris 2010: 287), or set con-ditions, as it did with the EU-South Korea PTA the same year. Thus, tensions between intergovernmentalism and supranationalism exist even at the heart of the Community system, even though the EU has a solid record of achievement in trade policy.

Increasingly, the EU seeks region-to-region agreements such as the EuroMed part-nership with the countries of the Mediterranean, and the Cotonou agreement, a trade and aid accord between the EU and 79 African, Caribbean, and Pacific (ACP) states. Such package deals require links between different systems for making European foreign policy. For example, most aid to the ACP states is distributed via the European Develop-ment Fund (EDF), which member states finance directly and is not part of the EU's general budget.

The Union's aid policy has faced serious challenges in recent years. Evidence that EU aid programmes are not very effectively managed has contributed to 'donor fatigue'. The new wisdom—reflected in World Trade Organization (WTO) rules—is that poorer countries need trade more than aid. Trade is seen as helping poorer countries to grow from within in a sustainable way, while aid is often wasted, especially through corruption. The labelling of the twenty-first century's first global trading round as the Doha development agenda both reflected the new wisdom and focused global atten-tion on the EU (and US) for their reluctance to open (especially) their agricultural mar-kets to developing countries.

The world's poorest countries continue to insist that they need large injections of aid, and remain wary of the EU's new preference (driven by WTO rules as well as political choices) for creating free-trade areas. Large transfers of EU aid continue to flow to the Cotonou countries, most of which are in Africa. The EDF's budget, set at €13.8 for 2000–7, was increased to nearly €23 billion for 2008–13. Besides Africa, the Mediterranean and the Balkans are also priority areas for Community spending on development.

The Union has also become the world's largest donor of humanitarian aid through the European Community Humanitarian Office (ECHO), located within the Commission. It announced the largest contribution of any donor to humanitarian aid in Afghanistan within days of the start of the 2001 war. ECHO also contributed more relief than any other donor to areas affected by the 2004 Asian Tsunami and 2010 Pakistani floods.

Bad 'plumbing' often mars the EU's good deeds. ECHO was slammed for its lax spending controls by the Committee of Independent Experts whose 1999 report sparked the mass resignation of the Santer Commission. For years, EU development funds helped prop up dictators who were overthrown in Egypt, Tunisia and elsewhere in the 2011 Arab Spring. EU aid delivery certainly has become more efficient over time. But the Commission still has some distance to go before it escapes the memorable charge (made by a UK Secretary of State for International Development) that it is the 'worst development agency in the world' (Short 2000).

BOX 10.3	How it really works

The EU and the Libyan crisis

The Union's response to the 2011 Libyan crisis was widely criticized for being slow, incoherent and ineffective. Constituting the first major foreign policy crisis since the entry into force of the Lisbon Treaty, expectations that the EU could deliver a decisive response were high. However, the crisis revealed yet another gap between the Union's rhetoric and action, and showcased how 'uncommon' its foreign, security and defence policies continued to be.

The EU's response to a potential humanitarian disaster on its Mediterranean doorstep revealed an imbalance between its military and civilian crisis management capacities and a lack of any integrated civilian-military capacity. The Union was at least partially successful in civilian crisis management by implementing 'soft' security actions, such as civil protection and humanitarian assistance. European heads of state and government also agreed to impose sanctions authorized by the United Nations Security Council on the Gaddafi regime and went even beyond them with tougher measures. However, while member states eventually agreed on the need for Gaddafi to cede power, they remained at odds on the use of military force. Germany refused to support a UN Security Council Resolution (1973) authorizing (amongst other measures) the implementation of a no-fly zone over Libya, abstaining on the vote and withdrawing its military assets from the Mediterranean once a NATO military action began. After an extraordinary European Council failed to endorse the no-fly zone, the UK Prime Minister, David Cameron, told the press 'Of course the EU is not a military alliance and I don't want it to be a military alliance. Our Alliance is NATO' (Nicholas and Traynor 2011). An attempt to set up a CSDP military mission, EUFOR Libya, to support the UN in the delivery of humanitarian aid

Cont. ➤

> **Cont.**
>
> seemed not only ill-defined but was opposed by multiple member states, including Finland and Sweden. Although France and the UK eventually took the (European) lead in implementing the no-fly zone over Libya, the NATO operation relied heavily on US military assets.
>
> The divided European response and the lack of sufficient military capabilities and structures once more underlined the weaknesses inherent in the CSDP. Yet, disappointment at the EU's crisis response was also linked to a lack of leadership, with the High Representative being pulled in different directions by national leaders, as well as to the still immature institutional set-up of the EEAS. Critics argued that the EU's defence policy—and the CFSP more generally—'died in Libya', fuelling the glass half-empty argument. Yet, a more optimistic view saw the Libyan crisis as a lesson learned and an opportunity to address existing flaws and obstacles. The EU subsequently undertook a review of its crisis management procedures and sought to reinforce the so-called 'comprehensive approach', whereby a full range of EU policy tools could be deployed to prevent, defuse, or manage future crises. Lower profile EU military actions in Chad, Central African Republic, and off the Somalian coast are seen as successful, if less spectacular, as are police support missions in Bosnia and Macedonia.

Externalizing internal policies

In a sense, the EU has no purely internal policies: its market is so huge that every decision it makes to regulate it (or not) has international effects. When the Union negotiates internal agreements on fishing rights or agricultural subsidies, the implications for fishermen in Iceland or farmers in California can be immediate and direct. The ultimate act of externalizing internal policies occurs when the EU enlarges its membership, as it did when it more than doubled in size from 12 to 28 member states after 1995.

A rule of thumb, based on a landmark European Court decision (see Weiler 1999: 171–83), is that where the EU has legislated internally, a corresponding external policy competence for that matter is transferred to it. The Union has frequently taken this route in environmental policy, and now participates in several international environmental agreements. Where internal lines of authority are clear, the EU can be a strong and decisive negotiator. The Commission has become a powerful, global policeman for vetting mergers between large firms. When the Union seeks bilateral economic agreements, whether with China, Canada, or Cameroon, the Commission negotiates for the Union as a whole.

The Union's most important international task may be reconciling rules on its single market with rules governing global trade. The EU sometimes does the job badly, agreeing messy compromises on issues such as data protection or genetically modified foods that enrage its trading partners. External considerations can be a low priority when the Union legislates, and treated as someone else's problem. Most of the time, however, the internal market has offered non-EU producers better or similar terms of access than they were offered before the internal market existed (Young and Peterson 2014: 150).

Meanwhile, EU enlargement has been widely hailed as the most effective tool of European *foreign* policy, in terms of exporting both security and prosperity (Nugent 2004; Smith 2011). But it has also produced enlargement fatigue and rising concerns in longstanding member states about migration from less-developed newcomers. One result has been the European Neighbourhood Policy, a framework for cooperation with states on or near EU borders such as Ukraine or Belarus which, in the Brussels jargon, do not have the 'perspective' of membership anytime soon (Dannreuther 2004; Weber et al. 2008). It is difficult to see how the powerful lure of actual membership could ever come close to being replicated by a policy that forecloses that possibility (see Chapter 8).

The Common Foreign and Security Policy

The gap between the Union's growing economic power and its limited political clout was a source of increasing frustration in the early 1990s. Thus, a distinct system of making foreign policy was created with the CFSP at its centre. This new system overlapped with but did not replace the Community system. Over time, it incorporated a nascent Common Security and Defence Policy (CSDP). Confusingly, the Common Foreign and Security Policy (CFSP) and CSDP are mainly labels for 'institutions that *make* [policies] but *are* not proper policies' in themselves (Jørgensen 2006: 509).

The CFSP unveiled in the Maastricht Treaty marked a considerable advance on the European Political Cooperation mechanism. But it still disappointed proponents of closer foreign policy cooperation (see Box 10.4). The CFSP gave the Commission the right—shared with member governments—to initiate proposals. It even allowed for limited qualified majority voting, although it was always clear that most actions would require unanimity. Compliance mechanisms in the CFSP were not made as strong as those in the first pillar, with the European Court of Justice mostly excluded. The CFSP (like the initial JHA policy) remained largely intergovernmental, even if links to the Community system were gradually strengthened.

Established habits of exchange between foreign ministries meant that member governments were able to agree a considerable number of common positions and joint actions in the early years of the CFSP (see Nuttall 2000: 184–8). Some measures, such as the 1993 Stability Pacts to stabilize borders in Central and Eastern Europe, or support for democratic elections in Bosnia (in the 1990s) went well beyond the usual EPC declarations. Nevertheless, critics scorned the CFSP's inability to deal with more complex or urgent security issues, above all the wars in ex-Yugoslavia.

BOX 10.4　　**How it really works**

Making foreign policy decisions

Provisions in the Maastricht Treaty for **Qualified Majority Voting (QMV)** on foreign policy seemed to mark a major change from European Political Cooperation. However, QMV was rarely used in the second (or third) pillar. The glass remained (at least) half-empty: rules on when QMV could be used were far more complex than in the first pillar, and nearly all important CFSP decisions required a consensus. Because it could not agree a unanimous position on Iraq (far from it), the EU was completely sidelined during the drift to war in 2003. It is difficult to identify any major foreign policy decision of the George W. Bush administration that was influenced by any CFSP decision, except perhaps a softening in tactics for dealing with the Iran nuclear dossier. The CFSP's annual budget is in the range of a paltry €150 million. Looking to the future, foreign policy by unanimity seems impractical, even impossible, in a EU of 28 plus. Procedurally, it is clear how the CFSP works. Substantively, there is controversy about whether it works at all.

But perhaps the glass is half-full. Following the terrorist attacks of 9/11, the EU agreed a raft of statements or decisions within days. Subsequently, the EU moved decisively—sometimes controversially so—and gave its consent to counter-terrorist agreements with the US on issues such as airline passenger records and container security (see Rees 2006). The EU's diplomacy (through the 'EU-3') on Iran, its participation in the Middle East Quartet (on an equal footing with the US, Russia, and the UN), a range of actions in central Africa and the Balkans, and the (admittedly slow) maturation of the Lisbon Treaty's new foreign policy 'machinery' suggest, for optimists, a steady integration of European foreign policy.

The 1997 Amsterdam Treaty's main foreign policy innovation was the creation of a new High Representative for the CFSP (who also served as Secretary-General of the Council). The High Representative was meant to help give the EU a single voice and the CFSP a single face. After his appointment to the post in 1999, former NATO Secretary General Javier Solana at times proved a skilful coordinator of different actions and instruments, whether sourced in Brussels or national capitals. He fronted the Union's diplomatic efforts, in cooperation with NATO, to head off civil war in Macedonia in 2001, and had a leading role in nuclear dialogue with Tehran. However, the EU continued to be represented externally by its *troika*, with Solana joined by the Foreign Ministers of the state holding the Council presidency and the European Commissioner for External Affairs. There thus was never a clear answer to the legendary (and apparently apocryphal) question asked by the US Secretary of State, Henry Kissinger, in the 1970s: 'What number do I call when I want to speak to "Europe"?'

After the rejection of the 2004 Constitutional Treaty, the Lisbon Treaty assigned that single number to a new model High Representative, who would do the same job the Constitutional Treaty gave its EU Minister for Foreign Affairs (even if that title was rejected as too provocative). The High Representative, Catherine Ashton in the first instance, combined the role of the previous High Representative with that of the

Commissioner for External Affairs. Ashton also served as a Vice-President of the Commission and chaired EU Councils of Foreign Ministers, in perhaps the most audacious attempt ever to combine the supranational with the intergovernmental in one position. Doing so involved tricky compromises: for example, the High Representative had the (non-exclusive) right to propose CFSP initiatives without passing them through the entire College of Commissioners.

Ashton spent most of her first year (2010) in post navigating a minefield of institutional bickering between the Commission, Council, and Parliament about the precise composition of the EEAS. As there was no blueprint for the creation of the EEAS, one intrinsic feature of its setting-up was to ensure that all parties, the Council, the Commission, and the member states were included. Member states took different and often ambiguous positions towards the EEAS and the HR. By the end of Ashton's mandate (2014), diverse attitudes continued to undermine the EEAS's ability to provide for a more effective CFSP. Ashton's successor, the former Italian Foreign Minister, Federica Mogherini, will have to continue to grapple with such dynamics.

Moreover, member states showed considerable reluctance to grant the High Representative room for manoeuvre. For instance, political reactions to the Arab Spring often came in the form of statements by European foreign and prime ministers—quickly and before consultations at the EU level—given the historic importance of the events. Although foreign ministers agreed to downscale on public diplomacy for the sake of a single message from Brussels, the High Representative has so far not been given the flexibility to react to events without prior consultation with national EU capitals (Balfour and Raik 2013). In order to be more effective, the CFSP post-Lisbon 'requires an enhanced sense of ownership if the member states, which have to accept the new structures, feel represented by the different policy choices as well as convinced [that] the EEAS provides added value' (Helwig et al. 2013: 1).

Theorizing the EU as a Global Actor

The expansion of the EU's foreign policy role confounds many international relations (IR) theorists, particularly those in the realist tradition. Most realists make two assumptions. First, power in international politics is a zero-sum commodity. Second, all alliances between states are temporary (see Mearsheimer 2001; Waltz 2002). On the one hand, realists claim to be able to explain why the EU is often weak or divided on matters of high politics, such as Iraq or Russia. Facing forward, one confidently predicts that 'the European [Union's] best days are probably behind it' (Rosato 2011: 255). On the other hand, realists find it difficult to explain the EU's international ambitions and activities (see Box 10.5), or even why it does not collapse altogether. More generally, twenty-first century works of IR theory often barely mention the EU, or ignore it altogether (see Elman and Elman 2003; Burchill et al. 2005; Devetak et al. 2012).

One consequence is that research on European foreign policy 'has come to resemble an archipelago' (Jørgensen 2006: 507), which is only barely connected to the study of IR more generally. Consider intergovernmentalist approaches to European integration, which themselves are derived from liberal theories of international politics (see Moravcsik 1998). Liberal intergovernmentalists assume that governments respond to powerful, domestic economic pressures. When governments agree policy deals that benefit national economic interests, they try to lock in those gains by giving EU institutions powers of enforcement. In contrast, governments face far weaker incentives to delegate foreign or defence policy powers to EU institutions, which explains why the EU's trade policy is far more integrated than the CFSP. Beyond that insight, however, intergovernmentalists have shown little interest in the EU's global ambitions. As such, what has been described as 'the most suitable theoretical tradition' for explaining European integration also seems to be 'currently running out of steam and relevance' to European foreign policy (Jørgensen 2006: 519).

BOX 10.5	Compared to what?

The EU and Russia

The EU's relationship with Russia is a classic glass half-empty or half-full story. A pessimist would note the EU's dependence on Russia for energy, particularly since price disputes between Moscow and former Soviet republics or client-states led to repeated interruptions (or threats of them) in flows of Russian natural gas in the 2000s. The EU's concern for its energy security is often viewed as making it the weaker partner in its relationship with Moscow. One upshot, according to this view, is that the Union is reluctant to speak truth to power about the erosion of Russian democracy, the 2007 cyber-war waged (apparently) by Russia on Estonia (an EU member state), and Russia's 2014 annexation of the Crimea region of Ukraine.

In practice, the EU and Russia are mutually and heavily interdependent. The EU relies on Russia to supply more than a quarter of both its oil and natural gas. Russia equally relies on its sales of raw materials to the EU for most of its hard currency earnings, which fund nearly 40 per cent of Russia's federal budget. Around 60 per cent of Russia's export earnings come from sales of energy, most of it to the EU.

The EU needs to co-exist with Russia but it is difficult to imagine that the two could ever be 'partners'. Russia's intervention in Ukraine in 2014 followed the overthrow of a pro-Russian Ukrainian government by citizens motivated in large part by the rejection of an agreed EU-Ukraine trade deal by President Viktor Yanukovych. The contempt of the Russian President, Vladimir Putin, for the EU was reflected in his courtship of far right, Eurosceptic parties in Union member states. This wooing was done alongside a Cold War-style crackdown on domestic dissident media in Russia amidst portrayals (ironically) of the new, post-Yanukovych Ukrainian government as dominated by 'fascists'. The words of a former EU diplomat remain appropriate a decade after they were uttered: 'Europe should clearly work for a comprehensive partnership with Russia, but at the moment it is nonsense to suggest that this will be based on shared values' (Patten 2005: 178).

In contrast, one of the oldest theories of European integration—neofunctionalism— may still have mileage, at least by proxy. Institutionalism, a theoretical cousin of neo- functionalism (see Haas 2001), focuses on how the EU produces habits that eventually mature into institutionalized rules of behaviour (see Smith 2003; Menon 2011). For example, habits established through 20 years of foreign policy exchanges within EPC led to the CFSP. The EU often creates new roles or organizations—such as the High Representative or the Political and Security Committee—which develop their own interests, missions, and escape close intergovernmental control.

Yet the leading theory of European foreign policy remains constructivism (see Tonra and Christiansen 2004; Bretherton and Vogler 2006; Meyer and Strickmann 2011). Constructivists depart from realists and liberals in insisting that the interests and identities of EU member states are not fixed before they bargain with each other. Rather, they are 'constructed' through bargaining, which is a highly social process. Constructivists, in contrast to institutionalists, insist that ideas matter as much as (or more than) institutions in IR. Alexander Wendt (1992, 1999), perhaps the leading IR constructivist, portrays the EU as more than a temporary alliance because its member states assume a measure of common identity through shared ideas, including ones about the desirability of multilateralism, environmental pro- tection, and so on. Many constructivists do not shy away from questions about what the EU *should* do in foreign policy, insisting on the importance of a 'normative power Europe' that stands up for its values and principles (Manners 2002, 2008; Forsberg 2011).

Arguably, however, constructivism sets the bar too low. Its proponents can become apologists for EU inaction or incoherence in global politics by always falling back on the argument that Europe remains 'under construction' as a global actor. As much as constructivists insist the glass is half-full, others—such as Toje (2010, 2011), who portrays the EU as a 'small power' analogous to Canada, Peru, or Switzerland—argue that it remains half-empty.

Conclusion

When the then British Prime Minister, Tony Blair, urged that the EU should become a 'superpower but not a superstate' in 2000, he provoked little controversy outside of his own country. The idea that the EU should take a lead in expressing European power internationally has become almost a mainstream view (see Morgan 2005; Peterson et al. 2012). The EU has come a long way from humble origins in foreign policy. But it remains an odd global power, which has difficulty living up to its ambi- tions. It has increased its potential international power each time it has enlarged but simultaneously increased the difficulty of reaching consensus. Yet EU foreign policy is only as good as the quality of the consensus amongst its members, and it is often of poor quality in an enlarged EU of 28 member states.

One reason why assessments of European foreign policy vary so widely is because it is unclear how the EU's success should be measured. There is no question that the Union is far more active internationally than its founders ever imagined it could be. In several policy areas, especially economic ones, it is a global power. No other international organization in history has even tried, let alone claimed, to have a 'common' foreign policy.

There were signs post-Iraq that foreign policy was being reclaimed by European national capitals, or groups of states acting together, even if none appeared to be giving up on the CFSP altogether (see Hill 2004). The Lisbon Treaty's institutional reforms aimed to move the EU closer to a truly common foreign policy (see Rogers 2009). Consider the US Secretary of State, Hillary Clinton's, view: 'These are historic times for the EU. I expect that in decades to come, we will look back on the Lisbon Treaty and the maturation of the EU that it represents as a major milestone in our world's history' (*EU Observer* 2011).

Five years after the entry into force of the Lisbon, it was still too early to tell whether the new institutional set-up would provide for a more coherent CFSP in the long run. In the immediate aftermath of the Treaty's implementation, it seemed as if the EU's foreign policy was characterized by even *more* complex institutional inter-actions. The High Representative and the EEAS were placed as additional administrative structures between the existing key actors in EU foreign policy—the rotating Council Presidency and the Commission. The new set-up thus called for more coordination of all external policies, which was further complicated by the fact that the EEAS is not part of the Commission (Helwig 2013: 240).

The future of European foreign policy will be determined largely by two factors: the EU's relationship with the US (see Toje 2009) and its ability to wield its 'soft power', or its power to persuade rather than coerce (Nye Jr. 2004; 2011). Whether the George W. Bush era marked a glitch or a watershed in transatlantic relations is an open question. The failure of hard (mostly) American military power to achieve US policy goals in Afghanistan or Iraq, let alone Iran or North Korea or the Middle East, rekindles questions about whether Europe's soft power might make it an alternative source of leadership in the twenty-first century (Rifkin 2004; Leonard 2005). Yet the Libyan crisis could be taken not only as an example where Europe was (again) reliant on US support and resources, but also one that exposed the limits of Europe's soft power approach (Menon 2011).

Alternatively, Europe's declining population and military weakness might foreclose such questions. One of the EU's top diplomats argues that Europe will never maximize its soft power until it invests far more in hard power (Cooper 2004a), a prospect that became increasingly remote in a climate of post-recession austerity in the second decade of the twenty-first century. Yet, there is no question that the EU faces powerful incentives—especially as it loses economic ground to states such as China, India and Russia and faces security challenges in its neighbourhood—to become more united in foreign policy: As Howorth (2007: 22) argues, 'The pressures for the EU to speak to the rest of the world with a single voice will become intense.

The refusal to make collective EU choices in the world of 2025 will be tantamount to an abdication of sovereignty'.

It is easy to see why debates about Europe as a global actor are so lively. The EU is likely to remain an often uncertain and hesitant global power but one that never stops trying to be more coherent and effective. It will no doubt continue to frustrate its partners, but sometimes show surprising unity, and fascinate—probably as much as it confounds—future students of international politics.

DISCUSSION QUESTIONS

1. Define 'European foreign policy'. Explain why this term has assumed wide usage amongst those who study the EU's international role.

2. Why are member states reluctant to entrust the Commission with responsibilities for the political side of foreign policy, while they have done so for important areas of economic external relations?

3. Why is the most effective way for the EU to promote development in the less-developed world increasingly seen as 'trade not aid'?

4. How best to characterize the EU as a global actor: Civilian power? Normative power? Market power? Small power?

FURTHER READING

The best single source text on Europe as a global actor is Hill and Smith (2011). Useful overviews include K. Smith (2008), Laïdi (2008), and Toje (2010). Good historical treatments are available, told both from the points of view of a practitioner (Nuttall 2000) and an academic institutionalist (M. E. Smith 2003). Useful recent treatments of EU external economic policy are Woolcock (2012) and Young and Peterson (2014). The Union's contribution to the United Nations, as well as multilateralism more generally, is considered by Bouchard et al. (2013). On the idea of the EU as a 'civilian power', see Sjursen (2006).

Bouchard, C., Peterson, J. and Tocci, N. (eds) (2013), *Multilateralism in the 21st Century: Europe's Quest for Effectiveness* (London and New York: Routledge).

Hill, C., and Smith, M. (eds) (2011), *International Relations and the European Union*, 2nd edn. (Oxford and New York: Oxford University Press).

Laïdi, Z. (ed.) (2008), *EU Foreign Policy in a Globalized World: Normative Power and Social Preferences* (London and New York: Routledge).

Nuttall, S. (2000), *European Foreign Policy* (Oxford and New York: Oxford University Press).

Sjursen, H. (ed.) (2006), 'What Kind of Europe? European Foreign Policy in Perspective', Special Issue of *Journal of European Public Policy* 13/2.

Smith, K. E. (2008), *European Union Foreign Policy in a Changing World*, 3rd edn. (Oxford and Malden MA: Polity).

Smith, M. E. (2003), *Europe's Foreign and Security Policy* (Cambridge and New York: Cambridge University Press).

Toje, A. (2010), *The European Union as a Small Power: After the Cold War* (Basinstoke and New York: Palgrave).

Woolcock, S. (2012), *European Union Economic Diplomacy: The Role of the EU in External Economic Relations* (Farnham and Burlington VT: Ashgate).

Young, A. and Peterson, J. (2014), *Parochial Global Europe: 21st Century Trade Politics* (Oxford and New York: Oxford University Press).

WEB LINKS

A good place to start researching the EU's external policy role is the website of the Paris-based Institute for Security Studies (**www.iss.europa.eu**), which formally became an autonomous European Union agency in 2002. Other specific areas of EU policy have their own, dedicated websites:

* External relations and foreign and security policy: **www.europa.eu/pol/cfsp/index_en.htm**
* Humanitarian aid: **http://europa.eu/pol/hum/index_en.htm**
* Justice/home affairs: **www.europa.eu/pol/justice/index_en.htm**
* Trade: **http://europa.eu/pol/comm/index_en.htm**
* Development: **http://ec.europa.eu/europeaid/index_en.htm**

The Commission's site (**http://ec.europa.eu/index_en.htm**) has general information about EU foreign policy, but the websites of national foreign ministries often reveal more. On the EU's relationship with the US, see: **http://www.euintheus.org** and **www.useu.be** Weblinks on the EU's other important relationships include ones devoted to the Cotonou convention (**www.acpsec.org**), EU–Canadian relations (**www.canada-europe.org**), and the Union's relationship with Latin America (**http://aei.pitt.edu/view/subjects/D002022.html**). To see how closely linked the EU's trade and aid policies are see: **http://ec.europa.eu/trade/policy/countries-and-regions/development/aid-for-trade/** The European Council on Foreign Relations offers an annual assessment of European foreign policy in the form of a scorecard: **http://www.ecfr.eu/scorecard/2014**

Visit the Online Resource Centre that accompanies this book for additional material: **www.oxfordtextbooks.co.uk/orc/kenealy4e/**

CHAPTER 11

Conclusion

John Peterson, Daniel Kenealy, and Richard Corbett

▮ Overview

The EU is exceptional, complex, and in important respects unique. This concluding chapter revisits three key themes that guide understanding of the EU, before returning to the question: how can we best *explain* the EU and how it works? We review some leading theoretical approaches, and identify what each approach claims is most important to explain about the EU, and why. Finally we confront the question: 'where do we go from here?' Does knowing how the EU works give us clues about how it might work in the future?

Introduction

This book has offered a *basic* introduction to how the European Union works. A vast body of work has emerged in recent years to satisfy those who wish to know more. Much that has been written about the EU may seem confusing or unintelligible to the curious non-expert. Together with our co-authors, we have tried to be simpler and clearer, particularly by illustrating how the Union works in practice, not just in theory. We have also tried to show that the EU is not so exceptional that it resists all comparisons.

Yet, it does not take much study of European integration before one is struck (or becomes frustrated) by how complex and ever-shifting it seems to be. Most of our 'compared to what' exercises have ended up drawing contrasts—some quite sharp—between politics and policy-making in Brussels and these same processes elsewhere. There are very few analytical 'bottom lines' about how the European Union works, except that it works quite differently from any other system for deciding who gets what, when, and how.

Three Themes

We have offered (Chapter 1) three general themes as guides to understanding how the EU works. The first is experimentation and change. The European Union refuses to stand still: perhaps the only thing that can be safely predicted about its future is that it is unlikely to remain static for long, even if change in the years to come may be incremental rather than revolutionary. Second, EU governance is an exercise in sharing power between states and institutions, and seeking consensus across different levels of governance. Getting to 'yes' in a system with so many diverse stakeholders often requires resort to informal methods of reaching agreement, about which the EU's Treaties and official publications are silent. Third and finally, the gap between the EU's policy scope and its capacity—between what it *tries* to do and what it is *equipped* to do—has widened. The EU has been a remarkable success in many respects. But its future success is by no means assured. We will now briefly revisit each of these themes.

Experimentation and change

Every chapter in this book, from a different angle, has painted a picture of constant evolution and change. Few could deny that the European Union has developed into more than an 'ordinary' international organization. However, its development has not been guided by any agreed master plan. Rather, it has evolved through messy compromises struck after complex political bargaining between member states (Chapters 2 and 4), institutions (Chapter 3), organized interests (Chapter 5), and competing visions.

One consequence is that when the EU changes, it usually changes incrementally. Radical reform proposals tend to be scaled back in the direction of modesty in a system with so many different kinds of interest to satisfy and in which change to the basic rules (the treaties) needs the agreement of every Member State. The unsuccessful attempt to establish a Constitutional Treaty for the EU proves the point: although ratified by a large majority of Member States, it proved a step too far, at least in terms of its symbolism, for all to accept. Yet, the Lisbon Treaty carried forward most of the institutional changes contained in the Constitutional Treaty while stripping out references to an EU flag, anthem and the provocative designation 'EU Minister for Foreign Affairs' (renamed, in the EU's familiar jargon, 'High Representative'; see Box 11.1).

However, apparently unexceptional acts of fine-tuning, such as slightly increasing the EP's power or sending an encouraging political signal to an applicant state, can sometimes gather momentum like a snowball rolling down a hill. Moreover, the EU's potential for fundamental change, as illustrated by the launch of single currency or dramatic decisions by the European Court of Justice (ECJ), cannot be denied. Perhaps because the EU is such a young political system, it is sometimes surprisingly easy to change its structure or remit. In recent years, it has created large bail-out funds, rewritten rules, and restructured the debts of struggling member states to keep the Euro intact. Yet, by late 2014 the Eurozone was in danger of slipping into its third recession in six years, with youth unemployment above 40 per cent in Spain and Italy. The EU's everyday mode of relying on compromises and incremental, modest changes appeared inadequate in the face of a political and economic climate that led the new European Commission President to declare 'we are last-chance Europe' (quoted in *The Economist*, 25 October 2014).

The more general point is that the EU is a fundamentally experimental union (Laffan et al. 2000). Nobody argues that it always works like a smooth, well-oiled machine. It has become far more difficult to shift it in any particular direction as its membership has nearly doubled in the space of about a decade. Equally, almost no one denies that it is remarkably successful in coaxing cooperative, collective action out of sovereign states that regularly, almost routinely, went to war with each other a few generations ago. Increasingly, the Union is seen as a model or laboratory worthy, in some respects, of mimicry by other regional organizations in other parts of the world (Farrell 2007; Checkel 2007; see also Box 2.4).

Sharing power and seeking consensus

A second theme that cannot be avoided in studying the EU is that power is distributed widely between states, institutions, and organized interests. At the same time, consensus and compromise are highly valued. Enormous efforts are often required

| BOX 11.1 | What's in a name (revisited)? |

As we have seen, the terms used to refer to the EU's artefacts often stir up controversy. A word can have different connotations in different languages or cultural contexts. Examples include:

Assembly or Parliament?

The designation of a European 'Parliament' was initially a term too far for some. The drafters of the original Treaties prudently used the term 'Assembly'. The Assembly decided to call itself a Parliament in the early 1960s. For a long time, some governments strictly avoided the term. However, in 1986, they agreed to amend the Treaty to include the name European Parliament.

Commission or Executive?

Although many saw the Commission as an embryonic European government when what is now the EU was created, others did not. The authors of the Treaty thus shied away from even describing it as an executive. In French, it is often referred to as the *Commission exécutive* to distinguish it from the *Commission parlementaire*, which is the French term for a parliamentary committee.

Constitution or Treaty?

The Treaties are sometimes described as the EU's constitution (see Weiler 1999). The European Court of Justice has itself referred to them as a constitutional charter. However, the attempt to replace the Treaties by a single text formally described as a Constitution failed in 2005 when it was voted down by France and the Netherlands. Member states instead agreed to amend the existing Treaties without formally labeling them as a constitution.

Federal or Supranational?

The Schuman declaration, the basis for establishing the European Coal and Steel Community, referred to the ECSC as the first step towards a European federation. But this definition of the *finalité* of the Union has always been controversial. Definitions of 'federal' are highly divergent. The term supranational emerged instead.

Foreign Minister or High Representative?

The merged post of Vice President of the Commission/High Representative was originally described as the EU Minister for Foreign Affairs in the unratified Constitutional Treaty. The term was dropped in the Lisbon Treaty, although it is still used informally in Brussels.

Representative or Ambassador?

The heads of the EU's representations in third countries have ambassadorial status, and are commonly referred to as ambassadors, though they are officially just representatives.

Why 'President'?

The EU gives the title 'President' to all kinds of functions that might have been named otherwise—at least in English. For Anglophones, it might make more sense to use 'Speaker' of the Parliament, 'Governor' of the Central Bank, 'Chair' of the Council, and maybe 'Prime Commissioner'?

to strike agreements that are acceptable to all who have a slice of power to determine outcomes. Just being able to agree is often viewed as an achievement in itself. Once sealed, EU agreements are almost always portrayed as positive sum, that is, bringing greater good to a greater number of citizens than did the previous policy. Of course, nearly every policy creates losers as well as winners. But the perceived need to preserve support for the Brussels system means that heroic attempts are usually made to avoid creating clear losers (or at least to compensate them). After being named as the first post-Lisbon President of the European Council, Herman Van Rompuy declared: 'every country should emerge victorious from negotiations. A negotiation that ends with a defeated party is never a good negotiation' (*Los Angeles Times*, 20 November 2009).

It follows that coming to grips with how the EU works means more than mastering the Treaties. The formal powers of institutions and member states, and formal rules of policy-making, are not unimportant. But they do not come close to telling the whole story, since informal understandings and norms are crucial. Most of our investigations of 'how it really works' have accentuated the importance of unwritten rules that have emerged almost organically, as opposed to being mandated in formal or legal terms. These rules and norms have then been learned and internalized by EU policy-makers. For example, it is widely accepted in Brussels that formal votes in the Council should be avoided whenever possible, even if they have become more common and perhaps more necessary in a radically enlarged Union. Still, the idea that consensus should be the ultimate aim, and that long negotiations and manifold compromises are an acceptable price to pay for it, is powerfully engrained. These norms often matter far more than what the Treaties say about which state has how many votes, what constitutes a qualified majority, or where QMV applies and where it does not. The enlargements of 2004 and 2007 suggested that representatives of new states learn the rules of the game rather quickly. To illustrate, they were able to lend their weight to a broad alliance supporting further liberalization of the services sector not by threatening a blocking minority, but by constructively arguing their case.

Moreover, the EU is a uniquely multilevel system of governance. Even the most decentralized, federal nation-states such as Germany or the US have a government and an opposition. The European Union has neither. As such, it often suffers (not least in foreign policy) from a lack of leadership. Rarely does one institution or member state, or alliance thereof, offer consistent or decisive political direction. Instead, grand bargains to agree quasi-constitutional change, as well as many more mundane agreements, result from a unique kind of power sharing across levels of governance, as well as between EU institutions and member states. It is this diversity and mix of actors—regional, national and supranational, public and private—the wide dispersal of power between them, and the need to try to increase the number of 'winners' without the paralysis of most international organizations, that make the European Union unique.

Scope and capacity

Third and finally, we have suggested that the EU's scope, both in terms of policy remit and constituent states, has grown faster than its capacity to manage its affairs. Chapters 5 and 6—and perhaps especially Chapter 9—outlined the uneven yet unmistakable expansion of EU policy responsibilities. Chapter 8 focused on why, and with what consequences, the Union has continued to enlarge its membership and tried to improve its relations to countries in its near abroad. Chapter 10 showed how the EU has evolved, almost by stealth, into a global power. With no agreed upon 'end goal', the Union has taken on new tasks and members, but without always obtaining a concomitant increase in capacity, or tools and resources to perform its designated tasks. For instance, Chapter 3 highlighted the institutional limits of the EU. Can the Commission, equivalent in size to the administration of a medium-sized European city, manage an ever larger and more ambitious Union? Perhaps its emphasis under the Presidency of José Manuel Barroso on a 'Europe of results' reflected, in part, a rebalancing of the traditional argument that most problems require integration to solve them. Similarly, Majone (2005) argues that EU policies need to solve actual problems, as opposed to serving the political purpose of further political integration, which often seemed to be their primary goal in the past. Now that we have that integration, the EU must demonstrate that it is actually solving policy problems. But does it have the capacity to do so?

The Commission is far from alone in confronting a gap between scope and capacity. Can one Parliament adequately represent nearly 500 million citizens? Can 28 or more ministers sit around the Council table and have a meaningful negotiation? The EU's political and geographic scope has increased, sometimes without explicit support from its citizens. This gap between scope and capacity (institutional and political) raises broader questions about the Union's future. A specific one concerns the future membership of the United Kingdom, whose Foreign Minister, Philip Hammond, said his (Conservative) party's commitment to an in or out referendum was 'lighting a fire under the EU', which he described as a 'putative superstate' that commanded only 'fragile' public consent (*Financial Times*, 18 October 2014). It seems risky to assume that the EU can continue to take on ever more tasks and member states (or even keep its existing ones), while retaining its status as the most successful experiment in international cooperation in modern history.

Explaining the EU

While seeking above all to describe how the EU works, we have also introduced, and tried to demystify, debates about what are the most important forces driving EU politics. Just as there is no consensus on the desirability of European integration, there is no consensus about what is most important about it. Social scientists disagree over what it is about the EU that is most important to *explain*. The position they take on this question usually reflects their own approach to understanding the EU: as an international organization (IO)? A polity in its own right? A source of constructed identity? Or a factory for public policies?

We have seen how theory can help us frame interesting questions and help us determine what evidence is needed to answer them. If it is accepted that the European Union is exceptionally complex, then it stands to reason that there can be no one 'best' theory of EU politics. What a former Commission President, Jacques Delors, once called an 'unidentified political object' is a little bit like other IOs such as NATO or the United Nations, a little bit like federal states such as Germany and Canada, and a little bit like the other leading system for generating legally binding international rules: the WTO. But it closely resembles none of them. It makes sense in the circumstances to approach the EU with a well-stocked tool-kit of theoretical approaches, and to be clear about what each singles out as most important in determining how it works.

International relations approaches

International relations (IR) scholars bring important insights to the study of the EU. They can be relied upon to ask hard, stimulating questions about the nature of power in international politics, and the extent to which cooperation is possible or durable in the absence of any 'international government'. In seeking answers to these questions, students of IR add value, in two principal ways, to debates about the nature and significance of European integration.

First, approaching the EU as a system within a system—a regional alliance in the wider scheme of global politics—encourages us to ask why European states have chosen to pool a large share of their sovereignty. For neofunctionalists, the answer lies in the way that the choices open to states narrow after they decide to establish a common market (Börzel 2005). EU institutions, in alliance with interest groups, guide and encourage 'spill-over' of cooperation in one sphere (the internal market) to new spheres (such as environmental policy). States remain powerful but they must share power with each other and with EU institutions and non-institutional actors in Brussels, as well as those in national and regional political capitals. For neofunctionalists, what is most important to explain about EU politics is how and why European integration moves inexorably forward. There are crucial differences between EU member states and ordinary nation-states in international politics, to the extent that European integration is largely irreversible.

For intergovernmentalists member states remain free to choose how the EU should work (Moravcsik 1998; Moravcsik and Schimmelfenig 2009). The Union is built on a series of bargains between its member states, which are self-interested and rational in pursuing EU outcomes that serve their economic interests. Of course, conflict may arise in bargaining between states, whose preferences are never identical. But, ultimately, the status quo changes only when acceptable compromises are struck between national interests, especially those of its largest states. The EU's institutions are relatively weak in the face of the power of its member states, which can determine precisely how much authority they wish to delegate to the Commission, Parliament, and Court to enforce and police intergovernmental bargains. For intergovernmentalists, what is most important to explain about the EU is how national interests are reconciled in intergovernmental bargains. European states are 'ordinary' states, whose national interests happen to be compatible often enough to produce unusually institutionalized cooperation. The EU 'occupies a permanent position at the heart of the European landscape' (Moravcsik 1998: 501), but only because member governments want it that way. Much about European integration remains reversible, and always will be.

A comparative politics approach

As the European Union's policy remit has expanded, many comparativists (at least those who study Europe) have found themselves unable to understand their subject—centrally, the state—without knowing how the EU works. In particular, new institutionalists, whose work has become deeply influential in the study of comparative politics as well as across the social sciences, have developed insightful analyses of how the EU works. Institutionalists view the EU as a system where cooperation is now normal and accepted. Policy-makers in Brussels have become used to working in a system where power is shared, in particular between its major institutions. Bargaining in the making of day-to-day, 'ordinary' EU policy is as much between institutions as it is between governments. Usually, it contrasts with bargaining—primarily intergovernmental—in episodic rounds of Treaty reform. Yet, some analysts view institutionalism as better at 'capturing' and explaining negotiations than intergovernmentalism—even intergovernmental negotiations that alter the Union's Treaties (see Slapin 2008). A key determinant of actual outcomes in any EU negotiation is the extent to which 'path dependency' has become institutionalized and radical change is precluded.

Institutionalists share important assumptions with neofunctionalists, particularly about the need to view European integration as a continuous process (see Pierson 1996; 2004). But institutionalists tend to study the Union as a political system in itself, analogous to national systems, as opposed to a system of international relations. For them, institutions develop their own agendas and priorities, and thus 'load' the EU system in favour of certain outcomes over others (Meunier and McNamara 2007; Pollack 2009). The European Union is extraordinary, above all because it has such extraordinary institutions.

A public policy approach

Studying EU politics without studying what it produces—actual policies, is like studying a factory but ignoring the product it manufactures. We have seen (especially in Chapter 5) that most EU policies are regulatory policies, which often aim to create a single rulebook for the single market, and that many are highly technical. We have also seen how resource-poor the EU's institutions are, and how reliant they are on expertise and resources held beyond Brussels and/or by non-public actors. Advocates of policy network analysis insist that EU policy outcomes are shaped in important ways by informal bargaining, much of which takes place outside formal institutions or policy process (Peterson 2009). By the time that ministers vote in the Council or MEPs vote in plenary, legislative proposals usually have been picked over and scrutinized line-by-line by a huge range of officials, experts and, usually, lobbyists. Often, the proposal bears little or no relationship to what it looked like in its first draft. As we saw in Chapter 7, democratic controls are embedded in the EU more than in any other international organization. But policy network analysis assumes that most policy details are agreed in a world far removed from the political world of ministers and MEPs.

Moreover, the EU is distinctive in its lack of hierarchy: it has no government to impose a policy agenda, so policy stakeholders bargain over what the agenda should be. No one actor is in charge, so they must work together and exchange resources—legitimacy, money, expertise—to realize their goals. For policy network analysts, what is most important to explain about the EU is its policies and who determines them. Making sense of policy outputs means investigating how sectoral networks are structured: are their memberships stable or volatile, are they tightly or loosely integrated, and how are resources distributed within them? The EU is, in effect, a series of different and diverse sub-systems for making different kinds of policy. What is common across the full range of EU activities is interdependence between actors: even those with the most formidable formal powers—the member states and EU institutions—are highly dependent on one another, and indeed on actors that have no formal power at all.

A sociological/cultural approach

For constructivists, the most important feature of the European Union that requires explanation is how interests and identities are constructed. EU decision-makers are the same as anyone else: they are fundamentally social beings. But they are also different from most other political actors in that they interact intensively and extensively with actors whose national identity, language, and culture are different from their own. Brussels (along with Luxembourg and Strasbourg) is a truly multinational crossroads. There is no other political capital in the world that features a more diverse cultural mix. In a sense, Brussels is unlike the rest of Europe and one effect is to encourage a sort of disconnect between the EU and its citizens. But the European identity which often seems barely to register amongst a majority of citizens in Europe's heartlands is very much in evidence amongst those who are closely involved in EU politics and policy.

Again, it is worth reiterating that constructivism is not a substantive theory of regional integration comparable to intergovernmentalism or institutionalism (see Risse 2009). It is a philosophical, even 'metaphysical' position that insists that our social reality is constructed by human beings and reproduced in day-to-day practice. The main upshot is that we cannot explain how the EU works simply by calculating what is in the material interest of each member state, institution, or lobbyist and then assuming that Brussels is a vacuum in which those interests are unchanging. We cannot assume that negotiations between these actors are unaffected by the informal rules of the game, or untouched by how those at the centre of the EU system view themselves as part of a major collective, political endeavour. Of course, EU decision-makers are self-interested and egoistic. There is much about the European Union that does not work very well. But it produces far more collective action than any system ever invented, or 'constructed', for the reconciliation of multiple national interests. The insights of constructivism are inescapable and essential to explaining why.

There is no one approach with a monopoly of wisdom on EU politics. All shed important light on key features of how the EU works. All downplay, even ignore, factors that others argue are important—or can be in the right circumstances —in determining who gets what from the European Union. A first step in making sense of the EU is deciding what it is about this unidentified political object that is most important to explain.

Where Do We Go From Here?

When we ponder where the European Union may be headed, we have to remember where it has been. For over two decades, the Union has been either preparing, negotiating, or ratifying a new treaty. In the 25 years after 1985, the EU modified its basic treaties five times. No Western nation state has ever made so many major changes to its constitution, including hundreds of amendments, within a similar span. By way of comparison, the US Constitution has been subject to fewer than 30 amendments over nearly 225 years.

Agreeing to reform the EU's institutions, disagreeing on the details, and then agreeing to try to agree again in a future intergovernmental conference (IGC) has become routine. Furthermore, the impact of the global financial crisis after 2008, and the emergence of the Eurozone crisis in 2010, triggered a flurry of activity by member states and EU institutions on monetary policy, fiscal policy coordination, and banking union. The economic impact of the economic crisis continues to pose a challenge to the Union and its members, and the policy responses to that challenge have, in themselves, triggered disagreements amongst member states. Against this backdrop, where does the EU go from here?

Debating the future of Europe

Sometimes it seems as if a debate on the future of EU is 'much of the same old . . . '. The debates of the 1950s dealt with many of the same challenges that the EU faces today. Institutional reform, enlargement, policy remit, money, and foreign policy have always been on the EU agenda. The changes over the past 50 years might seem incremental in the short term. However, measured over time, the EU has actually experienced a radical metamorphosis from an institutionally weak and small club with a limited policy arsenal, separate currencies and no foreign policy, to an institutional powerhouse of 28 members, an elected parliament, a plethora of policies, a single currency and an important role in world politics.

The first decade of the new millennium brought with it new themes to the European agenda. Peace, prosperity and security remain the cornerstones of integration. But the agenda has shifted markedly towards economic reform, climate change and energy. On one hand, the economic reform agenda resists simple solutions because an EU of 28 is far more economically diverse than ever before. And Europe was hit very hard by the post-2008 global recession.

On the other hand, there were signs of fresh life in the EU's economy by the middle of the second decade of the 2000s, even given crises in the Eurozone. Macroeconomic coordination, banking union and fresh efforts to extend the single market to services were all illustrative. The Union took a global lead on climate change by pledging to cut greenhouse emissions by at least 40 per cent by the year 2030 and encouraging the rest of the industrialized world to follow its lead. But it also was marginalized by emerging economy states at the 2009 Copenhagen climate change summit. The Union remained far from having a common energy policy. At the same time, it at least encouraged European citizens to see connections between energy security and environmental protection.

However, the second decade of the twenty-first century has, at least so far, been dominated by the EU's response to the Eurozone crisis. Since May 2010, when Greece stood on the brink of a sovereign default, the EU has provided emergency assistance funding to three of its members (Greece, Portugal, Ireland). Through an intergovernmental treaty, euro members established the European Stability Mechanism (ESM), a permanent crisis resolution mechanism, in 2012. The ESM helps finance loans and other forms of financial assistance to euro members. It is an intergovernmental organization based in Luxembourg with a maximum lending capacity of €500 billion. In parallel, a series of measures referred to as 'the six pack' and 'the two pack' have been agreed since 2011 to try to strengthen the Stability and Growth Pact by enhancing surveillance of public spending and enforcement provisions. In 2013 a Fiscal Compact signed by 25 of what were then 27 EU member states (the UK and the Czech Republic did not sign), required member states to enshrine in national law a balanced budget rule.

Perhaps most dramatically, the EU's member states have moved towards a banking union, involving a single supervisory mechanism for approximately 6,000 banks across the EU and a single rulebook with which all European financial must comply. Still, much remains to be done to ensure that member states hit hardest by the Eurozone crisis can find a path back to economic growth and that the highly complex banking union can operate effectively.

How *will* it work?

We conclude with a few thoughts, we will not call them 'predictions', about how the Union may evolve in the years to come. There is no shortage of controversy or disagreement about what is most important in determining how the EU really works. Be that as it may, models or visions of how the EU *should* work are useful in stimulating thinking about different potential futures. These models are by no means mutually exclusive. On the contrary, the European Union has always been a hybrid of the:

1. *Intergovernmental*
2. *Federal*; and
3. *Functional*.

Intergovernmentalism denotes both a school of theory in the study of European integration and a descriptive term to describe an EU that is dominated by its member states. An intergovernmental outcome to the 2007 IGC would have meant a repatriation of competences, a weakening of the institutional triangle between the Commission, the Council and the EP, and a return to unanimous decision-making; with many decisions taken outside the current institutional framework. In some ways, the outcome was the opposite. The Lisbon Treaty extended qualified majority voting to some 30 new areas of policy. The pillar structure was collapsed. The EU was given a legal personality and all of its key institutions were strengthened (see Chapter 3). All member states realized that if the EU wanted to be a serious player on the international scene, strict intergovernmentalism was not an option. However, the response to the Eurozone crisis has seen member states, particularly Germany, come to the fore. The response to the crisis has been a reminder of the importance of the Franco-German tandem, especially given the rift between them: in 2014, France submitted a budget that violated (again) the Growth and Stability Pact while Germany stubbornly insisted on fiscal rectitude.

A fully *federal* Europe would have meant the adoption of something closer in form and substance to the Constitutional Treaty. In symbolic terms, it would, at least in some EU states, have been called a Constitution and would have included constitutional symbols such as the European anthem and flag, a president and a foreign minister. But a truly federal EU, at least for ardent enthusiasts of the idea, would mean going beyond the Constitutional Treaty and giving the Union a more powerful central authority with wider competences. Supporters argued that a federal structure could be more transparent and democratic. Power sharing in most federal regimes is governed by the subsidiarity principle (see Box 2.2), with powers formally divided in a way that brings government as close to the citizen as possible.

Put simply, most member governments and their publics remained unwilling to take a quantum leap to a federal state. The French and Dutch rejections of the Constitutional Treaty proved the case, which was further underscored by the results of the 2014 European Parliament elections. The UK seemed to drift ever closer to leaving an ever closer union, with its Prime Minister opining '[i]t may appeal to some countries. But it is not right for Britain, and we must ensure that we are no longer subject to it' (*Daily Telegraph*, 16 March 2014). Many of the hallmarks of a federal state—a large central budget funded through direct taxation, an army, or constitutional amendment by less than unanimous agreement amongst component states—are unlikely. There is no mass political movement or demos pushing for a European federation.

To be sure, as the history of the European Union shows, there can be federalism without a federation. The euro and European Central Bank are nothing if not federative elements. Thus, we find another apparent contradiction: the idea of a federal Europe—a nightmare to Eurosceptics—is both a utopian pipe-dream and a practical reality in some areas of policy. But if it ever arrives, a United States of Europe will not arrive in the near future. In some ways, political agreement on the Lisbon Treaty, as an alternative to the Constitutional Treaty, was a major setback to those who support a federal Europe.

A final, *functional* model of the future is a mix between the previous two. It is in essence what the Lisbon Treaty represents. More than either the intergovernmental or federal variants, the functional model favours continuity in European integration and is sceptical of radical change. It embraces a largely functional path of integration, which is practical and utilitarian rather than decorative or symbolic. It accepts that the EU does not yet (and may never) operate in policy areas such as child care and most forms of taxation. It accepts that the Community method of decision-making, with powers shared between the EU's institutions, is inappropriate (at least initially) for some areas where European cooperation makes sense, including defence and border controls (see Chapter 9). The response to the Eurozone crisis to date has demonstrated this functional logic. Member states played a crucial role in shaping the framework of that response, but the roles of the Commission and (perhaps most critically) the European Central Bank were of crucial importance. The Commission has played a leading role in putting flesh on the bones of the policy response, while the ECB was instrumental in calming financial markets and ensuring that countries such as Spain and Italy avoided having to draw on the European Stability Mechanism.

The functional model can accept a 'core Europe' in some areas of policy. As in the cases of Schengen or the Eurozone, some EU states may forge ahead with cooperative agreements that others choose not to support on the assumption that outsiders might become insiders later on (see Box 11.2). But the functional model also values power sharing for its own sake. It favours pragmatic cooperation extending to all EU members based on strengthening the institutional triangle between the Commission, Council and EP with the ECJ adjudicating disputes between them.

A basic assumption underpinning this model is that the EU—warts and all —has worked to further the greater good of European citizens. But form should follow function, not vice versa as in the federal vision. The functional model represents a

> ### BOX 11.2   Two-speed Europe?
>
> Debate abounds about a 'two-speed Europe', a vanguard of countries that integrate further. The holding of Eurozone summits and the establishment of a Fiscal Compact with 25 participating states stimulated a further round of such discussions. Reality is more complex than the label 'two speed Europe' would suggest. In practice, a striking variety of speeds and configurations exist. Some examples include:
>
> - Non-participation in defence cooperation: Denmark;
> - Non-participation in all aspects of Schengen: Cyprus, Croatia, Ireland, and the UK (but participation of Norway, Iceland, and Switzerland from outside the EU);
> - No obligation to join the euro: UK and Denmark; no intention to join the euro soon: Sweden, Czech Republic;
> - Right to opt-in (or not) to measures in the field of freedom, justice, and security: Denmark, Ireland, UK;
> - Exemption from the single market rules regarding the acquisition of secondary residences on its territory: Denmark, and;
> - Exemption from the primacy of EU law regarding anything affecting abortion: Ireland.
>
> Thus, we do not find any straightforward group of slow states, nor an *avant-garde* group of leading member states. Instead, there is a variety of *arrière-gardes*, in each case rather small and with a different configuration, sometimes a single country. The general unity of the Union remains largely intact, even if the growing number of special situations regarding the UK is frequently commented upon.

path that has been followed from the earliest beginnings of European integration in the 1950s. It may well live on in the EU of the future simply because, in the past, it has worked: most say reasonably and some say remarkably, even if a minority says not at all.

Conclusion

The reality of European integration is naturally more complex than the simple models we have just outlined. French EU policy illustrates this point. On some federal projects, such as the euro, France has been instrumental. At the same time France has often given intergovernmentalists reasons to be happy by putting a halt to further European integration: in 1954 by blocking the European Defense Community, in 1966 by refusing to move to QMV and in 2005 by rejecting the constitution. Yet, France has been a vocal advocate of the Common Security and Defense Policy, thus revealing its affinity for a Europe that is a more 'functional' global actor.

The EU has always been a combination of these three models. It is more than an ordinary international organization, but less than a state (Wallace 1983). It is likely always to be a multilevel system in which the supranational, national and regional co-exist. It is a unique and original way of organizing cooperation between states, whose governments (if not always their citizens) genuinely see themselves as members of a political union.

The EU of the future will remain an experimental system, always in flux, with plenty of scope to be reformed and competing ideas about how to do it. It will continue to be, above all, an exercise in seeking consensus and trying to achieve unity, where it makes sense, out of enormous diversity. As such, how it really works will never match one vision of how it should work.

▌ APPENDIX: Chronology of European Integration*

1945 May	End of World War II in Europe
1946 Sept.	Winston Churchill's 'United States of Europe' speech
1947 June	Marshall Plan announced
	Organization for European Economic Cooperation established
1949 Apr.	North Atlantic Treaty signed in Washington
1950 May	Schuman Declaration
1951 Apr.	Treaty establishing the ECSC signed in Paris
1952 May	Treaty establishing the European Defence Community (EDC) signed
Aug.	European Coal and Steel Community launched in Luxembourg
1954 Aug.	French parliament rejects the EDC
Oct.	Western European Union (WEU) established
1955 May	Germany and Italy join NATO
June	EC foreign ministers meet in Messina to relaunch European integration
1956 May	Meeting in Venice, EC foreign ministers recommend establishing the European Economic Community (EEC) and the European Atomic Energy Community (Euratom)
1957 Mar.	Treaties establishing the EEC and Euratom signed in Rome
1958 Jan.	Launch of the EEC and Euratom
1961 July	The UK, Denmark, Ireland, and Norway apply to join the EEC
1962 Jan.	Agreement reached on the common agricultural policy
1963 Jan.	French President Charles de Gaulle vetoes the UK's application; de Gaulle and German Chancellor Konrad Adenauer sign Elysée Treaty
July	Signing of Yaoundé Convention between EEC and 18 African states
1964 May	EEC sends single delegation to Kennedy Round negotiations on tariff reduction in General Agreement on Tariffs and Trade (GATT)
1965 July	Empty Chair Crisis begins
1966 Jan.	Empty Chair Crisis ends with Luxembourg Compromise
1967 May	The UK, Denmark, Ireland, and Norway again apply for EEC membership
July	The executive bodies of the ECSC, EEC, and Euratom merge into a Commission
Nov.	De Gaulle again vetoes the UK's application
1968 July	The customs union is completed 18 months ahead of schedule
1969 Apr.	De Gaulle resigns
July	The UK revives its membership application

*Compiled by Desmond Dinan, Andrew Byrne, and Daniel Kenealy.

1970	Oct.	Council agrees to create Euopean Political Cooperation (EPC) mechanism Luxembourg's Prime Minister, Pierre Werner, presents a plan for Economic and Monetary Union (EMU)
1972	Oct.	Meeting in Paris, EC heads of state and government agree to deepen European integration
1973	Jan.	The UK, Denmark, and Ireland join the EC
	Oct.	Following the Middle East War, Arab oil producers quadruple the price of oil and send the international economy into recession
1975	Feb.	Lomé Convention (superceding Yaoundé Convention) agreed between EEC and 46 African, Caribbean, and Pacific (ACP) states
	Mar.	EC heads of state and government inaugurate the European Council (regular summit meetings)
	June	In a referendum in the UK, a large majority endorses continued EC membership
	July	Member states sign a treaty strengthening the budgetary powers of the European Parliament and establishing the Court of Auditors
1978	July	Meeting in Bremen, the European Council decides to establish the European Monetary System (EMS), precursor to EMU
1979	Mar.	Member states launch the EMS
	June	First direct elections to the European Parliament
1981	Jan.	Greece joins the EC
1985	June	The Commission publishes its White Paper on completing the single market
1986	Jan.	Portugal and Spain join the EC
	Feb.	EC foreign ministers sign the Single European Act (SEA)
1987	July	The SEA enters into force
1988	June	EC and Comecon (East European trading bloc) recognize each other for first time
1989	Apr.	The Delors Committee presents its report on EMU
	Nov.	The Berlin Wall comes down
1990	Oct.	Germany is reunited
1991	Dec.	Meeting in Maastricht, the European Council concludes the Intergovern-mental Conferences on political union and EMU
1992	Feb.	EC foreign ministers sign the Maastricht Treaty
	June	Danish voters reject the Maastricht Treaty
1993	May	Danish voters approve the Maastricht Treaty, with special provisions for Denmark
	Nov.	The Maastricht Treaty enters into force; the European Union (EU) comes into being
	June	Copenhagen European Council endorses eastern enlargement
1994	Apr.	Hungary and Poland apply to join EU

1995	Jan.	Austria, Finland, and Sweden join the EU
1995	Mar.	Schengen Agreement implemented by seven EU member states
1995–6		Eight additional Central and Eastern European countries apply to join the EU
1997	June	European Council agrees Amsterdam Treaty, which creates post of High Representative for the CFSP
	Oct.	EU foreign ministers sign the Amsterdam Treaty
1998	Mar.	The EU begins accession negotiations with five Central and Eastern European countries, plus Cyprus
		UK and France agree St Malo Declaration on European defence
	June	The European Central Bank is launched in Frankfurt
1999	Jan.	The third stage of EMU begins with the launch of the euro and the pursuit of a common monetary policy by 11 member states
	Mar.	The Commission resigns following the submission of a report of an independent investigating committee; the Berlin European Council concludes the Agenda 2000 negotiations
	May	The Amsterdam Treaty enters into force
	Dec.	The European Council signals 'irreversibility of eastern enlargement'; recognizes Turkey as a candidate for EU Membership
2000	Feb.	The EU begins accession negotiations with the five other Central and Eastern European applicant countries, plus Malta
	Dec.	Meeting in Nice, the European Council concludes the intergovernmental conference on institutional reform
2001	Feb.	EU foreign ministers sign the Nice Treaty
	June	Irish voters reject the Nice Treaty
2002	Jan.	Euro notes and coins enter into circulation
	Feb.	Convention on the 'Future of Europe' opens
	Oct.	In a second referendum, Irish voters approve the Nice Treaty
2003	Feb.	The Nice Treaty enters into force
	June	The Convention on the Future of Europe promulgates a Draft Constitutional Treaty
	Oct.	An intergovernmental conference opens to finalize the Constitutional Treaty
2004	May	Cyprus, the Czech Republic, Estonia, Hungary, Latvia, Lithuania, Malta, Poland, Slovakia, and Slovenia join the EU
	June	The intergovernmental conference reaches agreement on the Constitutional Treaty
	Oct.	National leaders sign the Constitutional Treaty in Rome
2005	May	French voters reject the Constitutional Treaty
	June	Dutch voters reject the Constitutional Treaty
		The European Council launches a year-long 'period of reflection' on the stalled Constitutional Treaty

	Oct.	The EU opens accession negotiations with Turkey
2006	June	The European Council decides to prolong the 'period of reflection' and calls on Germany to find a solution to the constitutional impasse during the country's presidency in the first half of 2007
2007	Jan.	Bulgaria and Romania join the EU
		Slovenia adopts the euro
	June	European Council agrees mandate for new 'Reform Treaty' to replace Constitutional Treaty
	July–Oct.	Intergovernmental conference drafts the Reform Treaty
	Dec.	National leaders sign the new treaty in Lisbon (the Lisbon Treaty)
2008	Jan.	Cyprus and Malta adopt the euro
	June	Irish voters reject the Lisbon Treaty
2009	Jan.	Slovakia adopts the euro
	Oct.	In a second referendum, Irish voters approve the Lisbon Treaty
	Dec.	The Lisbon Treaty enters into force
		The possibility of Greece defaulting on its soaring national debt causes its cost of national borrowing to increase rapidly and sparks crisis in the Eurozone
2010	Apr.–May	Greece applies for emergency support and concludes a loan agreement with the EU and IMF
	May	EU leaders create the European Financial Stability Facility (ESFS) to make financial assistance available to troubled Member States in the Eurozone. The EFSF is given capacity to offer up to €750bn in loans, €250bn of which will be contributed by the International Monetary Fund (IMF)
	Nov.	Ireland agrees an emergency loan programme with the EU and IMF
2011	Jan.	Estonia becomes the 17th member of the Eurozone
	Feb.	Eurozone finance ministers agree to establish a permanent emergency funding mechanism, the European Stability Mechanism (ESM)
	Apr.	Portugal becomes the third Eurozone country to apply for an EU loan assistance programme
	May	Portugal receives rescue package worth €178bn
	June	EU leaders agree to a new €120bn bailout of Greece, imposing further austerity measures as a condition. Talk of Greece leaving the euro grows.
	July	A second rescue package, worth €109bn, is agreed for Greece
	Aug.	ECB says it will purchase Spanish and Italian bonds as their yields rise to dangerous levels
	Oct.	Opposition to austerity in Greece erupts into scenes of violence outside parliament
	Nov.	Greek and Italian prime ministers both resign and are replaced by technocrats. Mario Draghi replaces Jean-Claude Trichet as president of the European Central Bank
	Dec.	Fiscal Compact agreed as an intergovernmental treaty between all EU states (except UK and Czech Republic) following David Cameron's veto

2012	Feb.	More protests in Greece as further austerity demanded in exchange for further rescue package
	Mar.	Eurozone finally approves second rescue package, worth €130bn, for Greece
	May	Socialist Francois Hollande succeeds Nicholas Sarkozy as president of France
	July	Mario Draghi says that the European Central Bank will do 'whatever it takes to preserve the euro'
	Sept.	Mario Draghi announces plan to buy the bonds of struggling Eurozone economies, called Outright Monetary Transactions (OMT), against wishes of Germany
	Oct.	The ESM is formally launched
	Nov.	Cyprus formally requests emergency assistance
2013	Jan.	UK Prime Minister, David Cameron, delivers his 'Bloomberg' speech setting out his plans for renegotiating the UK's membership of the EU ahead of a planned referendum on UK membership in 2017
	Mar.	Cyprus receives rescue package after controversy over its banking sector delayed the deal
	July	Croatia joins the EU
	Dec.	Ireland becomes first country to exit its rescue programme
2014	Jan.	Latvia becomes 18th state to adopt the euro
	May	Portugal exits rescue programme European Parliament elections see significant gains for Eurosceptic and populist parties, including the UK Independence Party and the French *Front National*
	Nov.	Jean-Claude Juncker becomes 12th President of the European Commission
	Dec.	Donald Tusk succeeds Herman Van Rompuy and becomes the 2nd President of the European Council
2015	Jan.	Mario Draghi unveils new ECB bond buying scheme Anti-government rebels in Ukraine seize Donetsk airport Alexis Tsipras, leader of Syriza (Coalition of the Radical Left) party, becomes Prime Minister of Greece on a platform of renegotiating the EU rescue package Extraordinary session of European Council to discuss developments in Ukraine Peace negotiations between Ukraine, the rebels, Russia, and the OSCE collapse
	Feb.	Eurozone agrees a four month extension to the Greek rescue package Ukraine, Russia, Germany, and France agree to end hostilities in eastern Ukraine at talks in Minsk
	Apr.	P5+1 conclude a framework agreement with Iran regarding their nuclear programme

GLOSSARY

Several of the terms which follow are defined and elaborated in more detail in the concept boxes of each of the chapters. Where this is the case, the box number is provided.

The EU also has its own official EU glossary which can be found at: **http://europa. eu/scadplus/glossary/index_en.htm**

Absorption capacity (see Box 8.1) Refers to the EU's ability to integrate new members into its system.

Accession (see Box 8.1) The process whereby a country joins the EU and becomes a member state.

Acquis communautaire (see Box 4.1) Denotes the rights and obligations derived from the EU treaties, laws, and Court rulings. In principle, new member states joining the EU must accept the entire *acquis*.

Assent procedure (see **Consent Procedure**)

Asylum Protection provided by a government to a foreigner who is unable to stay in their country of citizenship/residence for fear of persecution.

Battle groups combine national military resources at the 'hard end' of European capabilities in specialised areas. The EU decided in 2004 to create 20 Battle Groups, which would be deployable at short notice for limited deployments.

Benchmarking (see Box 5.1) The use of comparison with other states or organizations with the aim of improving performance by learning from the experience of others.

Bicameralism (see Box 7.1): from Latin *bi*, two + *camera*, chamber. The principle that a legislature should comprise two chambers, usually chosen by different methods or electoral systems.

Cabinet The group of staff and advisers that make up the private offices of senior EU figures, such as Commissioners.

Candidate countries (see Box 8.1) Refers to a country whose application is confirmed by the EU but is not yet a member.

Charter of Fundamental Rights Adopted at the Nice Summit in 2000 but not legally binding, the Charter was made binding on the EU's institutions and law by the Lisbon Treaty. It seeks to strengthen and promote the fundamental human rights of EU citizens.

Civil society (see Box 6.1) The collection of groups and associations (such as private firms and non-governmental organizations) that operate between the individual and state.

Co-decision procedure Under this decision-making procedure the European Parliament formally shares political and legal responsibility for legislation jointly with the Council of Ministers.

Cohesion policy Introduced after the first enlargement in 1973, its aim has been to reduce inequality among regions and compensate for the costs of economic integration.

Common Foreign and Security Policy (CFSP) (see Box 10.1) Created by the 1992 Maastricht Treaty as a successor to the European Political Cooperation mechanism. It has been embellished by successive new Treaties and given (by the Treaty of Nice) a

Brussels-based Political and Security Committee to prepare Foreign Ministers' meetings and (by Lisbon) a 'new look' High Representative and the EEAS.

Common Security and Defence Policy (CSDP) (see Box 9.3). Formerly known as ESDP: the European Security and Defence Policy. It was created in 1999 to engage in the so-called 'Petersburg tasks' (see later) humanitarian and rescue missions, peacekeeping, crisis management, and the vaguely-specified task of 'peacemaking'.

Community method Used especially in areas where common EU policies replace national policies (such as the internal market) the community method is a form of supranational policy-making in which the Union's institutions wield considerable power. Usually contrasted to the intergovernmental method.

Conditionality (see Box 8.1) Means that accession is conditional on fulfilling the criteria for membership.

Consent Procedure: (see Box 6.3) Previously known as the **assent** procedure, requires the EP's approval in a simple yes/no vote on international treaties, the accession of new member states, and some other decisions. The EP cannot amend proposals subject to consent. For enlargement, the approval of an absolute majority of Parliament's members is necessary.

Constructivism (see Table 1.1) A school of thought drawing on cultural and sociological studies and emphasizing the non-rational 'social construction' of the collective rules and norms that guide political behaviour.

Consultation procedure (see Box 6.3) Decision-making procedure whereby the Council seeks the opinion of the European Parliament but need not heed that opinion.

Coreper (the Committee of Permanent Representatives) The most important preparatory committee of the Council, Coreper is composed of heads of the Permanent Representation (EU ambassadors) and their supporting delegations maintained by each member state in Brussels. (See also '**Perm Reps**'.)

Cotonou agreement (see Box 10.1) Agreed in the African state of Bénin in 2000 and then revised repeatedly (lastly in 2010). It is the successor to the Lomé Convention and is claimed to be a 'comprehensive partnership' between former European colonies and the EU.

Council of Ministers The EU institution representing the interests of the member states. National ministers from each EU member state meet in the Council to adopt laws and coordinate policies. For most EU law the Council co-decides with the European Parliament.

Court of Justice of the European Union The judicial authority ensuring that EU law is applied and interpreted uniformly throughout the Union. It consists of three courts: the Court of Justice, the General Court, and the Civil Service Tribunal. Since 1952 the Court has delivered approximately 28,000 judgments.

Customs union This is a core component of the EU's single market. A customs union involves elimination of all customs duties and restrictions among a group of states and the introduction of a common customs tariff between these states and third parties. The external dimension of a customs union is a common commercial (or trade) policy.

Demandeur (see Box 4.1) French term often used to refer to those demanding something (say regional or agricultural funds) from the EU.

Democratic deficit (see Box 7.1) Refers broadly to the belief that the EU lacks sufficient democratic control. Neither the Commission, which proposes legislation, nor the Council, which enacts it, is directly accountable to the public or national parliaments.

Demos From the ancient Greek, refers to 'the people', 'populace', or 'citizen body'.

Direct effect Established in the 1963 *van Gend en Loos* case, the doctrine has become a distinguishing principle of Community law. Under direct effect Community law applies directly to individuals (not just states) and national courts must enforce it.

Directive (see Box 5.1) The most common form of EU legislation. It stipulates the ends to be achieved but allows each member state to choose the form and method for achieving that end.

Directorates General (DGs) The primary administrative units within the Commission, comparable to national ministries or Departments. There are about 20 DGs, each focusing on a specific area of policy such as competition or trade.

Economic and Monetary Union (EMU) A package of measures designed to harmonize the economic and monetary policies of participating member states. It includes the free movement of capital and convergence of monetary policies. Its most visible element is a single currency— the euro—adopted in 1999 with notes and coins circulating in 2002. By 2015 19 member states were members of EMU.

Elysée Treaty (1963) A treaty of friendship signed between Germany and France signalling greater political cooperation.

Empty Chair Crisis (see Box 2.2) Protesting the Commission's plans to subject more decisions to Qualified Majority Voting, French president De Gaulle pulled France out of all Council meetings in 1965 thereby leaving one chair empty.

Europe Agreements Signed in the early 1990s, these cooperation agreements between the EU and several east European countries were viewed as a first step towards accession. The agreements cover economic cooperation, cultural exchanges, and some foreign policy coordination.

European Commission The EU's executive body, representing the interests of the Union as a whole. The Commission proposes legislation, enforces European law, manages and implements EU policies and the budget, and represents the Union outside of Europe.

European Convention on Human Rights (ECHR) (see Box 7.1) formally the *Convention for the Protection of Human Rights and Fundamental Freedoms* is an international treaty drafted in 1950 by the then newly formed **Council of Europe**. All (the now 47) Council of Europe member states are party to the Convention. Any person who feels his or her rights, as defined in the Charter, have been violated by a state can appeal to the **European Court of Human Rights**. Judgements finding violations are binding on the States concerned

European Council Made up on the heads of state or government of the EU member states, the European Council is the political apex of the EU. It defines the general political direction and priorities of the EU.

European Court of Justice (see Court of Justice of the European Union).

European Defence Agency (EDA) (see Box 9.3) Created in 2004 'to support the Member States and the Council in their effort to improve European defence capabilities [particularly] in the field of crisis management and to sustain' the ESDP. It aims to move the EU towards more cooperation in arms production and procurement.

European Defence Community (EDC) A French-inspired, American-backed proposal for a European army. Tabled in 1950, the plan collapsed following its rejection by the French National Assembly in 1954.

European Economic Area (EEA) (see Box 8.1) An arrangement which extends the EU's single market to Norway, Iceland, and Liechtenstein.

European External Action Service (EEAS) (see Box 10.1) Created by the Lisbon Treaty and became active in 2010. It works under the authority of the High Representative and brings under one roof EU (Commission and Council) and national diplomats. One intended effect of the EEAS is to make the Union's missions in foreign capitals more like real embassies, with clout and resources.

European Parliament The only directly elected body of the EU. Its 751 members (MEP's) represent the EU's citizens. Elections are held every five years. The Parliament has gained power over the decades and is now a co-legislator (along with the Council) for nearly all EU law.

Europeanization (see Box 4.1) The process whereby national systems (institutions, policies, governments) adapt to EU policies and integration more generally, while also themselves shaping the European Union.

Europol (see Box 9.4) The European Police Office designed to improve the effectiveness with which police forces across the EU could cooperate across national borders.

European Political Cooperation (EPC) The precursor to the Common Foreign and Security Policy (CFSP), the EPC was launched in 1970 as a way for member states to coordinate their foreign policies and speak (and sometimes act) together when national policies overlapped.

European Security and Defence Policy (ESDP) See CSDP.

Eurozone (see Box 5.1) The countries that are part of the Economic and Monetary Union (EMU). By 2015 19 member states belonged to the Eurozone.

Federalism (see Box 5.1) Principle of sharing power and sovereignty between levels of governance, usually between central or federal level, and substate (state, provincial, Länder) level.

Free trade area (see Box 2.4) An area in which restrictive trading measures are removed and goods can travel freely among its signatory states. These states retain authority to establish their own tariff levels and quotas for third countries.

Frontex (see Box 9.3) is the EU's agency for the management of its external border. It was created in 2005 to coordinate Member States' operational cooperation in external border controls, provide training to national border guards, carry out risk analyses, organise joint control operations, and assist Member States in migrant return operations.

GDP (gross domestic product) An index of the total value of all goods and services produced by a country, not counting overseas operations.

Globalization (see Box 1.5) The process by which the world becomes increasingly interconnected and interdependent because of increasing flows of trade, ideas, people, and capital.

GNP (gross national product) An index of the total value of all goods and services produced by a country, including overseas trade. Most common measure of a country's material wealth.

Governance (see Box 1.5) Established patterns of rules, principles, and practices that enable a community to be governed even without a government or ruler. The term is usefully applied to the EU because of its lack of identifiable government.

IGCs (Intergovernmental Conferences) Conferences bringing together representatives of member states to hammer out deals and consider amendments to the treaties, or other history-making decisions such as enlargement.

Integration, European (see Box 1.5) The process whereby sovereign European states relinquish (surrender or pool) national sovereignty to maximize their collective power and interests.

Integration, flexible Also called 'reinforced' or 'enhanced cooperation', flexible integration denotes the possibility for some member states to pursue deeper integration without the participation of others. Examples include EMU and the Schengen Agreement.

Integration, negative Integration through market-building and the removal of obstacles to trade. Less ambitious than positive integration.

Integration, positive Integration through the active promotion of common policies which effectively replace national ones.

Intergovernmentalism (see Box 1.5) Process or condition whereby decisions are reached by specifically defined cooperation between or among governments. Sovereignty is not directly undermined.

Internal market More than a free trade area, an internal market signifies the free trade of goods, services, people, and capital. Also known as the single market.

Legitimacy The right to rule and make political decisions. More generally, the idea that 'the existing political institutions are the most appropriate ones for society' (Lipset 1963).

Liberal intergovernmentalism (see Table 1.1) A theory of European integration which argues that the most important decisions taken concerning the EU reflect the preferences of national governments rather than supranational institutions.

Lisbon Treaty The treaty was intended to make the EU more democratic and efficient as well as giving it a voice in global affairs. Amongst other things, the treaty enhanced the power of the European Parliament, changed voting procedures in the Council, and established the new positions of President of the European Union and Higher Representative. It was signed in 2007 and in force from 1 December 2009.

Lobbying (see Box 6.1) An attempt to influence policy-makers to adopt a course of action advantageous (or not detrimental) to a particular group or interest.

Luxembourg Compromise (see Box 2.2) Agreed in 1966 to resolve the 'Empty Chair Crisis', this informal agreement established that when a decision was subject to Qualified Majority Voting (QMV), the Council would postpone a decision if any member states felt 'very important' interests were under threat.

Market (Box 5.1) A system of exchange bringing together buyers and sellers of goods and services.

Marshall Plan (1947) (see Box 2.2) A US aid package of $13 billion to help rebuild West European economies after the war.

Multilevel governance (see Box 1.5) A term denoting a system of overlapping and shared powers between actors on the regional, national, and supranational levels.

Neofunctionalism (see Table 1.1) A theory of European integration which suggests that economic integration in certain sectors will provoke further integration in other sectors, and can lead to the formation of integrated supranational institutions.

New institutionalism (see Table 1.1) As applied to the EU, a theoretical approach that suggests that institutions, including rules and informal practices, can mould the behaviour of policy-makers (including national officials) in ways that governments neither plan nor control.

Non-tariff barriers (see Box 5.1) Regulations, such as national standards, that increase the cost of imports and thus have the equivalent effect of tariffs.

Ordinary Legislative Procedure (see Co-decision procedure)

OSCE (see Box 10.1) The Organisation for Security and Cooperation in Europe—brings together 57 (as of 2015) states from Europe and beyond in what is the world's largest regional security organisation. It claims to take a 'comprehensive approach to security', extending especially to human rights. The OSCE works on the basis of unanimity and its decisions are politically, not legally, binding. It thus is criticised as toothless, even though its predecessor—the Conference on SCE—was important in putting into motion the changes that led to the end of the Cold War.

Path dependency The idea (developed especially by new institutionalists) that once a particular policy path or course of action is taken, it is extremely difficult to turn back because of the 'sunk costs' (time and resources already invested). Used to explain why even those policies that have outlived their usefulness remain unreformed.

'Perm Reps' Eurospeak for the Permanent Representatives (EU ambassador) and the Permanent Representations (similar to embassies) of each member state. Together the 'Perm Reps' from each of the member states make up Coreper.

Petersberg tasks (Named after a German hotel where an earlier summit devoted to defence was held.) A series of security tasks designed to strengthen European defence capability and the EU's role as a civilian power. These tasks include humanitarian, rescue, and peacekeeping operations as well as tasks involving combat forces in crisis management.

Pillars (see Box 1.2) A shorthand term for describing the 'Greek temple' architecture created by the Maastricht Treaty, with the first pillar (the pre-existing European Community) and the second (foreign and security policy) and third (justice and home affairs) pillars together constituting the 'European Union'. The Lisbon Treaty collapsed the EU's pillars into one institutional structure.

Policy networks (see Table 1.1) Clusters of actors, each of whom has an interest or stake in a given policy sector and the capacity to help determine policy success or failure. Scholars applying this notion argue that analysing such networks can reveal a great deal about day-to-day decision-making in the EU.

Public policy (see Box 5.1) A course of action (decisions, actions, rules, laws, and so on) or inaction taken by government in regard to some public problem or issue.

Qualified Majority Voting (QMV) (see Box 2.2) Refers to the most commonly used voting method in the Council of Ministers. Under this system each member state is granted a number of votes roughly proportional to its population.

Rapporteur (see Box 6.1) The Member of the European Parliament responsible for preparing a report in one of the Parliament's committees.

Schengen Agreement (see Box 2.2) An agreement stipulating the gradual abolition of controls at borders. By 2015 26 EU member states were signatories including non-EU states: Switzerland, Liechtenstein, Norway, and Iceland. The UK and Ireland have not signed, and Denmark has opted out of certain aspects.

Schuman plan (see Box 2.3) A plan proposed by the French Foreign Minister, Robert Schuman, in 1950 to combine the coal and steel industries of Germany and France, thus making war between them impossible. It eventually became the basis for the European Coal and Steel Community, launched by the 1950 Treaty of Paris.

Single market (See internal market)

Soft security (see Box 9.3): is a post-Cold War concept that refers to security that is obtained through non-military policy instruments (except in cases of peacekeeping) and does not involve territorial defence of the state. It is related to the ideas of 'human security'—defence of the citizen, as opposed to the state—and 'homeland security', obtained via policies designed to eliminate internal security threats.

Sovereignty (see Box 1.5) refers to the ultimate authority over people and territory.

Subsidiarity (see Box 2.2) The idea that action should be taken at the most efficient level of governance, but as close to the citizens as possible.

Supranationalism (see Box 1.5) Above states or nations. Supranationalism means decisions are made by a process or institution which is largely independent of national governments. The term supranationalism is usually contrasted with intergovernmentalism.

Tour de table (see Box 4.1) In the Council of Ministers a 'tour around the table' allows each delegation to make an intervention on a given subject.

Transparency (see Box 6.1) refers to the process of making (EU) documents and decision-making processes more open and accessible to the public.

The Glossary was compiled with the assistance of Louise Maythorne (University of Edinburgh) and Andrew Byrne (Universities of Köln and Edinburgh).

■ REFERENCES

Acosta, D. and Geddes, A. (2013), 'The Development, Application and Implications of an EU Rule of Law in the Area of Migration Policy', *Journal of Common Market Studies*, 51/2, 179–93.

Armstrong, K., and Bulmer, S. (1998), *The Governance of the Single European Market* (Manchester and New York: Manchester University Press).

Aspinwall, M., and G. Schneider (2000), 'Same Menu, Separate Tables: The Institutionalist Turn in Political Science and the Study of European Integration', *European Journal of Political Research*, 38/1: 1–36.

Avery, G. (2004), 'The Enlargement Negotiations', in F. Cameron (ed.), *The Future of Europe, Integration* and Enlargement (London: Routledge): 35–62.

Avery G., Bailes J.K., and Thorhallsson B. (2011), 'Iceland's Application For European Union Membership', *Studia Diplomatica*, Royal Institute for International Relations, Brussels, 64/1: 93–119.

Avery, G. (2014a), *Independentism and the European Union* (Brussels: European Policy Centre).

Avery, G. (2014b), *Could an independent Scotland join the European Union?* (Brussels: European Policy Centre).

Aydin, U. and Thomas, K.P. (2012), 'The Challenges and Trajectories of EU Competition Policy in the Twenty-first Century', *Journal of European Integration*, 34/6: 531–47.

Bache, I. (2008), *Europeanization and Multi-Level Governance: Cohesion Policy in the European Union and Britain* (Lanham, MD: Rowman & Littlefield).

Bachtler, J., Mendez, C., and Wishlade, F. (2013), *EU Cohesion Policy and European Integration* (Farnham, United Kingdom: Ashgate).

Balfour, R. and Raik, K. (eds) (2012), 'The European External Action Service and National Diplomacies', *EPC Issue Paper,* 73/March, available at: http://www.fiia.fi/assets/news/The%20EEAS%20and%20National%20Diplomacies.pdf

Barber, T. (2010), 'The Appointments of Herman van Rompuy and Catherine Ashton', *Journal of Common Market Studies*, 48/1: 55–67.

Bartolini S. (2005), *Restructuring Europe Centre Formation, System Building and Political Restructuring between the Nation State and the European Union* (Oxford: Oxford University Press).

Barysch, K., Everts, S., and Grabbe, H. (2005), *Why Europe Should Embrace Turkey* (London: Centre for European Reform).

Baun, M., Dürr, J., Marek, D., and Šaradín, P. (2006), 'The Europeanization of Czech Politics', *Journal of Common Market Studies*, 44/2: 249–80.

Baun, M. and Marek, D. (2008), *EU Cohesion Policy after Enlargement* (Basingstoke and New York: Palgrave Macmillan).

Bergman, A. and Peterson, J. (2006), 'Security Strategy, ESDP and the Non-Aligned States', in R. Dannreuther and J. Peterson (eds) *Security Strategy and Transatlantic Relations* (London: Routledge).

Best, E., Christiansen, T., and Settembri P. (eds) (2008), *The Institutions of the Enlarged European Union: Continuity and Change* (Cheltenham and Northampton, MA: Edward Elgar).

Bindi, F. with Cisci, M. (2005), 'Italy and Spain: A Tale of Contrasting Effectiveness in the EU', in S. Bulmer, and C. Lequesne (eds), *The Member States of the European Union*, 2nd edn. (Oxford and New York: Oxford University Press): 142–63.

Bogdanor, V (2007), *Democracy, Accountability and Legitimacy in the European Union* (London: Federal Trust for Education and Research).

Börzel, T. (ed.) (2005), 'The Disparity of European Integration: Revisiting Neofunctionalism in Honour of Ernst Haas', Special Issue of *Journal of European Public Policy*, 12/2.

Bouchard, C., Peterson, J. and Tocci, N. (eds) (2013), *Multilateralism in the 21st Century: Europe's Quest for Effectiveness* (London and New York: Routledge).

Bretherton, C., and Vogler, J. (2006), *The European Union as a Global Actor*, 2nd edn. (London and New York: Routledge).

Bulmer, S., and Lequesne, C. (2005a), 'The EU and its Member States: An Overview', in S. Bulmer, and C. Lequesne (eds), *The Member States of the European Union* (Oxford and New York: Oxford University Press): 1–24.

Bulmer, S., and Lequesne, C. (2005b), *The Member States of the European Union*, 2nd edn. (Oxford and New York: Oxford University Press).

Burchill, S., Linklates A., Devetak, R., Donnelly, J., Paterson, M., Reus-Smit, C., and True, J. (2005), *Theories of International Relations* (Basingstoke and New York: Palgrave).

Cafruny, A., and Ryner, M. (eds) (2003), *A Ruined Fortress? Neoliberal Hegemony and Transformation in Europe* (Oxford and Lanham, MD: Rowman & Littlefield).

Caporaso, J. (2001), 'The Europeanization of Gender Equality Policy and Domestic Structural Change', in M. GreenCowles, J.Caporaso, and T. Risse (eds), *Transforming Europe: Europeanization and Domestic Change* (Ithaca, NY: Cornell University Press): 21–43.

Cardwell, P. J. (2011), 'Euromed, European Neighbourhood Policy and the Union for the Mediterranean: Overlapping Policy Frames in the EU's Governance of the Mediterranean', *Journal of Common Market Studies*, 49/2, 219–41.

Carlsnaes, W. (2006), European Foreign Policy, in K. E. Jørgensen, M. A. Pollack, and B. Rosamond (eds), *Handbook of European Union Politics* (London and Thousand Oaks, CA: Sage): 545–60.

Chalmers, A. W. (2013), 'Regional Authority, Transnational Lobbying and the Allocation of Structural Funds in the European Union' *Journal of Common Market Studies*, 51/5: 815–31.

Checkel, J. (1999), 'Social Construction and Integration', *Journal of European Public Policy*, 6/4: 545–60.

Chekel, J. (2001), 'Why Comply? Social Learning and European Identity Change', *International Organization*, 55/3: 553–88.

Chekel, J. (2004), 'Social Constructivisms in Global and European Politics; A Review Essay', *Review of International Studies*, 30/2: 229–44.

Chekel, J. (2006), 'Constructivism and EU Politics', in K. E. Jørgensen, M. Pollack, and B. Rosamond (eds), *Handbook of European Union Politics* (London: Sage): 57–76.

Chekel, J. (2007), 'Social Mechanisms and Regional Cooperation: Are Europe and the EU Really All That Different?', in A. Acharya and A.I. Johnston (eds), *Crafting Cooperation:*

Regional International Institutions in Comparative Perspective (Cambridge and New York: Cambridge University Press).

Chevenal, F. and Schimmelfenning, F. (2013), 'The Case for Democracy in the European Union', *Journal of Common Market Studies*, 51/2: 334–50.

Christou, G. and Croft, S. (eds) (2012), *European 'Security' Governance* (London and New York: Routledge).

Closa, C., and Heywood, P. S. (2004), *Spain and the European Union* (Basingstoke and New York: Palgrave).

Coen, D. and Richardson, J. (2007), *Lobbying in the European Union: Institutions, Actors and Issues* (Oxford and New York: Oxford University Press).

Coker, C. (2009), *War in an Age of Risk* (Cambridge and Malden, MA: Polity).

Commission (2007b), *The Official EU Languages*. Available at: http://ec.europa.eu/education/policies/lang/languages/index_en.html

Commission (2007c), Translation Directorate General 'Frequently Asked Questions' at: http://ec.europa.eu/dgs/translation/navigation/faq/faq_facts_en.htm

Commission (2010a), *EU 2010 Budget in Figures* (Luxembourg: Publications Office of the European Union). Available at: http://ec.europa.eu/budget/library/publications/budget_in_fig/syntchif_2010_en.pdf

Commission (2010b), *EU Budget 2009—Financial Report* (Luxembourg: Publications Office of the European Union).

Commission (2013a), *EU Budget 2012—Financial Report* (Bruxelles: Commission).

Commission (2013b), *30ᵗʰ Annual Report on Monitoring the Application of Community Law* (Bruxelles: Commission).

Conceição-Heldt, E. (2011), 'Variation in EU Member States' Preferences and the Commission's Discretion in the Doha Round', *Journal of European Public Policy*, 18/3: 403–19.

Cooper, R. (2004a), 'Hard Power, Soft Power and the Goals of Diplomacy', in D. Held and M. Koenig-Archibugi (eds), *American Power in the 21st Century* (Oxford and Malden, MA: Polity): 168–80.

Cooper, R. (2004b), 'Untitled', in N. Gnesotto (ed) *EU Security and Defence Policy: the First Five Years (1999–2004)* (Paris: Institute for Security Studies).

Copsey, N. and Pomorska, K. (2014), 'The Influence of the Newer Member States in the European Union: The Case of Poland and the Eastern Partnership', *Europe-Asia Studies*, 66/3, 421–3.

Corbett, R (2002), *The European Parliament's Role in Closer EU Integration* (Basingstoke: Macmillan).

Corbett, R. (2014), 'European Elections are Second-order Elections: Is Received Wisdom Changing?', *Journal of Common Market Studies*, 52/6: 1194–8.

Corbett, R., Jacobs, F., and Shackleton, M. (2010), *The European Parliament*, 8ᵗʰ edn. (London: Cartermill).

Cottey, A. (2013), *Security in the 21ˢᵗ Century Europe*, 2ⁿᵈ edn. (Basingstoke and New York: Palgrave).

Cowles, M. G., and Curtis, S. (2004), 'Developments in European Integration Theory: The EU as "Other"', in M. G. Cowles and D. Dinan (eds), *Developments in the European Union II* (Basingstoke and New York: Palgrave): 296–309.

Damro, C. (2010), 'Market Power Europe', MERCURY e-paper.

Damro, C. (2014), 'Market Power Europe: Externalization and Multilateralism', in C. Bouchard, J. Peterson, and N. Tocci (eds) *Multilateralism in the 21ˢᵗ Century: Europe's Quest for Effectiveness* (London and New York: Routledge).

Dannreuther, R. (ed.) (2004), *European Union Foreign and Security Policy: Towards a Neighbourhood Strategy* (London and New York: Routledge).

Dannreuther, R. (2007), *International Security: the Contemporary Agenda* (Cambridge and Malden, MA: Polity).

Daugbjerg, C. (2012), 'Globalisation and Internal Policy Dynamics in the Reform of the Common Agricultural Policy', in J. Richardson (ed), *Constructing a Policy-Making State?* (Oxford: Oxford University Press).

De Grauwe, P. (2012), *Economics of Monetary Union*, 10ᵗʰ edn. (Oxford: Oxford University Press).

Deutsch, K. Burrell, S., Kann, R., Lee, Jr. M., Lichterman, M., Lindgren, R., Loewenheim, F., and Van Wagenen, R. (1957), *Political Community and the North Atlantic Area: International Organization in the Light of Historical Experience* (Princeton, NJ: Princeton University Press).

Devetak, R., Burke, A., and George, J. (eds) (2012), *An Introduction to International Relations* (Cambridge and New York: Cambridge University Press).

Dinan, D. (2014a), *Europe Recast: A History of European Union*, 2ⁿᵈ edn. (Boulder, CO: Lynne Rienner and Basingstoke: Palgrave).

Dinan, D. (ed.) (2014b), *Origins and Evolution of the European Union*, 2ⁿᵈ edn. (Oxford: Oxford University Press).

Donnelly, B. and Bigatto, M. (2008), 'The European Parliament and Enlargement', in E. Best, T. Christiansen, and P. Settembri (eds), *The Institutions of the Enlarged European Union: Continuity and Change* (Cheltenham and Northampton, MA: Edward Elgar): 82–99.

Dryhauge, H. (2014), 'The Road to Environmental Policy Integration is Paved with Obstacles: Intra- and Inter-organizational Conflicts in EU Transport Decision-making', *Journal of Common Market Studies*, 52/5: 985–1001.

Duchêne, F. (1994), *Jean Monnet: The First Statesman of Interdependence* (New York: Norton).

Dyson, K., and Featherstone, K. (1999), *The Road to Maastricht: Negotiating Economic and Monetary Union* (Oxford: Oxford University Press).

Eilstrup-Sangiovanni, M. (2006), 'The Constructivist Turn in European Integration Studies', in M. Eilstrup-Sangiovanni (ed.), *Debates on European Integration: A Reader* (Basingstoke and New York: Palgrave): 393–405.

Elgström, O. (2007), 'Outsiders' Perceptions of the European Union in International Trade Negotiations', *Journal of Common Market Studies*, 45/4: 949–67.

Elman, C., and Elman, M. F. (eds) (2003), *Progress in International Relations Theory* (Cambridge and London: MIT Press).

Epstein, R. and Sedelmeier, U. (eds) (2009), *International Influence beyond Conditionality: Postcommunist Europe after EU Enlargement* (London: Routledge).

Eurobarometer (2007), *Standard Barometer 67, First Results Spring 2007* (Brussels: European Commission). Available at: http://ec.europa.eu/public_opinion/archives/eb/eb67/eb_67_first_en.pdf

European Union (2009), *EU 2010 Budget in Figures* (Luxembourg: Publications Office of the European Union).

Eurostat (2007), *Statistics in Focus. Population and Social Conditions*, 41/2007. (Luxembourg: Eurostat). Available at: http://epp.eurostat.ec.europa.eu/cache/ITY_OFFPUB/KS-SF-07-041/EN/KS-SF-07-041-EN.PDF

Eurostat (2012), 'External Trade', *Statistics in Focus 3/2012* (Brussels: Eurostat).

Everts, S. (2002), *Shaping a Credible EU Foreign Policy* (London: Centre for European Reform).

Faber, G. and Orbie, J. (2009), 'Everything but Arms: Much More than Appears at First Sight', *Journal of Common Market Studies*, 47/4: 767–87.

Falkner, G. (2000), 'How Pervasive are Euro-Politics? Effects of EU Membership on a New Member State', *Journal of Common Market Studies*, 38/2: 223–50.

Falkner, G., Treib, O., and Holzleithner, E. (2008), *Compliance in the Enlarged European Union* (Aldershot: Ashgate).

Farrell, M. (2007), 'From EU Model to External Policy? Promoting Regional Integration in the Rest of the World', in S. Meunier, and K. McNamara (eds), *Making History: European Integration and Institutional Change at Fifty* (Oxford and New York: Oxford University Press): 299–316.

Forsberg, T. (2011), 'Normative Power Europe, Once Again: A Conceptual Analysis of an Ideal Type', *Journal of Common Market Studies*: 49/6: 1184–204.

Gallagher, T. (2009), *Romania and the European Union: How the Weak Vanquished the Strong* (Manchester: Manchester University Press).

Galtung, J. (1973), *The European Community: A Superpower in the Making* (London: George Allen & Unwin).

Gebhard, C. and Smith, S. J. (2014), 'The Two Faces of EU-NATO Cooperation: the Case of Counter-Piracy', *Cooperation and Conflict* (details forthcoming).

Geddes, A. (2008), *Immigration and European Integration: Towards Fortress Europe*, 2nd edn. (Manchester: Manchester University Press).

Geddes, A. and Boswell, C. (2011), *Migration and Mobility in the European Union* (Basingstoke and New York: Palgrave).

Gillingham, J. (1991), *Coal, Steel and the Rebirth of Europe, 1945–1955* (Cambridge: Cambridge University Press).

Gillingham, J. (2003), *European Integration, 1950–2003* (Cambridge: Cambridge University Press).

Ginsberg, R. (2001), *The European Union in International Politics: Baptism by Fire* (Boulder, CO, and Oxford: Rowman & Littlefield).

Glencross, A. (2011), 'A Post-national EU? The Problem of Legitimising the EU without the Nation and National Representation', *Political Studies*: 59/2: 348–67.

Goergen, P. (2006), *Lobbying in Brussels: A Practical Guide to the European Union for Cities, Regions, Networks and Enterprises* (Brussels, D&P Services).

Goetz, K. H. (2005), 'The New Member States and the EU: Responding to Europe', in S. Bulmer and C. Lequesne (eds), *The Member States of the European Union* (Oxford and New York: Oxford University Press): 254–84.

Grabbe, H. (2006), *The EU's Transformative Power: Europeanization through Conditionality in Central and Eastern Europe* (Basingstoke and New York: Palgrave Macmillan).

Grant, W. (2010), 'Policy Instruments in the Common Agricultural Policy', *West European Politics*, 33/1: 22–38.

Greenwood, J. (2011), *Interest Representation in the European Union*, 3rd edn. (Basingstoke: Palgrave Macmillan).

Gross, E. (2009), *The Europeanization of National Foreign Policy: Continuity and Change in European Crisis Management* (Basingstoke and New York: Palgrave Macmillan).

Haas, E. (1958), *The Uniting of Europe: Political, Social, and Economic Forces* (Stanford, CA: Stanford University Press).

Haas, E. (1961), 'International Integration: The European and the Universal Process', *International Organization*: 15/3: 366–92.

Haas, E. (1964), *Beyond the Nation-State: Functionalism and International Organization* (Stanford CA: Stanford University Press).

Haas, E. (2001), 'Does Constructivism Subsume Neo-functionalism?', in T.Christiansen, K. E. Jørgensen, and A. Weiner (eds), *The Social Construction of Europe* (London and Thousand Oaks, CA: Sage): 22–31.

Habermas, J. (2008), *Europe: the Faltering Project* (Cambridge and Malden, MA: Polity).

Hadfield, A. and Fiott, D. (2013), 'Europe and the Rest of the World', in N. Copsey and T. Haughton (eds), *The JCMS Annual Review of the European Union in 2012* (Oxford and Malden MA: John Wiley and Sons): 168–82.

Hagemann, S., and De Clerck-Sachsse, J. (2007), *Decision-making in the Council of Ministers before and after May 2004*, Special CEPS Report (Brussels: Centre for European Policy Studies).

Hall, P. and Taylor, C. (1996), 'Political Science and the Three New Institutionalisms', *Political Studies*, 44/5: 936–57.

Hancke', B. (2013), *Unions, Central Banks, and EMU: Labour Market Institutions and Monetary Integration in Europe* (Oxford: Oxford University Press).

Hayes-Renshaw, F., and Wallace, H. (2006), *The Council of Ministers*, 2nd edn. (Basingstoke: Palgrave).

Heinsenberg, D. (2005), 'The Institution of "Consensus" in the European Union: Formal versus Informal Decision-making in the Council', *European Journal of Political Research*, 44/1: 65–90.

Heinsenberg, D. (2007), 'Informal Decision-Making in the Council: The Secret of the EU's Success?', in S. Meunier, and K. McNamara (eds), *Making History. European Integration and Institutional Change at Fifty* (Oxford and New York: Oxford University Press): 67–88.

Helwig, N. (2013), 'EU Foreign Policy and the High Representative's Capability-Expectations Gap—A Question of Political Will', *European Foreign Affairs Review*, 18/2: 235–54.

Helwig, N., Ivan, P., and Kostanyan, H. (2013), *The New EU Foreign Policy Architecture, Reviewing the First Two Years of the EEAS* (Brussels: Centre for European Policy Studies).

Henderson, K. (2007), *The European Union's New Democracies* (London and New York: Routledge).

Hill, C. (1993), 'The Capability-Expectations Gap, or Conceptualizing Europe's International Role', *Journal of Common Market Studies*, 31/3: 305–28.

Hill, C. (1998), 'Closing the Capabilities-expectations Gap?', in J. Peterson and H. Sjursen (eds), *A Common Foreign Policy for Europe? Competing Visions of the CFSP* (London and New York: Routledge): 91–107.

Hill, C. (2004), 'Rationalizing or Regrouping? EU Foreign Policy since 11 September 2001', *Journal of Common Market Studies*, 42/1: 143–63.

Hill, C. (2006), 'The European Powers in the Security Council: Differing Interests, Differing Arenas', in K. V. Laatikainen and K. E. Smith (eds), *The European Union at the United Nations* (Basingstoke and New York: Palgrave).

Hill, C. and Smith, M. (eds) (2011), *International Relations and the European Union*, 2nd edn. (Oxford and New York: Oxford University Press).

Hillebrandt, M.Z., Curtin, D., and Meijer, A. (2014), 'Transparency in the EU Council of Ministers: An Institutional Analysis', *European Law Journal*, D20/1: 1–20.

Hillion, C. (2008), 'The EU's Neighbourhood Policy towards Eastern Europe', in A. Dashwood, M. Maresceau (eds), *Law and Practice of EU External Relations: Salient Features of a Changing Landscape* (Cambridge: Cambridge University Press): 309–33.

Hix, S. (2008), 'Towards a Partisan Theory of EU Politics', *Journal of European Public Policy*, 15/8: 1254–65.

Hix, S. (2009), *What to Expect in the 2009–14 European Parliament: Return of the Grand Coalition?* (Stockholm: Swedish Institute for European Policy Analysis).

Hix, S. and Hoyland, B. (2013), 'Empowerment of the European Parliament', *Annual Review of Political Science*, 16/1: 171–89.

Hix, S., Noury, A., and Roland, G. (2007), *Democratic Politics in the European Parliament* (Cambridge: Cambridge University Press).

Hix, S., Noury, A., and Roland, G. (2009), 'Voting Patterns and Alliance Formation in the European Parliament', *Philosophical Transactions of the Royal Society B*, 364: 821–31.

Hodson, D. (2010), 'Economic and Monetary Union', in H. Wallace, M. Pollack, and A. Young (eds), *Policymaking in the European Union*, 6th edn. (Oxford: Oxford University Press): 157–80.

Hoeksma, J. (2010), *A Polity called EU: The European Union as a Transnational Democracy* (Amsterdam: Europe's World).

Hoffmann, S. (1966), 'Obstinate or Obsolete: The Fate of the Nation-state and the Case of Western Europe', *Daedalus*, 95/3: 862–915 (reprinted in S. Hoffmann (1995), *The European Sisyphus: Essays on Europe 1964–1994* (Boulder, CO, and Oxford: Westview Press)).

Hoffmann, S. (1995), *The European Sisyphus: Essays on Europe 1964–1994* (Boulder, CO, and Oxford: Westview Press).

Holzinger, K. and Sommerer, T. (2011), '"Race to the Bottom" or "Race to Brussels"? Environmental Competition in Europe', *Journal of Common Market Studies*, 49/1: 315–39.

Hooghe, L. (2005), 'Many Roads Lead to International Norms, But Few Via International Socialization: A Case Study of the European Commission', *International Organization*, 59/4: 861–98.

Hooghe, L. and Marks, G. (2001), *Multi-Level Governance and European Integration* (Lanham and Oxford: Rowman & Littlefield).

Hooghe, L. and Marks, G. (2003), 'Unravelling the Central State, but How? Types of Multi-level Governance', *American Political Science Review*, 97/2: 233–43.

House of Lords (2006), *The Further Enlargement of the EU: Threat or Opportunity?* European Union Committee, Report with Evidence, HL Paper 273 (London: Stationery Office Ltd.). Available at: http://www.publications.parliament.uk/pa/ld200506/ldselect/ldeucom/273/273.pdf

Howorth, J. (2007), *Security and Defence Policy in the European Union* (Basingstoke and New York: Palgrave).

Hug, A. (2010), *Reconnecting the European Parliament and its People* (London: Foreign Policy Centre).

Hurrelmann, A. (2014), 'Democracy Beyond the State: Insights from the European Union', *Political Science Quarterly*, 129/1: 87–105.

Jabko, N. (2006), *Playing the Market* (Ithaca, NY: Cornell University Press).

Jeffrey, C. and Rowe, C. (2012), 'Social and Regional Interests: The Economic and Social Committee and Committee of the Regions', in J. Peterson, and M. Shackleton (eds), *The Institutions of the European Union*, 3rd edn. (Oxford: Oxford University Press).

Jones, E., Menon, A., and Weatherill, S. (2012), *The Oxford Handbook of the European Union* (New York and Oxford: Oxford University Press).

Jordan, A. and Schout, A. (2006), *The Coordination of the European Union: Exploring the Capacities for Networked Governance* (Oxford: Oxford University Press).

Jørgensen K. E. (2006), 'Overview: The European Union and the World', in K. E. Jørgensen, M. A. Pollack, and B. Rosamond (eds), *Handbook of European Union Politics* (London and Thousand Oaks, CA: Sage): 507–25.

Jørgensen, K.E.Pollack, M., and Rosamond, B. (eds) (2006), *Handbook of European Union Politics* (London and Thousand Oaks, CA: Sage).

Journal of European Public Policy (2007), Special issue on 'Empirical and Theoretical Studies in EU Lobbying', 14/3.

Journal of European Public Policy (2015), Special issue on Demoicracy in the European Union', 22/1.

Judge, D. and Earnshaw, D. (2008), *The European Parliament*, 2nd edn. (London: Palgrave Macmillan).

Judge, D. (2002), 'No Simple Dichotomies: Lobbyists and the European Parliament', in *Journal of Legislative Studies*, 2nd edn. 8/4: 61–79.

Karakatsanis, G. and Laffan, B. (2012), 'Financial Control: the Court of Auditors and OLAF', in J. Peterson and M. Shackleton (eds), *The Institutions of the European Union* (Oxford and New York: Oxford University Press): 241–61.

Kassim, H., Peters, B. G., and Wright, V. (eds) (2001), *The National Co-ordination of EU Policy: The European Level* (Oxford and New York: Oxford University Press).

Kassim, H., Peterson, J., Bauer, M., Connolly, S., Dehousse, R., Hooghe, L., and Thompson, A. (2014), *The European Commission of the 21st Century: Decline or Renewal?* (Oxford: Oxford University Press).

Kaunert, C. (2011), *European Internal Security: Towards Supranational Governance in the Area of Freedom, Security and Justice* (Manchester: Manchester University Press).

Kenealy, D. (2014), 'How Do You Solve a Problem like Scotland? A Proposal Regarding Internal Enlargement', *Journal of European Integration*, 36/6: 585–600.

Kenealy, D. and MacLennan, S. (2014), 'Sincere Cooperation, Respect for Democracy, and EU Citizenship: Sufficient to Guarantee Scotland's Future in the Union?', *European Law Journal*, 20/5: 591–612.

Knill, C. and Liefferink, D. (2007), *Environmental Politics in the European Union* (Manchester: Manchester University Press).

Kostakopoulou, D. (2006), 'Security Interests: Police and Judicial Cooperation', in J. Peterson and M. Shackleton (eds), *The Institutions of the European Union*, 2nd edn. (Oxford and New York: Oxford University Press).

Krasner, S. (1999), *Sovereignty: Organized Hypocrisy* (Princeton, NJ: Princeton University Press).

Krotz, U. (2009), 'Momentum and Impediments: Why Europe Won't Emerge as a Full Political Actor on the World Stage Soon', *Journal of Common Market Studies*, 47/3: 555–78.

Laffan, B. and O'Mahony, J. (2008), *Ireland in the European Union* (Palgrave: London).

Laffan, B., O'Donnell, R., and Smith, M. (2000), *Europe's Experimental Union: Rethinking Integration* (London and New York: Routledge).

Laïdi, Z. (2008), *La Norme sans la Force: l'Enigme de la Puissance Européene*, 2nd edn. (Paris: Presses de Science Po).

Lavenex, S. (2006), 'Shifting Up and Out: the Foreign Policy of European Immigration Control', *West European Politics*, 29/2: 329–50.

Lavenex, S. and Wagner, W. (2007), 'Which European Public Order? Sources of Imbalance in the European Area of Freedom, Security and Justice', *European Security*, 16/3–4: 225–43.

Leonard, M. (2005), *Why Europe Will Run the 21st Century* (London and New York: Harper Collins).

Lewis, J. (2013), 'The Council of the European Union and the European Council', in M. Cini and N. Perez-Solorzano Borragan (eds), *Politics in the European Union*, 4th edn. (Oxford and New York: Oxford University Press): 143–58.

Lindberg, L. (1963), *The Political Dynamics of European Economic Integration* (Stanford, CA: Stanford University Press).

Lindberg, L. and Scheingold, S. A. (1970), *Europe's Would-Be Polity: Patterns of Change in the European Community* (Englewood Cliffs, NJ: Prentice-Hall).

Lindberg, B., Rasmussen, A., and Warntjen, A. (eds) (2008), 'The Role of Political Parties in the European Union', Special issue of *Journal of European Public Policy*, 15/8.

Ludlow, P. (2010), *Eurocomment*, 7/8: 7.

MacCormick, N. (2008), 'Constitutionalism and Democracy in the EU', in E. Bomberg, J. Peterson, and A. Stubb (eds), *The European Union: How Does it Work?*, 2nd edn. (Oxford and New York: Oxford University Press).

Majone, G. (1999), 'The Regulatory State and its Legitimacy Problems', *West European Politics*, 22/1: 1–13.

Majone, G. (2005), *Dilemmas of European Integration: the Ambiguities and Pitfalls of Integration by Stealth* (Oxford and New York: Oxford University Press).

Manners, I. (2002), 'Normative Power Europe: A Contradiction in Terms?' *Journal of Common Market Studies*, 40/2: 235–58.

Manners, I. (2006), 'Normative Power Europe Reconsidered', *Journal of European Public Policy*, 13/2: 182–99.

Martin, P. (2010), 'The US Supreme Court', in G. Peele, C. Bailey, B. Cain, and B. Guy Peters (eds), *Developments in American Politics 6* (Basingstoke and New York: Palgrave Macmillan).

Mayhew, A. (1998), *Recreating Europe: The European Union's Policy towards Central and Eastern Europe* (Cambridge: Cambridge University Press).

Mearsheimer, J. J. (2001), *The Tragedy of Great Power Politics* (New York and London: Norton).

Menon, A. (2011), 'Power, Institutions and the CSDP: the Promise of Institutional Theory', *Journal of Common Market Studies*, 49/1: 83–100.

Merand, F. and Saurugger, S. (2010), Special issue of *Comparative European Politics*, 8/1.

Merand F., Foucault, M., and Irondelle, B. (eds) (2011), *European Security Since the Fall of the Berlin Wall* (Toronto: University of Toronto Press).

Messerlin, P. (2001), *Measuring the Costs of Economic Protection in Europe* (Washington, DC: Institute for International Economics).

Meunier, S., and McNamara, K. (eds) (2007), *Making History: European Integration and Institutional Change at Fifty* (Oxford: Oxford University Press).

Meyer, C. O. and Strickmann, E. (2011), 'Solidifying Constructivism: How Material and Ideational Factors Interact in European Defence', *Journal of Common Market Studies*, 49/1: 61–81.

Miller, V. (2013), 'Voting Behaviour in the EU Council', House of Commons Library Standard Note SN06646.

Milward, A. (1984), *The Reconstruction of Western Europe, 1945–51* (Berkeley: University of California Press).

Milward, A. (2000), *The European Rescue of the Nation-State*, 2nd edn. (London: Routledge).

Moravcsik, A. (1993), 'Preferences and Power in the European Community: A Liberal Intergovernmentalist Approach', *Journal of Common Market Studies*, 31/4: 473–524.

Moravcsik, A. (1998), *The Choice for Europe: Social Purpose and State Power from Messina to Maastricht* (Ithaca, NY, and London: Cornell University Press and UCL Press).

Moravcsik, A. (2002), 'In Defence of the Democratic Deficit: Reassessing Legitimacy in the European Union', *Journal of Common Market Studies*, 40/4: 603–24.

Moravcsik, A. (2013), 'Did Power Politics Cause European Integration? Realist Theory meets Qualitative Methods', *Security Studies*, 22/4: 773–90.

Moravcsik, A. and Schimmelfennig, F. (2009), 'Liberal Intergovernmentalism', in A. Wiener and T. Diez (eds), *European Integration Theory*, 2nd edn. (Oxford and New York: Oxford University Press).

Naurin, D. and Wallace, H. (2008), *Unveiling The Council of the European Union: Games Governments Play in Brussels* (London: Palgrave).

Neheider, S. and Santos, I. (2011), 'Reframing the EU Budget Decision-Making Process', *Journal of Common Market Studies*, 49/3: 631–51.

Neustadt, R. E. (1991), *Presidential Power and the Modern Presidents: The Politics of Leadership from Roosevelt to Reagan*, revised edn. (New York and London: Free Press).

Nicolaidis (2012), 'The Idea of European Demoicracy', in J. Dickson and P. Eleftheriadis (eds), *Philosophical Foundations of European Union Law* (New York and Oxford: Oxford University Press).

Nicolaidis (2013), 'European Demoicracy and Its Crisis', *Journal of Common Market Studies*, 51/2: 351–369.

Norheim-Martinsen, P. M. (2010), 'Beyond Intergovernmentalism: The European Security and Defence Policy and the Governance Approach', *Journal of Common Market Studies*, 48/5: 1351–65.

Nugent, N. (2004), *European Union Enlargement* (Basingstoke and New York: Palgrave).

Nugent, N. (2010), *The Government and Politics of the European Union*, 7th edn. (London: Palgrave Macmillan).

Nuttall, S. (2000), *European Foreign Policy* (Oxford and New York: Oxford University Press).

Nye, J. S. (2004), *Soft Power: The Means to Success in World Politics* (New York: Public Affairs).

Nye, J.S. (2011), *The Future of Power* (New York: Public Affairs).

OECD (2013), *National Accounts—Volume IV—General Government Accounts* (Paris: OECD).

Orbie, J. (2009), *Europe's Global Role: External Policies of the European Union* (Farnham: Ashgate).

Panke, D. (2010), *Small States in the European Union: Coping With Structural Disadvantages* (London: Ashgate).

Papadimitriou, D., and Phinnemore, D. (2007), *Romania and the European Union* (London and New York: Routledge).

Patten, C. (2001), 'In Defence of Europe's Foreign Policy', *Financial Times*, 17 October. Available at: www.ft.com

Patten, C. (2005), *Not Quite the Diplomat: Home Truths About World Affairs* (London and New York: Allen Lane/Penguin).

Peterson, J. (1995), 'Decision-Making in the EU: Towards a Framework for Analysis', *Journal of European Public Policy*, 2/1: 69–73.

Peterson, J. (2001), 'The Choice for EU Theorists: Establishing a Common Framework for Analysis', *European Journal of Political Research*, 39/3: 289–318.

Peterson, J. (2008), 'Enlargement, Reform and the European Commission: Weathering a Perfect Storm?', *Journal of European Public Policy*, 15/5: 761–80.

Peterson, J. (2009), 'Policy Networks', in A. Wiener and T. Diez (eds), *European Integration Theory*, 2nd edn. (Oxford: Oxford University Press).

Peterson, J. (2012a), 'The College of Commissioners', in J. Peterson, and M. Shackleton (eds), *The Institutions of the European Union*, 3rd edn. (Oxford: Oxford University Press).

Peterson, J. and Bomberg, E. (1999), *Decision-Making in the European Union* (Basingstoke and New York: Palgrave).

Peterson, J. and Shackleton, M. (eds) (2012), *The Institutions of the European Union*, 3rd edn. (Oxford: Oxford University Press).

Peterson, J., Byrne, A., and Helwing, N. (2012b), 'International Interests: The Common Foreign and Security Policy', in J. Peterson and M. Shackleton (eds), *The Institutions of the European Union*, 3rd edn. (Oxford and New York, Oxford University Press).

Pierson, P. (1996), 'The Path to European Integration', *Comparative Political Studies* 29/2: 123–63.

Pierson, P. (2000), 'Increasing Returns, Path Dependence, and the Study of Politics', *American Political Science Review*, 94/2: 251–67.

Pierson, P. (2004), *Politics in Time: History, Institutions and Social Analysis* (Princeton, NJ, and Woodstock: Princeton University Press).

Pinder, J. (1999), *Foundations of Democracy in the European Union* (Basingstoke and New York: Macmillan and St Martin's Press).

Piris, J-C. (2010), *The Lisbon Treaty: a Legal and Political Analysis* (Cambridge and New York: Cambridge University Press).

Pollack, M. A. (2009), 'New Institutionalism', in A. Wiener and T. Diez (eds), *European Integration Theory*, 2nd edn. (Oxford: Oxford University Press).

Pollack, M. A. (2010), 'Theorizing EU Policy-Making', in H. Wallace, H., M. Pollack, and A. Young (eds), *Policy-Making in the European Union*, 6th edn. (Oxford and New York: Oxford University Press): 15–44.

Posen, B. (2004), 'ESDP and the Structure of World Power', *International Spectator*, 30/1: 5–17.

Quaglia, L. (2007), *Central Banking Governance in the European Union: A Comparative Analysis* (London and New York: Routledge).

Quaglia, L. (2010), *Governing Financial Services in the European Union* (London and New York: Routledge).

Redmond, J. (2007), 'Turkey and the EU: Troubled European or European Trouble?' *International Affairs*, 83/2: 305–17.

Rees, W. (2006), *Transatlantic Counter-terrorism Cooperation: The New Imperative* (London and New York: Routledge).

Rees, W. (2008), 'Inside-Out: The External Face of EU Internal Security', *Journal of European Integration*, 1: 97–111. Available at: http://www.informaworld.com/smpp/title~db=all~content=t713393849~tab=issueslist~branches=30-v3030

Richardson, J. (2005), *European Union: Power and Policy-Making*, 3rd edn. (London and New York: Routledge).

Rieger, E. (2005), 'Agricultural Policy: Constrained Reforms', in H., Wallace, W., Wallace and M. Pollack (eds), *Policy-Making in the European Union*, 5th edn. (Oxford: Oxford University Press): 161–90.

Rifkin, J. (2004), *The European Dream* (Cambridge: Polity Press).

Risse, T. (2009), 'Social Constructivism', in A. Wiener and T. Diez (eds), *European Integration Theory*, 2nd edn. (Oxford: Oxford University Press).

Risse, T. (2010), *A Community of Europeans: Transnational Identities and Public Spheres* (Ithaca, NY: Cornell University Press).

Roche, M. (2010), *Exploring the Sociology of Europe: An Analysis of the European Social Complex* (London: SAGE).

Rodrick, D. (2011), *The Globalization Paradox* (New York: W.W. Norton and Company).

Roederer-Rynning, C. (2010), 'The Common Agricultural Policy—The Fortress Challenged', in W. Wallace, M. Pollack, and A. Young (eds), *Policy-Making in the European Union*, 6th edn. (Oxford and New York: Oxford University Press): 181–205.

Rogers, J. (2009), 'From "Civilian Power" to "Global Power": Explicating the European Union's "Grand Strategy" through the Articulation of Discourse Theory', *Journal of Common Market Studies*, 47/4: 831–62.

Rometsch, D., and Wessels, W. (1996), *The European Union and Member States: Towards Institutional Fusion?* (Manchester: Manchester University Press).

Rosamond, B. (2000), *Theories of European Integration* (Basingstoke and New York: Palgrave Macmillan).

Rosamond, B. (2013), 'Theorizing the EU After Integration Theory', in M. Cini and N. Pérez-Solórzano Borragán (eds), *European Union Politics*, 4th edn. (Oxford and New York: Oxford University Press).

Rosato, S. (2011), *Europe United: Power, Politics and the Making of the European Community* (Ithaca, NY, and London: Cornell University Press).

Rosato, S. (2012), 'Europe Troubles: Power Politics and the State of the European Project', *International Security*, 35/4: 45–86.

Roth, K. (2007), 'Europe must Pull its Weight on Human Rights', *Financial Times*, 12 January.

Rüger, C. (2012), 'From Assistant to a Manager: The High Representative for Foreign Affairs and Security Policy After the Treaty of Lisbon', in F. Laursen (ed.), *The EU's Lisbon Treaty: Institutional Choices and Implementation* (Farnham and Burlington, VT: Ashgate).

Sandholtz, W., and Stone Sweet, A. (1998), *European Integration and Supranational Governance* (Oxford: Oxford University Press).

Sbragia, A. (2001), 'Italy Pays for Europe: Political Leadership, Political Choice, and Institutional Adaptation', in M. GreenCowles, J.Caporaso, and T. Risse (eds), *Transforming Europe: Europeanization and Domestic Change* (Ithaca, NY: Cornell University Press): 79–96.

Scharpf, F. W. (1999), *Governing in Europe: Effective and Democratic?* (Oxford and New York: Oxford University Press).

Schimmelfennig, F. (2003), *The EU, NATO and the Integration of Europe* (Cambridge: Cambridge University Press).

Schimmelfennig, F., and Sedelmeier, U. (eds) (2005), *The Politics of European Union Enlargement: Theoretical Approaches* (London: Routledge).

Schmidt, V. (2013), 'Democracy and Legitimacy in the European Union Revisited: Input, Output *and* "Throughput"', *Political Studies* 61: 2–22.

Schneider C. J. (2008), *Conflict, Negotiation and European Union Enlargement* (Cambridge: Cambridge University Press).

Schultz, M. (2013), 'Europe's Budget Deal is Flawed', *Financial Times,* 17 February.

Settembri, P. (2007), 'The Surgery Succeeded: Has the Patient Died? The Impact of Enlargement on the European Union', Paper Presented at the Global Fellows Forum, NYU Law School, New York, 5 April. Available at: http://www.nyulawglobal.org/ fellowsscholars/documents/gffsettembripaper.pdf

Short, C. (2000), 'Aid that Doesn't Help', *Financial Times*, 23 June. Available at: www. ft.com

Siedentop, L. (2000), *Democracy in Europe* (Harmondsworth: Allen Lane/Penguin Press).

Sjursen, H. (ed.) (2006), 'What Kind of Europe? European Foreign Policy in Perspective', Special Issue of *Journal of European Public Policy,* 13/2.

Sjursen, H. (ed.) (2006), *Questioning EU Enlargement: Europe in Search of Identity* (London: Routledge).

Slapin, J. B. (2008), 'Bargaining Power at Europe's Intergovernmental Conferences: Testing Institutionalism and Intergovernmental Theories', *International Organization*, 62/1: 131–62.

Smith, K. E. (2014), *European Union Foreign Policy in a Changing World*, 3rd edn. (Cambridge and Malden, MA: Polity).

Smith, M. E. (1997), 'What's Wrong with the CFSP? The Politics of Institutional Reform', in P.-H. Laurent and M. Maresceau (eds), *The State of the European Union*, Vol. 4 (Boulder, CO, and Essex: Lynne Rienner and Longman): 149–76.

Smith, M. E. (2003), *Europe's Foreign and Security Policy* (Cambridge and New York: Cambridge University Press).

Söderbaum, F. and Sbragia, A. (2010), 'EU Studies and the "New Regionalism": What Can be Gained from Dialogue?', *Journal of European Integration*, 32/6: 563–82

Stakeholder.eu: The Directory for Brussels (2011) (Berlin: Lexxion).

Stolfi, F. (2008), 'The Europeanisation of Italy's Budget Institutions in the 1990s', *Journal of European Public Policy*, 15/4: 550–66.

Stolfi, F. (2013), 'The Monti Government and the European Union', in C. Radaelli and A. di Virgilio (eds), *Italian Politics 2012* (New York: Berghahn Books).

Tatham M. and Thau, M. (2014), 'Territorial Interest Representation in the European Union: Actors, Objectives and Strategies', *European Union Politics*, 15/2: 256–77.

Taylor, S. (1999), 'Union Comes of Age in Helsinki', *European Voice*, 16 December. Available at: http://www.europeanvoice.com/article/imported/union-comes-of-age-in-helsinki/39845.aspx (accessed 27 August 2010).

Tocci, N. (2011), *Turkey's European Future: Behind the Scenes of America's Influence on EU-Turkey Relations* (New York and London: New York University Press).

Toje, A. (2009), *America, the EU and Strategic Culture: Renegotiating the Transatlantic Bargain* (London and New York: Routledge).

Toje, A. (2010), *The European Union as a Small Power: After the Post-Cold War* (Basingstoke and New York: Palgrave).

Toje, A. (2011), 'The European Union as a Small Power', *Journal of Common Market Studies*, 49/1: 43–60.

Tonra, B. (2001), *The Europeanisation of National Foreign Policy: Dutch, Danish and Irish Foreign Policy in the European Union* (Aldershot and Brookfield, VT: Ashgate).

Tonra, B. and Christiansen, T. (eds) (2004), *Rethinking European Union Foreign Policy* (Manchester and New York: Manchester University Press).

Torreblanca, J. I. (2001), *The Reuniting of Europe: Promises, Negotiations and Compromises* (Aldershot: Ashgate).

Vachudova, M. (2005), *Europe Undivided: Democracy, Leverage, and Integration after Communism* (Oxford: Oxford University Press).

Vachudova, M. (2009), 'Corruption and Compliance in the EU's Post-Communist Members and Candidates', *JCMS Annual Review of the European Union in 2008*, 43–62.

Van Middelaar, L. (2013), *The Passage to Europe: How a Continent Became a Union* (New Haven, CT, and London: Yale University Press).

Van Rompuy, H. (2012), Speech at the Humboldt University, Walter Hallstein Institute for European Constitutional Law, 'The discovery of co-responsibility: Europe in the debt crisis', 6 February. Available at: http://www.consilium.europa.eu/uedocs/cms_data/docs/pressdata/en/ec/127849.pdf

Vanke, J. (2010), *Europeanism and European Union: Interests, Emotions, and Systemic Integration in the Early European Economic Community* (Palo Alto, CA: Academica Press).

Wallace, W. (1983), 'Less than a Federation, More than a Regime: The Community as a Political System', in H. Wallace, W. Wallace and C. Webb (eds), Policy-making in the European Community, 2nd edn. (London: John Wiley and Sons).

Wallace, H. (2000), 'The Policy Process', in H. Wallace and W. Wallace (eds), *Policy-Making in the European Union*, 4th edn. (Oxford and New York: Oxford University Press): 39–64.

Wallace, H. (2005), 'Exercising power and Influence in the European Union: The Roles of Member States', in S. Bulmer and C. Lesquene (eds), *The Member States of the European Union*, 2nd edn. (Oxford and New York: Oxford University Press): 25–44.

Wallace, H., Pollack, M., and Young, A. (eds) (2015), *Policy-Making in the European Union*, 7th edn. (Oxford and New York: Oxford University Press).

Waltz, K. N. (2002), 'Structural Realism after the Cold War', in G. J. Ikenberry (eds), *America Unrivaled: the Future of the Balance of Power* (Ithaca, NY, and London: Cornell University Press).

Weber, K, Smith, M. E., Baun, M. (eds) (2008), *Governing Europe's Neighborhood: Partners or Periphery?* (Manchester and New York: Manchester University Press).

Weiler, J. H. H. (1998), 'Ideas and Idolatry in the European Construct', in B. McSweeney (ed.), *Moral Issues in International Affairs* (Basingstoke and New York: Macmillan).

Weiler, J. H. H. (1999), *The Constitution of Europe* (Cambridge: Cambridge University Press).

Wendt, A. (1992), 'Anarchy is What States Make of It: The Social Construction of Power Politics', *International Organization*, 46/3: 391–426.

Wendt, A. (1999), *Social Theory of International Politics* (Cambridge: Cambridge University Press).

Wessels, W., Maurer, A., and Mittag, J. (eds) (2003), *Fifteen Into One? The European Union and its Member States* (Manchester and New York: Manchester University Press).

West European Politics (2011), 'Linking Inter- and Intra-institutional Change in the European Union', Special Issue, 34/1.

White, B. (2001), *Understanding European Foreign Policy* (Basingstoke and New York: Palgrave).

Wiener, A., and Diez, T. (eds) (2009), *European Integration Theory* (Oxford and New York: Oxford University Press).

Wolf, M. (2004), *Why Globalization Works* (New Haven CT: Yale University Press).

Woolcock, S. (2012), *European Union Economic Diplomacy: The Role of the EU in External Economic Relations* (Farnham and Burlington, VT: Ashgate).

Wurzel, R., Zito, A. and Jordan, A. (2013), *Environmental Governance in Europe: A Comparative Analysis of New Environmental Policy Instruments* (Cheltenham: Edward Elgar Publishing).

Young, A. R. (2002), *Extending European Cooperation: the European Union and the 'New' International Trade Agenda* (Manchester and New York: Manchester University Press).

Young, A. and Peterson, J. (2014), *Parochial Global Europe: 21st Century Trade Politics* (Oxford and New York: Oxford University Press).

Zielonka, J. (2007), *Europe as Empire* (Oxford: Oxford University Press).

▌ INDEX